The Next Taboo

Curing Cancer Through Cannibalism

By

Avery Weisman

ISBN: 0-7596-9848-1

This book is printed on acid free paper.

1stBooks - rev. 04/11/02

In Memory of My Parents

Idea for a frightening story: It is discovered that the only remedy for cancer is living human flesh. Consequences.

(from the notebooks of Paul Valéry)

Table of Contents

Chapter 1—Simon, Simon, Not So Simple

Simon Simon was never sure who he was, what he was, or where he belonged. Although he had been raised by an affectionate and imposing woman he called Aunt Gina, his origins were obscure and she was never inclined to enlighten him. The mystery was so complete that he had no alternative but to deal with himself as a stranger, always ready to be surprised by alien and abrupt whims and passions that yielded to nothing until he was able to reach prompt and prevailing satisfaction. It was not that he was nobody's boy, poor and forlorn. Indeed, he was strongly somebody's boy, except for the question of whose. And this perplexed him from his youth on, as he grew up and shed his reliance on Aunt Gina and her directives.

Ordinarily he feigned normality, and did it well, but it was fictitious and he knew it. Nevertheless, through practice and for convenience in dealing with the world, the fiction was largely successful. After all, he was accustomed to it. So well did his apparent normality screen out anything else that might betray him, but to acquaintances who knew him well he was the real thing, a regular fellow, whatever that meant.

Now in his mid-twenties Simon was handsome, energetic, and engaging. People spontaneously liked him, drawn to assume an immediate friendship, even intimacy that was not there. Well proportioned, fit, even robust by conventional standards, he was also articulate in speech, and impressed most people as someone of breeding and education, which was in fact not far from truth. He was usually an agreeable listener who met the other person with respect and even an implied interest. With women, his warm gaze revealed a sympathetic attraction, with a gentle promise of an intimacy yet to come. He could laugh with appreciation at someone's sallies and witticisms but had no apparent humor of his own. Simon voiced opinions occasionally, and never judged a mere listener. Nevertheless, Simon was not a man of strong beliefs, rarely devoting any time to thinking about one issue or another.

Generally, people were attracted to Simon although others were simply indifferent and forgot him as soon as the evening's activities were over. A few unexpectedly found themselves wary and uncomfortable in his presence, as if there were more to him or much less than met the eye. Only someone unusually astute would have noticed that despite his open amiability, Simon seemed hardly there at all. A forthright manner nevertheless disclosed ambiguity and uneasiness, when not pretending and performing. Simon was not the regular guy he appeared to be, but regularly set a screen to deceive and disappoint their expectations. Simon seldom came close to forging a close connection; it was pretense at best, a mark of a talented actor, that is, if he had any acting talent.

Since college, Simon traveled widely, meeting people from various stations and under a variety of circumstances, exotic and ordinary. During his various journeys, he practiced different identities, pretending to be a designated character for one group, and someone entirely different for another, according to whim and fantasy. Simon could not have told you himself why he acted as he did, but each role prepared him for another. Most people he came in contact with were utterly taken in, and never knew the deception when he left, usually without a farewell.

It was during a variety of unconventional and thoroughly illicit affairs, most of which were what others would surely call immoral, unethical, forbidden or scandalous that Simon came closest to feeling a strong sense of engagement. In fact, he regularly sought out and went beyond the limitations of ordinary social custom, transgressing the norm, pursuing taboos to break, but stopping just short of culpable offenses, as a rule. He rarely was sure of how forbidden his actions were, and he didn't much care, since who was he to feel responsible for anything? Had he ever been arrested, and there were a few close calls, the police blotter would have been blank about physical characteristics, other than eye color, hair, height and weight, pretty banal stuff. Nevertheless, for no reason except curiosity, he once underwent cosmetic surgery a few years earlier. It was not to change his appearance as much as to find if there was anything or anyone under the skin that would unequivocally affirm who he really was and where he came from. It was intended to disclose, not to hide. No one else really cared. He was not being pursued, and far from being an actual fugitive. The stranger was hardly a role thrust on him, nor was it welcome. It came naturally, a habit of life and quirk of character that only a person without enduring connections could understand. He aroused no antagonism, because he was not genuine enough to annoy anyone. He did manage a few pseudo-intimate attachments, which were of course temporary, as well as concocting a number of utterly fictitious friendships, which often resulted in cruel and frustrating consequences for the other person.

Simon could readily fool people into trusting him, and this was potentially hazardous. Such relationships scarcely mattered enough to remember. He could be called a reliable hypocrite, who said one thing but meant another. Nevertheless, combining natural as well as honed intelligence with a skillfully deceptive manner, Simon usually managed to make connections wherever he went, and to realize in a short time whatever he wanted. When it came to jobs, he could turn himself into a seemingly dependable employee in a very short time, even encouraging a modicum of trustworthy responsibility. Nevertheless, he was never totally engrossed or attached to what he did, nor did he feel even minimal loyalty to his employers, or anyone else who played a part in fulfilling a fantasy.

No job ever lasted more than a few months. He played his role well until the flavor of regularity wore off and something more appealing and just as temporary crossed his path. Before then, however, he seemed to fit in well, friendly and capable enough to be respected and even promoted. However, it was only superficial sheen and not substance. That was his way. It was unlikely that he could have handled a steady job or a permanent relationship. Meanwhile he was just as unattached from his own enigmatic self as he was from various people who were unwitting participants in his schemes.

Simon's preoccupation with his origins, and questions about a real family somewhere led to a game in which he accosted strangers on the street, under a pretext of recognizing a resemblance to someone he might once have known. Walking along, for example, he surreptitiously peered at men coming towards him. He did not expect to find a real double, but just someone suggestively similar to how he fancied a family member might look. From time to time, his imagination did stretch enough to spot an oncoming man matching his anticipation. If their gazes happened to meet at that moment, he would stop and with a friendly smile, disarm any suspicion and begin a conversation.

"Excuse me, Sir," he would say, "But you look enough like someone I knew very well in college (or the army, old neighborhood, former church, etc) to ask if you were really that person or someone related to him. It's really uncanny; you must excuse me. Does the name Henry Watson (or John Ingersoll, or any name he thought of) mean anything to you? He was an old friend. There's such a close resemblance that maybe you're a relative."

He was always careful to pick a name that seemed plausible. Plain John Smith would never do and he liked names that sounded like one of the gentry. Once in a while, he used a famous name but with a slight twist, such as Henry Wadsworth or Rollo Emerson. The gambit, "I've seen you before," was, of course, far too stale for a convincing pick-up line. Besides, not every man stopped at his intrusion. Many simply walked on. Others responded warmly and seemed to welcome the intrusion, occasionally suggesting that they walk along together. Such friendly overtures were usually a homosexual prelude, which Simon rarely responded to. That was not what he was after, nor was it a part of the game. Its purpose was not pickup for pick-ups sake, and he liked pretending to be someone he was not.

Simon knew that the game was futile because it stemmed from total ignorance about his true family. And unless he knew of a valid connection to authentic parents, he was nothing at all, only a fiction he hardly believed in. No one, of course, could resemble a member of a family he never knew. Nevertheless, the goal of finding an imaginary family member made him continue to play at it, until he began to wonder who in fact these strangers actually were. He always had a clear but unlikely hope that one day he'd be recognized, and without asking his name, the stranger would embrace him affectionately. Finding an unknown connection could turn him into the real thing, not a ghost of a person, or a phony who just happened to be where he was.

Whenever he thought about his own existence he had to confront the realization that aside from fleeting attachments, bleak and empty, he was starkly and absolutely bereft and alone. Moreover, such fictitious and trivial encounters, which amounted to parodies, had to be more authentic and sustaining than vapid empty solitude. The personal world he lived in was spurious, while worlds of public reality, other people and things, were at least constant and solid. Of this, he was sure. Otherwise, he doubted the ordinary facts of his own everyday existence. Sometimes, coming home to his apartment at night, he felt unsure that the key in his hand was right and would fit the lock. In the morning while dressing, he looked at clothes in the closet. Were they really his, or had he accidentally stumbled into someone else's home and spent the night? Being a stranger never truly became familiar, so he always looked for some unexpectedly strong emotion or attachment that might grab him and testify that this was real and proper for him.

Simon might have manufactured a lasting identity, just as a method actor puts himself completely into a role and almost forgets it is only a play. After all, Simon rehearsed different roles often enough. However, the actor sincerely tries to be a good actor and knows all along that he is an actor, while Simon was only sure that he was a fake in whatever he tried to be. Simon's only lasting attachment, however, one that filled him with dread, but his enduring certainty, was that some day he had to face death. It was the ultimate, absolute, unswerving calamity, and he was terrified. In one sense, death made him just like everyone else. Since he did not want to believe in premature death it meant getting old, too, in order to die. Perhaps death could be postponed so long that it might never occur.

Suicide never tempted him because it required a sense of futility that just wasn't there, and he was never that depressed. Indeed, absence of strong emotion, save that of ecstatic passion, was his way. But death, an irreversible fate, was genuine and permanent regardless of when it occurred by putting an end to everything, including his fakery and the taboos he was obliged to find and violate. Taboos were uppermost in whatever incentive in

4

life that Simon found. The forbidden always aroused preemptive intentions towards transgression and in its intensity seemed to be an antidote to fear of death. Death was disintegration, but violating a taboo was like an organic fascination just as ultimate. Through igniting an ecstasy that defied everything else he might do or pretend to accomplish, the actuality of his demise could be held off for a time, even neutralized. A taboo strong enough might bring him together with himself into a state of delirious fulfillment, fleeting but assuring that somewhere another reality existed.

Simon's singular attitude towards people, jobs, and everyday existence was not a voluntary withdrawal from the mainstream of life. It was a fact of being. He had, in fact, very little sense of linkage between one person and chapter in his life with another. Regardless of how engaged he seemed to be, when the time came that he lost interest or felt overbearing ennui, he simply walked away without a goodbye, regret, or explanation. His qualified attachment suddenly palled. He was sickened and had to put it behind him, as if to breathe again and relieve his boredom. Simon himself had no terminal forewarning nor did he ever regret or rejoice in abandoning what he left behind. Almost immediately, it became a matter of no further consequence.

Despite Simon's general lack of purpose, he had no trouble being admitted to and graduating from a prestigious university with more than average distinction. He had neither attraction nor aversion to whatever college might offer, and certainly no determination to make a go of his studies. There were other classmates who attended college at the behest of interested adults, without any special motivation of their own. Simon attended college simply because Aunt Gina expected him to, and she expected it only because of what Simon must become. Although he was a dabbler in whatever he pleased, he was smart enough to follow directions, cautious enough to keep out of trouble, and able to avoid detection as someone inherently fallacious and possibly reprehensible. He absorbed information readily; and unwittingly, even developed a taste for certain cultural things that he later found useful. At graduation he was a thoroughly qualified dilettante, a certification that he henceforth practiced to perfection.

Unencumbered by conventional goals or ambition, Simon usually followed his whims wherever curiosity led. This tendency evolved into a lasting appetite for travel. Reluctant to attach himself permanently, he went from job to job, country to country, always at loose ends, fearful of convention and regularity. Were he ever to write a resume, it would look like the yellow pages of a small town telephone book. At various times, he was a chauffeur, waiter, parking lot attendant and other menial jobs that required no special qualifications. But he also found himself becoming a fairly competent legal assistant, almost a paralegal, and then a practical nurse, the latter based on common sense about the body's ills and patients' wants. As a plumber's assistant he carried tools and observed closely, doing enough simple tasks until he became quite competent at that. For a short period, he was a security officer, another almost invisible job requiring willingness to wear a uniform and accept low pay for long hours spent alone and at night. At another extreme, however, he also managed to be hired as a temporary teacher at a private school, faking only his credentials, and performing quite credibly in the assignment he was given. Students and fellow-faculty liked him. Although he never truly became attached to the work, he was a somewhat colorful teacher who amused classes with anecdotes just on the respectable side of being racy. Episodes from his travels, suitably bowdlerized, kept the young peoples' attention. But then, as always, one day he dropped out of sight, without warning, near the semester's end, leaving colleagues and students to wonder whatever happened.

One of his more colorful but typical adventures, however, was a stint as ship's doctor on a cruise sailing to Caribbean ports of call. The employment interview did not require much camouflage, beyond a statement of schools attended, which was never checked, and a perfunctory conversation about past experience, almost totally made up. Simon had gleaned enough knowledge and skill from close observation as a practical nurse to deal with common physical complaints and dispense non-prescription drugs. A deeper knowledge of medicine was never required. Passenger problems were slight, and he handled them deftly and competently. How easy to be a quack, he thought, except for the risk of discovery. There was nothing to it, really, only a gift for talking glibly and seeming to be sympathetic, with just a smattering of technical information and somewhat larger doses of flattery. Most of his voyages were spent dallying with older women on board who welcomed a cultivated dinner companion, dance partner, and more often than not, a temporary lover.

All went well for about two weeks into his final cruise. Then the ship docked at one of the larger ports of call. There was a well-known and especially notorious nightlife that Simon wanted to explore further, even when the ship was due to depart. Regardless of his job, the call to abandon ship was more urgent. He packed his few belongings, always traveling light, and took off, intending to stay in port for a night or two, discover what he could about the disreputable parts, and then depart for nowhere in particular. Disappointing or causing a problem for his shipmates and favorite passengers was not an issue. When he failed to return that first night and was still missing the following morning, the Captain became alarmed and sent a couple of officers to look for him. The search was fruitless, but a local policeman reported that a man matching Simon's description had been seen in several waterfront bars only the night before. He was not alone, but the policeman could not describe Simon's companions, who were probably pick-ups.

Two days later, another policeman said that a man resembling Simon sailed earlier on a freighter bound for New Orleans. His shipmates worried about a mishap, then flabbergasted and now angry when they finally realized that Simon had simply abandoned them. Deserters are not uncommon on shorter cruises, but this trip was somewhat longer and extensive, and they had become rather attached to this attractive companion. Leaving the ship in the lurch without medical coverage was unethical, they agreed, still not suspecting that his medical qualifications were all falsified. The Captain had to make do with a local medical student and a registered nurse, hastily recruited. Simon had no more qualms than if he'd decided not to claim a reservation in a restaurant somewhere. After all, he thought, he wasn't a regular doctor anyway, so they shouldn't have any trouble finding a replacement.

While Simon had little or no sense of blame, shame, or obligation, he showed traces of sentimentality occasionally and unexpectedly. Music, sweet and sentimental, meant to be nostalgic, stirred unfamiliar pangs of sadness, discontentment and loss. A young mother holding a small child frequently evoked a wistful glimmer of yearning and pity, but nothing more. Mostly, however, he was reluctantly satisfied by being an authentic faker with a sincere wish to be someone else, if only he could be sure who that hypothetical person might be.

It would be erroneous to exaggerate Simon's friendships, temporarily formed in the course of travel and during various flings of employment. Preponderantly, they were minimally gratifying, except perhaps to the other person. They were more or less impromptu attractions catering to the wishes and wants of the people involved, while Simon maintained a qualified distance. While exploiting to the utmost such attachments, Simon never seriously duped his 'friends', say, by bilking them out of funds or promising much of anything else that betrayed trust. Simon had ample funds of his own, so cheating was never necessary. He was always an upright deceiver, never stooping to dishonest practices. Moreover, his erstwhile friends were usually pretty indulgent about Simon, rarely criticizing him even after he disappeared, unless, as with the ship, he put them into a painful predicament. Some thought of him as just an unpredictable rascal, and soon forgot. Others were not so forgiving, especially if he truly let them down.

Pondering his own origins was one of Simon's predominant preoccupations, rivaled only by a strong sexual attraction for older women to bed with. Despite years of reflecting, he always came up against a blank wall of ignorance, without facts to nourish and support various conjectures. First, there was the question of his curious redundant name, Simon Simon, which he arbitrarily changed from time to time, anyway, depending on the circumstances. How he got to be called such a stupid name got no satisfactory explanation from Aunt Gina, who considered the question trivial and couldn't be bothered. He knew of no one else with such a duplicitous moniker. Which Simon was his first name, or the last, if either? It read the same backwards or forward. Not Simons, Symonds, Simmons, or even Simone. He could be comfortable with any surname but one that copied the first. It increased his doubt about who he really was. His best guess was that persons unknown patched it onto him like bad joke without a punch line. Maybe he was a foundling, left in a department store by a mother who fled. Perhaps she had good reason to run away, but what reason was good enough? Simon could have been a misbegotten bastard, unwanted and then turned over to an unscrupulous adoptive agency that didn't know or care what to do with him. Maybe the two names were just a clerical error hastily written for the record and never corrected. Possibly, where he came from, a first name was good enough, and last names were usually suspect. Throughout these ruminations, he had the utmost distaste, if not antipathy, with a rare flicker of yearning and pity for the mother who must have abandoned him. Paternity seldom entered into his questions, as if his father could have been anybody, a sperm donor, perhaps, a hit or miss one-time partner, but a figure of no special significance.

He knew the nursery rhyme about Simple Simon, but couldn't figure out what it had to do with him. Some anonymous intern in a foundling or free hospital might have played a prank, just to see if anyone noticed, which they didn't. As a boy he discovered a game called Simon Says. The gist was that Simon is the leader and all the players have to do as he says. They follow instructions, or they're out of the game, ridiculed or humiliated. If anyone survives to the last, it would be by paying strict attention to his orders and carefully obeying. He liked the idea of being the Boss. Long after he stopped playing the game, he kept the spirit. At parties, he might say, "Simon says, get me a drink!" or, under more intimate circumstances, Simon says...whatever he might fancy at the moment.

As a child, however, Simon Simon was dutiful and not at all rebellious, living as he did, an only child in a household presided over by Aunt Gina, a devoted, but formidable figure who certainly influenced the direction of his life without comparison to anyone else. Nevertheless, he went to local schools, did ordinary things, played innocent pranks, and was just bright enough, athletic enough, friendly enough, attractive enough, and appealing enough to get along well without making other children envious. This was comfortable because even at an early age he realized, without being told, that his normality was an unchallenged disguise for whatever else he imagined, did, failed to do, thought about doing, or had done to him.

There were a couple of classmates his age that became his pals for sport and adventure. They would sneak into movies, hitch rides to nearby towns, and watch sailing vessels, yachts and freighters, huge and mysterious to his eyes, whether passing by or anchored in the town's harbor. Simon wondered who could own such magnificent ships, where they went, or came from, and how rich the people must be who traveled on them. The grand house he lived in however had a special distinction that set it apart from the town's other opulent residences. It was at the top of a hill, higher than every other hill. The very location fostered an illusion of a castle, which at night and through fog gave a shadowy hint of an imaginary moat that made the great house look even more unapproachable. Majestic and remote as the ships seemed, he had similar questions about the place in which he grew up. A manor that large should have had a name, but it didn't, leaving even more to an imagination seeking stability.

Such an imposing structure, almost a mansion, was certainly more than a mere residence. Its presence almost dominated newer, larger, and costlier residences. Passersby might be excused for thinking that wealthy gentry must have occupied this edifice for generations, just like nobility in another land. Actually, whoever lived there in years past were not distinguished citizens, but a series of well to do occupants, known for their intractable aversion to inquisitive outsiders. All the owners in bygone years seemed to share a common insistence upon privacy. That is what they got. Not even official records told much more. Former residents held the property in trusts, without specific names, and were known largely by reputation and rumor.

The documents on file said just as little about the woman who now was the lady of the manor. It remained through preceding owners and current a house of mystery. A rare intruder or delivery man looking for directions venturing to use a huge brass knocker on the massive oak front door, or to ring an almost hidden bell, loudly announcing an arrival with a throaty chime, would have to be very bold, indeed. Strangers were not welcome, and, regardless of their mission, were turned away. Besides privacy, there was a dignified grandeur about the place, admired only from afar. The combined effect worked very well, to be securely cut off from the outside world.

Appropriately, the high house was surrounded by about two acres of wooded land, some undeveloped, but otherwise carefully patterned by flowerbeds, fruit trees, gardens and shrubs. At the edge of the property, partially hidden by tall trees, was a former stable, now used as a garage with a second floor apartment for a chauffeur or caretaker. It, too, although of humbler origin, defied strangers to come near. The style of the house could with tolerable accuracy be called Victorian, were anyone to ignore its subdued eclecticism. Less charitable observers might call the total effect, Secular Gothic, but in truth, it was a conglomerate of style, a mixture from everywhere. A massive, intimidating roof covered a large verandah, creating a frontal promontory. No one ever was observed actually using the porch although it could easily accommodate several dozen people, with much space. Why individuals seeking seclusion wanted such a large and extravagantly unused expanse could scarcely be guessed at, except for deliberate distance. Each corner of the heavily shingled roof had its distinctive turret or small tower, like lingering watchtowers of a bygone age. The towers themselves had several small windows for a fancied sentry to watch the oncoming hordes that never came. On perpetual duty, such guards protected and preserved the castle from intruders.

An architect would be stumped to explain just why so many different and perhaps incompatible materials were put together in such a way. There was wood in abundance, fieldstone, granite, bricks, and of course a heavy slate shingled roof. The general effect was contradictory, secretive, absurd and assertive. That was the baroque place where the young Simon grew up.

Simon was not immune to a general myth that his home was once upon a time an European castle, taken apart illogically and with mixed materials long ago set down in this moderate town, once a colonial village. It was surely generously sized, but actually not as large as the neighbors who called it the "mansion on the hill" imagined. The young Simon explored the house for years, always in secret, never satisfied that his explorations were thorough enough. His sense that there was always something else deepened its mystery. Rooms on the third floor were called "guest rooms," but hardly anyone stayed overnight. When Simon peeked into one of these ornately furnished bedrooms, the pungent aroma of stale disuse always met him. Keen of scent, Simon failed to find tell tale odors of people.

The rest of the house was furnished in a curiously sturdy, obsolete mixed style from another era. Victorian heavy chairs were covered in tapestry cloth or black leather. There were a few spindly chairs too frail to bear anyone's weight. However, almost every article had a dignified air, as if plucked long ago from a British gentlemen's club or purchased at some long ago auction. Drapes were unflinchingly damask, deliberately lined to curtail light. Rococo floor lamps provided meager illumination. Walls were decorated with paintings of foreign scenes, cloudy mountains, peasants wearing unlikely garb, and inevitable bridges over unidentified rivers, leading nowhere. There were several small statuettes of mythical figures, carefully placed on tables, balanced by lamps that shed only very dim decorative light.

On the vast first floor, the ceilings of which were proportionately high, there was a baronial dining room, adequate for dinner parties of at least twenty guests. An adjoining great reception room shared the immensity. Guests were never expected to venture far beyond these two rooms unless into fancy washrooms, ornately marbled and mirrored. Inevitably, a large grandfather clock presided at the landing of a curved staircase, leading upwards to unknown quarters. Tolling out regular hours, as if time were a precious heirloom, the clock also seemed to caution visitors not to go up the stairs without special authorization. There were at least two more floors above the second. Bookshelves regularly adorned the walls where paintings were absent, filled with matching volumes whose titles quelled any interest in reading, unless the rare visitor wanted to know about dead statesmen and battles fought long ago. Only Simon was likely to investigate closed doors and locked cabinets. However, the larger of the second floor rooms, thoughtfully arranged and elegantly furnished with a large desk, also kept locked, with a few chairs, for just sitting and for work, ostensibly designed as a study, was reserved for Aunt Gina. Here, she spent most of her time while in residence, writing letters, talking on the telephone, sometimes conversing with guests, reading, or visiting with Simon.

The musty and open space of Simon's mansion on the hill contrasted with the easy and open congeniality of his friends' homes. Mothers were always at home, and fathers were apparently at work and out of the way. These ordinary houses were ample enough by almost any standard. The intensity of living so close to others was not at all consoling to Simon, although the abstract idea of family life had another appeal. He became uncomfortable by the notion of such close quarters, each family member knowing the other's habits so casually, without privacy.

Although Simon was usually surrounded by solitude, sometimes more than he liked, he did not altogether live by himself. There were two caretakers, Steve and Ingrid, who lived in an apartment on the ground floor, but also used the rooms over the former stable for storage and overflow. Simon never visited either place. Steve had many functions. He was the gardener and sometime driver of two cars in the garage, a handyman responsible for maintenance of the house itself, and general caretaker of the premises. When an electrician or plumber showed up, it was a special occasion, marked by much discussion. Steve must have been very strong and vigorous as a younger man, because, even now, slowed up and weighed down by years and arthritis, his hands and arms showed surprising power, when called for. He still impressed Simon by easily moving heavy furniture and carrying large packages coming to the house, never asking for help, as if a boy could not be trusted with such serious matters. Steve was now old, however, walked slowly, and not given to speaking more than a few sentences in response to questions. While they could have been friends, Simon and Steve rarely conversed, and then only when Simon insisted on talking and making company for himself on rainy days.

Ingrid was in charge of everything inside, from housekeeping to the kitchen where she prepared daily meals. She also supervised part-time help hired mainly for dinner parties, which she prepared meticulously. Ingrid was no more talkative than Steve, except when speaking to her married daughter over the telephone. Simon never knew the daughter's name, and saw her only a few times. Nevertheless, Ingrid often allowed the young Simon to watch her doing something special, especially elaborate preparations for Aunt Gina's dinner parties.

These mundane activities were steeped in conventional regularity. Still, there was an atmosphere of unanswered questions that no one fully understood, pretended not to know about, or did not want to mention. The somber upstairs with its silence and rococo decorations interspersed with sturdy furniture did not welcome intrusive questions. Simon suspected that somewhere there had to be hidden valuables and incriminating documents, a notion fueled by movies. He went about looking for places where panels, if touched just right, combined with a magic formula, might spring open to reveal a narrow stairway running between the walls from floor to floor, ending up in enigmatic rooms. But this was only his young vivid imagination, working hard against the stolid silence and secrecy that Aunt Gina did not deign to explain. When he touched the walls in what he guessed were the right places, nothing actually happened.

The reigning overseer of the mansion on the hill was its owner, Aunt Gina to the boy whom she raised, but Madame Benett to everyone else. She was the Lady of the Manor. How long she'd lived in this great house was not known, and no one ever dared to ask. Although Ingrid and Steve had worked for her a long time, Madame Benett was inclined to do no more than issue directives and not converse with them at all for any length of time. Nevertheless, she was always friendly, composed to the utmost and not at all forbidding to the help. She spoke in a soft contralto voice that carried the authority of an easy but confident assurance. While given to hearty laughter at times, usually at some inner humor that she decided not to share, she was rarely boisterous and seldom vulgar, except when annoyed at some stupidity. Rarely did she descend to frivolity, and then only at one of her dinner parties. Simon, a fascinated onlooker since earliest boyhood, discovered that she had a gently raucous side when one of her guests told a joke that Simon could not make out, and everyone burst out laughing.

Gina's gracious manner and lively spirit would quickly impress anyone meeting Madame Benett for the first time. She could be both down-to-earth and guarded with unexpected loftiness. Although often absent on unexplained and sometimes lengthy trips, her felt presence was never gone, even down to variations in small details that might have escaped a lesser person. If a piece of furniture had been moved, she noticed it. Silverware had to be immaculately shiny, and the tables were clean but never glossy. A fresh bush did not pass without a comment, often complimentary, because she knew, it seemed, that Steve and Ingrid tried very hard to please her.

Simon always enjoyed seeing Aunt Gina riding her horse, Dusty, in the early morning when the grounds of the house seemed to open magically into an intricate lattice of paths. Being taller than most women enhanced her stately bearing, but she managed still to retain a delicacy that did not detract from her occasionally firm and somewhat imperious manner. She seemed fully confident on all occasions, as if beauty, wealth intelligence, and whatever else she harbored endowed her with an ample security for benign control over her surroundings. One of the intriguing phenomena that added to her uncommonly arresting and attractive composure was that she looked older when young, and still seemed young as she aged. Thus, her actual age was always the same, timeless, impervious to change, and, of course, no one's business. If there were authentic Olympian goddesses come to life on this ordinary planet, they would have been like Madame Benett, whether Aphrodite or Diana.

Women friends occasionally visited Gina during the day, usually at what an older generation called teatime. They seemed fond of Simon, although he was never sure about their names. Generally, Gina's friends seemed ageless, too, always dressed immaculately and correctly in keeping with current fashion, he later noted. Gina was relaxed and hospitable with her women friends, judging by the light conversation, tea service, and gifts at birthdays. Although occasional men visitors came and went, it was never for very long. If a man were present, it was always with a woman companion, never by himself. Sometimes, however, long after teatime, a gentleman did call, driven to the occasion in a chauffeured limousine. Simon was never introduced. There was no light conversation or tea served. The gentleman and Aunt Gina quietly went upstairs, leaving Simon to be inconspicuous in another part of the house. Once or twice over the years

Simon came face to face with a man visitor. This was highly unusual and accidental.

To Simon's knowledge, Gina had never been married, which was strange, since she was both cultured and attractive, along with considerable wealth. Her poise and style would have pleased and fascinated the most exacting suitor. But Simon was understandably prejudiced about his beloved Aunt Gina. Presumably, she was the only relative he'd ever known, although their actual blood relationship was vague. His actual origins were as unknown as the source of her income. Gina's life, both inside and out, was so clearly and unambiguously cloaked that a similar secrecy had inevitably insinuated itself into the mansion itself. But beneath all the apparent mystery and secrecy, and certainly beyond speculation, there was a most heavily guarded and anomalous secret, shared with no one else. No outsider would have believed, should the unlikely information ever been disclosed, that the roots of Simon's future deviant behavior and perversities were first planted, inculcated, and nourished by his Aunt Gina.

Gina was more than an aunt: she was his tutor, preceptor, guide, oracle, and devoted regent. She fulfilled innumerable roles that a mere blood relative could not, and her influence permeated Simon's behavior and thought throughout his life. From boyhood until early teenage, she never hesitated, indeed, encouraged explicit talk about sex, including graphic description of what went on between men and women, men and men, women and women, without implying what was acceptable or not, better or worse, except that she was adamantly opposed to hypocrisy and prudery. Periodically, with his eager consent, Simon was allowed to join her in bed, where he learned to explore the warm, wet hidden places in her body. Her other efforts at educating Simon, aside from cultivating perverse and premature sexual desire, took place in her study, where they listened to classical music, and when old enough, read aloud from books that were supposed to be elevating and tilting towards culture and literacy. Without specifically giving him direction, Gina trained him to fit her values and never doubted but that her aims were within his range. Simon was never sure about the freedom she wanted for him, or what he was supposed to be free about, but sooner or later, he came to believe that liberty and libertinism were almost if not exactly the same thing. How he was to achieve all this depended on being able to recognize what society expected, what it staunchly held to be taboo, and then transgress such restrictions, with fervor and fascination.

Chapter 2—Aunt Gina's Secret Stairway

So far as anyone could tell, and there was really no one to wonder, Aunt Gina was not just fond of Simon, her putative nephew and protégé, but truly devoted to him in a singular fashion she conferred on no one else. Nevertheless the sphere of mystery surrounding them both was never breached. Absence of other family was not discussed, and at his first question, brushed aside. Perhaps in connection with her unspecified work, but certainly in response to an outside demand, from time to time, and without warning or preparation, Gina would leave on a trip, and be absent for several weeks or occasionally just for a few days. The duration was not relevant. Then she returned, with no explanation, usually bringing gifts for the young Simon who was overjoyed to see her again. Her abrupt departures always made him feel abandoned, as if left alone in that vast mansion, wholly deprived of the deep pleasure she gave him.

Birthdays and Christmas were celebrated generously, including a large tree, festooned with lights, symbols and tokens of the season. Such occasions were usually spent alone, although Aunt Gina held another Christmas celebration when her many friends were invited. Steve and Ingrid might peek in and share Simon's birthday cake, but they were not considered real guests.

As he grew up, Aunt Gina and Simon spent many evenings together, reading to each other when he was old enough, listening to music and opera that was emphatically uplifting and educational. He might just sit quietly when Gina spoke on the telephone with some one unidentified, often in French, Spanish, or Italian. How she learned other languages was as secret as almost anything else about her. Simon asked no questions, because often just the sound of her voice was comforting enough. When he read by himself, she would interrupt to talk about school, but then pick out books not on the school's curriculum to read in her absence. These weighty efforts at education and culture kept them from personal things, and Simon had little opportunity to ask about urgent and perplexing problems. As long as reports about school and teachers were satisfactory, Gina preferred discussing impersonal matters, which, like a travelogue, covered colorful descriptions of foreign countries, exotic inhabitants, and strange and compelling customs. They seldom watched television unless a momentous event demanded concentrated attention. At times, she filled him in on the background of important programs, especially if the story had political implications.

Otherwise, Simon was left alone. Her attempts at inculcating education and culture were put aside. He used these periods to explore the empty house, instead of a reading assignment. When he was older, he and his two friends explored the outside world; seldom did they dare enter the house, and then only on the first floor and verandah. Steve sometimes let them visit Dusty in the stable. Upstairs was off limits entirely. Simon came to know however that Gina frequently shared her bed with someone else, whose sex or identity was never clear. He was exiled to his own room at the other end of the third floor, although he managed to sneak around, even listening at her door. Without questioning the propriety of this or anything else about his life, he was still envious of the person who made her laugh, murmur, or fall into silence.

Years passed so quickly that in retrospect Simon hardly recalled his childhood and early adolescence at all, and then through sporadic events. Time obliterated itself, as if nothing had happened. Until he became completely independent, Aunt Gina continued to inquire and supervise his activities, but as a principle, never overtly passing judgment about whatever he told her about. Still, far from feeling free to do whatever he chose, Simon felt an invisible push, pull, and drag towards certain behavior, and silent disapproval of another. When they patronized upscale shops for his clothes, a custom that lasted until he left for college, the managers seemed to know her well. Perhaps it was only Simon's impression that their attraction to Gina took the place of shopping for her nephew. Nevertheless, Simon acquired a fine taste in clothing, however, as well as a precise pattern of speech, which coupled with a fine baritone voice, endowed him with an air of down to earth breeding. This seemed to satisfy Gina, who wanted to prepare him for a gentleman's life.

He had a fine sports car in adolescence, but hardly had any place to go. Despite being well to do with ample funds, Gina was not at all pretentious, nor did she expect specifics from him, except about cultural and sexual matters, where nothing but detailed exploration would do. Her purpose was not to prepare him for a career; indeed, she scorned such ambitions. She simply wanted Simon to grow up with an eager appetite for taboo, and a discriminating and selective preference for matters of education and culture, but never a hint of vocation. What she wanted was to avoid complacency while enjoying the lush benefits and privileges of an easy and effortless life. That this encouraged indulgence was a risk she was willing to take. Aunt Gina's secret stairway, if there at all, was never found.

These were not standards for high accomplishment, but rather a way of life consistent only with people convinced of their inborn superiority to everyone else. As a result, Simon was left to wonder at such indoctrination.

Since he was to become one of the self-serving, self-infatuated rich, it would never be necessary to prove his status. Nevertheless, he was not supposed to become a fop, practice social climbing, and be a total nothing in everything else. She despised this type of man, whom they read about and laughed at. In fact, Gina seldom expressed admiration or respect for any man.

Disdain for conventional moral issues was unexpectedly more difficult for Simon than being an arrogant wastrel, which Aunt Gina would have fought. Money only provided the means to do whatever he wished. Questions of what is good and bad, true and false, right or wrong got little attention except to emphasize how arbitrary such judgments are.

Taboos and social prohibitions were to be sought, scorned and transcended. This was a directive to obey and put before anything else. Whenever he asked about what made something right or wrong, better or worse among options, she quietly brushed aside his doubts, chiding him for even thinking about such things. Everything was wholly a matter of individual inclination and taste. Informed impulse dominated almost everything else, with the 'almost' left open. Yet she did not encourage hedonism, pleasure for pleasure's sake. He was left to conclude that right and wrong behavior depended only on choice, not on any absolute principle besides that of whimsy or preemptive passion. He was schooled to do whatever pleased him, seemed opportune, just interesting, regardless of social approval, and always expect impunity. A mercenary attitude, however, was to be stamped out vigorously. Money was good to have, the more the better, but it was not a primary mission in life. Gina was puritanically insistent upon that. Indeed, being wealthy was an opportunity, not a sign of superiority.

The young Simon treasured every available moment with his Aunt Gina, in her bedroom or study. Had they been aware of it, his friends would have considered him a lucky boy. Under her warm and luxurious quilt, he was cared for and enormously comforted by her soft skin, hands, arms and voice. But this sentiment did not last long. As he grew older, verging on but not quite adolescence, his emotions became stronger, defined, and then perplexing, especially after beginning surges of unadulterated sexual desire. He yearned, even more, for those hidden places in her body that she helped him to explore from childhood on. A mature woman's sorcery had schooled, tantalized, and indulged Simon. Tension became too intense. But the gradual transition from a child's warmth and intimacy to an adolescent's incandescent passion was inevitable. In Simon's case no less than in others, boyish delight gave way to strong desire presaging manhood that could not be quelled. Fires had been banked yet kept smoldering by Gina's sensuality. Womanly intuition along with unequivocal observation finally forced Gina

17

to face Simon's growing up, so that she began now to speak about other women, hoping to divert his appetites.

By this time, henceforth for many years, Simeon continued to be puzzled that, despite a variety of carnal intimacies, penetration never occurred. Indeed, Gina expressly forbade it, regardless of limitless exploration. As he further came into adolescence, however, he could barely restrain himself. She rebuffed him gently but firmly, repeating over and over that this was not for them, but meant for someone else. Finally, after one heated episode, they stopped sleeping together completely, and from that point on, maintained separate bedrooms. It was Gina's belated decision; surely not Simon's. The barrier was firm, and never breached.

The rift was hardly unfriendly and neither was at all angry. Simon kept silent about the arrangement with Aunt Gina, saying nothing whatsoever to Eddie and Jimmy, who were struggling with their own frustrations. Only much later, and then only with women, did he refer to his precocious initiation and training in sexuality. However, there was never a doubt but that his early indoctrination with Aunt Gina contributed mightily to his enduring, almost exclusive passion for older women.

"That is not for us, Simon," she would say over and over, in one way or another, "You will have real sex with other people, starting very soon, I imagine. Not with me. For you, it's not soon enough. But now you know enough to get around any woman, as often as you want, no more, on your terms, with anyone you choose, no one else's. No bargaining or begging. No deals for one thing or another. With us, it's been just love. But with everyone else, regardless, I say, fuck the rest of the world! And fuck them any way you want!" Aunt Gina was never one for euphemisms and circumlocution. She always laughed whenever she used a forceful expression. She could be earthy and down to earth, but just to make an emphatic point. Generally, her tone of voice was gentle and modulated, and about the same whatever she spoke about. She never hesitated to talk about sex explicitly, except, of course, while listening to the classical music she cherished. It was all part of Simon's education. However unorthodox her methods, she did not pretend to be a traditional parent or that she was merely using her body to graphically explain the so-called facts of life. That would have been misleading and hypocritical. Gina was open at all times, in describing what went on between men and women, men and men, women and women. Behind it all was an entrenched revulsion against prudery and hypocrisy, which she insisted went together. Consequently, Simon knew as much as she could teach about the shortcomings and secret hang-ups of people professing public virtue. Above all, he was expected to be knowledgeable enough not to be fooled, hemmed in and made a prisoner of convention and popular taboos. She preached about freedom at such an early age that Simon was not at all clear what he was supposed to be free from, free for, and free about. There was hardly any difference between the grand concept of liberty and the point of view of libertinism. Those who practice one would inevitably practice the other, she assured him confidently.

When he grew sophisticated, or at least more highly informed, Simon understood that taboos were never to stand in his way. Indeed, confrontation and deliberate violation conferred the best that life could offer in terms of human freedom. Whenever something was expressly forbidden by society, and there were many differences from one group to another, then, like an age-old and mighty adversary, it was always to be sought out and overcome. Transgression was both an obligation and a temptation. He found that defiance of an established taboo was both arousing and fascinating. It was a little like his namesake game, Simon Says. Everyone must obey and follow orders, or the players were out of the game. A taboo violated, custom defied, convention scoffed at, hypocrisy stripped naked, all held an exciting promise of consummation yet to come. He was to be one of those special, fortunate people who would not submit to moral or social pressure, and had the means to carry out desires, regardless of how critical and punitive the rest of ordinary society might be. Unfortunately, it was Simon's destiny not to have a grand cause or worthy purpose to go with his qualities and capacity to see through pretense.

Gina's challenge of taboo was never wholly explained. Simeon could hardly believe she meant all she said, since their life together was comparatively quiet and not given to controversial situations requiring defiant courage and rebellion. And there were exceptions to her professed candor and confrontation with the forbidden. Simon's origin, steeped in secrecy, certainly seemed to be forbidden. Yet, whatever information Gina had, and it must have been enormous, was never disclosed. How had he come to live with this woman whom he called Aunt Gina? What was he to her, and why were there so many other secrets and so much mystery? Where did she go during her travels? What did she do when not being his mentor?

"Why don't I have an Uncle Gina?" he once asked. In his friends' homes there were mothers and fathers, brothers and sisters, all sorts of visible relatives, not just an Aunt who might not be an aunt at all. Gina laughed indulgently. This was her custom.

"Why, you've had lots of uncles, Simon, but none called Gina that I remember," she answered, "I have men friends you could call Uncle, if you wanted to. I don't keep them around very long, that's all." This answered nothing but it stirred the little Simon to wonder if he too would be discarded some day, like these anonymous men. When she spoke of men, he could not help but notice, her lips curled slightly, sneering, as if the entire sex was contemptible and responsible for most of the misery in the world.

"Do you throw them away? Do they die?" he asked, wondering who these men were. He had never met the men whose voices he heard coming up from the first floor during her dinner parties, or the men who drove away in the early morning. Gina shook her head, still smiling. Nothing more was said that she intended to talk about. The subject was closed, before it was suitably opened, and in effect, forbidden. Judging by the number of times that he broached the subject, he might well be transgressing a taboo, except that he never prevailed.

Simon was never a true innocent. His disingenuous talk hid a certain paradoxical precocity. His initiation by Aunt Gina, whatever the pretext, cancelled a part of childhood that he never revisited. Nevertheless, the nebulous innocence that did remain was never completely extinguished. He was inquisitive enough during her extended absences to explore on his own, still seeking a secret stairway leading somewhere else, certain it was to an entirely different kind of world.

"You won't learn anything by snooping around," she said firmly, on occasions when he was bold enough or discovered in the act of prying. "I'll tell you what I want you to know, nothing else. It matters that I'm here, and that you are here. I go away, but I always come back. We care for each other. That should be enough. No mother or father could do any more." While these affectionate words provided consolation, she never did tell how he came to live with her, and in fact, what she was to him.

The adolescent Simon generally avoided risky adventures outside his home. Violations of local prohibitions and customs weren't worth taking a chance on. From time to time, however, whenever the opportunity seemed attractive, Simon peeked into the girls' toilet at school, using an ancient hole in the wall, never plugged by sympathetic janitors. The prank was not very original, and did not qualify as a social taboo of much magnitude. Once or twice, still with an adolescent voice, feigning a guttural basso, he made obscene phone calls to women whose numbers he randomly found in the telephone book. Most women promptly hung up, but a few were frightened, which made Simon ashamed as well as excited. He was ashamed to feel ashamed, because he also enjoyed the consternation he caused.

While still in high school, a couple of friends urged him to visit a local brothel, just beyond town limits. Brothels were technically forbidden, but still tolerated by authorities. Surprisingly, Aunt Gina had never mentioned the subject. Naturally, Simon was curious and went along but found the experience rather drab, unexciting, and far less than liberating. There was something about the openness that flattened desire. Nevertheless, for sociability, he went on other forays without much taste for the women and none for the fleeting pleasure. It occurred to him that girls his own age might be as willing as he and with Aunt Gina's urging and prediction, found this to be true. Even at that age, however, he was aware of a nascent preference for older women.

He told Aunt Gina nothing about his trips to brothels, relishing a little secret of his own. However, very soon, for no particular reason, he mentioned visiting the brothels to Aunt Gina shortly before starting to date local girls. Gina's response was non-committal at first, almost as if she hadn't heard him. However, when he and friends next went to an establishment known to be higher class and more discriminating about clientele, the madam singled him out, took him aside, and politely told him to take his business elsewhere. She even knew his name, which embarrassed him. He was puzzled about the encounter but didn't question the madam, and never went back. He was pretty sure that Aunt Gina did not approve, but how she managed to reach and close the doors did not occur to him.

Later, he found his way into adult movies where he witnessed sexual taboos beyond imagination being violated right before his eyes. He concluded that unless pornography is strictly forbidden, there is nothing to violate and therefore nothing to seek. Taboo must be forbidden to awaken his preemptive interest. He was an old hand, even at a comparatively young age. In fact, he came to feel that erotic literature or porno movies were not so remarkable or even taboo, but exist merely to disseminate certain kinds of information unlikely to be taught in school or found in newspapers. After all, his education had been not very conventional. The actors were doing only what the script called for in the course of working for a living, and had no cause to confront conventional society. It had nothing to do with being liberated. Depending on local mores and preferences, there was no taboo at all.

All this made sense. When is a taboo not a taboo, if not forbidden? Erotic movies and books therefore were, therefore, not a temptation, even to the curious and as yet insatiable Simon. If the purpose of taboo is first to excite, and then do away with itself through repeated transgression, what evil has to be addressed? What makes the evil go away? Perhaps conventional men were only aroused by second hand portrayals of sexual freedom that most people are forbidden. But what is forbidden about freedom, a concept ubiquitous enough to be found in all sorts of documented history, in most countries dominated by censorship and dictators? Was taboo only freedom to do what seems desirable? Not all desires have to be forbidden, but is this only an ingrown idiosyncrasy of Simon's? Perhaps being free means to do away with freedom itself and be controlled by a stronger power or passion coming from somewhere else. As time went on, Simon became even less clear about taboos. Yet, here he was, enmeshed in a set of directives to oppose prohibitions, regardless of what purpose they served. Even sexual taboos had to hold dozens of other taboos. Which ones was he supposed to violate? Some taboos were just violations of law. He left them alone because he had no appetite for them. Simon was never tempted to steal, or even to pilfer a trinket from a store, just to get away with it. And so far as learning more about a class of liberated people for whom the law did not seemingly apply, such as celebrities or psychopaths, Simon was carefully law abiding, even scrupulous about keeping within society's bounds.

Aunt Gina had no inclination to be specific about these abstract questions. It was enough to teach him that some prohibitions should be emblematic challenges, but not all. She would not have allowed or encouraged Simon to commit a crime, for example, just to test himself out and by chance, forfeit his freedom. Aunt Gina could be good, generous, perverse and incestuous, preaching freedom and yet condoning and practicing a kind of unconventional orthodoxy. Her tolerance for almost anything considered forbidden by nature was an assumed given without giving examples.

Ultimately, he realized that taboos must be tempting as well as forbidden. In one way or another, however disguised, most taboos were about local and tribal sexual customs. It was forbidden to curse sacred things, but Simon had nothing to do with religion anyway. Aunt Gina never forced church attendance, and did not urge him to believe in anything said to be divine. Sacrilege was not something he was interested in, yet when he heard friends mouthing pieties about God, divine indignation, and whatever else went along with religion, he was tempted to exercise freedom and belittle what they kept holy. But he kept silent; taboos were a private province. Taboos about hurting children, exploiting the aged or helpless, or torturing the afflicted were principles that Aunt Gina would urge him not to violate, and therefore, he was never tempted. Violations went on daily, forbidden and then punished. It was very explicit. On his own, Simon obeyed these injunctions, such as carefully protecting the vulnerable, partially because he was not tempted to do otherwise.

He stayed puzzled for years, knowing that transgressions, which preemptively must be challenged, first have to be tempting as well as forbidden. The test of a successful transgression was a refreshing liberation and exemption from the oppressive rules of established society. If successful in understanding and following these instructions, Simon would only be matching up to his Aunt's expectations. Aunt Gina knew this when she taught him to shun compromising entanglements, like a latter-day George Washington. Finally, Simon drew his own conclusion that any taboo worth violating must have its own intrinsic appeal beyond specific regulation, and needed to have a strong sexual quality that was hard to resist. And this varied with any special group of people who would not dream of doing otherwise. While wildly divergent, every group and tribe is special, with its symbolic prohibitions and directives that characterize its uniqueness and bizarre attraction for outsiders. It was getting far too complex. True to his teaching, Simon concentrated on locating the forbidden without heavily pondering its remote implications.

On one of his late adolescent forays into the city, something of a secret adventure in itself, Simon was picked up by a slightly older youth, called Jed. It was probably a phony name. They developed a kind of illicit friendship. Jed, a long ago high school dropout, lived at home where he obeyed no rules and yet depended on his parents' indulgent generosity to sponsor his explorations. His vocation was to be an unemployed bum and would-be con man, sponging off as many people as possible. Jed supplemented his parents' ample but unspecified allowance by petty thievery and minor confidence games. Often he found the vulnerable elderly to be the most promising and safest victims. Jed tried to persuade Simon that robbing an old man sleeping in a park at night was a ridiculously easy mark. Although the score in money might be slight, Jed also found the old man's helpless protests both funny and exhilarating, because the old man could do nothing but protest. It was surely a safe taboo to break, which Simon understood, but shrunk from imitating. To his alarm, one night he watched Jed rob a much older man, dressed somewhat better than the ordinary homeless person. Apparently passed out from drinking, the victim was sleeping on a bench at a bus stop in a scruffy part of the city where no one paid attention to events on the street. The victim had no way to retaliate or defend himself except to hand over his money and beg not to be hurt. Simon did not enjoy the escapade at all, and had no wish to repeat the unsavory episode. People weren't supposed to do that, but it didn't feel like a taboo, only a brutal act that demeaned the perpetrator and humiliated the victim even more. It was reprehensible and the robbery made the criminal something less than human. He was afraid to tell Aunt Gina, who would most certainly disapprove. In Aunt Gina's terms, a transgression worth its salt must heighten a sense of triumph and liberation, not mean gratification about picking up spare change from a defeated old man's pockets. It certainly lacked any trace of sexual domination and excitement about violations yet to come.

Breaking the law deliberately for obscure emotional satisfaction is a compulsion often relieved temporarily by the act itself. Kleptomania, stealing trifles from large stores, is without supplementary sexuality unless through a series of devious assumptions. Some men, old and young, like to exhibit before a woman of any age, hoping to shock, fascinate, or cause her to be instantly aroused by his mighty phallus. It is hardly a sacred taboo that is violated, however, except to the harmless and timid exhibitionist. For Simon nothing about law breaking appealed to him. The real taboos were hallowed symbols unquestioned and avoided by custom and supported by tradition, not specifically forbidden by law. They aren't on the books. Although these issues were perplexing to Simon, even at this age, late adolescence, he was already firmly fixed into a pattern of obeying the order to transgress.

When the time came to put his adolescence behind, graduate from high school, and leave for college, Simon readily obeyed Aunt Gina's expectations, although he had no special ambition. Whether Aunt Gina had anything to do with his prompt acceptance was a question not to be asked. He subsequently found it easy to get good grades without being particularly interested in any subject. He simply looked for what the professors expected and dutifully gave it back to them, with a strong slathering of admiration. It was Gina's method and strategy all over again. It was not difficult.

In avoiding real attachment to people and things except as they served a purpose, his talented inclination to be a glib pretender developed into a fine art. Thus he acquired an excellent reputation, which meant someone of charm, talent, and, of course, unrealized potential, although without vocational direction. He sought no popularity among other students, but kept his own counsel and selected acquaintances elsewhere. Simon had something about him of the drifting typical C student, except that he managed to curry favor and accumulate an excellent academic record, while exerting no interest or special talent. He hardly studied and spent most weekends exploring a large city nearby, sometimes venturing to another metropolis where assorted taboos and promiscuous sexuality abounded.

Despite her antipathy about conventional values, Aunt Gina was exceedingly proud of Simon's academic record, understandably confusing it with accomplishment. She was not disturbed by his aimless attitude about the future, because vocations and jobs were, to her, just ludicrous excuses for accumulating money, and Simon already had plenty of that. Privately, however, she was just as worried that he might opt for some career or other, as she was afraid he'd meet a woman near his age and settle for less than nothing. There was little risk of either happening.

As he grew further into adulthood it became clearer that his major goal and single-minded ambition was just to seduce as many older women as possible. It was more than an obsessive preoccupation, but the obvious outcome of his early training and indulgence, uninfluenced by education or casual sex with young women his age. Occasionally, pursued by younger women, he bedded them reluctantly, but without the passion he reserved for older women. While most young men his age would have been pleased to fornicate with almost any female contemporary, Simon's interest was tepid and perfunctory. His ruling passion concerned much older women, usually of another generation, that many young men would find totally uninteresting. Simon did nothing to outrage the community. His sexual appetite, however slanted and unusual, proved difficult to satisfy. Despite his charm and experience, he found it less than easy, with the exception of a few older women in the larger cities. In single-minded pursuit, he saw less and less of Aunt Gina, who was apparently satisfied with his way of life, although she remained uninformed. Simon found himself drawn to larger cities, where armed with curiosity, plenty of money, and a commanding erotic passion, he managed to get into the local underground. Discreet advertisements helped him find what he was looking for. In this way, he met a number of men and women. Sometimes older married couples found this young man most amusing and diverting. They were indulgent and helpful about his professed preference. In exchange for his services, a few older women readily volunteered. Then certain couples introduced him to others, and soon he acquired a retinue that he regularly visited.

Chapter 3—Chester

Of his new friends, who remained pleasantly anonymous or used names that were colorful but vague, Simon soon learned who was worth cultivating, which ones were too risky, emotionally unstable, or even verging on early senility. He used them judiciously, for his own ends, managing to detach himself when their arrangements promised nothing of interest and novelty.

Midway through his junior year in college, Simon decided to visit Aunt Gina and doing something even less common, chose to hitchhike. He was somewhat weary of visiting his big city acquaintances, anyway, and indeed, halted his weekend forays a month earlier. Hitchhiking was a somewhat puerile but economical means of travel, but for Simon, there was always the prospect of an adventure. Getting into a car with a total stranger generated many sorts of fantasies, few of which materialized. But he did meet a number of strange, often troubled people who confessed their shortcomings, current problems, and, often enough, their innermost wishes to this unknown young man. Occasionally, a woman picked him up, but despite a few hints, nothing came of it.

Now, as he stood curbside, just at the town limits where drivers in large numbers passed by, Simon had little time to waggle his thumb. Very quickly, a man in a large sedan stopped and offered a ride. His host, a well-dressed man in his midforties, introduced himself by first name. It was an unusual and hasty thing to do. Most often, drivers were content never to exchange names, because it was unlikely that they'd ever meet again. Consequently, Simon was alerted to something a little more personal.

Chester was not only friendly, but also talkative to a fault, rambling on and on about his job and peppering Simon with questions about college. He was a manufacturer's representative, on the road a good deal; more than a mere salesman, other salesmen in effect worked under his supervision. Simon wasn't sure what Chester represented, and didn't care. Chester emphasized that he was well paid, a topic that Simon would have hesitated to ask about. Few men offered such information unless there was a reason. Soon, as they talked, Chester's reason for candor became apparent, when his affable questions became more focused.

"How are the girls here?" Chester began, casually enough. There was not much originality or surprising about this overture. "Pretty sexy, I suppose. A lot different than when I went to school back there." Chester turned out to live not far from where he picked Simon up. Simon was hardly naïve, and realized what his host was after. However, if sexy conversation was what Chester wanted, it was a cheap way to pay for transportation.

"Oh, some are sexy enough, but not all. I don't know that many, but I know enough. There's plenty of stuff around. No trouble getting it, if you know where to find it." He acted nonchalant, but was prepared to talk about what Chester wanted to hear. The pitch would be coming soon.

"I'm married," Chester said, "But I'm on the road a lot, traveling like this but I fly to either coast every month or so. I don't know people where I happen to stay, except the businessmen, so I'm at loose ends most of the time. I get restless, know what I mean?" He might have said that he spent his time away from home loosely. "I have to be careful; everyone should be these days. I watch out where I go and who I'm with." Simon nodded sympathetically; Chester had identified himself as a lonely but horny businessman away from home.

"What do you do mostly when you're on your own in a strange town?" Simon asked, knowing his cue. But Chester would have told him anyway.

"It's easy enough finding someone if you're not too particular. No whores, nothing like that. Have you ever heard about these places where there are young guys to fool around with? I don't mean a real young boy; that's dangerous. Just fellows in their early twenties, around that age. Sometimes I read ads in the local paper for any kind of action; that's one action I think about. Never tried it though. Fool around any way you like." Simon was noncommittal, sure that Chester would soon make a move.

"Oh, I've heard about lots of places," he said, "Can't tell you more than that. Never came across the real thing. It sounds pretty fancy, if that's what you like. How come you never tried it?" He waited for Chester to continue the conversation. Chester said nothing but then started talking faster and driving slowly. As if pacing his own mounting excitement, Chester clutched the steering wheel, controlling himself as well as the car.

"If you'd like to go with me sometimes, I'd be glad to pay for both of us," Chester continued amiably. "I still do my duty at home, but when I'm away I get to do stuff that never happens there. My wife is very broad-minded, but frankly, I like to go both ways." Simon was sure that Chester's invitation was for real, although going to a male brothel might be just talk. Nevertheless, Simon wasn't ready for either kind of adventure, not having desire for men. He knew from weekend friends about male hustlers, but they sounded pretty seamy and not too healthy. A man like Chester with cash and connections could usually find what he was looking for. Chester might be all right for a passing fling, but a stranger who had been with other strangers was hazardous. But it was another taboo, not yet completely breached.

Although that was stimulating to a degree, Simon wasn't ready to accept the invitation.

Simon was becoming more attentive to Chester's line of talk by imagining Chester's broad-minded wife. He had to conjure up a fantasy about her. Without that, any proposal from Chester was just idle conversation, destined to go nowhere. Does this unknown woman suspect Chester's tastes? Did she accept his conduct, or play around herself? How old could she be? If she was as old as Chester that was fine, but if not, how much younger? His fantasies were going in all directions, leaping toward the time when he'd find out. Meanwhile, Chester was almost pleading with Simon, even clutching his groin, and making sure Simon noticed.

"I'd be glad to pay," he repeated, "With something left over for you, if you like." Their trip was soon coming to an end, and Simon had to do something about keeping Chester in tow but refusing anything else for now. That Chester solicited a hitchhiker meant that he wasn't so careful.

"No promises, this time, Chester," Simon was coy and cautious, still imagining Chester's wife. "I'm just not that interested in going that far, for now. Maybe another time."

Even that delayed promise seemed to arouse Chester, but he couldn't persuade Simon. In Simon's mind, Chester's wife was becoming older and more attractive by the minute. That was uppermost, but a careful plan had to be worked out. He wondered what Aunt Gina would say. She was still his mentor, guardian, and the only woman at the center of his life. Every other woman he'd been with remained distant and utterly peripheral. Simon was clear about that. Thus, when the ride finally came to an end, he and Chester shook hands warmly, and exchanged names and telephone numbers. Simon smiled in anticipation, but not really expecting to hear from Chester again.

It had been several months since he'd last seen Aunt Gina. Evidently she was satisfied with such minimal visits, not chiding him. It was with more than casual custom that he let himself into the house, knowing that Aunt Gina was probably in her upstairs study, talking on the telephone. She seemed a little surprised, however, and almost immediately ended a conversation she'd been having with someone unlikely to be identified. Nevertheless, pleased by the unexpected visit, she listened without comment when Simon explained how busy he'd been. It was difficult to avoid subjects that were always beyond her willingness to enlighten him, and still show warm interest in what each other had been doing. Neither one probed and seemed to accept the visit without questioning the elapsed time. There was never a kiss of greeting, but amenities came easily. Rather too quickly, Simon told Aunt Gina about his ride with Chester, not hesitating, indeed, eager to tell her about Chester's proposition and his own fantasy about Chester's wife.

Aunt Gina listened well, without interrupting to register an opinion. Of course, she condoned almost every new opportunity to deal with a taboo, which usually meant a forbidden but intriguing experience. This time, however, she seemed reserved, because it was hard to disguise how dubious she was.

"Chester? That's the name? Sounds like your average married middle-aged man; out to get what he can, before it's too late. Wants to keep safe in whatever he does. Likes it both ways and wants it both ways. Young college boys, preferably straight, of course, are what he wants, not hustlers. But willing to pay for it. College boys always need the money, or almost all, not you, of course. You should have seen right through him, except for that teaser about his wife. Maybe he didn't mean it that way. He sounds pretty ordinary; you don't know if he even has a wife." Aunt Gina was her skeptical self about men, but she was concerned about Simon's apparent enthusiasm. The invitation to a male brothel didn't sound right. "It's unheard of around here. That's why gay men go overseas. Probably a come-on, bait to see if you're willing. If you aren't he'll come up with something else to hook you. Maybe he'll dangle his wife in front of you." Everything she said made sense. She didn't suggest that he'd never hear from Chester again.

"Might not work out with the wife, even if he has one. He wants to get you in the sack. If that's his proposition, remember that you aren't gay, and never will be, though I suppose you want to try it out. I don't see you pretending to be something you're not, even to get something more to your liking. Gay guys would accept or flatly turn him down, not let him go with a maybe. It's up to you. If you like the idea of letting some poor slob go over you, I don't imagine he'd stop at much, including promising you a fling with his wife. She might not exist or be interested. Think about it some more. I see how eager you are. But don't jump into something you don't want. For God's sake, do it if you can't help yourself!"

Gina had seldom expressed herself so strongly, and Simon knew she was right. There were enough older men cruising around the campus, a pretty pathetic lot; he wanted no part of them. But he was already overheated about Chester's wife. If it weren't for this mythical woman, Simon would not be talking about Chester at all. Gina could not stop with her disapproval.

"Chester evidently goes both ways. Bisexual men are risky. They do both sides and use any port of call. Don't ever take money from him, even for the game. That gives him power over you that he shouldn't have and makes you into a hustler, the lowest form of life I can imagine. Don't kid yourself that Chester's just a horny yokel, a frustrated husband looking for a clean-cut college boy. Don't imagine you're the first, either. You know better than that. No telling who or what he's been with. His wife may be all wrong for you, if it happens at all."

It was sage advice. Simon no longer wondered where she had learned and knew so much, and not from books. Back in her study after dinner, their conversation continued; there was not much else to talk about. However, Simon had never seen her so overtly against anything as now, especially a taboo topic like dabbling in the gay life. She did not want him to be drawn into a situation he could not control. Being in charge not only meant superior power but protection against the disreputable people he was bound to meet. Simon's penchant for much older women did not displease her. She had certainly fostered this craving. Old women were for Simon's protection; and certainly were unlikely to trap a young man by pleading pregnancy or wanting marriage. Gina had a dilemma: how could she discourage him about Chester, and yet approve of pursuing Chester's alleged wife? Simon had had so few older men in his life; he might even like Chester, and get to enjoy being in bed with a man. This could be risky.

Afterward, sitting by herself, Gina thought hard about various dour possibilities. Privately, she considered tracing the man, should Simon pursue what he was imagining. They might never contact each other again, but that would not take care of future Chesters who surely will come along, offering more than a ride. Gina knew that like most people she had a hypocritical streak running strongly inside. Violating every taboo wasn't necessary, and a homosexual encounter might only endanger Simon. While holding much hope for strengthening Simon, and making him different from the contemptible men she usually dealt with, she had little corners of doubt shared only with herself. Of all the fates she feared such as an unwanted marriage or simply imprisonment by swarming prejudices and pretenses, Gina surely didn't want Simon to turn gay. That was a hard life, regardless of a man's other traits and qualities. Somewhat ruefully, she wanted to hang onto that boy as long as possible, even longer. A gay Simon would be unthinkable; she was nauseated at the picture it evoked. Simon might turn out to be just another promiscuous lecher, hanging around bathhouses for pickups. All that meant was that she'd practically adopted a boy, raising him according to what the world considered corrupt standards, but all for nothing. Gina despised failures, and didn't want to be one. Something had to be done, and done quickly, just to prevent him from being victimized by a bisexual prowler. No longer could she pretend to be absolutely open-minded; no one could be, anyway. The next morning was not too soon, but first, late as it was, she had to make plans.

Breakfast was delayed, so Gina had a little more time.

"Simon, I must tell you, frankly, having thought about it, I worry that this Chester could cause a problem. I'm not sure just what. He may be all right; I told you to get it over with, if you're tempted to experiment. That's what it is, since you're not gay. Events have proved that, I must say. But it's hard to keep things experimental. Ask any gay man with his pants up or down, even if you dabble from time to time, as some men do. Don't be reckless just because you have a notion about a woman who might not even exist. It's easier to fall into something than to jump out."

This was vintage Aunt Gina, more voluble and just as considerate, but still a sheathed sword. Simon had to heed her words, although a night's sleep did nothing to restrain his fantasies.

Long after ceasing to sleep together, Simon and Aunt Gina cultivated candid and honest talk, steeped in a unique upside down conventionality. The earlier incestuous years had given way but solidified an intimacy that many more legitimate families might envy. While Simon struggled against her dogmatism from time to time, he had to listen to her words with obedient respect. Unflinching insistence on drawing limits and resisting exploitation were cautions that held Simon firmly, and were designed to prevent him from being victimized then or in the future. Both knew that sexual desire, powered by perverse inclinations, tolerates no amount of prudence standing in its way. It imperiously sets the momentum and model for transgressing taboos.

Nevertheless, he was both surprised and a little annoyed when Gina called soon after he returned to college, almost insisting that he come home the following weekend. This in itself was unusual because Gina seldom urged, and even more rarely imposed any pressure to do anything. She did not have to use pressure or persuasion; it was already there.

When the weekend arrived, he took no chances and came home using his own car. Neither mentioned Chester; the topic was only slightly submerged. When, after dinner, they settled down again in her upstairs study, she calmly said that during the week she'd found an alternative to playing around with Chester just to meet his wife, a dubious strategy at best. What she offered was an intriguing proposition, something altogether new for Aunt Gina.

"I've wondered if you'd like to meet this woman I know slightly. A woman very substantial, a widow, but I believe you and she might get along very well, the two of you together." Her proposal was almost casual, quite in contrast to the loaded talk of the week before. Never before had she actually offered to be an intermediary. He hadn't needed one.

"You are certainly old enough, and I'm happy to say, attractive, well-behaved enough, and discreet enough to handle a very delicate situation. This lady is certainly much different and much higher class than some of the specimens I'm afraid you've hung around with." Simon immediately came to attention, waiting for details. "She's been a widow, say, about ten years, not a young woman, of course, but mature enough and lively enough. She's not like some widows, hot for a new man, but she lives alone, very private, with grown children. There are plenty of women looking for adventure, cruises and all that. She's not like that. She's been doing what wealthy women of her class do for the community with their time and money. The family has been prominent because of that, with plenty of culture to go with their money. I doubt if she's had an affair since her husband died. I wouldn't know, though. She is certainly not the kind to take up with a young man, unless…unless she could be sure. I do think she's at the point of spending a little time, at least at night, doing things for herself besides grandchildren, meetings, and sponsoring one good cause after another. She needs a cause of her own. She's not a common person at all." Gina did not have to wait for Simon's answer; he was conspicuously enthralled. Gina let it all sink in, and then continued. "Of course, she wouldn't consider it if you weren't who you are. She insists on discretion, absolutely, not a word to anyone else. I told her she could count on you in every respect. Yes, I talked with her; she agreed, at least tentatively. It is completely new for her, and I suppose also for you."

Simon did not miss Gina's emphasis on *insists*. Gina had not only spoken with this woman, whom she referred to only as Sophia, an odd and somewhat foreign sounding name, but had brokered the meeting. He was astonished. The encounter with Chester rattled her into quickly setting up a plan. The arrangement was intended to quell any desire for Chester, by appealing to Simon's very well entrenched fantasies. Gina had known, of course, about some of his adventures with older men and women. If she was worried or dubious, she had said nothing, not considering it more than playful exploration. Sophia was safe in all respects, too cautious and discriminating to compromise Simon in any way or to claim him for her own. If everything worked out, Chester might fade away entirely.

Simon scarcely understood, much less fathomed his beloved Aunt Gina, even after prolonged intimacy and candid conversations over the years. He had suppositions and theories, of course, but only glimpses of her own experience here and there. Friends, both men and women frequently visited Gina. What they talked about he did not know. Simon assumed that some were simply seeking counsel, and willing to reveal private things. Evidently they understood that she was absolutely trustworthy and totally capable of keeping a confidence. Without a scrap of evidence, Simon also suspected that Gina kept a file about people and when needed, it provided a subtle leverage. Perhaps this happened when she needed someone like Sophia.

What would she do with confidential information? Aunt Gina did not seem to need very much from anyone. Did she influence the people she knew about, or who owed her for past favors? How did his aunt come to meet, know about, and persuade a woman like Sophia to agree to a position alien to her way of life? Or was it so alien? Class standing had nothing to do with passion, he already knew. However, such a candid proposal had to be confidential. Gina must have been very sure about Sophia.

The prospect of meeting Sophia was so irresistible, however, that he put aside the technicalities of how it all happened so quickly. Simon wanted to meet Sophia as soon as possible. He almost ignored a warning that his ardor might frighten her away. This woman needed to be cautious, and preserve her dignity and reputation.

Nevertheless, the next evening, rather late, but according to precise instructions, he telephoned Sophia, introduced himself, and after a subdued, friendly conversation, arranged a meeting. While somewhat brief, it was most agreeable. Her soft cultivated voice and speech were gracious, stimulating, and inviting, indicating that she was not only prepared but also rather eager. Simon could scarcely believe that Sophia was as inexperienced as Aunt Gina suggested. She was not at all like the other overheated women he had anything to do with before. This was a classy person, quiet, but responsive and prepared to undertake something most unconventional for her. Simon, brought up as he was, was equally soft-spoken, restrained and tactful. He felt privileged to be part of a new venture. Aunt Gina was right, and Sophia was surely right for him. It was a vote of confidence.

He was more than willing to stay over an extra night or two, just to see Sophia. While just as willing as Simon, however, she put him off until the following weekend, late at night, around eleven, when they were unlikely to be disturbed by telephone calls or seen by others. Gina had prepared him for that. Sophia was frankly concerned about his visit, but that plan was preferable to anything else. She gave Simon specific directions and would alert the doorman that he was a guest and allowed in.

The week dragged slowly. Saturated with erotic expectations, he thought of little else but the adventure awaiting him. Simon had no difficulty finding her apartment hotel, long accustomed to wealthy and prestigious residents. The tall building was not very old but still new enough to be a prideful addition to the upgraded center of the city, near the fashionable places, but far enough away to confer an aura of baronial privacy.

There was no difficulty about being shown the elevator to her lofty residence. The initial meeting went far beyond his imagination. Although she greeted him warmly and after comfortably settling in her living room, and conversing easily about things other than the primary reason for being there, little time was wasted on social amenities. Even with his elaborate expectations Sophia was everything Aunt Gina said, and more. She was no means beautiful, but far from unattractive. Now in her late sixties, exceedingly well groomed, especially for this nighttime encounter, she seemed to be well poised and in excellent physical health, most assiduously taking advantage of whatever salons and vacations at spas had to offer. Despite Simon's already extensive experience, he realized that this situation was unique. Sophia was so far beyond the older women he had been with that any comparison would be offensive.

Simon was awed by his surroundings, quietly reeking of wealth, taste and tradition. Nevertheless, Sophia was exceedingly easy and pleasant to talk with. Her large apartment overlooking much of the city was nothing like the grandeur of his own mansion on the hill, but its subtly fashionable style provided a luxurious background for Sophia and the situation in which Simeon found himself. They talked comfortably about general matters, while at first cautiously refraining from the unspoken but clear purpose of being there. She asked about college, which she knew about, and in turn told anecdotes from years before. Nevertheless, the conversational atmosphere soon became thick with sexual innuendo, which crept in along the edge of whatever they found themselves saying. Both commented that they liked the idea of the age difference, without saying why. As they spoke, warmly and confidentially, it seemed less and less like an inappropriate liaison, even a social deviation, but rather like an enchanting alternative to pairing with someone of comparable age. He did not hesitate to express genteel compliments, which she reciprocated, as if this were a mutual seduction and not an assignation. Simon's youthful sophistication complemented her mature but naïve charm, making everything seem natural and spontaneous, not at all pre-arranged.

Prior to meeting Sophia personally, Simon had qualms and misgivings about living up to whatever Gina described him to be. That he was Gina's own nephew, and to be trusted had to be a strong reason to accept Gina's offer. Nevertheless, Simon continued to be unreasonably afraid of being received as little more than a delivery boy, there to offer a service to the lady of the house. That was all before meeting her. Because she made him feel welcome, stimulated and at ease under the circumstances, he now could fully appreciate how, like a precious gem, she fit precisely into this setting. He was moving up in the world, and liked it immensely.

From the moment that she opened the door, her warm invitation mostly alleviated his concern. Clad in a smooth and sensuous robe, bare feet comfortably shod in expensive slippers, she had tastefully prepared herself. She offered a drink, which he cautiously accepted, as they sat on comfortable chairs, almost directly facing each other. The flickering lights of the city shining far below provided a silent distant reminder of their mutual mission, far away from intrusion. Simon was sure that her attire was intentional, because he could easily see her bare legs below the edge of her robe. She carefully crossed and uncrossed her legs, restlessly indicating, perhaps inadvertently, that words were but a preliminary. The purpose of being there was as bare as his desire and her body.

"Your aunt did not exaggerate, Simon," she said at last, music playing unobtrusively in the background. "She promised that you'd be just right for me, considering my inexperience. And I am a little embarrassed. Gina is a very understanding woman. She seemed to know without being told what I never talk about to anyone. It's good to know someone who is so frank and sympathetic. This is very new to me. Whatever happens must be very confidential. Your aunt assured me that you were trustworthy, *and* very attractive. I believed her and can see for myself that you are a very special and discreet young man. It's a compliment to all three of us that your aunt offered her nephew, whom she thinks so much of."

Simon sensed that almost anything Sophia said had a double-edge. Her misgivings had not vanished. She talked around the subject, not asking the obvious question that she was hesitant to put in specific words, which was "How do we go about shedding our clothes and getting on with it?" He relieved her restless indecision by slowly reaching over and touching her robe. She immediately responded in comfortable anticipation, awaiting something further. Preliminaries were over. He got up and moved next to her with a quiet embrace. It was reassuringly subservient and yet Simon controlled the pace. No words seemed necessary. She did not have to be afraid.

Simon caught himself several times. He had to be very deliberate and gentle with this lady. In his own mounting passion he could not strip off his clothes as he would in a locker room or with one of the elderly bawds he customarily made out with. He could only have what she was willing to share. Aunt Gina was unquestionably a most perceptive tactician. Simon knew better than to overwhelm Sophia. Momentarily he had to curb himself. Sophia was alert to her own excitement, concealed so long from anyone else and relieved only in solitude. Mutual nakedness and Simon's ingenuity aroused her in unaccustomed ways that she once, a long time ago, considered indelicate. Urged to reciprocate according to Simon Says, she showed herself to be an eager and apt pupil.

Oblivious to time, entranced and engulfed with an after-glow, Sophia was the first to break the silence.

"Your aunt was right. You have a way that any woman would relish. I've missed so much that I never had, and I think I want more of now." She laughed at being so bold. Simon tried to respond, but his mouth couldn't form intelligible sounds. He too had transcended the hour, more than even he imagined, considering prior adventures and partners. Her words kindled a renewed appetite then and there. However, in the midst of a groping second chance, he was suddenly reminded of his ungratified lust for Aunt Gina. While Aunt Gina consistently frustrated his efforts, Sophia clearly welcomed them, as if attempting to make up in a flurry what was denied during that long interlude.

Subsequently they met almost weekly, always late at night, ostensibly keeping a secret from curious neighbors prone to gossip. Simon's departures were when the night was still dark, but not long before daybreak. He was reminded of Gina's guests whom he spied on as a young boy. Careful not to awaken Aunt Gina as he silently climbed the stairs he could only wonder if Gina were listening as he once did, years before. Gina asked few questions on the morning after, largely because she didn't need to. As the weeks went on that Simon came to anticipate so keenly, he became fearful that Sophia would suddenly and without warning call everything off. When he invited her to meet at other places, she steadily refused, telling him that he was too eager and ardent and that this worried her.

Meanwhile, he could scarcely think of anything but his times with Sophia. It was entirely fresh for him who had long been sheltered from infatuation. Always prepared to walk away, this time there was no hint of waning interest. He was rapturous and impatient about every meeting with Sophia, while feigning a cadence of control that he did not feel. Although it was a preposterous suggestion, he urged her to visit his college town and stay at his apartment. It would be less hurried and not at all risky, he insisted. She refused quietly but firmly. It always reminded him of how Aunt Gina adamantly pushed him away with tender refusal, when he wanted to mount her. Surprisingly, another less familiar feeling overtook him, frightening but endearing. Sophia became just about the closest friend he ever had.

Simon found it strange that Sophia seemed to know next to nothing about Gina, in contrast to how quickly and confidently Aunt Gina arranged things. Knowing each other went in only one direction. Once Sophia asked about his uncle, assuming that Gina had been married and Simon was a legitimate nephew. When he questioned her about how she came to know Gina in the first place, Sophia instantly became vague and uncomfortable. Gina had certainly been so familiar and well informed about Sophia that her unusual and intimate suggestion got a prompt agreement. Simon, always discreet and unlikely to share information, said nothing about how he came to be considered a nephew. Once or twice, however, Sophia did relent and visited him at college where it was not unusual for an older woman and a young man to be seen together, and for others to assume it was family. But these were only brief visits, and aroused no comment, so far as either knew, even when she stayed the night.

With every week that passed Simon's infatuation increased. Their talks together offered Simon companionship he never had known, and might never be matched again. Along with their growing affection, heavily weighted on Simon's side, an agonizing conviction also grew, that it had to end sometime. When this disaster might strike could not be foretold, only postponed. Sophia never hinted at termination, but she never gave Simon any reason to think it would not occur. Simon dreaded the mourning and dismay at the wretched loneliness to come.

Fear of abrupt abandonment led him at last to confide in Aunt Gina who had already surmised the problem. What began as a pleasurable rendezvous protecting Simon from Chester now had gone far beyond what Gina originally planned. Gina was seriously concerned for her beloved but distraught nephew, at a loss how to prevent the harm that she had not intended. Simon was strangely, and actually in love with a woman so much older as well as inappropriate in every other way. It was not like breaking up with a girl his own age and then after a few weeks, finding someone else with whom he'd be just as infatuated. An explosive perhaps potentially tragic situation was inevitable. He was totally engulfed by a gathering tempest that could have violent ramifications.

Gina's favorite nephew was in danger. Until now, she had stood by silently concerned about unforeseen consequences. Simon now came home practically every weekend, spending very little time with Gina before rushing off again to Sophia. Then he would return before dawn, dissatisfied and disconsolate, so far as Gina could tell the following morning. His college work, of course, was in shambles. She resolved to drop false neutrality and confront him, just about the time that he decided to confess his helplessness and terror.

Once again, he came home, eager as ever to see Sophia, looking harassed, as if he lost whatever autonomy remained. He found Aunt Gina solemnly looking out her window at the distant horizon, when he let himself in and climbed the stairs to her study, just like old times.

"I didn't hear you come up the stairs," she said, with just a hint of chiding him.

"I'm sorry, I just didn't think," he said, close to an apology, "I was in a hurry to see you."

"You seem to be in more of a hurry these days than I ever remember," she said, "What's the matter? You're not in any hurry to see me. You're rattled, but why play games? I never like to interfere but I know that it's about Sophia." Simon was anxious to talk it out, but more than a little defensive about admitting how deeply the affair had taken hold of him and compromised the independence she had striven to develop. He was entangled, and still didn't want to be freed.

"You don't have to wonder why I'm here. It's true, I'm a mess, and I do visit a lot more than I used to. Yes, yes, it's all about Sophia and where I'm going. I mean what if she decides to break it off? I don't think I could stand it; that's hard to admit. You have always been so on top of things, and I'm not. What's going to happen? I'm in a nightmare."

"Simon, neither one of us is stupid, but you are so upside down that you forget from one moment to the next that we haven't talked at all about what's ailing you. It's more than that now, and I am worried about your health, too. The whole thing has gotten out of hand. It's a kind of insanity. You know that something must be done quickly or you'll be done for. It used to be that you were away, away at school, I presumed, doing great things, I hoped. I knew about your expeditions, too. They seemed pretty harmless. I wouldn't hear from you at all but that was all right. Now it's a regular thing, back here with Sophia, and it has nothing to do with missing me," she said, ironically, "You know, I still think about you, now and then."

She was more than a little impatient, and faintly sarcastic, while still trying to contain herself and keep from denouncing him for being such a traitor to her principles. For her, he was a callow fool duped into an affair and now crying to her. She was ashamed for him. He was hurting, but he was a disappointment, this man in love. Gina, truth be known, despised anyone in love. She could be stern when called for, but Simon was almost bleeding with dread and fear. In desperation, seeking to absolve himself, and looking for an acceptable face-saving excuse, Simon thrust back to an old and familiar lament: blaming Gina for her long ago absences and token desertions. His complaints, of course, were not unlike his present problem. He was afraid that Gina, too, might leave, break it off and never return.

"I do disappear like you used to and come back without warning," he said "And no bulletin about where I go. No apologies, no explanation. I worried that you'd disappear and never come back, but you did, and everything was O.K. again, for awhile." He knew he was prattling, marking time lest he talk about Sophia, avoiding what truly scared him, and of course, Gina understood it all. Complaints about where she'd been years ago were by now threadbare, except when Simon needed to haul them out of storage and berate her again. It was easier to blame her than Sophia or most of all, himself, for violating what he'd been taught and had instilled, ending up a mess, a self-pitying adolescent, belatedly going through first love.

"Oh, that's it? Tell me something I don't already know. The point right now is that you can't stay away from Sophia, and I know it only has to do with Sophia and the struggle you're having inside. In fact, you are becoming more a pain in the ass than I like you to be, and I hope, you'd like to be. You're a pain because you're caught up in such drivel, and acting so helpless. You'd like to switch blame back on me, but that's such an old story. Spare me your tears and moans. I wanted you to be above all that, sorry though I am that you're moaning and groaning. Carrying on like this. What's eating at you is Sophia. You have to face it, my dear, and not keep running back to her and away from something else. What are you going to do about it before she does it for you?"

"You're right," he admitted, soberly, "I worried about losing you and now it's worry about losing her. Only this time it's much worse. I know I can count on you, and in a way I count on her. But I'm afraid I mostly count on her to leave me some day, and I can do nothing about it. What's more, it has to end, but not now, please! What can hold us together? It's not exactly one-sided, but I am so afraid. It's like she'll die and that will be the end, and of me, too." For a moment he again wept, and Gina could only stare at his weakness.

Simon looked out the window at nothing in particular, struggling to control himself. Still more tears were already in his eyes that he didn't want Aunt Gina to see. It wasn't that Sophia would die, but that she'd banish him and they'd never meet again. Gina continued to stare at him, almost fuming, while worried and concerned that Sophia was giving her nephew a very hard time, as only the upper crust knows how to do. She was angry with Sophia for letting it happen, but more deeply disappointed that her insistence on keeping a superior and controlling position had now been undermined. She refused to call what was happening "lovesickness." That was the rubbish she could not tolerate. His suffering was far too special to have any conventional name for what her nephew was going through, the poor slob!

There was suicide to consider, too. Suicide was now really not very far from Simon's mind and unhappy spirit. Staring out of the window, off to that familiar and distant horizon, he wondered how window-washers manage to climb so high, without falling. He pictured a much younger Steve, slowly twisting in a free fall towards his death. Falling from this high window was easier by far than falling in love; there, death, much as he feared, could be a consolation. Everyone would pity him, and breaking Sophia's pledge about secrecy and confidentiality might be a suitable revenge. Simon so simple had fallen in love, stupidly, and now weeping a bucket full of tears. Simon couldn't tell if the windows were open or not. People could fall out of open windows, if they aren't careful. He was grimly amused by his inane dilemma: open windows were a temptation to jump, and closed windows risked getting slashed. What if he threw himself out the window, without getting cut, but dying with a thud and a shattering splash on the ground below? It was just this painful uncertainty. Suicide would put his mind at ease, but he'd have to pay a price and leave Aunt Gina, too!

"The fact is, Aunt Gina," he said, "I never told you this, but I was jealous. But there's no one to be jealous about now. That's it. Not just lonely. You were leaving me for someone I didn't know. Some grown up guy, not a kid like me. I envied him. I didn't know where you were and with a guy I didn't know. I've complained about this before, but now I feel like an under-aged reject again. Pain in the ass? Yes, any reject has to be a pain in the ass, unless he just tucks his tail in and sneaks away. I was jealous of all the people you had so much fun with at your parties, laughing so much, and afterward, too. They must have had fun because some of them didn't leave until the next morning."

He was on forbidden ground, and trembling inside, as if an earthquake was about to destroy them both. There had always been strict rules about intrusion into private matters, and here he was, violating them. It also went against her uncompromising principle about feeling too deeply about anyone.

"Jealousy? Oh, spare me that crap!" Gina almost exploded with wrath, "Where did you learn to be jealous? Not from me! What do you expect me to do? You have such damned excuses! I taught you that jealousy or any other feeling about someone only rips you apart, right down the middle. It's like shit getting on your shoes. Who's going to scrape it off? No, the shit is in you, inside where it really festers. Some shit! That's what it means to me. It's shit and you're full of it! I hoped you were above all that, but here you are; ready to bawl your eyes out, whimpering like a puppy dog. Here you are, all grown up, screwing your head off with God knows who, and now you're in love! Asking over and over about why I did what I did, then complaining about Sophia, and that it's my fault for setting you up in the first place. Snot-nosed nonsense, just like a fucking cry-baby!" She was clutching her hands, not to keep from striking him, but to hold back her own unwelcome tears. She had not cried in years, not since that which remains nameless happened.

This was a drastic denunciation, something rare coming from Aunt Gina. Her reserved, dignified and yet affectionate front always seemed so natural, and impervious. She was furious, not at all sympathetic, and cruder in words and grimaces than he had ever seen her. Simon took her scolding as needling, demanding that he go back to the way he was before getting into this ignoble affair. But he was helpless, a pitiful wreck, and fearing something still worse. Falling in love was the crime. This was a fervent taboo that he'd broken. Gina couldn't find a way to forgive such a transgression.

"You sent me to her, and we've gone at it ever since. It worked fine for a while. Now it's much more. You know that, and I'm ashamed that I'm not ashamed of breaking our rule. And she was no close friend of yours, either. I still don't know how you knew her. But for some reason, you knew her; you knew she was ready for anybody or me. I feel good with her; I hate to say it, but it's what I imagine feeling normal is like. But it hurts me, and I know it has to go one of these days. Not for awhile, until I figure things out or get more control over myself." He actually wanted Gina to approve of falling in love, which she was most unlikely to do. She would sneer and deride instead of comforting him with painless wisdom. He had violated the warnings. It was like a family of atheists and a youngster who wants to sing in a church choir. He shouldn't be surprised or insulted to be called a black sheep and a renegade.

Aunt Gina got up, walked over to her desk, riffled through some papers lying there, purposely unanswered, and then threw them aside impatiently. The moment seemed endless. He was being upbraided for a haunting and demeaning confession. Simon admitted that his infatuation and dismay were reprehensible, a dereliction of what he was supposed to be. Moreover, he dared to ask forgiveness and consolation. Falling in love, of all things, was anathema, a curse. It was an affront to Gina and what she stood for. Now, in some fragile incarnation of guilt, he was ashamed and knew that falling in love was a punishment for misdeeds unspecified.

"I'm glad you decided to come clean with me," she finally managed to say, in a less agitated voice. "I suppose it ought not to be a surprise. I can't go against nature, if that's what it is. But I don't like it for your sake, Simon." She slowly shook her head in rueful puzzlement. "I brought you up to be what you would choose, not to be somebody else's idea, and I can't blame Sophia, either. I'm sure she's as shocked as I am. I assume she cares for you, too, though she has to live and work by her rules. I hope she's bothered by what was supposed to be only a diversion, nothing more. That's what I thought, too. It's dangerous. You taste poison because the skull on the label is smiling. It's death and you're staring right at it, and afraid it'll change. It can only change for the worse! Now I'll break my own rule, and tell you something. I had a family once, a long time ago. I won't tell you where or when or even what happened, but I did. Then, for reasons I won't go into, I went away and never saw any of them again. Oh, how I wanted revenge on those self-righteous, low down, criminal assholes that'd never, never think of breaking any rules! That's what I call the criminal mind! I love to get revenge; one of life's sweet pleasures is enjoying someone else's misery. I never heard from them, but I still hate what they did, or didn't want to do! Self-righteous shitheads! Whether I'm your aunt or something else means nothing to me. And I hate that you care one way or another about me, Sophia, yourself, almost anyone. Indifference is control, but only if you want it! Call it gentle domination. That's what I mean and wish for you! Now I find you don't value it as much as I do!"

Gina caught herself saying hate and revenge. She didn't want even these sentiments, and wasn't sure she meant them deep down. That was the irony of it. She couldn't really hate that renounced family as much as all that. It was unseemly to want revenge.

"I am just very disappointed," she corrected herself, calming down as much as she could. "Go ahead. Make up a family for yourself. What good are they, anyway? They don't know, understand, or care that much. Go look for a long lost cousin selling insurance somewhere. Make your own toys to play with. Stick yourself with expectations. Be a fraud, live up to your fiction. I believe in fictions, too. They're not really lies, but very convenient for their commercial value, lots better than jerking yourself off about truth. If you still don't know what I'm saying, it's really too bad. I'm sorry if you don't, because you should know better."

Deep inside, something more was stirring in Gina. It might be regret for sending Simon to Sophia. She was now sensing something nostalgic and nonsensical about her own long ago family. Had she really taught him how to be independent, scorn taboos, rise above ordinary people, and resist ordinary compunctions? Now that he was doing something outrageous, like falling in love, it was like a blasphemy. She was shocked at being abruptly confronted with her own fictions.

Having heard her semi-confession, Simon momentarily became less distressed about his own plight. A slight crack in her imperturbable composure seemed briefly to relieve his suffering. Aunt Gina's profanity also seemed to have a theatrical quality. Were her serenity and defiance real? How much else was pretentious fiction?

"I do make things up," he said, "I wish I made up all this and then could switch it off completely. Pull the curtain, the play's over, and no encores. I always pretend this and that. I may be fooling myself now that I don't want to be as I am now. I've fooled myself very well. My imagination runs wild."

"If your imagination gets over-heated, so does mine, trying to keep up with the fictions you believe," Gina responded, unforgiving but relenting a little as she clutched at a hope that this was only a temporary delirium. Gina made a strong effort to rein in the conversation and temper the malice she had allowed herself to show. She wanted to take back her confession, too. "Forgive me for the show I've put on. But you can't forgive any more than I can. I enjoy revenge too much. I don't know what it is I'm asking, but, believe me, I don't care whatever you're doing with Sophia, it's all right. She's too fucking old for you, anyway, and much too well bred! Harmless enough relaxation, just that. So get it out of your system now. Fuck her and be done with it." She wanted to rid herself of the noxious thought of Simon in love.

His passion for old women had accidentally spilled over into infatuation. She tried to see it as a trivial side effect of good intentions. Gina arranged an affair with Sophia just to get rid of Chester and spare Simon from another kind of poison. One reason strengthened the other, so that no real harm was done. Something indelibly unforgiving took place when Gina said that the love between them made everything else unnecessary. That was no fake, to be cast aside indifferently. But if that, too, were a fiction, then Simon's professed love for Sophia was also a total sham, another incandescent blistering fiction. What he still wanted was Aunt Gina. Sophia was only a stand-in, whatever other drama was being played out. Gina would have been enough for him; that was both forbidden and true.

"There's not much room inside me," he said, practically to himself, "I have to be sure that I really and sincerely don't care. You and I think the same way. We're special and can get away with anything, just by believing our own fictions. How I want to believe that I've just made up how I feel and by willing it, turn my back! We can be untouched, except in bed somewhere, maybe. My current fiction right now is to want Sophia and not care for her at the same time. I feel grown up and big, and that has to be all pretending, all my imagination. And being afraid of my grief when it ends, why that could be all fake, too." And so the deceiver in deceiving himself knows better than to believe what he pretends.

Prodded by her own memories, Gina did not have to be reminded that pretense aside, yearnings are like a relentless river that cannot be dammed up permanently. She pitied such sufferers who drown in self-pity while trying in vain to swim against the tide. It made her ashamed of having a soft spot for Simon, and for lying to him.

"You are special, Simon," she said, almost tenderly, and then, catching herself, "But not in the way you imagine. What the future holds for you, I try not to imagine. I can't, and neither can you. It's just as well. You'll have to figure it out for yourself. I don't want to."

By this time, her vituperation had already dissipated. This serious chatter must end. She had already slipped and said more than was tolerable. Gina resolved once again to maintain her fortress. Sternly, she'd have to live with that decision. She donned once again the dignity of self-control, like a suit of armor that made her all but invisible from the outside.

"Now, Simon, I have some things to do, those papers over there. Have to get them done," she said, too brightly and nonchalantly, "And, oh, by the way, in case I forget, please remember me to Sophia. We'll have to get together for lunch one of these days." If her casual offhand reminder about Sophia seemed gravely ironic, it was small price to pay for restoring her familiar self. Now she could leave Simon and his moaning lovelorn nonsense aside, and get her letters done.

Chapter 4—Virtual Fictions

Shortly after his conversation with Gina, Sophia broke off their affair. Dread of abandonment never left him and only amplified his attachment to Sophia. Simon would have continued indefinitely. While trying to adopt a more rational and less helpless attitude towards the certain break-up, Simon still hoped it would not be permanent, but only a temporary interruption, until their mutual passion brought about reconciliation and resolution. But when the break came he was incredulous. It should not have come so quickly and conclusively. At first, she simply failed to return telephone calls, which he always placed at the same time, late at night. Then, she left a message, canceling the next meeting, followed by another and another Simon knew, of course, that something was happening. He pleaded for another time together while fearfully certain that whatever she had to say was beyond negotiation. Finally, they met at her apartment, but from the moment he came in, the atmosphere indicated that a different kind of session was about to occur. There was no welcome in the way he'd been accustomed to. Sophia barely waited until they were seated, before talking about her decision.

"Simon, I've put off seeing you, or even talking with you until I settled things for myself," she said, after a few moments. "I intend to end this, our meeting together, whatever it is, whatever we've been," she said, sounding very firm and resolute, "It's just become too intense, gone far beyond what I intended at first, and maybe for you, as well. We are going nowhere. It is over, finished. I know you've wanted even more. But I'm not ready to go on, any further. You've been more than a friend, much more than just someone to go to bed with, too. If you know me at all, please don't argue or try to change my mind. It's difficult enough. That's not to be. Try to see that what we had is over with. I can manage and I'm sure you will too."

She went on, repeating herself but not wavering. Sophia was inexperienced ending affairs, just as she was in having affairs. Nevertheless she was accustomed to making her own decisions and was not to be swayed. Simon tried to change her mind, at first calmly, and then pleading with her to grant a reprieve, settle for something less drastic, anything but an immediate and final break. When he saw that her decision was firm and not open to anything but a total termination, he became more agitated, just what he'd been afraid of.

Erotic stories and elaborate fantasies ordinarily excited her immensely. Now, breathless and desperate, he tried the same stratagem by embellishing what they could do together. He was surprised when it had no effect.

Impassively staring at him, she seemed almost embarrassed by his ranting. There was to be no compromise, nothing more, no further meetings anyplace. That was all. She was not aroused and did not deviate. Panicked, with composure long gone, he raised his voice and began to swear, saying anything that crossed his mind, grasping for whatever raving might break through her resolve, a desperate verbal throttling that could do nothing more but solidify her stand. At last, partially out of exhaustion, he, too, realized that pleas and reproaches were futile. If Sophia were intimidated or hesitant, her silence and expression did not show it. From her manner, she was sorry for him, not frightened, and anything but regretful. He had made a pitiful scene, which only confirmed that a split was necessary.

Simon left without a good bye, thrusting himself out the door, angrily refusing to take her extended hand in a final good bye. It was impossible to manage a token gesture of an amicable inevitable departure. Unable to glance back before she closed the door, he was agitated, confused, clenching his fists in helpless anger, incredulous and incensed that fear had become fact. He tried to remind himself of Aunt Gina's insistent dictum, so recently repeated, about not caring too much about anyone or anything. It was more than good advice, but useless. Now, despair and fury were almost beyond control. To be without Sophia, never to lie with her in bed again, not to hear her voice or touch her, was like an abrupt, agonizing, and devastating death. Preparation for a break had been wholly ineffectual. His agitated, brutal departure seemed to herald an even more serious and calamitous future.

During the next few bewildered days he rashly considered calling again, with more pleas, but realized that this would only demonstrate once more her solid resolve. He had to accept her decision and turn away for good. How could he endure? Leaving suicide aside as a mere fantasy of retaliation, he wondered if perhaps he could throw himself into some outlandish orgy with his older friends in New York or Chicago, perhaps that might alleviate the agony. This plan, too, however, turned into another disappointment.

He found that they too were inexplicably gone in an eerie evaporation. In fact, their telephones were cut off. When asking for them by name at the old haunts, nobody, not the owner, nor the bartender, knew where these anonymous people had gone. They were simply customers who came and went, like many others. It was a mystery in which the characters abruptly disappear without explanation or forewarning. Had any of them, whom he thought he knew so well, really existed? Where had they gone? Was it by consensus or under duress? Did they, too, like Sophia, decide to disappear and have nothing further to do with him? Could he have just imagined the affair with Sophia as well as these people he hardly knew? Simon was suddenly even more desolate. The world was empty, and the familiar vanished. What next?

He hesitated to face Aunt Gina again, afraid that she, too, had gone away. After all his protests and her disclosures, he was too embarrassed to report that Sophia ended everything so soon afterwards. It never occurred to him that the timing of the break was suspicious, just like their initial introduction, and that Aunt Gina herself might have had something to do with it. Unable to continue at school as if nothing had happened, he took a leave of absence, now completely bereft, and went to New York, where he took a pathetically seedy room in a low-grade hotel. Flashing lights just outside his window all night and a constant din from the subway made sleep almost impossible, unless aided by unaccustomed drink. Although well able to afford first class accommodations, he felt so devastated and worthless in the empty world he happened still to inhabit that this lodging seemed appropriately bereft and debilitated. Frantically, he went from bar to bar every night until almost dawn, dance halls, clubs and dives, trying to put everything out of mind except raw impulses and ill-formed fantasies which would not be repudiated. Throwing himself into one risky or mortifying situation after another, his aimless wanderings eroded the little restraint and caution he had left. There were older women to be picked up. In exchange for substantial amounts of money and booze they were amenable to whatever he asked. However, their compliance gave him little or no relief beyond the moment. He could not shake the image of Sophia, nor could he successfully pretend that these women were anything but grimy substitutes. How could any of these old besotted harridans be other than humiliating reminders of what he lost? His pick-ups were willing to do anything. Paying to be soiled in any way imaginable, he was left with hollowness and resentment.

When he tried to visualize Sophia, he only managed to see her totally expressionless face at their final meeting. Humiliation and deep resentment were all that was left. Solitary and miserable, Simon was a prisoner of his mistakes. Alcohol helped even less. Once, after maneuvering two fairly young and callous prostitutes into bed, the women were amused by what he urged on them. One of them apparently sensed his suffering. She even asked what could bring this attractive young man with plenty of money to look for and do what he did. Another prostitute was afraid that she had got herself a weirdo, perhaps a sadistic freak who meant her harm, and threatened to call the police if he didn't leave at once. They could not, of course, know that Simon courted a state of numbed indifference through whatever corrupt or defiling sex he thought up. He was mocked by his own mortification, and wanted simply to die in the midst of defilement.

He lost count of nights spent in this way and days lying in a stupor. But then Simon succeeded only in degrading himself further. What he needed amounted to rebirth, not obliteration, at least a fresh start for another self. Finally, scraping together fragments of his fractured self, but exhausted, hungry and unwashed, still reeking of bad smells and sweaty stinks, he got himself back to college, tumbling back into old haunts, looking for old habits. Although half-intending to resume where he left off, he wanted to become another person inside his skin, cleansed and reformed, inexplicably better for his bottomed-out experiences. Of course, such resolution did not last. No one missed him except a few teaching assistants who casually noted his absence from classes and conferences. There were only messages from Aunt Gina that he put off answering, but nothing, only silence from Sophia.

As if by pre-arrangement, the telephone rang one morning. It was Chester responding to an almost forgotten message from Simon days before. During his affair with Sophia, Simon put aside plans about Chester and his wife, although not entirely forgotten. Aunt Gina's solution for Simon's dilemma had worked too successfully. Although Simon still had no appetite for Chester, he was discouraged, aimless, and empty enough to experiment with just about anything to clear his mind and raise his spirits. Exercises in degradation had opened him up and more amenable to another meeting with Chester. Nothing could be objectionable, restraint was in shreds, and anything between them could hardly matter. Consequently, he greeted Chester's call with a good imitation of enthusiasm, after a moment in which he did not recognize the voice. They started off an exchange of teasing with Simon feigning a sexual interest he did not truly feel. Strangely, as they spoke, Simon recognized a slight renewal of control over himself, a welcome change.

"How you doing, old friend?" Chester disregarded that they hadn't spoken since that first meeting in his car. "I've been on the road a lot. Haven't answered your call, but I've thought about you a lot. What are you up for these days? Handling things pretty well?" His voice was husky with poorly disguised innuendo.

"Not as well as you'd handle them, I'm sure," Simeon responded, wanting to get to the point as quickly as possible. He didn't have patience or time enough for verbal seduction, but had to simulate caution and deliberation.

"Well, when can we get together?" Chester answered. "I have plenty of open time now. The sooner, the better?"

"But where and when?" Simon said, "I'm pretty busy most evenings, and days, too. You must be too, unless you've been combining too little business with too much pleasure." Pretty corny stuff, but it was no time for witticisms. Now they were talking about details, not whether to meet. Chester made no allusion to male brothels. Probably, as Aunt Gina surmised, they existed only in his imagination. After more flirtatious bantering and teasing, Simon ended up inviting Chester to his apartment that very evening. His inner urges could not wait, and Chester's appetite tolerated no further delay. Simon then became more than a little apprehensive. Aunt Gina said to get it over with. Jousts with older women other than Sophia had not worked. It couldn't be worse with an older man. By this time Simon was beyond making sexual distinctions. Besides, Chester did want him and that must mean Simon's still worth something.

Simon hung up with a surprising calm, clearer in resolve than in a long time. He had formulated the strategy long ago, and was prepared to carry it out with a few variations. Let Chester do what he wants, fool around, but be sure to keep it one-sided, holding out a succulent bait for another time. Stay in control; keep Chester dangling in anticipation until Simon was ready. Chester must get both hooked and enamored. Sooner or later, he would be willing to serve Simon in any way, just to keep him, including getting his wife to join them.

At this time Simon had a mental picture of Chester's wife. She was to be everything he fantasized about older women, without any limitations and flaws. She would exceed Sophia, and in so doing; his imagination turned Sophia into a decrepit old lady, dried up and alone, and, of course, full of remorse that she had sent him away. The only hitch in Simon's plan was that Chester's wife in reality might fall far short of what he dreamed of, as well as not at all interested. But if all went well…This phrase repeated itself over and over until it seemed certain to Simon that all would go well. Chester truly was nothing but the bridge to his wife. Simon was not gay, nor did it matter, after all he had been through. Sex with men in any fashion scarcely appealed to him except to see what it was like. He knew that many straight men had just such exploratory fantasies. The plan surely confirmed that Simon was only using Chester for his one uppermost passion. His strategy was by now a three-way session with Chester's wife a very willing participant. She was Simon's prize, if all went well. However, what if Chester refused to go along? In that case, Simon decided, that would be the end of Chester. He'd be down the drain and Simon would be off to something better, whatever that might be. Simon says it all; that was the game, now real enough to make plans about.

Chester was early, and his eagerness showed. Although they had only been together once in the car, Chester embraced Simon like a dear old friend, hugging and reminiscing without true memories about a past they never shared. But they quickly turned to matters sexual, exchanging provocative stories. It didn't seem to matter that the stories were merely intended to get them aroused. During their ride, Chester offered Simon a euphemism for a fee, to pay his way to a male brothel. Gina strongly advised against it, not only because it seemed like prostitution, but also that money would give Chester a fulcrum of power he was not supposed to have. However, here tonight two taboos were ready to be violated: sex with a man and being paid for submission, except that Simon decided to try the first and refuse the second.

Chester did not mention money or imply anything hinting at prostitution. He acted as if two consenting adults were about to show friendship for each other in bed. Simon was no longer surprised to find himself less apprehensive and far less agitated about Sophia. He hardly thought of her since Chester called. That was a very agreeable change, and convinced him that he had made the right decision.

"I can't tell you how glad I am to get together, how great this is, here in your apartment and all," Chester exulted, "Much better than going somewhere, like a hotel. Everything private, except our own privates." He laughed, almost giggling at his good fortune and bad joke. Simon was ready to listen. They sat down to continue the eager conversational foreplay.

"What do you like to do? Remember, we didn't talk about details in the car, but you must have something special in mind," Simon said, smiling seductively as he slowly and gently rubbed what Chester eyed so avidly. Feeling calm and at last rid of nagging images of Sophia, it was Simon for sure who was ready for anything. The bed was just a few feet away, but it was a serious turning point in his image of himself. Breaking a new taboo did not thrill him as it had. This was business to get over with.

"Chester, I want to see and do what you like best, but let's get one thing straight. Right now, tonight, I am not going to do anything to you. Maybe another time, if you're good, of course, or better yet, very bad." He was about to update his old game, Simon Says, by arch comments and vague promises. Of course, Chester could not know that Simon's plans included a specific version of the game and were not at all vague. Only a timetable was lacking.

It did not take but a few minutes for Simon to undress, go into the other room and lie on his bed He deliberately turned the light very low, not just to hide the sight of another naked man, but better to imagine that this was Chester's wife. When Chester came into the bedroom, Simon was surprisingly and genuinely stimulated. It was not like this with the older men and couples in New York. With them, it was a frolic, a group sport with wives or friends. For Chester, however, there was nothing playful. It was serious, something to be reached, an obstacle to overcome, and a desire to fulfill. On his weekend jaunts, Simon had mostly confined himself to consorting with the women, while the men did whatever they chose. Now, he was really involved with a man, and despite pretending to be a passive partner feigning submission, he was in charge, and about to give orders. Simon found himself enjoying the naked glow of Chester, coming out of the darkness, pretending that it was Chester's imaginary wife.

When Chester first saw the naked Simon, lying spread-eagled, he let out a low moan of appreciation and was about to fling himself onto the bed besides him. Simon put up both hands and stopped him. They were not to be equals. Chester was to be submissive and wait upon Simon's orders. Simon Says.

"No, Chester. Take it easy. Remember what I said. Don't lie down. Get down and I'll tell you what to do. Be careful." Chester did not protest, but obeyed with alacrity, ready for his orders, gently fondling Simon and himself with anticipation. He was still grateful that this attractive young man was available. Of course, he knew nothing of Simon's recent struggles, nothing at all about Sophia, Gina, or anything else, except Simon's availability. Simon kept his own eyes closed and remembered Aunt Gina saying, "Try it, but you aren't gay." He wondered what truly gay men got out of this. Then he found that it was not altogether unpleasant, once he forgot that it was Chester doing adeptly what he liked best. In his erotic delirium he imagined that she was doing what Chester did. It acted like an aphrodisiac. Simon hoped that Chester would be as compliant when the time came to talk about a threesome, as surely it must. A few more sessions like this might bring Chester to a point of promising almost anything.

The tide rose and fell several times. Simon stayed silent and motionless, when Chester got up and began to prattle about nothing in particular, except his delight about what just went on. For Simon, it had been a key experience, never to be repeated in quite that fashion. Even considering his childhood with Aunt Gina and countless sessions with others afterwards, this event had no parallel. Curiously, Simon felt as if he had just lost his virginity, or had it taken from him compliantly, without force. Nevertheless, Chester was only the vehicle, a substitute for the real thing. Chester's wife was out there, a conquest yet to be made. Her image was incandescent. Best of all, his torment about Sophia had at last abated. Soon, her image might vanish entirely. Despite hesitant misgivings, Chester had helped Simon forget and restore his hope.

Chester and Simon met regularly during the next few weeks, without mentioning Maggie, his wife. Simon had at last learned her name, without yet suggesting that they meet. The opportune moment had yet to arrive. Chester kept pestering Simon about reciprocating, and while Simon refused, he promised it would not be long. Chester's imploring and insistence, coupled with mounting frustration made postponement difficult. Finally, there was a moment one evening when Chester seemed both cooperative and tormented, that Simon decided to ease into the proposal.

"Doesn't Maggie have any idea about you, Chester, that you like young guys, too? I've had to wonder about her. I know you've seen other fellows like me, but as regularly as we have?" Chester had taken pleasure in details of previous lovers, but never mentioning names. Like Simon, he often used earlier experiences, true or not, as stimulating anecdotes.

"I won't kid you, Simon," he answered, "You know I've been with other guys before, but nothing like this, even though you're holding out on me. No one fills me up the way you do, all warm and wet. Maggie and I still make love now and then. We've been married a long time. It's still OK, but I always want more than that, more than we manage, even when I get to screw another woman, which has happened. I am getting too hard up waiting for you to make up your mind. Maybe I'll have to get someone else." He hadn't answered Simon's question about whether Maggie knew about his penchant for young men. Simon knew he was only teasing, not threatening, and that he was ripe for Simon's next suggestion. Maggie was still Simon's enigma that not even Chester could anticipate.

"I wonder what Maggie would think," Simon went on, "If she knew about us? How open-minded do you think she'd be?"

"Well, I'm sure open-minded about swinging, I'll tell you that," Chester answered, without questioning whether Simon would ever tell. "I couldn't swear about Maggie. We never mentioned swinging. It would be a great idea, though. I've talked to fellows who swing with their wives, but I don't think I could ever get used to seeing Maggie with a stranger. It's just me, and ideas about my wife. I might be all wrong She's a great gal, but sex is something we don't talk about."

"How do you think swinging with me might go over?" Simon asked, "I'm a close friend, after all, not a swinger type. And I wouldn't take advantage. Just imagine the three of us together. How about that? What do you think about that idea? That might be the best time for me to do you, with Maggie watching? Appeal to you?" Chester didn't seem shocked, or surprised at the idea, as if he'd thought about it before. Simon had brought it into the open. "Just think. The three of us in bed together, watching and doing one another."

"I don't know. I never know what she thinks and knows. And what about you?" Chester nodded towards Simon. "You seem content having it all one-way. Swinging is nothing like that, from what I hear everything goes. And I mean everything." Simon's comment about not being a swinging type was something his New York and Chicago friends would dispute. But these vanished friends could not interfere. Chester did not know about them. For Chester, Simon still was a nice, quiet college boy, just trying to turn taboo on its head without having any other motive in mind. Simon kept this image burnished for Chester, knowing that a pretense of modest inexperience helped his cause.

"It's an idea, something you'd like but haven't had," Simon said, "I know I've not returned any favors, not that I don't want to, Chester, but it would have to be in the right situation." He tantalized Chester with a whispered, "If I ever got it into my head, with Maggie watching, I could see you'd like it fine." He heard Chester gasp, and with sudden anticipation, knew that Maggie would soon hear about it all.

Simon was so surreptitious and disingenuous by this time that Chester soon thought that a threesome was his idea all along. But he was torn between habitual reticence with Maggie, and the consummation that Simon had so far denied him. He could even picture Simon with Maggie, a stimulating and shocking image in itself. It was a lot more acceptable, especially with Simon's promise, than swinging with God knows whom.

Chester's opportunity came several nights later, lying in bed with Maggie. She seemed particularly receptive to talking, and he found courage to ask if she'd ever thought about having sex with anyone else but him. It was a simple enough question. However, the correct answer could hardly be given without considerably more candor than Maggie usually showed. In effect, however, Chester wanted both answers, Yes and No. Somehow Chester realized that despite total fidelity, few people are entirely monogamous in their thoughts. She might be hesitant, however, but by his question she'd immediately understand that he'd been having thoughts along those lines, and just wanted to check out her past, which was, in fact, none of his business.

Maggie surprised him completely. Instead of answering his question with a modest, if misleading "No, of course not," she declared, with a little laugh, "After all these years, you're just getting around to asking that? Chester, what brings this on tonight?"

"You mean it's not such a new idea?" he said, "I just wondered if…you know, since it goes on, whether…" He was now more embarrassed than his wife. Maggie was surprisingly matter-of-fact.

"Chester, my dear, I've not only thought about sex with others, but I'm also sure you've had much more experience along those lines than I have. I'm not an innocent, you know, and I have a pretty good idea what you're up to when you're away. I've seen how you look at young couples, and I often wonder which one you're interested in, the man or the woman. Now I see that it's both." Chester managed to say almost nothing, thunder-struck by her forthright openness. She also seemed to understand that no one swings without at least an overt homosexual tinge. Another night, perhaps, they'd talk a little more until he could tell her about Simon, his current young man. He did not have long to wait.

The very next night, shortly after dinner, Maggie, now pretty direct despite Chester's hesitation and with a gift of humor that seldom deserted her, brought up the subject again.

"How was it that just last night, you asked me about sex with others? I've been thinking about that all day," she said.

"I was just curious, that's all," Chester answered, without conviction, preferring to drop the subject and talk about anything else. He was now wavering in his intention to talk about Simon.

"Just curious, last night? Bullshit! Something's going on, and it's not just a quiet affair on the side that you want to keep quiet. I'm no schoolgirl, after all. Either you've been shacking up with a woman who wants to get it on with me, or with some fellow who wants the same thing. Otherwise you wouldn't be sounding me out. Which one is it?" She was clearly amused and insistent, not at all censorious.

"I don't know what to say, Maggie. A lot of what you guessed might be true. I'm not saying. But I do think about it. Honestly, I do think about it, and glad you aren't horrified by the idea." He couldn't quite get beyond that, so he repeated himself.

"Horrified?" she exclaimed, now laughing, "You remember my old friend from college days, Jeff? You met him a couple of years ago when he came through here for a medical convention. Well, the good doctor went both ways. You know what I mean. I'm sure you do. We slept together back then, and listening to him talk about other men put an extra something into what we did. I hear that men get off on watching two women. Lots of men and women like it both ways. So you're not that unusual." Chester was now embarrassed and flabbergasted by Maggie's open confession about Jeff. Maybe there were others, and he would have asked, but expected only to be rebuffed. She had told him enough, and he learned enough.

"It's not your business," she said, again smiling secretively, and guessing what else he wanted to ask "But you're my business, who you go with, and it might not be safe. I've suspected something was going on, and you've kept it from me." Maggie was forthright, more candid than he, certainly. He was not at all sure about her private life now. He could be sure, however, that she would not be outraged about Simon, his student friend, who promised him something. He had to take that chance and tell her about maybe a threesome.

"You've already guessed, Maggie, but I didn't plan to be so open about it," he said, "But some time back, I met this very nice fellow here, good-looking, has it all together, quiet, discreet, smart about the right things…He's a student, but not just another horny undergraduate. He's very sophisticated too. He's traveled a lot, good background, not at all promiscuous. I like him. I think you'd like him, too. Maybe the three of us could…" He didn't know how to finish his pitch. "Well, maybe you'd like to see for yourself."

Maggie was smiling with relief; at least it wasn't another woman. She knew that Chester must be smitten. His description was so exaggerated. Probably his friend is a little older, or older in experience and discretion than Chester imagines. So Chester's is having an affair with another guy. Why not? Perhaps it isn't too late for an adventure.

"I have to think about it, having the three of us right here on our bed. I'd want to meet him here, of course, see that his head is on straight, not just his pecker. I'd have to check that out later."

Chester was accustomed to Maggie's pseudo-tough talking. Usually it didn't mean very much. Now he was ready to believe anything. In fact, he was ready for anything, especially since she now confessed to having an affair of her own. It wasn't unreasonable to imagine others.

"Tell me about him, Chester," she said, "What kind of guy is he? What's he look like? Is he really a student? Where does he come from?" Relieved by her conditional acceptance, Chester became very voluble, talking about the Simon he knew. He was impatient to get back with the news.

Simon was enthralled when Chester told him about the conversation. Maggie sounded just like his Aunt Gina, although he had no reason besides occasional tough talk to think so. Maybe they looked alike. But she was no Sophia, despite her good education and teaching job at a local high school. Sophia had to be aroused and her desire revived, time after time. Maggie was not only ready and willing, but had some experiences of her own, with a suitable appetite for exploration. He was disappointed, however, to learn that she was not quite the idealized older woman he'd imagined. She was younger than Chester by at least a decade, still youthful, not yet middle-aged, and not prim and neither proper, nor very repressed after the surface was scratched a little. And she had a sardonic humor, which appealed to him. Although lacking Aunt Gina's magnetism and Sophia's breeding, she was far closer to the quintessential female he sought than the old women of recent past he'd been forced to consort with. He recalled with disgust the older prostitutes and casual pick-ups. Now that things at last were working out, he was eager to fulfill his longing.

When the three actually met for dinner and whatever was to follow, Simon was immediately intrigued by Maggie's cordiality, spontaneous humor and attractive appearance, which didn't quite fit in with Chester's somewhat unflattering description of what she was like. He had already been aware that to be plain was a mask that allows a person, man or woman, to pass unnoticed and then voluptuously shed, just as soon as the opportune moment presents itself. This evening was surely opportune for him. Whether it was true for Maggie, he wasn't so sure, but didn't need to know at that moment. Maggie greeted him warmly and informally, dressed with certain flair as she would for any other dinner guest. They shared a good dinner, and a wine that Chester said he kept for special occasions. They even spoke a little about Simon's background, not quite like checking his credentials, but certainly she was curious. He told the usual lies about Aunt Gina, and about being an orphan. Maggie told him outright that she was pleased that Chester's friend was so charming and handsome. They had had several of the same courses at college, and this provided a curious conventional aura for the evening. Chester said little, glancing frequently at his two companions, preoccupied and incredulous about what was taking place. Simon said at one point during dinner that Chester had been surprised at Maggie's forthright questions and some of her answers. Maggie smiled with an air of someone with many secrets, still unshared. Chester was not his typically verbose self, seeming at times to be glum, listening as the other two carried on no less than a flirtation.

Simon was more than a little astonished however when almost immediately after dinner Maggie took the lead by suggesting that they waste no time before going upstairs. Simon quickly agreed, as if it were casual lark, though with some unspoken trepidation. He had made a bargain that if Maggie joined them, Chester would finally get his wish, a prospect that while not entirely new to Simon had unwelcome overtones. But he did not let this get in his way. He had waited a long time for Maggie.

Chester seemed to lag behind, saying that he'd be right up. Why he tarried was unclear. But this was not a disadvantage to the other two. It allowed a brief interlude for Maggie and Simon to watch their own arousal. Both of them without hesitation experimented, and by the time Chester finally arrived, later than expected and still fully clad, they were already busy with each other.

Chester quietly sat in a bedroom chair; solemnly surveying the scene, as if it could never happen just like that, and he was not sure he approved. When the other two at last noticed him, they laughed at his reserve, almost an outsider, but without the excitement of a true voyeur. So different from the way he talked. They had to coax him to join them.

"Show me what you and our new friend usually do," Maggie said impatiently. Still reluctant, Chester finally was able to get into the action on his own. Maggie was delighted but Simon was a little perturbed seeing that it was now his duty to perform. Nevertheless, he reluctantly proceeded to fulfill his end of the bargain. Afterward, he was troubled by a vagrant thought that Aunt Gina, while sanctioning the experience as a whole, would disapprove of what Simon had just done.

The three got together frequently after that first convivial evening. He came to like them, long after the taboo inherent in their relation was exhausted. Predictably, he cautioned himself that an end would inevitably arrive, and that it had to be permanent and painless with neither regret nor longing. It came simply enough when Simon graduated and left town. Like proud relatives, Maggie and Chester attended the ceremonies, and were introduced to Aunt Gina, too. When Gina first heard that the three in bed was a regular occurrence, she was somewhat relieved that it had not just been Chester and Simon and that Simon and Maggie had been together more often.

Simon spent the next few years attempting to discover something worth doing beyond his customary transgressions, but failed. Violation was wearing thin, and like any career lecher, he needed always something more to provide a sense of purpose. Nothing materialized, and he was bored. He traveled from one city and country to another, not as a tourist who arrived one day and was gone the next, but a permanent visitor who managed to spend enough time to learn local customs and discover what was both fascinating and forbidden. His quick intelligence and endearing ways gained him access to many places, even into homes where the ordinary outsider would be met with a polite rebuff. Unwittingly, and notwithstanding his general indifference, he had developed a curious career of his own. Language was never a serious problem in visiting foreign countries. Always facile and gifted with the capacity to listen well and recognize sounds, he had a quick capacity to communicate very soon in the common phrases and soon the native language. His linguistic aptitude was astonishing, but never put to a purpose other than setting up an unsuspecting partner. Seeking always to gratify himself in devious ways, while professing tolerance, he was often intolerant and beset with righteous indignation whenever he found customs and practices in other countries that were beyond limits of his acceptance. He was outraged, for example, by slavery, child abuse, mutilation, bestiality, and sadistic torture, even when approved by authorities that conveniently looked the other way, when paid enough. The underground had its own rules. Many prohibitions, though practiced by many, and sanctioned by bribery and connivance, did not appeal to him at all. He was puritanical and fastidious in a sense, discriminating beyond distaste and indifference. There had to be something in it for him, something strongly sexual, specifically, not unlike what aroused him about Sophia.

Criminality meant nothing to Simon, who considered the ordinary lawbreaker far beneath anything he craved. Like every other good citizen he had no respect whatsoever for gross lawlessness and little patience for the career criminal. Although Chester's fascination with brothels for young men had been only a product of lively fantasy, Simon ran across just such places in foreign countries. He was deeply offended by tourists who paid and by parents who made children sexually available, and tried to mitigate his indignation by reporting such offers anonymously to the police. This was, of course, a fruitless mission, since houses of accommodation like these could not exist without tacit connivance of authorities. Simon had no urge to be a reformer, although he was sternly against hypocritical morality, which opposed, but tacitly tolerated, even encouraged child prostitution.

Convoluted conduct is a way of life in every country, depending on how it is defined and the company it keeps. What is profitable matters, regardless of preaching to the contrary. It is far more dangerous to be a political revolutionary in most countries than to practice any sexual aberration. Straight society makes perversity popular by forbidding it. But being caught in an aberration is taboo, more deplorable than the offense itself.

Dearth of desirable taboos not only spurred Simon's travel and exploration of strange corners of the world but also made him a snob about what to do next, and whom to do it with. In quiet dissatisfaction, and for lack of any other diversion, he revived a suppressed interest in cultural matters he had left behind in earlier days. Faced with a poverty of perversity, he made excursions into the arts and drama, seeking to learn more and expand his education. He was careful to remain a dabbler, not a serious student, however, and this circuitously led him back to America, where he was more comfortable, anyway.

Identifying himself by another name was hardly a problem, but putting an untried role into practice was a feat of another dimension. His theatrical experience was, indeed, very limited. However, for sport, during his peregrinations, particularly in small towns, he joined the local dramatic club. Amiable folks of all ages and occupations effectively shared and enjoyed a game of "Let's pretend" by putting on a show and assuming a variety of temporary roles. Simon almost always fitted in, just long enough to meet the Chester and Maggie of that community.

When he set up a temporary residence in Los Angeles and Hollywood, he needed a more elaborate and extended plan to establish himself. Most people he met were outsiders yet alert and savvy to local con games of all sorts. Because almost anything he could imagine was based on playacting, better called pretense, there was very little forbidden or significantly hidden. Claiming to be an unemployed actor of which there were many, but also one with lots of money, he let it be known that he might also sponsor the right productions for low-budget or no-budget independent filmmakers. An assortment of would-be producers avidly sought him out. His ample funds were, of course, a ticket to almost any aspect of non-mainstream movie making. For fun, he was also able to get small parts in films of no consequence, and even spoke a few words in never-shown commercials. His only interest was in pretending, not acting as a career. He was already a dilettante, a talented faker, but hardly an ambitious actor, willing to hone a career.

Out of curiosity, but still seeking taboos, he migrated to makers of pornography, who seldom lacked for money but could always use more. The camera's eye was neutral, and the production staff didn't care. It was business, and the moviemakers were indifferent to anything else. The male performers were seldom free of fear about aging and with it, quick descent from popularity to unemployment. It was less difficult for women who could continue for years before being replaced. One such woman, named April Breeze, attached herself to Simon. While older than he, careful use of cosmetic surgery and make-up helped her appear younger than many other women of her vintage. Besides knowing her true age, Simon found her surprisingly intelligent, vastly uninformed and under-educated, with a natural wit that amused him. She was corruptible by just about anything. April Breeze was not her real name, of course. When asked, she always replied that she could blow as gentle as an April breeze, which Simon found to be exactly true. She used drugs more often than Simon appreciated, however, and boasted about being bisexual. If there had been more than two sexes, April surely would have been pansexual, but polymorphous was just as accurate. Furthermore, Simon became fonder of April than he planned. They shared the same apartment, and many of the same thoughts, but she was frequently away on special assignments. He did not know with whom, and according to an unspoken agreement, did not dare to ask. Simon was glad when she returned, but that he cared enough to miss her company made him uneasy. He was also reminded of Aunt Gina's unexplained trips, and Sophia's regrettable severance.

In the end, April was capable of no more than an affectionate but casual attachment. One day, turning the tables on Simon, she left a note, thanking him, and he never saw her again. Presumably, her love affair with drugs and women prevailed. At least that is what Simon believed. She might have found a new man but that was too painful to consider. It didn't matter, because he was ready for a better fiction. Soon after April's disappearance, Simon left Hollywood; he found that some important doors were always closed. Other powerful people had much more money than he did and resented interlopers. Simon contracted a disease called terminal boredom, which tenaciously depleted him of whatever ambition, hope or anticipation still lingered.

A few more years passed. Simon traveled almost constantly, to other out of the way societies, like an amateur anthropologist without affiliation anywhere. Whenever he stopped awhile, he was again the stranger who belonged nowhere, only fitting in temporarily, and under false pretenses. In his pursuit of ways to alleviate his crushing boredom, he was obliged to seek novelty not just in what was taboo, but also in everyday existence. A steady job therefore seemed like a bizarre but feasible idea. It was not a game to be stopped at any moment, but a curious commitment, strange in itself. He was a little tickled by the challenge, especially by an urge to act the way he imagined ordinary blue-collar people might spend their entire life. The mundane routine of everyday work was surely unfamiliar, but held out a novelty that was refreshing in itself. He would not be at loose ends.

Travels had taken him to many places in search of the forbidden and novel. Then one day, wandering across Canada, looking for the right place to experiment with a plain but lasting job, he came to a medium sized city near the United States border. It seemed to be undistinguished enough, but from what he observed, its citizenry didn't seem to mind, or if they knew, didn't care, or know the difference. The curse of incessant boredom had not reached the town. Simon found this fascinating. What would it be like to settle into this middle-class, blue-collar town, where he could cease fruitless meandering and become a day-to-day jobholder? Plain towns to Simon were exotic locales where anything might happen.

He found it not very difficult to become a plain citizen. At first, he took a room in a small hotel, truthfully explaining to instant acquaintances that he was a newcomer, looking for a job. Very soon he found a job working in a large printing plant. His credentials, easy to fake, were not questioned. While his entry job was modest, it still required a certain amount of energy, even aptitude, which he readily called upon. It was only prudent to hide his urbane demeanor, lest he be suspected of being a fugitive and hiding something sinister. Nevertheless any job was a challenge because he wanted the bosses to recognize competence and promote him, just like an ordinary worker. He was too naïve to know that ordinary workers can stay in an unrewarding job indefinitely. His first job required no technical knowledge, but he carefully asked questions, and did what he was told.

Simon had a natural knack for absorbing information and acquiring new skills, most of which he put to no discernible use. Within a month or two, he learned enough about printing to be noticed and promoted several times. His job was now far from menial, but still comfortably blue collar, which suited him fine. It just fitted his talent for quietly fitting in while actually belonging nowhere. His buddies at work accepted him as one of their own. Then, just as he began to find being ordinary tolerable, his life turned suddenly.

One bright Canadian morning in the early autumn, as Simon was busy at his work, even enjoying his newly established efficiency while warmed by the mutual appreciation of his crew, his immediate foreman, Ed Flannery, shouted over the public address that he had a telephone call, in itself a strange event. To his knowledge, no one was aware of his whereabouts or what he did, except his fellow workers and a few acquaintances in the town.

"Hey, Simon, long distance call! A woman on the phone. What have you been up to? She tracked you down." Kidding from the men around him was a sign of affectionate acceptance.

Ed's bantering had its accidental truth. Because personal calls at work were discouraged, Simon found himself doubly apprehensive when he closed the office door to answer the phone. He was even more astonished when the woman turned out to be Sophia, sounding the same, and speaking across the bridge of years as if no time had elapsed. She did not pause for amenities. There was little warmth in her voice, only a hint of formal urgency.

"Simon, this is Sophia. I was sure you'd want to know that your Aunt Gina died yesterday." Stunned into silence, Simon was hardly able to respond.

"Dead? Aunt Gina? It can't be!" he said, foolishly. How did Sophia find him? Moreover, like a child who expects parents to live forever, ageless and immune to illness and misfortune, Simon assumed that Aunt Gina would always to be there, accepting his neglect with forbearance. He sent her a postcard from time to time, never often, and deliberately omitted a return address, especially since he was usually moving about. Now, shocked by the sudden news, abrupt and meaningless questions came to his mind, the receiver pressed tightly against his ear. "What happened? How did you find me? Where are you?" Sophia chose not to answer any of these questions, but slightly amplified her original announcement.

"I can't give you any medical details, Simon. She had been sick at home for some time. I visited her now and then, but she apparently didn't want anyone to know how sick she was. That must have included you. She was not one to interfere or impose. I am not sure myself what she died of. Maybe heart, cancer, perhaps, she didn't say. She could be very secretive, that dear woman. Ingrid found her dead yesterday morning. Your number was in the address book in the bedside table drawer. I do not know any more than that, of course. Anyhow, there will be a wake a day or two before the funeral, or some other ceremony afterward. I am not sure what the custom is. So far as I know, you are or were her only relative. The funeral comes very soon after the wake, but I really am not sure which is first. I think they're planning something for the public. If you feel like getting away for a couple of days, there is room at her house for you to stay. I think the priest expects you."

Sophia did not urge him, and seemed to call only to inform him about the death. Come only if you care to. She was pleasant enough, but very impersonal, as if there had never been anything between them. No coercion, of course. No sympathy. No reproach for his absence. If Simon expected more responsiveness, he got none. He was left to wonder about Sophia visiting his aunt. He had no idea that they were friendly enough to visit. He had to get leave from Ed, explaining only that there'd been a death in the family. It felt strange, saying even that much. An old aunt who'd been very good to him had died. Ed was properly sympathetic but quickly asked when he'd be back. There was work to be done. Simon had to say, "As soon as possible, maybe a couple of days, that should be enough." But he was not at all sure when, if ever, he'd be back.

On the trip home, disbelief mingled with melancholy and memories. After all, he wasn't supposed to grieve. Mourning was discouraged, but there were some feelings of sadness he couldn't help. Even enjoyment had to be endured and parceled out in small increments. Nevertheless, it was hard now to feel neutral about Gina's death. Who and what she was continued to be an enigma, but neutrality be damned! That was too much to expect. He was sad, and knew that he was really alone now, more an orphan than ever, more bereft than he ever had been.

Steve and Ingrid welcomed him impersonally, without showing surprise or warmth. There were no embraces, not even a handshake. For someone they had known since childhood, this was a strange rebuff. So much for stoicism, a term they would never have understood, anyway. Were they as indifferent or wary? Ingrid wept, however, when speaking of Mrs. Benett, and Steve seemed more solemn and taciturn than ever. Simon did not ask about their health, nor did he inquire about Aunt Gina's final days. But there he was, and his old room had hardly changed. Only after unpacking did he recall that he neglected to ask and was not told about Aunt Gina's sickness and demise. Simon got the clear idea that he was not just a familiar stranger, but also a neglectful intruder.

On the following day another gathering besides the wake was held in the chapel of the most prominent Catholic Church in town, as if everyone had waited for the arrival of the prodigal. Surprised by the event, Simon had not supposed that Gina had an affiliation with established religion, Catholic or not. He had never thought about it. Gina never seemed to care about religion and Simon had no instruction in the principal teachings of any creed. Even at an early hour, there was a sizable number of people coming into the chapel, paying respects and shaking hands with Simon. Gina evidently cared enough about the Church, Simon concluded, still astonished, to merit a gathering with a large crowd in attendance.

Simon was Gina's sole surviving relative. Many people came up to him and talked of her as an old friend. They were utter strangers, but offered condolences to him and briefly spoke of her fondly. It was indeed ironic that the one person presumed to be most affected by her death returned after a long absence and still wasn't sure who he was in the first place, and now was mystified by an entirely different view of his aunt. At last, he met Steve and Ingrid's married daughter, now considerably older than when she was only a voice on the telephone. Her children were almost grown, and fond of their grandparents, he could see with a momentary pang.

Then he spotted Sophia across the room, walking slowly towards him, with an elderly, white haired gentleman at her side. She was, of course, older than he remembered, but still attractive in his eyes. They shook hands politely and with sincere cordiality, before she introduced her companion.

"Simon, I want you to meet my husband, Edgar Wright," she said, turning then to Edgar, "This is Simon, Gina's nephew. We haven't seen him for a long time." Simon extended his hands to both simultaneously. Edgar acknowledged the introduction politely, offering condolences, adding that they would certainly miss Gina. Simon had to assume from this that his aunt and the Wrights were at least social friends. Edgar was friendly but quietly reserved, giving no indication that Simon was anyone other than a nephew of the deceased. He did not attempt further conversation, nor did Sophia. Later, Simon mused that no one could ever call Edgar by any other name. Still, he was faintly jealous, and hoped that they slept well in bed together, nothing more.

As Simon peered around the room, he found himself looking for someone among these strangers who resembled Gina and might be a family member. One young woman did remind him of Gina, but she turned out to be only a neighbor. The heterogeneous crowd signified that she had many acquaintances, not all from the town. Gina might have been aloof and mysterious in some ways, but she evidently had close attachment to the Church. Maybe this had all quietly developed after he left home. He wished that he could talk to them individually, and find out more about Aunt Gina than he knew. It was incredible that Gina had somehow touched these lives, without his being aware of it.

Then there was Father Fogarty who was in charge of everything and did not hesitate to embrace Simon heartily. Stocky, plethoric and verbose, Fr. Fogarty had a wide genuine smile that exposed gleaming white teeth. He greeted visitors, calling almost everyone by name, but introducing himself to those he did not know with warm thanks for being there.

"Simon, at last we meet! Your late aunt talked of you so often and always with so much affection! It was a truly auspicious day for her when you graduated from college. She told me all about it. Very proud of you and all your accomplishments, whatever they were. She never went into details. But she did tell me that you were on the road a lot and that your business kept you from visiting even occasionally. She missed you and enjoyed hearing from you whenever you called or wrote. Gina was a very special person. My sympathy and God's divine help to you in your grief, my boy." Fr. Fogarty did not ask what business he was in, nor did Simon inquire about which of his accomplishments Gina was proud of. As Fr. Fogarty continued to speak expansively about Gina, Simon gathered that her interest in the Church was not recent, nor was it simply in anticipation of death.

"She and I spoke together many times over the years. A very good friend. I will miss her. I'll miss her worldly wisdom and her unlimited generosity. I don't want to repeat my eulogy but there is so much I leave out when I talk about her. Sorry you couldn't make the funeral, but I'll have something to say later today. She was so kind, and philanthropic. I could always call on her. How will we get along without her? You will understand that, I'm sure. You must have very warm memories, indeed." Fr. Fogarty paused, pondering the enormity of it all, as if her death were something beyond human understanding. It was apparent that Gina was more active in the Church and community than Simon could have imagined. Through all their years together she had hardly mentioned religion or the Church, except scornfully, in a rare bout of anger, and then only with blasphemy. She must have been more than a closet Catholic. The traditional Church would have represented almost everything she preached against. But Fogarty lauded her as someone devout and with great wisdom and generosity, a useful combination for a loyal church member. Who was this woman? He opted to play along with Fr. Fogarty, just to see if he was on the level, or merely exaggerating to ensure a further contribution in her memory.

"True, Fr. Fogarty," he said, "I have been away far too long, and now nothing can be done about it. I did not know about her failing health or the worthy causes she must have supported for the community and you." Simon smiled sadly at his own loss and remorse about his late aunt.

"Many causes and many people, all worthy, and others that I knew very little about. Not just with money, although that helped, but her natural sympathy and care were important, too," Fr. Fogarty added, "Acts of kindness right up until the end. We always counted on her. Her benevolence and generosity, that is. She never failed us."

"She must have been more devout than even I realized," Simon said, not altogether ironically. "My aunt was pretty private person, you know."

"Private, yes," Fr. Fogarty said, still extolling Aunt Gina, "A truly modest person seldom makes public noise about good deeds. And she always refused public thanks or recognition, although God knows she deserved it. Kept away from banquets and committees, that kind of stuff, social gatherings, you know. Preferred to work behind the scenes. She set up a home for neglected and unwanted children of any faith, most born out of wedlock. Also, much support for houses and shelters for battered, abused women." Simon could believe that, and found that he nodded gravely in new appreciation of his aunt. He wanted to ask if he had been one of the foundlings.

Fr. Fogarty interrupted his private panegyric to ask if Simon would be willing to share a private prayer, as Gina's only kin. He agreed, and leaving the multitude still thronging the chapel and reception, retreated to Fr. Fogarty's study. Simon, of course, was unfamiliar with prayer, but he must have put on a good imitation, because Fr. Fogarty embraced him again at its conclusion. Afterward, Fr. Fogarty left Simon to speak with new arrivals, turning to greet as many visitors as he could. Sophia's younger son, whose name he never caught, went out of his way to meet Simon and grasp his hand firmly, then told him that he was running for state office. A politician is always at work. Nothing personal, Simon reminded himself. Not one of Simon's old schoolmates showed up, including several who were his buddies. Most of the people were of Gina's age, but this was also ambiguous, too, since Simon was never sure how old she was. Another man, Burt Edelson, clearly Jewish, which was unusual in this crowd, introduced himself as Gina's attorney. Burt was respectful but primarily concerned about business, and not given to empty condolences.

"I understand you're away a lot, and probably will be leaving soon. It's important that you stay over, if you can. Come by my office, so we can go over your aunt's Will." Burt gave Simon his address and left before Fr. Fogarty could begin another eulogy. Apparently, there was enough good in Aunt Gina to support several eulogies, possibly more.

"Our beloved sister, Virginia Benett, is no longer with us, but she is still here in spirit, in memories, and in good works that will go on and on, without her physical presence. *Your* presence here shows how much she meant to us all, and how hard it will be to replace her. She was a true and a wonderful example of strong faith and duty. Her lasting deeds of mercy testify to her compassion and care. She will never be forgotten, this true daughter of our Church. So modest and self-effacing about her benefactions, she always insisted on staying in the background, never seeking recognition and thanks, and actively avoiding the limelight. But you, her friends and admirers, who are here today, know, as I do, that the private Virginia was always available for counsel, which was unfailingly wise. A precious jewel beyond price need not be on display. Its rare value only grows with the passage of time. So it will be with Virginia whose love was shared by so many. I will miss her, along with many others, for her enduring love and generous spirit. Shelters and homes for the homeless and battered are monuments to her good works she provided for those in need. They will continue and memorialize her wise and kindly soul, so deeply representative of the true Christian spirit. May the Lord continue to share his grace on all of us through her example."

As Fr. Fogarty concluded his brief message, the assemblage was silent except for scattered sobs, throat clearing, and visible tears. Simon himself was more than touched by the sentiments. After all, she'd been very generous with him, too. He could truly believe what Fr. Fogarty said. He might have been a foundling, too, needing shelter and a home. It was so like Aunt Gina to love without any tangible reward or reciprocity. As the muted Simon, still standing, reflected, there was no contradiction between this Virginia and his familiar Aunt Gina. Nevertheless, love had been an alien notion for the Gina that Simon knew, except the love between them. Now he understood more than he had only hours before. She had separate areas of conviction and different kinds of love, including loving kindness that she satisfied without allowing intrusion of one upon the other. Whether she admitted it or not, Gina had a certain kind of love in abundance, stored up and reserved for her causes, which she never disclosed. What was he to her? She accepted his neglect, but how did she get along without recognition for everything else that she gladly gave? Simon caught himself almost blushing at his sentimentality.

After speaking once more to Fr. Fogarty who was busily taking leave of visitors, Simon walked to the far end of the reception room, putting himself at a distance from those offering condolences. There, an older man, quite distinctive, although Simon had not noticed him before, approached the periphery of Simon's solitude. In dress and appearance, this slightly swarthy and tastefully groomed gentleman seemed completely at ease although clearly out of place in this pale white suburban crowd. His dark jacket, faintly striped, expertly tailored to an experienced eye, was made more elegant by light gray slacks, black alligator loafers, tattersall vest, pale blue shirt and a correctly somber modest necktie. He was hardly in mourning, but dressed respectfully for the occasion, despite a little incongruity. Nevertheless, it was not clothes that made this man seem so quietly poised. Without saying a word, he exuded undisputed authority. While not pretending that they had met before, he nevertheless called Simon by name as he shook his hand.

"Simon, I am Bruno Lorenzo, and I am very sorry about Gina's death." He did not call her 'your late Aunt', and by using the word, "death," he acknowledged her absence in a way that uttering a euphemistic "passing away" could not. "I hope you are sorry, too," he added, unexpectedly. It sounded like an admonition, but also a sympathetic inquiry about Simon's grief. He could not have guessed, however, that Simon's grief now wavered between sadness and a benign distance that Aunt Gina herself might have approved of. Without having met Mr. Lorenzo before, Simon was instantly convinced that this stranger knew more about Gina and Simon than anyone else in the whole room, so recently murmuring with banal sympathy.

Mr. Lorenzo spoke slowly and precisely, with just a trace of an accent that Simon did not readily identify, despite his travels in foreign countries. Then he noticed two young men, also dressed soberly, standing not too far away, watching the room empty itself. They hardly spoke to each other and certainly not to anyone else. Although neither could overhear the conversation between Simon and Mr. Lorenzo, it was clear that they were with him, and not there as mourners.

Mr. Lorenzo made no move to leave, as if ready for a longer conversation than the circumstances allowed. However, his deliberate manner also indicated that he was more accustomed to being listened to, not hurried, interrupted, or required to tolerate ordinary conversation. His smile was soft, unobtrusive, cordial and pleasant. Not only did he listen carefully to what the other person had to say, but perhaps gleaned more from the words than the person intended. Handsome teeth, evidently the best money could buy, flashed quietly in that smile, not necessarily with amusement. His age notwithstanding, Mr. Lorenzo was almost handsome, except for an incongruously large, turned up nose, somewhat more prominent than it should have been. Simon was a little intimidated, without knowing why, although Mr. Lorenzo showed him nothing but courtesy and interest.

"How did you know my Aunt, Mr. Bruno?" Simon ventured to ask, "She knew so many people that I never met, and I think most of them are here today. I can't try to put them all together with their connections." He had momentarily forgotten Bruno's last name. Mr. Lorenzo did not seem to mind but promptly corrected him.

"Please, I am not Mr. Bruno," he said, "But Mr. Lorenzo, if you choose. A few old friends call me by my first name. At my age, I am venerable enough not to be a buddy to anyone. For my associates, my last name does well enough. I am not an excessively formal person." Mr. Lorenzo was not about to say how well he'd known Gina. Simon could see that this was not a real conversation at all, but an audience in which he was not expected to ask any further questions, regardless of Lorenzo's remark about not being excessively formal.

"I am truly sorry we never met before now, Mr. Lorenzo, but I wish we had." This gentle compliment was surprising but not insincere. It apparently moved Mr. Lorenzo to answer Simon's original question, but in his own fashion.

"Gina and I worked together for many years. We were loyal friends. She was very capable, as you know, attached to her work, compassionate and generous, just as Fr. Fogarty said, competent, surely, and very kind." Fr. Fogarty had alluded to nothing specific about Gina's occupation, only her philanthropies. Simon never knew the source of her income, always supposing it was both enough and enormous. How she came by it was never mentioned.

"I knew nothing about my Aunt's work, Mr. Lorenz. Things she did were always kept very private, even from me, living right in the same household. Whatever the work was, it gave her a good income." Simon laughed a little indulgently, but Mr. Lorenzo's face was an unresponsive neutrality. "What Gina did with her money or where it came from was her business too. According to Fr. Fogarty she put it to good use."

"We have a family business," Mr. Lorenzo said, "Gina was an important and essential part of our organization. That is, until she was forced, no, chose to retire, and then not quite recently." Mr. Lorenzo did not elaborate or seemed inclined to offer any details, except to add, "She was like one of the family. Even during the last illness, although we didn't expect her to die just then, her advice and counsel were a great treasure, just as Fr. Fogarty said."

Simon had been around the world often enough to recognize a genuine and complimentary cliché for what it was. When an imposing person like Mr. Lorenzo says that someone is 'like one of the family', he usually means that family inclusion is actually closed. Long-term employees always have been and remain complete outsiders. Such people, though well liked and respected, are anything but members of the family. So it must have been for Gina, never an insider, well compensated, but out of the inner circle. Furthermore, vaguely described 'family business' is designed to discourage all inquiries whether from the IRS, unions, or anyone else choosing to ask unwelcome questions. Mr. Lorenzo was not about to disclose any more information about what it was that Gina was so good at, made her so appreciated, and what kind of business she worked for. He was not more specific than Fr. Fogarty had been.

It was time to leave. The reception room was practically empty. Even Fr. Fogarty was no longer bidding people good bye and was nowhere seen. The conversation between Mr. Lorenzo and Simon dwindled amiably, until it, too, came to a comfortable end. At a nod, the two young men approached, but were not introduced. Simon made no move towards them, taking a cue that they were expected to be anonymous and practically invisible.

"I hope we'll meet again, Mr. Lorenzo. Of all the people I've met today, I shall remember you most. Please understand that I am intrigued by what you have not told me about my aunt." Framed in a smile it was a heartfelt, spontaneous comment. "Thank you, Simon We both have much to thank Gina for. And we shall meet again. When that time comes, I shall find you. I always have." Simon was puzzled by this enigmatic comment, said teasingly in jest with a slight laugh. Before he could respond, however, Mr. Lorenzo had turned away, and walked to the door with his two cohorts slightly behind him. He spoke briefly with Fr. Fogarty who had reappeared. Both men smiled at something that was said, contrary to the sober atmosphere that still clung to the chapel.

Simon had not forgotten Burt Edelson, and the next day arranged a meeting, late the following afternoon. Burt Edelson's name almost headed a long list of other attorneys on the top floor of a downtown building. Although he was unmistakably a senior partner in a huge law firm and entitled to due respect, Burt, unlike Lorenzo, did not mind being called by his first name. He got right to the point, without conversational niceties. Simon's polite efforts to expand the conversation and learn more about Aunt Gina were disregarded.

"I asked you to come in right away because Gina's Will does not have to be probated," he said, not explaining how this was managed or wasting any time. It was only a business transaction. "Your Aunt and I made everything clear and simple. Practically everything goes to you, except for bequests to several non-profit organizations, such as shelters and private agencies for women and children. Orphans were a big interest for her, next to the Church. Ingrid and Steve are given a steady life income, which ends with their deaths. A sizable amount goes to a facility for elderly women in Ohio, somewhere around Dayton, called the Sara Maxfield Home." Burt knew little more about the place other than it seemed like a nursing home for elderly and disabled women. He did not have information about Sara Maxfield. There were smaller contributions to philanthropic causes, all tax-free. The house is to be sold immediately with its contents. Nothing will be left over. No other gifts and no strings. "I have a list of investments and so forth that will make you or keep you a wealthy man for the rest of your life, barring some calamity. I understand you're on the move a lot, but I may need to get in touch. I am the executor, and I'll want an address for you."

Burt did not waste a word. If he had any thoughts about Gina or doubts about Simon, there was no indication. His answers to the few questions Simon asked were terse and professional.

"She invested in different companies that were not on the exchange, but others were." This was typical of Burt's response to Simon's questions. When the meeting seemed intentionally to lag, Burt stood up, shook Simon's hand perfunctorily, and was more than willing to let him go. He had other appointments, and the Will had now been discussed. The rest was a legal matter. However, Simon suspected that Burt knew substantially more about Bruno, Gina and her work than he needed to say. He tentatively tried to inquire.

"I met a man at the wake who seemed to know my aunt better than the others, except Fr. Fogarty. His name is Bruno Lorenzo. Gina used to work for him in some family business. Do you know anything about that?"

"Whoever he is," Burt responded, "He wasn't mentioned in the Will, and probably was a friend. She knew many people. That's about all I know. About her work, we never got into that. Ms. Benett preferred to tell me only what I needed to know." His tone discouraged further discussion. Another brisk handshake and Simon was out the door, richer than he expected, but no clearer about Gina. She was as secretive about legal affairs as her heir was uninformed. However, her kindly and loving thoughts about him could not be doubted. Simon might have been written off entirely; he deserved no more. But he hadn't and he wondered what to read into that. Of course, his job at the printing plant was for practical purposes almost forgotten. Simon felt no further obligation, even though he'd told Ed to expect him back. Maybe he'd just clear out his locker and resign on one pretext or another. It didn't matter. His only fixed location from now on would be a post office box somewhere.

Meanwhile, now that Gina was dead, the house and everything in it, secrets included, were to be completely sold or discarded. He would have no opportunity to snoop around. Simon wanted to find out what he could about Bruno Lorenzo, Fr. Fogarty, Burt Edelson, and, most of all, Virginia Benett. Consequently, Simon decided to talk with Harry Gilday, a private investigator who seemed to have a good reputation based on inquiries from the local police.

Introducing himself to Gilday, Simon claimed to be a print-shop foreman, and, as befitted a blue-collar type, acted a little rough around the edges. Gilday immediately sensed that Simon was a pretender and not a regular workman. He was not even an unusual workingman. Polished speech, courteous manner, and uncalloused hands gave that away. Simon could use a little investigation himself. Why then was he trying to pass as something other than he was while asking about four people Gilday already knew something about? Halfway through the interview, Gilday agreed to take the case, along with a generous retainer.

Gilday jotted notes about Virginia Benett, whom Simon described as a recently deceased aunt who left him a sizable estate. Soft-spoken, not very talkative, asking a very few but precise questions, Gilday did not say whether he had knowledge of these four people, or anything else. It was professional neutrality, spun like a web. Nevertheless, all four would be investigated, he promised. He did stare a little longer than seemed called for, gazing at the wall and ceiling over Simon's head, as if reflecting on the substance of what Simon wanted. Simon had given vague and unconvincing reasons for the inquiry, and Gilday accepted this as deliberate dissimulation, also worth looking into. It was not uncommon in his business for clients to offer phony reasons for seeking his services.

One month later, almost to the day, Gilday had a preliminary report. Bruno Lorenzo was a prominent retired business executive, a consultant but not a board member of several organizations, well known and respected for his philanthropy and private grants to musicians, and occasionally other arts. He also sponsored struggling symphony orchestras and opera singers. Gilday then stopped, lowering his voice, as if afraid of being overheard. He had some confidential information. Even in the privacy of his office, Gilday called him "Mr. Lorenzo," an unwitting sign of respect. He was being careful for unknown reasons and curiously, after mentioning something confidential, evidently decided not to say what it was.

Mr. Lorenzo is very generous to artists, performers, and composers, Gilday explained, but takes a special interest in young sopranos. His patronage often continues after their careers are over, as they grow older. Carefully, Gilday explained that Lorenzo was not a playboy, but a wealthy man who appreciated opera and the arts, which included attractive and gifted women. He mentioned one quite celebrated star that was said to be a special protégé. Altogether, this did not seem either unusual or particularly confidential.

Gilday had more to say about the family business. After uncharacteristic circumlocution, he finally indicated that the 'family business' was nothing more or less than a conglomerate, with branches and connections all over, definitely connected to organized crime syndicates. Mr. Lorenzo's family also invested in legitimate businesses, real estate trusts, and banks. If lenders reneged on poorly secured loans, or balked at oscillating interest, well, the family settled accounts by taking over the business. That was not unusual in business, and was not necessarily outside the law. Clients usually managed to meet financial obligations.

In recent years, the family business had become semi-legitimate. Gilday's initial curiosity about Simon was easily satisfied. Through sources he found out that Simon did work in a print shop, but was by no means either a foreman or an ordinary manual laborer, but a trusted assistant who had worked his way up in a very short time. However, this was background, and Gilday did not interrupt his report about Mr. Lorenzo to quiz Simon further about himself. After all, he was being paid to gather information for a client, not about a client. Mr. Lorenzo had come into power at least thirty years before retirement, but Gilday was not sure how long he'd been 'retired'. He was still an active advisor, retaining considerable power, much of it unofficial. Although Mr. Lorenzo's earlier activities were not well known, there was no doubt, however, that he sought and achieved his position by all means possible, and that once upon a time, cultural interests notwithstanding, he had been a ruthless, uncompromising soldier, then becoming Chief, or however his position was designated. Of course the authorities had questioned him on a number of occasions. But now at his emeritus eminence he was better known for his unpublicized philanthropies.

With only a muted whisper, fundraisers of artistic organizations and highly placed officials were always ready to soften his reputation and take the money. Jokingly referred to as Lorenzo the Magnificent because of his munificence and patronage, he was never called the Godfather. He was still a figure to be wary of. Good causes never quite outgrow their corrupt or ruthless beginnings, but they manage to be concealed if the shady past can be ignored through abundant funds and prominent foundations.

At last Gilday turned to a briefer report about Burt Edelson. His reputation was that of a well-known, respected, and very tough attorney. In his early years, he was loosely connected with high level, somewhat unsavory defendants. Now he represented government officials, old-line families, and community leaders, who were prosperous and prestigious, and paid well for his services. Burt had never been a shady shyster, not at all, but always a reliable counselor whose dogged competence recommended his law firm and associates to many respectable families and established businesses.

Fr. Fogarty was just about as he seemed, a popular priest in a large, affluent Catholic diocese. There was nothing whatsoever to besmirch his reputation or compromise his noteworthy ability to solicit and get large contributions. However, Gilday did not know or care to investigate why Fr. Fogarty had remained in the same diocese for years without a significant promotion, even to Monsignor. Fogarty is an OK guy, Gilday said, but why was Simon interested in him? This was easier for Simon to answer than other questions, but he put his interest in simple terms. Fr. Fogarty was his aunt's priest, entrusted with many contributions to the Church, Burt was her attorney, and Lorenzo was a friend whom he'd met only once. His answers were simple, but did not explain why Simon chose to spend substantial money finding out about his late aunt's priest, attorney, and friendly employer. Gilday did not pursue his questions, but privately made another little note.

Gilday and Simon had been together for almost an hour. Finally, they turned to Virginia Benett, Simon's late Aunt. Who was she? What was her reputation? Gilday had startling information that quite justified leaving her to the last. Gilday silently handed Simon a photograph of a younger but unmistakable Aunt Gina. Under the photograph was her name, Virginia Benet (with only one T). However, the picture also listed other names, Verna Goldmark, Vivian Bennedetto, Velma Somebody or other. Simon was astonished and fascinated.

"I'm sure this is a great surprise," Gilday said, with professional understatement, "Your Aunt was once that young attractive woman known by several names, although why so many in view of a spotless record with the police is puzzling. She worked for and with the family, but while close to the top, at least for a woman, never was a true member. Women aren't given that much power in that world. Nevertheless, Gina had a lot to say about what went on in her division. She must have been very smart, with good connections, as well as better looking than a movie star, without much exaggeration. She was, well, almost like one of the family, but not quite." Simon was baffled. He nodded for Gilday to continue.

"These names are all phony but I wasn't entirely sure what her real name was. Virginia seems to be true, and Bennett, Benet, Benett come close, too. Most people are not given aliases without a reason but she was never arrested. Although questioned occasionally and informally, her record is absolutely clean. Possibly something was erased, but I found nothing. Virginia Benett was or became her legal name. She always used it, no disguise. How she came by it, I don't know. More investigation would probably not pay off. She managed to close off her past, so I doubt it's likely that another relative will come out of the woodwork for part of the inheritance. As for her work, there is no mystery. Your Aunt was in charge of the family's East Coast prostitution, a position of responsibility and very lucrative, too, as you might imagine. Her operations were very organized, it seems, recruitment, training, assignment, discipline, and when needed, termination, too. That picture you see is the only one my operatives found. With police files as skimpy as they are in her case, I'm surprised they found this." Gilday wanted to expand, evidently enjoying this part of his report.

"No arrests, very strange for someone in her line of work, but in spite of her high position, nothing was ever definitely proved about anything. She dropped out of working girl status, if any, almost as soon as she began, a very long time ago. Where she came from is not an unusual gap. Someone higher up might have protected her. In that family, people don't attend important meetings, take over responsible jobs, get promoted, and then up and quit without very convincing cause. No information on that. Nothing about you, I'm sorry to say, because I guess you wondered if you're mentioned at all. You were not, which is funny, since you were her only relative, at least that we know about."

"But she was a whore, beyond doubt," Simon said, lips tightening almost prudishly. Gilday answered laconically, in a world-weary voice.

"At one time, I suppose, when very young and very poor. Women had it very hard back then, and it's tough to be broke and despondent, with nothing going for you except looks and brains. That's a lot but you need something else. I can't imagine a woman like that having a pimp, but maybe a sponsor. Maybe she got into the business by another channel, but I doubt that. The life's too hard. She was too smart, unless she got a better job as she surely did very soon, in the upper reaches of the family. I'm only supposing now, but I think I'm right about that. A clean record in such a dirty business looks like she could take care of herself or someone very powerful took care of it for her."

Simon was silent, but not more flabbergasted than if Gilday said Fr. Fogarty was her original pimp. Maybe Simon and Gina were unrelated, maybe not. Gilday's report said nothing that could be construed either way. But there had to be a grain of mother love preventing her from having actual incest, or what a later generation called 'child abuse'. He recalled how she suddenly stopped sleeping with him, sending him to his own room, suffering from unrequited desire. But he never returned and she never relented.

Now Simon was ready to leave. He had heard enough. However, Gilday had more to say, after pointing out the hardship of a prostitute's life. A little speech about whores and call girls was superfluous, the last thing Simon wanted to hear. However, for his own reasons, Gilday insisted on treating him as if he were just a callow young man who lacked basic information about such matters.

"The way it works, prostitutes come from anywhere, from all over. As a rule, they're not forced into anything, and are glad to be protected by a family, not a street pimp who takes the money and beats them in the bargain. They make a lot of money faster and get to keep more of it when they work for a syndicate." This was trite talk. "Before the girls are accepted into the system, they are screened by someone in charge. That could have been Virginia Benett, your Aunt. They are checked very carefully, background, if possible and very quietly, as if they are going to work in an established high-grade organization, careful about its reputation, which they are. Also, they look into police records, pimp informers, drugs, booze, health, psycho stuff, any jobs, so on. If they pass, they're set up in places the family runs. No way if they don't match up. Then there's the training, but I won't get into that." Gilday made his speech, as if explaining how a high quality lady like Aunt Gina joined this organization and worked her way up to an executive position. As it turned out, however, he did neither.

So it came to this, after all the years of mystery and silence. Aunt Gina's trips were for business, and her job was to stock whorehouses or set up private establishments with the best stuff possible. No street people, perhaps a few unfortunate runaways. Boys, too, for gay customers. That had a familiar ring to Simon. Gilday did not sit in judgment, and, after his initial shock, neither did Simon.

Gina was no hypocrite, pretending to be something she wasn't. She was only secretive, which is no sin, but always challenged the forbidden. It was a test of character, and she was certain that transgression had its rewards. Protect yourself always, but mostly by carefully cultivating a do-not-care, impervious attitude. And she didn't care about the paradox. Whores will do almost anything that pays off, and if the price is right, whatever the customer wants. The supreme sin, Simon realized, is falling in love, which is also dangerous. It is practically fatal in the prostitution line. Make believe fantasies or virtual fictions are the whores' stock in trade. Simon could also understand a little about Gina's disdain for men. It was contempt in purest form, if purity is an issue here.

Gilday didn't speak about her generosity, philanthropy, compassion for abandoned children, support for abused women, and confidence in the larger purpose of the Church. Was 'Aunt' also an alias? Could her employees have called her 'Aunt' behind her back, like just an old Aunty? How he came to live with her, becoming her nephew and heir was not answered by Gilday's report. Was he a real or fictitious nephew? What difference would it make? At no point during Gilday's somewhat extensive report did Simon imagine an even closer connection than aunt and nephew.

Simon was better informed now; the price was worth it. He could not really resent Aunt Gina, be sanctimonious, and condemn what she did for a living. Indeed, despite his unexpected outburst about being a whore, her affection for him was genuine, not fictitious, and it lasted, despite his extended absences, just like hers. After all, people are seldom exactly as they seem. The front that shows is how they'd like to be seen, not as they are inside and to themselves. The inside person could be a fiction, too, since people fool themselves, too, while fooling others. He had no answers about who he was and what brought him to Aunt Gina. Simon himself presented several fronts to others, but all virtual fictions. Fiction or not, he no longer needed to be absolutely sure whether Gina was his aunt, or in fact who he was. They could both be counterfeit. If posing as Aunt Gina was done for a noble purpose, such as rescuing and raising an unwanted child or helping a mother in need, then she deserved something equally noble from her virtual nephew. So far, he had not matched up to all her expectations. Even violating taboos was a kind of hypocrisy.

Chapter 5—Simon called Simeon

It was just another glorious morning in the Caribbean. Glistening on the blue water, the sun came up almost abruptly, soon taking over the sky, proudly presenting hot rays to the sailboats and cruisers anchored in the bay or slowly wending to the port. St. Thomas was not yet as busy as it would be in a few hours. Prosperous tourists from the cruise ships had already eaten their breakfasts and were now preparing for disembarkation. Overhead, gulls swooped, ever searching for food, saluting and signaling each other with shrill cries.

Facing outward from his suite high in one of the more opulent hotels, Simon stood naked, just having risen and greeted the morning's expanse outside his window. The unimpeded vista assured him that, like the sun itself, the world revolved around his whims and desires and therefore belonged to him alone. His most recent woman friend had left, after a night that he had scarcely known since Sophia. Hermione was younger than Simon, who now called himself Simeon, by about fifteen years. Not so long ago, surely since he learned more exactly who Aunt Gina was when not being his aunt, Simon decided to divest himself of that freakish double name, Simon Simon, inflicted by someone unknown.

By accident, flipping through the pages of a book on biblical characters several months earlier, he came across an account of Simon who was called and perhaps became Peter, another person altogether. Simon was not a scholar, and his interest in the Bible was new. He read the Gideon with fascination, whenever he found himself in a hotel room, which was often. The name Peter did not appeal to him at all. It had slang and other unfortunate connotations. He wanted another name, preferably of a noteworthy person with power and status. Such interest in biblical or semi-biblical names as he acknowledged was surreptitious and, ironically, taboo. It had begun following Gina's death and the unexpected disclosure of her churchly interests. After some hesitation and consideration, he assumed the name, Simeon, which also had biblical connections. The several Simeons he read about all seemed to have much prestige, although some were pretty strange fellows. But it was now Simon called Simeon. The name became his, and in so choosing, Simon added his proper surname officially, becoming Simeon Benett, in honor of Aunt Gina. In that way, as her heir, Simeon Benett became her real nephew. By allying himself to famous Simeons, he detached himself forever from that perplexing Simon Simon.

Hermione was not only highly compatible but also an important person on the Islands. Attractive, intelligent and gregarious, she had returned to the island of her birth several years earlier. Her skills and education were desperately needed, if the local population was ever to emerge from its ingrained poverty, illiteracy, and low expectations. She was more than a match for Simeon in practically all respects, except that in dedication and ambition, she was far beyond the dilettante who so profligately wasted his talents.

Hermione's career demanded a very practical attitude, when dealing with the white world she had been thrust into and needed. Men in authority, from college professors earlier to influential politicians later, always sought her out. She had no illusions about what first attracted them. While well qualified for almost any job she wanted, it was just as true that men in power primarily sought her body. This, she knew, and used it selectively, but first sure that some significant advantage could be gained. Her rapid advancement was due to a variety of factors that she readily combined to get what she wanted and promote her agenda, helping black minorities on the Islands. Body and brain therefore worked together to improve conditions for those not nearly as well endowed. Seldom did she allow herself to be seduced into an affair for mere pleasure. Her body was too valuable to be frittered away on casual indulgence.

Hermione generally granted favors to powerful white men, although she occasionally made an exception. She chose Simeon however simply for her own enjoyment, not for what he could do for her. They met when Simeon attended a local assembly of teachers. He introduced himself as a former ship's doctor, but let it be known that at the present, he was simply seeking new opportunities on land. Immediately sizing him up, Hermione had no reason to believe anything he said, but liked the way he said it and found him attractive and amusing, in contrast to some of the solid citizens. She had no inclination or reason to expose his disguise because he was more to her taste than most of the men she'd met. Neither Hermione nor Simeon planned on more than a passing affair. It quickly became exceedingly intense, as if to pack as much as possible into limited time. He was highly aroused by her sophistication, quiet bawdiness, and graceful manner almost as much as by her sleek copper skin, long legs, firm breasts, and glossy black hair, just this side of oiliness. What also appealed to Simeon was an intangible but dusky aroma. It seemed primitive as well as worldly. Older black women frequently were attracted to Simeon, and he responded without hesitation, often finding that same scent. Hermione managed to quell his enduring appetite for older women, at least temporarily.

Simeon's humorous and engaging manner, combined with wealth, good looks, cultivation, and enough animal passion, quickly gained Hermione's approval. He made for a very acceptable interlude. However, at any unannounced moment, such as on this bright and cloudless morning, she too might decide not to return, and take up with someone else, just as Simeon spontaneously could leave on a whim. It was a thoroughly delightful, balanced, uncommitted equation, good for them both.

Simeon was unusually elated this morning. He had many reasons for congratulating himself on good fortune, a strong virile body, and wealth to support his appetites. Out of sheer robust exuberance, he sang a wordless aria of his own composition, rejoicing in the sunny vista that engulfed him. What unseen life there was beneath the glittering ocean waves aroused his imagination even more. The teeming surface, hinting of turbulence beneath, harmonized with his own scarcely satiable urges, lingering on in the faint but pungent body perfume left behind by Hermione.

He showered, enjoying the cascading hot water. Afterward, he proudly stood before a full-length mirror, admiring with approval his still turgid genitals. What diversions and excitement he'd known! What wonders did his transgressions discover! While vigorously and lovingly caressing himself with a luxurious warm white towel, he thought ahead to Hermione's promise to call that evening. But then again, she might not, and the uncertainty was stimulating in itself. As if it were not enough to be a dilettante, which he didn't mind at all, he enjoyed having the qualifications, means, and opportunity to be a true libertine in the style of ancient Roman emperors, whom he imagined were pretty much like himself.

Then, without warning, his enjoyment came to an abrupt stop. While rubbing himself, despite thick toweling, he discovered that his left testicle was about twice the size of the right. As he probed further, the testicle was slightly tender to a gentle squeeze. Instantly alarmed, he quickly went over events of the night before. He had not injured himself in any way, even during their erotic acrobatics. Savoring the memory, he recalled no residual fatigue, strain, or pain. He took a mirror and scrutinized the swollen testicle. Then he had to face the shocking possibility that it might be a sudden illness, but surely nothing serious, and certainly not an enduring impediment. His denial was loud enough to hear, because he spoke aloud in the empty room, "It's nothing, nothing at all!"

Panic did not fully set in until he tried to urinate. Regularly, the stream was free and powerful, especially in the morning, but now it was painfully difficult. There was only a trickle. He strained, ran water, nothing happened, then suddenly, with a gush, bright red blood exploded, splashing against the turquoise wall.

At that horrifying moment, almost unable to breathe, Simeon shuddered as if his whole life abruptly dissipated and was about to be irretrievably lost. A premonition swept over him that some evil force had sneaked up during the night and inflicted an illness that would kill him. The fulsome indulgent future he visualized just minutes before disintegrated at once.

"My God," he spoke fervently, as if supplicating an actual but hostile deity to let the bloody mess be all a mistake meant for someone else. "My God, what is going on?" By asking, he already had a dreaded answer, which he immediately wanted to dismiss. It might, of course, very remotely, be a sign of cancer. But, of course, that couldn't be. Simeon was so immobilized at that thought that he tried to stop thinking. Cancer then immediately capitalized itself in his mind, as if emerging like an unholy script on the bloody wall. CANCER, *cancer* the curse, the atrocity, and a death sentence were like a garish signboard suddenly before his eyes, without warning, marking a grim threat for the future.

Simeon was not unfamiliar with cancer, through stints as a nurse's aide and hospital attendant. But then it was always somebody else's, as if he were exempt. He had seen and heard much about this 'very bad disease' that people feared above all others. Nevertheless, he overheard doctors telling patients after an operation that their cancer seemed to be very small, and that they had caught it in time. That innocuous lump or annoying symptom often proved to be a little more tenacious, and most unwilling to give up its hold. Often enough, a month to a year or two later, despite assiduous treatment and heavy reassurances, the solitary lump became a set of unmistakably aggressive secondary tumors. The cancer had not only come back, but also reproduced and thrived.

While Simeon might not have known, there is no standard or uniform response to cancer, no matter how fast or slow it grows, how pressing the sense of mortality, and how distressed its victim. Nevertheless, few people confront cancer with calm and equanimity, including presumably mature doctors and nurses who may blanch, tremble, and attempt to deny when *they* become the unwilling patients. The future vacancy of time when they shall be dead cannot be imagined. When people talk about having had cancer, they are mistaken. *Cancer, CANCER, or in its familiar and, hopefully, less menacing guise, CA*, has *them* in its grasp, not the other way round. Simeon was about to confront just this challenge. Without quite realizing it, he had gone from the privileged domain of the invigorated, hale and hearty to the ranks of the vulnerable and afflicted.

For the unfortunate intimidated victims, cancer is now part of them, threatening body and mind, and whatever else keeps them whole. The sanguine physician who blandly called the cancer a minor and inconvenient problem that could readily be managed, no longer is able to hold back its spread. For some patients, cancer is like an unwanted intruder who comes uninvited, stubbornly refuses to leave, and then takes over the house. From that point on, few decisions or independent actions can be taken without heeding the potential restrictions of illness and the way of life it imposes.

In the space of a few minutes, Simeon had gone from a fine exuberance to corrosive doubts about life itself. Anxiety and fear of death shook him like a wriggling rat. He was still shaking when a chambermaid came in. Jarred by the sight of blood and an agitated naked man wandering around, she quickly withdrew.

Cancer became a new and obligatory challenging obstacle. It had to be dealt with, not just as a disease, but also a condition of life. Cancer has its own laws, which victims are obliged to follow haltingly and with dread. For the apprehensive and now pessimistic Simeon, still quaking with uncertainty and panic, the future could only be relentless death in much pain. Its evil proclivity towards suffering and death had quickly demonstrated what he had to endure. A true taboo is fascinating, whetting an appetite to violate it. But for Simeon, an inveterate seeker of taboos and forbidden pleasures, cancer was not a fascinating taboo but a dreaded fate, without qualification. Unlike taboo, cancer was about to violate Simeon, not the reverse.

After the first rush of panic and the chambermaid's hasty departure, prudence told Simeon to cool down and be checked by a doctor as soon as possible, today maybe, as if he were racing with lethality and about to lose. Although the official diagnosis was as yet uncertain, in his heart he was already sure. Simeon did recall that a couple of years ago, maybe five, both testicles had become acutely swollen and extremely tender one morning, with burning yellow ooze from his penis. A physician in Capetown, where he was visiting, pronounced his malady venereal, and treated him effectively with an antibiotic. Nothing more, but the doctor had something else to say. It was at once an admonition and a precaution.

"This happens all too often to young men visiting a strange country. They are incautious and impulsive, and want to feel totally free to do whatever they want with anyone. No one is entirely safe, anywhere. Under very attractive covering, there can be naked garbage. I would be remiss not to caution you, yet doubtful that my words have any effect." He was frank and not at all offensive or disrespectful. The well-meaning doctor whom he never saw again was both moralistic and realistic. He knew that his words would not restrain Simon. The doctor's words came back vividly, but now less like a sermon about promiscuity in strange lands than a warning about serious ailments still to come. Simeon would have willingly exchanged his provisional diagnosis for a venereal disease at this point.

Simeon chose to ignore the doctor's warning, defying it in every way possible, although he did not acquire another venereal disease to his knowledge, despite repeated and reckless exposure. At this moment, however, standing before a toilet bowl, surrounded by splattered fresh blood, he tried to hope that it might be no more than another case of clap, acquired from a symptom-less Hermione whom he supposed to be clean. But he knew better than to blame it on her, and look for another venereal disease that could easily be dispelled.

"There, you've got it again, done yourself in," he said, with scarcely a trace of conviction, "Just another twinge of bad luck, nothing really to worry about, happens to everyone." But worry he did. Not too long ago he returned from Southeast Asia where risk from one thing or another is as common as the rodents and insects. Local procurers, spotting another rich American, offered him a selection of adventures, with any number of people to help carry them out. There were temporary house slaves, male and female, of all ages, ready to service him in any fashion imaginable. The pimps' propositions did generate a sense of taboo that would horrify most people but attracted Simeon. Unlimited and extravagant sex was never to be rejected. That was a principle. If anything was taboo, or could be construed that way, then it was worth breaking. However, after a week or so, the variegated pleasures palled. Having indiscriminate sex around the clock was hardly worth the bother. He paid off the hired help with funds ample enough to buy freedom from their pimps, and still have money left over. Simeon, the benefactor, could ironically reflect that because of his generosity erstwhile slaves were now far better off than they had been before his money arrived. Had he also acquired another exotic ailment during this time that was just now showing itself?

Simeon knew no local physicians on the island. If his malady turned out to be merely another venereal infection from misadventure with Hermione or acquired lately from his trip, he did not want to be scolded like a schoolboy on his first fling. He remembered an elderly physician, perhaps still practicing in Miami, who seemed worldly wise and skilled enough to diagnose whatever was ailing Simeon and give him dependable advice without preaching. Along with enjoying Dr. Pochapin's funny Russian accent, Simeon also hoped he was competent. He called Miami immediately and was much relieved to find that the doctor was available two days hence. Exultant, he almost told the secretary all about his testicle. Without any hesitation, he packed up, checked out, leaving no forwarding address, and took off for Miami. Only when aloft did he recall that he hadn't notified Hermione. It was just as well. She might have been to blame, anyway. He never spoke with her again, although occasionally he was tempted to pluck their erotic strings again. But he didn't. The affair was abruptly over.

Dr. Pochapin turned out to be what Simeon remembered and anticipated. He was in fact an elderly, urbane, and thorough physician who carefully examined Simeon before making any pronouncement.

"No, no, Simeon," he said soberly, "I do not think you have an infection, but I shall check further. It is not uncommon to have tumors spring up over night, like poisonous mushrooms in the forest, and some doctors do mistake them for infections." Simeon did not appreciate the simile but listened quietly as Dr. Pochapin continued.

"Men your age get such things. To make an absolute diagnosis we need tests and that means a biopsy. A pathologist looks at a small bit of tissue from the testicle under a microscope." The doctor was candid and matter of fact. Simeon asked his questions, now not at all sure about venereal infection. He never had been, but only wishful for the blandest diagnosis.

"An antibiotic won't help? Will I have to have my testicle removed?" Simeon already knew that the answer to his first question was No, and the second, not now. He phrased other questions so ambiguously that any reassuring response would become a welcome certainty, bringing with it a momentary tinge of relief.

"Not just now, only the biopsy. Then we see." Dr. Pochapin said, "If positive, we shall talk about what next. I do not wish to play games, so I won't mention cancer until it is proven." Pochapin spoke of cancer boldly, yet with the courtesy due a respected enemy. He voiced the word cautiously, by speaking of cancer, not the threatening Cancer.

When Simeon next saw Dr. Pochapin the biopsy and other tests had been done and the results reported. Meanwhile the testicle remained large, and slightly tender. Simeon was happy, however, because the bleeding had not returned. This might be the optimistic omen he was looking for. But Dr. Pochapin was not pleased with the biopsy report and gave him no assurance that all would be well.

"Yes, Simeon, your biopsy shows cancer, not the usual kind that can be cured by just removing the testicle. I am sorry. The type of cancer you have is a little uncommon by coming on so quickly, and without warning. I must be frank, this type might be more difficult to treat." After listening to his chest again, the doctor put an avuncular hand on Simeon's shoulder, and added, "Your chest is not good, the x-ray showed that. Although you seem to be healthy enough, there are a couple of small shadows that should be frequently watched. There might also be a spread of the cancer already. In your groin, around the genitals, in your lower back, the x-rays show signs of what could be more cancer. This means trouble, I am sorry to say. I wish I had better news for you, but it is far better to know right away, to start the right treatment. Your bones look all right so far, and again, your previous health is in your favor. No, it is not venereal, a result of sexual abuse and misuse." Dr. Pochapin smiled for no particular reason. "Physically, you are quite a specimen. That's possibly an advantage, but perhaps no. Now, you may ask any other questions."

Simeon felt faintness as Dr. Pochapin spoke. Without hiding the discouraging facts, Dr. Pochapin openly used the diagnosis Simeon most dreaded, cancer. There it was, glaring at him like an insolent devil, daring him to protest. Simeon was silent, unable to phrase questions.

"This is not a death sentence, my boy," Dr. Pochapin said, "But make no mistake. Do not ignore it. You can see another doctor, if you wish, and you should, an oncologist, a specialist in cancer. That is your decision, but it is serious."

"I don't know if it's worth putting up with surgery and treatments like drugs and radiation. It's all very routine, I suppose, except to me. What else can I do?" Simeon said, sadly and bitterly, "I can hear the doctors being very upbeat, making light, sweet-talking me, or else very abrupt and off-hand. In such cases, sweet or sour, they don't care. They'll hedge, mince no words, and usually call a spade either a fancy teaspoon or a dirty shovel." Dr. Pochapin nodded in agreement, acknowledging that it was mainly a question of whether it was worth going through, including which doctor to trust.

"Hedge, most doctors must, one way or another," Dr. Pochapin tried to answer, but as an old timer, not defensively. "They may call cancer a shovel or a teaspoon. No one can pretend that it is OK. Being abrupt is inexcusable, but it happens for reasons I hope are not indifference. Sometimes the abrupt doctors care the most. It hurts them to be pessimistic. Nothing you did brought it on, that I know. What I do know is that cancer is not retaliation or punishment for some mistakes you made, or a bad thing deserving judgment from on high. If that were true, there would be hardly anyone left in the world without cancer. Cancer can be very bad, but some diseases are far worse. People don't seem to fear them so much. I told you that your cancer is unusual, but it isn't so rare in large medical centers where they see many cases of just about everything. I want to suggest that you must see a former student of mine, a colleague, younger, of course, but now a great cancer expert. He is Dr. Jeff Barton in Boston. I taught him briefly when I first came to this country, and he was a medical student. An outstanding specialist now, so I take some credit for his success and for being one of his teachers. But he is much more than a cancer specialist. He is also a very compassionate man who will not talk to the cancer as if you weren't in the room. No sweet talk or gruff talk."

Simeon later appreciated why Dr. Pochapin emphasized compassion along with competence. The doctor would appreciate the devastating loss of the ailing testicle, and still soberly advise him about the debilitating treatment that must follow. A foreboding again swept over Simeon as he faced an amorphous, ambiguous future. Naturally, he followed Dr. Pochapin's recommendation, without struggling further to find out if it was worthwhile in the long run.

Dr. Barton was everything that Dr. Pochapin promised, and from first impressions, he continued to be both competent and compassionate, without exuding excessive sympathy. He insisted at once that the offending testicle must be removed. Yielding to his authoritative advice, Simeon was in the hospital within a day, then out again the next, one testicle less, but with a program for treatment. Dr. Barton admitted that it was unusual to remove a testicle when so much of the cancer had already spread. Nevertheless, it had to be done. The wide distribution of secondary cancer had been noted in Dr. Pochapin's referral and Dr. Barton confirmed that sometimes taking out the primary could slow down the secondary tumors. Simeon privately noted that as a result, with that policy, Dr. Barton was never wrong.

"When will the other one go?" he asked Dr. Barton, "How bad do things look?"

"Not so good, I am afraid. You'll need treatment, however, starting very soon. I strongly advise against just letting nature take its course, without any treatment except for the fake panaceas you will be tempted to get in Mexico. You asked about removing the other one. My answer is No or Not yet. Not yet, I hope, and by that time, Never. Maybe is what I think now. In your favor is very excellent health in spite of the cancer, and your lack of symptoms. The apparent spread hasn't caused any pain, weakness, whatever. Were it not for the x-rays and other examinations, I would not have guessed that the cancer had spread so far and so fast. It won't interfere with sex, if that concerns you. I imagine it does. But chemotherapy will put you on hold for a while. That means of course, your sex drive will be dampened." For Simeon, being sexless was like suspended animation, life without living. It was a painful limbo for his libido, a prelude to partial death, at least to a vital part.

Dr. Barton then switched medical gears, leaving Simeon's clinical cancer aside, and spoke at length about Cancer, its implications for so-called normal quality of life, not just the medical facts. Cancer is the scourge of many, yet not without periodic signs of progress. Effective treatment for many types of cancer already exists that was not available just a few years ago. He went on to say that Cancer is a different way of life based on the limitations of the disease, and a special attitude about having cancer. Dr.

Barton understood this distinction. He hoped to keep cancer and Cancer as separate as he could, so that Simeon's life would not be drastically altered. His other remarks were also pertinent and kindly, but equivalent to explaining the unexplainable. Maybe it made Dr. Barton feel better. It was intended to offer a perspective, which Simeon was not in the mood to appreciate fully, although he perfunctorily asked questions, half-anticipating the answers.

Despite Dr. Pochapin's kindly reassurance, Simeon continued to believe that cancer had perversely picked out his genitals to invade, a part of the body that had always been dominant in his mind. If true that Simeon were so afflicted, would it mean that the punishment fit the crime? Surely, he had no guilt, and no crime had been committed. Had Simeon been looking to ease regrets, Cancer would be like paying a debt, a recompense for offenses and injuries to others. But to whom and for what? No one, not even Dr. Barton, could predict his future. That is, not unless Barton were to replace his testicle with a crystal ball. To the victor goes the spoiled man. With limited choices, he decided to accept Dr. Barton's recommendations for treatment, but with many misgivings.

As he doggedly followed the course of treatment, Simeon became bored with the routine. He experienced the nausea and distress of chemotherapy and knew this was expected. Nothing else bothered him, except lassitude. Simeon was tempted to answer the standard impersonal questions with smart aleck answers, but knew the nurses were just doing a job and there were many other people to see that day. The no nonsense professional optimism and prim competence had nothing whatsoever to do with effectiveness of chemotherapy. Had they given wolfsbane and promised that he'd feel better right after the full moon, the procedures would be just the same.

As cycles of treatment came and went, Simon began to believe that he was right about the routine, but wrong about his absolute doom. Apprehension faded as treatment itself and the process turned into a way of life. Fatalism was but a dreary accommodation to his commonplace situation. Nothing was left to deny except hope. His days melted down into one of unmitigated fatigue, interrupted now and then by sweeping nausea that medication only partially relieved. Doing nothing but lying on his hotel bed, between sessions at the hospital, he gazed indifferently at insipid television programs in which he had absolutely no interest. Otherwise, his daily denominator depended on radio voices droning on soberly or with laughter about inconsequential matters. He was alone, surrounded by solitude, confined to an impersonal room, while waiting for the next round. The cancer had not yet been subdued.

He moved from the hotel to a modest apartment, just to provide himself with a little fresh autonomy and a shadowy remnant of individuality. An elderly widow, Rita Glenn, came in daily to prepare tasteless meals, clean up, change bedclothes, shop, and do other chores. She had little to say except perfunctory greetings on arriving and departing. He considered this a blessing of sorts. Otherwise, he would be compelled to answer and deal with conversation. Usually, after six hours of slowly doing work that normally required about two, she left unceremoniously with a casual farewell, while Simeon dozed. It didn't matter, because most of the time he was not sure whether he was awake or asleep or if she'd been there or not.

Late one afternoon, as dusk crept silently in through the windows and across the room, the semi-somnolent Simeon was suddenly stirred into being awake and alert. Sensing the presence of something intangible, he did make out a hazy form at the other end of the room. More substantial than a mere dream, a ghostly apparition had settled in a far corner, shaded, but with a reality he could not dispel. There it was, unmistakably, a dim and misty figure with vaguely human form, silent and unmoving. The faceless body was covered with a dark gray mantle, like a shroud, concealing everything but its presence. Even from a distance, Simeon knew this specter was an emissary coming from the shadows and dusk, a first cousin to death. Nevertheless, eerie and disconcerting as it was, Simeon's visitor conveyed a reassuring calm that overcame fright and apathy, the two unlikely companions he was accustomed to. No words were exchanged. Then, as daylight further dimmed into the darkness of night, Simeon's hooded visitor slowly dissolved into the distant wall. When he turned on the bedroom light, it was gone. Simeon remained calm and mystified.

Most of the time, whether lying in bed or sitting slouched in an overstuffed chair near the window, fragmentary reminiscences entertained Simeon. Images spun out of nowhere were fantasies conjured up from fragments and filaments woven from unselected memories. It was a relatively amusing pastime, relieving to some extent his ennui. Nevertheless, from time to time, out of these vaporous images, like small flames erupting, came wavering visions and organized recollections of long ago. From among these came more vivid reminders of actual events and specific people. It was all very transient. He could not understand why anything had to be remembered at all. He was utterly by himself without visitors, free to wander through the past, and dip into the meandering stream of bygones.

Some of the floating memories were as real as when they first occurred, while others were no more solid than that ghost which never returned. Memory fooled him in other ways, such as endowing certain people with traits and sentiments they never had in the first place. Ronnie, for one, had been an unscrupulous young con man, drinking companion, and consummate trickster, always on the lookout for a profitable scam. Now, however, as Simeon recalled one fragment after another, Ronnie seemed to be a successful entrepreneur, an expert on finance and health, who carried himself with the assurance of authority. Was he really only a skillful faker or did Simeon recognize a side of Ronnie never in fact realized?

Among the half-recollections, Simeon thought that it might have been Chester who introduced him to Ronnie, but he didn't know how this happened and could only surmise. However, Ronnie never failed to fascinate Simon with his wild, yet plausible tales of intrigue, mischief, and scandalous behavior. Familiar with the good and bad, Ronnie didn't care which was which. Embracing evil gladly was clearly his preference. His arresting anecdotes and wily exploits became florid fantasies for the young Simon, who had not yet turned into the more sophisticated Simeon. Ronnie told Simon about various con games he perpetrated, including stories that certainly belonged to taboo territory. Simeon was particularly enraptured when hearing that Ronnie posed as a qualified masseur, advertising his services, and then carried out a variety of colorful encounters. Intrigued, Simon was curious enough to accept Ronnie's offer to try his own talent on a few clients, visiting their homes and hotel rooms. Certain episodes turned out to be so flamboyant that even Ronnie could not have anticipated the adventures in advance.

Ronnie had devious ways and tactics to do just about anything that attracted him. Maneuvering along a blurred boundary between the barely legitimate and the frankly illegal, Ronnie often tried to enlist Simon in other scams and schemes beyond spurious therapy. In his reveries, Simeon was sure they were not about mugging old people or abusing the homeless. Were Ronnie's stories real events or just contrived fables told to a willing and gaping listener? The massage game was real enough, but what about other escapades? Just because Ronnie was slick enough to keep out of prison, there was nothing forbidden that he hadn't once tried or said he had. He was a mentor, friend, and model for tricks Simon had not yet tried. Whatever happened to Ronnie, if that were his real name?

Recollections of Chester and Maggie replaced Ronnie. Was Maggie her real name or did Simeon merely make it up? Simeon's river of reveries suddenly stopped, as he recalled a series of unfortunate events with an elderly couple, the Professor and his wife. Ronnie had actually led Simeon into so many weird and astonishing adventures that all could have been a concocted figment of imagination based on what might have happened. But this was not true. Most were real enough, bizarre enough to be questioned, and not altogether synthesized from other events. Nevertheless, vivid recollections of the Professor and his wife swirled upward into Simeon's awareness, along with a painful claim of regret on Simeon's reluctant memory. There was no shaking off images of these two old people, regardless of how mortifying the recollections. Considering the offenses, it had been a shameful but perversely arousing intrusion. He wanted relief and release right now, next door to forgiveness, for what he could never wholly forget. The saga of the Professor and his wife made the Simon of yesterday singularly guilty for what he had perpetrated years before. Simeon still felt responsible for Simon's offenses towards these two who had been kind to him.

The Professor was a retired teacher and minister, dubbed "The Professor" by Simon and Ronnie, who laughed at his gullibility. His actual name was either Claude or Rollo, but Ronnie and Simon never called him other than "Sir". Claude or Rollo suffered from a not too disabling arthritis. Physicians recommended mild exercise and massage, which had not been very effective. Ronnie was not uninformed about physiotherapy and chiropractic, and somehow became the Professor's masseur. Maybe Chester made the referral, but perhaps not, since Ronnie had other acquaintances. To his credit, Ronnie's ministrations seemed to help his client, where regular doctors failed.

It was unclear however when and why Ronnie decided to transfer Claude to Simon. Ronnie might have been simply bored with the old man. He was also amused by Simon's strange fascination with elderly people, and curious to see what would happen. Ronnie's reasons were vague enough, but the transfer went smoothly.

Simon enjoyed the old man, while carrying out his job. Talking was easy, informal, and somewhat teasing, before turning into a kind of one-sided confessional. Encouraged by Simon's disingenuous questions, the Professor spoke openly and with slight hesitancy about bachelor exploits before marriage, when he was a young student in divinity school. Claude's adventures were comparatively tepid, but in order to encourage him further, Simon deliberately embellished the anecdotes he chose to tell the Professor. Claude was fascinated and clearly envious. Naturally, as with Chester and Maggie, it was all part of a plan. Soon, Claude's physical response became obvious. Without being asked, Simon did not hesitate to help his client along.

In due time, according to the familiar scheme, Simon wondered how to bring Claude's wife, Hannah, into the arrangement. It would be more difficult than with Maggie who was already more than acquiescent. Hannah was far too old, reserved and unprepared for what Simon had in mind. Would Hannah, whom Simon called by her first name, ever consider using his services? The suggestion seemed to come up quite naturally because the professor and his wife regarded Simon as a "nice young man working his way through college," and suspected nothing of Simon's intentions. It was, of course, not at all true, and nothing salacious was ever hinted at. Simon needed a far different strategy than the tantalizing promises he made to seduce Chester. Nevertheless, Ronnie laughed with conspiratorial glee when Simon reported how he asked Claude about Hannah. He couldn't fathom what Simon saw in older folks, but came up with numerous ideas about how to advance the plan.

It worked perfectly. Hannah did seem to feel better under Simon's care. At first she was embarrassed by partial nudity, but Simon, always very considerate and tactful, made sure that she was covered. In time, she accepted her treatment completely exposed, without comment. Inevitably, Simon proceeded to his own improvisations, finally to what he had in mind all along. However, Hannah found it far too upsetting and impossible to continue. For her it was an immoral, shameful, and mortifying affair that abruptly came to an end. Simon went away, chastened, and never saw Claude, Hannah or Ronnie again.

Lolling in his bed now years later, whiling away time between chemotherapy treatments, old images and new wishes blended dubious facts with a growing wish to exonerate himself. As he thought about Hannah, she became more delectable, seductive, and attractive than she actually could have been. Utterly solitary, free to improvise, the ailing Simeon felt the tension of fresh arousal. Memory easily became fantasy, and fantasy turned into what might have happened. By adding figments and details that even he knew never happened, reminiscence seemed very real and hard to resist. Nothing in the actual affair with Hannah had been as sensuous as he now imagined. Nevertheless, Simon spent several days and nights futilely attempting to get rid of what memory dredged up. Passage of time, lingering regret, resentment of his rebuff, and his present depleted physical condition were no barriers to imagination. Unable to control his own mounting tension, Simeon decided to act and found that their telephone number and address had not changed. Telephoning was utterly irrational and without reason other than to expect nothing but further mortification for Hannah, as well as the ailing Simeon, now quite out of his head. However, he made the call and immediately recognized Hannah's voice.

"Hello, Hannah," he began breezily, "This is Simon," using his old name. "I've been thinking about you and Claude, and just wanted to see how you are." He was sure she'd remember, and was thoroughly convinced that she'd welcome him, overlooking their acrimonious parting and the intervening years. It was immediately evident that Hannah remembered very well, but without the agreeable response he sought. His call was clearly disturbing, and her voice became tense, tremulous and scarcely audible.

"Of course, I remember you," she answered, irritation and fear showing, with a whispered quavering that could not be disguised. "Why do you call me now; after all these years? What are you up to? What is it that you want from me?" She was concerned, not without cause that this rascal had something devious and unscrupulous in mind, perhaps money. To her, as she clutched the telephone, Simon was a nuisance, at least, or a threat, at worst. She wanted to get rid of him quickly.

"No special reason, except that it's been such a long time, and I wanted to talk to two of my favorite people, you in particular. We had some warm memories, some good times together, maybe you remember. I've been laid up sick for a while, and have to stay put. But all this free time gives me a chance to call old friends." It was an unconvincing performance.

Hannah did not ask about his illness, nor where he was presently living. She had no such interest. There was no curiosity except for his motives, which she did not trust. She was alarmed that he might be nearby, and about to break into her life again. Simon persisted, trying to be friendly and flirtatious at the same time, asking questions that she answered with frightened curt and cautious monosyllables. Eventually, he asked solicitously about Claude. Hannah's response was even more antagonistic. Claude had been dead a long time, she said flatly, without offering details.

"What is it you want?" she insisted, "Please don't pretend you called just to renew old friendships with people you betrayed!" Simeon glibly tried to talk his way around her firm truculence. Finally, realizing that he'd made a dreadful mistake in disturbing her, he was tempted to hang up and break this spurious connection for good. He even thought of apologizing, for all the good that might have done. There was no good to be gained; it was all evil. As his fancied anticipation faded, reality forced him to see that he was just an ugly intruder shackled to skewed memories that he had inflicted on a very old lady, once a victim of his schemes.

"I'm sorry to hear about Claude," he managed to say, "I liked and admired him, just as I did you. You both were good friends, gave me advice I didn't always follow. But I appreciated that you cared, at least for a little while. Tell me something about yourself." He almost pleaded for some cordial reciprocity. She did not answer his questions.

"Simon, I still don't know what brought on this call. It is not at all welcome. What happened years ago shouldn't have happened. I regretted it and blamed myself. Claude knew nothing about it, I think, I hope. But I hold you as responsible as me. You used us both. That is also in the past. You are not an old friend, and you might have remembered that I wasn't so young even then and not experienced at all. I was just incredibly trusting. I'm an old lady now, trying my best to get along. You've chosen to make this pointless telephone call. I don't welcome it. You are gone, my husband is gone, all gone, and soon I will, too." Simeon started to protest, apologize, and make amends without revealing the real reason for the call, which would have been hateful. Hannah interrupted him.

"Please, please, I don't want to talk any further. I'm sorry you've been sick, and I'm willing to excuse you. Now, please leave me alone. I don't want to be rude unless I have to. And if I hear from you again, I'll have to do something about it." Simon tried to smooth things over. She broke in again. "I'm going to hang up. I see that you don't know enough to." And she did just that, leaving Simeon with humiliation, but only for a short time. Maybe he should try Chester and Maggie again. But he went to sleep thinking about Hermione, even managing to fuse her with the aged Hannah.

When he awoke an hour or two later, he was more troubled, especially after he got up, looked in the bathroom mirror, and witnessed with dismay the ravages of illness and its treatment. He was so weak, and lost so much weight that he would be thin fare, indeed, for a hungry cancer. His skin was like mildewed parchment, once treasured, and now repulsive, fit only for discarded rubbish. He was an ugly sight and turned away in disgust, glad for the privacy of his isolation.

When Rita came in two mornings later Simeon was still asleep. However, as soon as he awakened, he felt a stunning sense of rest, restoration, and renewal. In such contrast to his customary parlous condition, it was a miraculous change. Regardless of how it happened, or where it came from, it was a welcome relief from how ugly, depleted, and withered he had been. Pleased and puzzled, he wondered if at last he had become unshackled from regrets about Hannah, following their unhappy telephone conversation. It didn't make sense, but what did make sense? What gave him relief all of a sudden? In recalling Hannah's plea and response, and his regret afterward, he had abruptly lost any remorse. That in itself seemed like a potent tonic, not unlike the shivering satisfaction of making an anonymous obscene telephone call.

Perhaps the hungry cancer was also sated, for reasons best known to itself, and decided to let him be, while seeking others to feed on. The high mood continued. He even decided to get dressed. Wanting to tell someone who cared how well he was, Simeon now decided to call one of his doctors, just at random, past and present, regardless of whether the doctor would remember him or not. No doctor could be reached.

He was scheduled to have another transfusion on the following day. As a rule fresh blood temporarily invigorated him, but he was already feeling renewed and vigorous. However, he kept the appointment. The technician and then a doctor were puzzled that Simeon seemed to feel far better than his blood count and other tests actually could explain. He ought to have been much more fatigued and sick. Another transfusion was still in order.

The paradoxical invigoration lasted several more weeks, but without corresponding decrease of cancer. Nevertheless, during this interlude, Simeon found strength and ambition enough to make his own bed, read a little, and surprise himself by going out for an unaccustomed stroll. What was truly astonishing, he began to savor Rita's mediocre cooking and engaged her in conversation. Blood transfusions had boosted Simeon's energy before, but by this time, the effects should have worn off. Instead, he felt as healthy as he ever had since the cancer first showed itself in that hotel room, overlooking the sea.

He had not ever expected to feel so well again. It was a case of mistaken identity, except there was no one to share the joke with. But he did not doubt the laboratory and x ray reports. Another half-amusing thought crossed his mind. What if he were to refuse transfusions, and instead drink the blood? Would it have the same effect? If it did, why not just collect fresh blood, and periodically use it as a tonic at home? The idea of drinking fresh blood was like a new and challenging taboo, which excited him, even if he was reminded of old movies and Bela Lugosi. He wasn't sure where the blood would come from. Would he steal it from a blood bank or find donors somewhere? What would the hospital staff think of his idea? Why not? Of course, he said nothing.

Simeon was not unfamiliar with weird stories of people who ate strange repulsive things. Other than freaks that regularly performed by eating rats, mice and vermin, there were tales of bloodthirsty brigands who attacked and killed unfortunate travelers and ate their flesh. An Indian physician he once met talked of drinking urine, claiming that it prevented most diseases, and had a general purifying effect on the body and soul. After all, urine was cleaner than drinking water. The kidneys had already cleaned it of impurities, and only therapeutic ingredients were left. It was bad physiology but Simeon, of course, immediately tried it, only to feel nauseated.

There are no limits that a desperate person will not go to cure a fatal illness. Mischief and evil are everywhere, and it is possible that forbidden substances do have curative properties. Poison or something unsavory might have beneficial effects. In contrast, even the most established conventional medicine used for decades might still have hidden potential for unexpected harm. The principle seems to be finding a concoction that counteracts whatever it is that people complain about, regardless of its source and calling it medicinal. Sometimes, like cures like, and sometimes the unlike cures. Regardless of where the supposed cure comes from, or its source, gullible people are always willing to act upon it. Medical theories don't have to make sense, and surely don't need proof, if enough reputed testimonials approve. Could drinking blood help restore him for long periods? Anything whatsoever that comes from the body, properly prepared, might turn out to be an undiscovered boon. It was a crazy notion, but no more far fetched than other theories he'd heard about. The idea fascinated him. Wanting desperately to hang onto his strong turn of good health, despite persistent disease, Simeon looked everywhere for whatever far-fetched "nutritional supplement" might continue his well-being. Not every taboo had to be overtly sexual, although he was hard put to think of any. Just because society forbids or even criminalizes substances, maybe such stuff that seems disgusting or revolting might be secretly healthy.

Simeon continued to feel better than for a very long time, although cancer remained in control and could not be ignored. Like anyone else, he yearned for a state of healthy serenity, unafflicted. He once learned a little about Buddhism, and the promise of Nirvana in another life. He'd gladly opt for the eternal return instead of this infernal routine. There were plenty of believers in every religion who prayed incessantly, and died anyway, with no blessing or mitigation whatsoever from on high. Miracles couldn't be expected. Whoever is in charge of dispensing cures must be pretty choosy about who gets it. No, this was no miracle happening, but it has to be a freakish chain of unforeseen events. Where is this God when you need him most? If there were a god, then miracles should be his exclusive stock in trade. But why is he so stingy about them? Why not be more generous since plenty of people need all the help they can get?

A thread of awe and mysticism wound its way into him, like an insinuating worm masquerading as pious certitude. Simeon came to enjoy reading about mysticism and exotic medicines. Maybe a victim has to commit a very grievous sin before the divine dispenser of mercy grants an undeserved reward. It's more spectacular and confounding that way. The undeserving who never would think of praying, sacrificing, or paying a visit to some holy place sometimes seem to be beneficiaries of good fortune, too. Turn the story of Job inside out and a thoroughly bad guy might emerge, basking in prosperity and good luck. Self-help books were boring, repetitious and righteous to a fault. After thumbing through morale-boosting chapters in highly renowned moneymaking books, filled with inspirational and cautionary aphorisms, Simeon concluded that such books must help, but only help the authors who help themselves to fat royalties.

He was like a carrier of a dreadful infectious disease that left him feeling healthy, immune, and untouched, although fortunately, he could not give it to others without his protection. Good health must be a rare complication of any disease, especially cancer. It looked as if Simeon's fate was clear. He would die in the best of health. As Simeon gazed out of his apartment window, the sun seemed brighter, the sky bluer, and he was enjoying a remission. What ironic prank was this to play on a dying man? He remembered the apparition that appeared to be a delegate of death. Would this ghost tantalize him with a fictitious recovery, just to set him up for a great fall?

A letter from Dr. Barton interrupted his halcyon ease. What he wrote was also meant for other patients, but it was personally addressed to him. The message had just the right tinge of regret and good wishes. He was about to move away and accept a prominent post at a distant medical school. Although sorry to leave his loyal patients, the office would have a list of dependable replacements, all of which deserved the same trust and confidence that patients had always shown him. Etc. Etc.

Simeon crumpled the letter with dismay, before starting to speculate about his next doctor. He was surprised a day or two later by getting a real telephone call from Dr. Barton, who was very friendly and wanted to talk about continuing surveillance by another physician. However, instead of offering a perfunctory list of local colleagues, Dr. Barton had some unusual things to say. He came right to the point. There was only one physician for Simeon. This was an oncologist way off in Sydney, Australia, a doctor who had special knowledge about patients with the kind of refractory yet paradoxical cancer Simeon had. Barton seemed to emphasize Simeon's individuality, however, not just the disease. Simeon reminded Dr. Barton that he was doing very well now, and maybe he shouldn't see anyone, especially if it meant such a long trip.

"I'm certainly glad you're doing so well," Dr. Barton responded, "I already know that. That's fine, except that we both know that disproportionately healthy feelings are not all that unheard of, even with the extent of your cancer. Cancer is deceptive in many ways, even freeing a patient from symptoms temporarily. It's a false cure, however, just a remission, for which we're grateful anyway. It is far different than permanent cure, although very welcome. You have such a strange combination of good health and advanced cancer that I'm not sure just what is going on. Time will tell, as they say, but what time tells is very sketchy." Dr. Barton persisted in recommending a certain Australian physician.

"I hope you're one of the fortunate ones whose remission goes on and on until all signs of cancer fade away. Take my advice or not. That's your privilege. I am for sure not on a platform to promote anyone or anything. But just in case I sound like that, the doctor's name is Arim Narub and as considerate and competent a doctor as you'd ever want to meet. Compassion is not why I am referring him to you, or vice versa, I am never sure. All of us do the best we can. I have every confidence in Dr. Narub, even though it means a long trip. I think it might help because I don't find much that's promising around here except very experimentally, and you might not be eligible anyway for even the best of them."

Dr. Barton sounded as if he'd had his say; but Simeon was naturally curious about why he made a personal call, referring him to a doctor half a world away. Maybe Narub had unusual talent, but an unusual doctor for an unusual patient?

"The old question, Dr. Barton. Why me? What makes me so special? Could I stand it?" Simeon's impression, gathered during previous trips to Australia, was that Sydney was a grand city, but medically somewhat of an urban backwater, not a great medical center. He had nothing to back this up and didn't really appreciate that Sydney with ample reason could claim first rank as a medical center. Like most other travelers, Simeon carried his share of unfounded prejudices wherever he went. He mentioned a few such misconceptions about Sydney and Australia to Dr. Barton, and both men laughed. Simeon knew better than to voice the ignorance of a naive tourist. Still, he questioned what a presumably able oncologist was doing in such a faraway place.

"Not so," Dr. Barton replied, "And my answers may not be good enough to match your prejudices. Dr. Narub is up to date on cancer research and treatment, and so are most of his colleagues. I've visited Sydney and found it just as advanced as we are here. Dr. Narub has special interests and qualifications, however, that I think might fit your situation. I know him fairly well. He also knows much more than the average oncologist does about so-called alternative treatments, which could conceivably be of some help. While quacks will still quack, not all alternative treatment is worthless, and many colleagues are taking another look."

"By alternative treatments, what do you mean?" Simeon knew this euphemistic term covered a wild and wide variety of herbal medicines as well as other unproven methods for treating every ailment of man and beast. He did not want Dr. Barton to hang up. "I hope you're not sending me to some witch doctor or snake oil salesman on the other side of the globe. I don't really think you would, but I'm sure that you don't send all your patients down under, more likely you refer them to doctors down the hall."

"I know Dr. Narub," Dr. Barton continued, "I consider him ahead of his time. That's all. Alternative treatment is just a catchall term for a variety of practices and herbal products which may or may not make any difference, none of which I confidently recommend. Untested empirical stuff, yes, usually, but not always. A lot of respectable and accepted medicine began that way. And a lot has also fallen by the wayside. No mumbo jumbo, you can be sure of that. Dr. Narub works at a big cancer center in Sydney, as far from the outback mentality as you could imagine. I picked you and not someone else because your cancer has some strange characteristics. I'll let you know something else. Some patients live for a very long time with widespread metastases like yours. You can't be a cancer carrier because there aren't any, and carriers are free of the disease they carry, which you're not. And you can't be terminal because you are so well! But you are still, I regret to say, what we doctors call "post-therapeutic," which means we don't have much more to offer, even chemotherapy. How you happen all of a sudden to feel hale and hearty is an occurrence neither one of us can take credit for, but it's still weird. There it is, biding time because we can't be sure how long this strange combination will last. Besides, you of all people are adventurous enough to try something not yet ready or available for other patients. You of all people seem to have an inclination that makes you open to challenges and open to ideas out of the mainstream. That you're presently feeling OK only makes me think that you could stand the trip. Your only alternative, as it stands now, is just lying on your bed, waiting for a miracle, which I imagine would be to stay as you are, indefinitely. But you might not."

Simeon was gradually becoming more receptive as he listened, especially pleased after hearing Barton say, "You of all people." He was adventurous, yes, that part might be true. Maybe Barton surmised more than just a bent for travel, taking risks, and leading a somewhat deviant style of life. Sharp as he is, Dr. Barton could know no more. What was that special inclination that made him open to challenges? Simeon hoped that Dr. Barton was only being tactful, but his idea of Simeon was that only a very bizarre and borderline person would travel so far to get some outlandish and unaccepted treatment, as a last resort.

"I could die there, Dr. Barton," Simeon said, as if this were the last obstacle. "It's far away."

"Far away? From what? You told me you have no family, no one around here or anyplace else, which is too bad. I don't know any other patient with your peculiar equilibrium of advanced disease and practically no complaints, and who is also free to go so far, with something to gain. Give me credit for that, no witch doctors. I don't know any. But make your own decision, and call me if you want more details about Narub. Good luck." Dr. Barton was ready to close the conversation and in a moment, did hang up.

Faraway places always appealed to Simeon. Cancer can be very deceptive, like now, when for some unknown or supernatural reason, he inexplicably felt better. Yes, cancer can wait, but at other times, can't seem to wait. What is cancer like in Australia? How different could it be? What more can this Narub do? Maybe there are alternatives to alternative treatment just like alternatives to regular treatment? What do I have to lose?

The arrangements were easy enough for an experienced traveler. He discharged Rita with a good tip and thanks, terminated the apartment and got ready to leave for an indefinite period. An appointment with Dr. Narub was arranged just as easily. Dr. Barton sent the medical information, and gave Simeon enough medication just in case symptoms recurred. They met once more, mainly to bid each other Farewell and Good Luck. Dr. Barton had a new and prestigious job, and Simeon was off to never-never land, perhaps to die.

The long trip was uneventful and tiresome. There were few people Simeon wanted to converse with or listen to. Mostly he droned away the hours, musing about what might happen and the nothingness he left behind. After all, it might not be a bad place to die, if it came to that. He whiled away more time, imagining new adventures not related to cancer.

The Cancer Center in Sydney was readily located, with a little help from a taxi driver. It was something that the natives were justifiably proud of. Many foreigners visited the clinic there, prepared for many consultations and a big bill. The official entrance was in a recently completed and very tall imposing building that wealthy donors helped pay for. The main building had numerous floors, like a modern hotel, and the principal corridor, which seemed to go on and on, was lined with paintings by former patients and local artists. There was a huge semicircular information desk, staffed by dignified and helpful older men and women, and at either end, along the wall, plenty of soft seats for visitors who were still waiting.

In its entirety as seen only from the air by a friendly helicopter, the Center was a widely spread out, carefully designed assortment of old and new structures, showing that it was a venerable institution but also very modern. The older buildings, erected in the early years of the last century, seemed to represent solid tradition and past achievements, while those more recent glass and concrete monuments paid subtle but large scale tribute to affluent philanthropists and contemporary science.

Dr. Narub's office was tucked away on a higher floor of an older building, a little far from the grand principal building. There was surely grandeur here without beauty, perhaps intelligence, too, but without compassion. Simeon was fearful.

As he sat waiting patiently for Dr. Narub who shared a suite of offices with a common waiting room, Simeon watched the staff bustling about while doing its everyday chores. White coats were everywhere, and there was much to suggest that here was a thriving repository of current information about cancer. Nothing, no signs whatsoever pointed to a laboratory for alternative treatments. If miracles customarily happen in a sacred grove frequented by gods, this was not the place. Here however was a secular shrine dedicated to science, generous philanthropy, advancement of careers, medical teaching, and treatment of patients, perhaps in that order.

Dr. Narub turned out to be a pleasant, middle-aged swarthy man, wearing the regulation white coat, but clearly standing out from the others. His smooth and slightly bronze complexion seemed to be typical of what was probably an Indian heritage. Simeon immediately felt comfortable in his presence, however, because Dr. Narub came out of his office to greet him personally rather than first being formally ushered into his sanctum, there to wait further for the doctor's delayed appearance. By his name alone, Simeon would have known that Dr. Narub was not an Australian. His accent was decidedly that of a well-bred upper class Englishman, and at the same time, his mannerly somewhat austere appearance would have discouraged anyone curious enough to probe his origins. Many ethnic streams must have found themselves coursing through him. He was not instantly identifiable, with regular features, a beardless face, and a full head of graying hair, carefully combed. Taller than average, he might have been an athlete at one time instead of a doctor. It turned out that he was both.

He held out his hand to Simeon in welcome, as if he were a friend, not just another patient desperate and eager for a better treatment. His gaze was direct, and his cordial manner conveyed sincerity, without being patronizing. Simeon had to wonder why was he so very friendly to a mere patient from overseas and decided that it was Dr. Barton's referral that made a difference. Simeon was not about to ask for answers to such irrelevant questions. Dr. Narub just seemed like a very nice man, although slightly out of his element.

After Simeon was comfortably seated across the desk, Dr. Narub at first said nothing, but gazed politely and directly at his new patient. It was not by any means a suspicious and challenging stare. He had yielded to Simeon, as if to say that the time was his. Simeon's medical record was lying open on the desk and had been read before Simeon arrived, perhaps several times. Then, in a quiet modulated voice, avoiding both professional jargon and the lofty appearance of clinical wisdom beyond ordinary people, Dr. Narub briefly encapsulated Simeon's cancer history. The surprising split between the grievous extent of cancer and the apparent good health of the patient sitting before him was of course a matter of initial comment, but it was not why Simeon had been sent so far. Simeon had to assume that Dr. Narub knew much more than he let on. Nevertheless, Narub's comments were rather gentle under the circumstances, once he interrupted his initial silence. Gravely nodding and smiling as he spoke and questioned, Narub's style reminded Simeon of a reflective swami or rabbi, not necessarily a clinician, but highly learned and qualified, yet someone not in the academic loop. He had the aura of an alien, regardless of years in Australia. Quite aside from his reputed familiarity with both conventional and alternative treatment, "out of the mainstream," Dr. Narub was himself also the establishment's alternative doctor, and out of the mainstream, if only because he was not Caucasian. Simeon surmised that regardless of his credentials and achievements, Dr. Narub would always be the competent and congenial outsider, never admitted to the inner circle of those who ran the place. Dr. Pochapin also seemed that way, in contrast to Dr. Barton. Still, it was Dr. Barton who sent Simeon so far. Simeon's preoccupation with lineage and exclusion instead of his illness was only typical of lifelong questioning about who he was and where he belonged. He was quick to identify others sharing his predicament.

"What has it been like for you?" Dr. Narub asked, "Tell me how your morale has held up, principally." He implied that cancer was less a disease than a trial by ordeal. Being a captive of cancer was a credential that few untouched people could understand. "Almost everyone is frightened, then it gets less difficult, but never goes away. Doctors try to be reassuring but mainly for their own sake. What makes it hard to deal with is that the disease, cancer, always must be understood against its broader effect on life and outlook. No one can be casually confident about cancer; everyone is awed by it, or should be. If they are not awed by Cancer, the patient ought to see someone else who will understand how a person's life must change." Dr. Narub went on for a moment or two in this philosophical style of speech, trying to set the framework for understanding Simeon's cancerous situation. He was not behaving like a conventional physician, nor even an oncologist, but more like a humanist trying to establish the life of a cancer patient.

"My morale has been bad. I suppose by morale you mean my ability to tolerate sickness, or rather, the problem of not being so sick, but still needing treatment," Simeon said, "I hit bottom just before this surprising remission overtook me. It happened almost overnight. Now I'm afraid I'll relapse again. My morale needs more morale. It seems to be better now; otherwise I wouldn't be here, looking for something to make the good times last awhile longer. That's how I feel. Subject to change without notice, as they say. For better or worse, I've had few symptoms. The chemo had some strange effects. I have a reprieve, not a remission. For whatever reason, cancer gave me a holiday. Which I'm enjoying."

"It's the difference between Cancer the victimizer and Cancer, the perpetrator of more than sickness," Dr. Narub supplied, joining in, and sounding matter of fact, not oracular, now with an apparent grasp of Simeon the victim. "Like patients, every cancer has a personality of its own, but the larger problem is putting your illness to work for you, keeping up morale, not merely a bold front. You have to be more than your disease."

Narub did not explain what putting cancer to work might mean or being more than his disease. Evidently he expected Simeon to understand. Simeon began to wonder if Barton had sent him on a fool's errand. Narub's words were like inspirational self help chants that he'd read. Regardless of how Narub meant to sound, these encouraging words had an opposite effect, seeming to be nothing more than mere gibberish intended to buck up patients before they did in fact expire. Was this all Narub had to offer? Cancer wasn't going to be put to work. It was too busy eating him up inside to do a day's work. Cancer did not belong to the working class, and neither did Simeon, or Narub, for that matter. Was work supposed to be ennobling? A pitiful predicament, rather. Simeon felt outclassed in a struggle to quash Cancer. Simeon tried to put cancer in its place, wherever that was, but was only an unwilling victim, not someone in control of his nebulous future.

"I don't know what you mean by putting cancer to work," Simeon said, "It seems to me that it's already pretty busy at work. I'm feeling pretty good, and that's good enough for my morale. I'd like to plan a future, even if I know that it could end any time, right in the middle of planning. I'll tell you one thing, Dr. Narub, I have no confidence that anything will happen except one day, I'll get sick and then much sicker, going along with some kind of treatment that won't do me any good whatsoever." Simeon was not complaining and didn't mean to sound petulant, only cynical. He was just trying to be utterly clean and clear that he would not put up with bullshit, however enticing the aroma.

"You are correct that cancer is very busy, already working. What I mean is that you must, if you can, strive for something other than a miracle. Being at your wit's end, after following mainstream medicine, putting cancer to work means that you resolve it shall not devour you, that you will also make choices about your own treatment and your life, and act upon these choices, despite cancer. This, for sure, does not mean ignoring medical advice or submitting passively to whatever I recommend. There are options, always, maybe not good options, but still options. No one but a malicious quack with his private quirks could promise you a miracle or a cure." He spoke of "resolve" as if it were a strategy in a class by itself. Perhaps "resolve" meant nothing more than stubborn determination. "I cannot predict your future, nor my own. How long would anyone like to live, and what would you do with the time at your disposal, had you a choice? Cancer makes us face up to such questions, as I hope you already discovered. But if you've discovered anything, it's that these are not abstract philosophical nothings, but practical problems of what you choose to do and may be able to do."

Did Dr. Narub guess that he was talking to an expert dilettante who'd already pissed away his talents on chasing the forbidden for most of his life? Or that even before cancer set in, Simeon could easily resolve to pay no attention to anything serious, that he'd worked hard at doing nothing, encounters with nothing that had lasting value? His career had thus far consisted of diversions. Simeon had scarcely noticed in recent weeks that his cancer had already turned into Cancer.

"You're telling me to live as long and as well as possible before I die. Just live as long as possible without being an invalid or a vegetable, just put cancer to work," Simeon said, sardonically, "Here I am, in your hands, having come from half the world away, and the first thing you tell me is that I might die here, or that I might not. I knew that back in the United States." However, Simeon guessed that under the platitudes, Narub already had a plan in mind that would soon materialize into an option. That might be why Dr. Barton had been so quietly insistent.

"If you expect me to tell you something exact and tangible, be it known that I don't deal in promises, mine or yours. I don't know what Cancer has in mind for us." Dr. Narub had personified Cancer, not merely disease that the medical profession deals with. He personified the embedded experiences from everything he knew, but also seemed to turn Cancer into a person to be dealt with. Cancer or cancer, either has to be reframed, restrained, or diverted into something less formidable. The way Narub spoke, cancer was unpredictable and menacing, both as disease and a way of life. He intimated, without being told about it, that Cancer was the ghostly presence that was manifested to Simeon once in the twilight back home. Cancer and cancer were much more than a spooky shadow, but another world altogether, imposing itself alongside and into what passes for normality.

"You don't know why Dr. Barton selected you of all people to come here?" Narub said. Simeon had nothing to lose by being frank about his misgivings.

"I do, only up to a point. I'm rich and healthy enough to travel, strong enough, yet sick enough, no attachments or responsibilities, and without any regular treatment left to try. So I'm almost ready for anything. Barton's gone to greener pastures anyway, and can't do much for me. I like to explore things, not to a great extent, but just because it's new and challenging. If I'd made more of myself than I have so far, I'd still be a failure with disappointed ambitions. As it is, Sir, I have regrets but no disappointments. I don't play safe. I really had no choice, after Dr. Barton spoke to me. I was a good subject, willing, but now *you* tell me why I'm here!"

"There are always choices to go this way or that, even for you," Dr. Narub stated, "I do have some choices for you that we'll talk about. I do my own tests and find out what's inside. Yes, every cancer specialist has to do tests. It pays not to rely too much on other evaluations, other findings, or on other specialists. In your case, I'd be very surprised, however, if you did not have extensive cancer, as Dr. Barton reported."

After hearing this, Simeon left, wondering what to do with the rest of the day. However, when he returned to the hotel, Dr. Narub's secretary had already called. He had not stopped to talk with her before he left. Could Mr. Benett check into the hospital for a couple of days, say, tomorrow?

Simeon was surprised. Standard procedure must be different here than in the USA where hospital admission just for tests went out of favor years ago. Still curious about why, except for the doctor's convenience, the following day he checked in for evaluation. On his first day, one test followed another, some new and unfamiliar; most seemed standard. On the second day, however, early in the evening, long after the day's routines were over, Dr. Narub finally came to his room, holding Simeon's hospital chart.

"No more tests for now," he said, "There is certainly a lot of cancer inside, far more than I'd guess from your state of well being. Dr. Barton was absolutely correct. You are a paradox. You are like two different people, inside and out. Most patients feel sicker than their tests show. It's the other way round with you. I see that the chaplain dropped by earlier today."

"Oh, yes," Simeon answered, "That was the chaplain. I enjoyed her visit, but I didn't see what her chat had to do with cancer. We certainly didn't talk religion or how it feels to be sick. I'm grateful for that. She's a very attractive young woman, went to school in California. She seemed to be a lot more comfortable talking about the USA than about my missing testicle. We talked about nothing very spiritual, no more than with the others who dropped by, or took care of drawing blood or moving me around for x-rays. I wanted to show her the other testicle, but she scampered off. I told her to visit me any time, even tonight." Simeon laughed, almost bitterly, with his rueful joke. If she had come back, they could only talk. Dr. Narub was not amused. In talking about the chaplain, nevertheless, Simeon had told him what he wanted to know.

"You like to tease women. They must be a challenge to you," Narub said, "You have the night nurse fantasy," referring to the familiar wish of certain male patients that the night nurse would sneak in and have her way.

"A challenge only to get them into bed," Simeon said, "I never had a real love affair, not even close, but enough women." He knew he was lying, but did not want to talk about Sophia or even Hermione, certainly not Maggie. "I've known a few women better than others. But that is past. I'm pretty neutral, but not yet neutered. Might as well be." Narub must have more important things to talk about than Simeon's erstwhile sex life.

"I know you are a loner, no family, only the casual sex you seem to miss. But I really don't know that much more about you. These tests don't tell me, Simeon." It was the first time Narub called him by his first name. "You are pretty cagey; I don't know why but from what I imagine, there is much more. Otherwise, you wouldn't be here." Simeon was getting annoyed at this bothersome banter, too close to be comfortable.

"Are you just as curious about your other cancer patients?" he said, sarcastically, knowing that Dr. Narub didn't deserve a slight. "I don't mean to be rude, but I've always put a lot of space between me and everyone else. Except with women and they've mainly served a function. A few men might have served the same purpose, but I wouldn't let it. Now, I can't get away from cancer. I can't put enough space between cancer and me. There's too much inside, almost taking me over completely. Why this fooling around between cancer and me? I'm uncomfortable talking about Cancer, and something else I'm not sure about. If you were a shrink, I could understand probing questions that get nowhere. That's what shrinks do for a living." As he mouthed the words, Simeon simultaneously realized that Dr. Narub had not asked probing questions, but had merely shown a very human interest. Still, he felt probed and pushed towards something yet unknown. And he dreaded coming face to face with what fascinated him. It was like lusting for something that appalled him. He was angry and mistrustful of Dr. Narub's interest, believing it was a devious tactic intended to manipulate him into trying something exotic and distasteful.

"Some patients appreciate being talked as a person who just happens to have cancer, but others don't like it when I do ask personal questions. Some resent the implication that their life experiences have anything to do with how they'll manage to cope. It's hard to have it both ways, keeping a certain amount of privacy and wanting to be taken seriously as an individual. We are accused of being nosy shrinks, or worse. If I wanted to be a voyeur I'd peek in windows. You surely haven't lived in a vacuum. No one does. It was the kind of person you are that brought you here in the first place, not knowing what you'll be getting into but wanting to find out. Who you are and what you are, things that attract and repel you, whether you realize it or not, will decide your future."

Dr. Narub sounded much firmer, not so fuzzy, and more in control than when they'd first met, as if he were now sure that Simeon was the right person. Simeon therefore silenced himself.

"You may not put cancer to work, but Cancer will send you to places and make you behave in unimaginable ways, beyond anything that even you could dream of. Cancer will stick close, although it may not be the firmest friend you ever had. But it won't be your enemy."

"What cryptic bullshit is this?" Simeon asked himself, while waiting for a specific light to turn on, "What am I being set up for? This guy goes both ways at once!"

"Cancer will go with you everywhere, whether you want it or not, but it's always there," Narub continued. "Cancer is evil. It feasts on people, with no apparent rhyme or reason. I hate cancer because it eats you up inside, and ruins what you are. It keeps gnawing until you're an empty shell. Cancer is eroding you at this very moment, Simeon. It's there. I'm not yet sure where it will take you. It can turn a sensible doctor into a pretentious or arrogant fool. So doctors try anything, cut it, burn it, poison it, with doubtful results. It's too crafty and evil, like a demon set loose, determined to get its tribute, somehow. If it decides not to kill, then it either harasses you or lets you alone".

Simeon saw that Narub was talking faster, denouncing cancer, as if it was a supernatural enemy, almost, set loose to deny mankind its humanity. Is Cancer like Ronnie, say, a seductive companion conspiring all along to do evil? No, cancer may have another purpose. That purpose is to show good and evil dancing together without missing a beat, on the way to death. What kind of craziness is cancer making me think? Surely all this crap is getting to me. Can my wish to make sense make sense out of such ponderous drivel? Wrestling with the demon, CA? Maybe. But dancing? A dance to a dirge. Change partners. I'll sit this one out. Simeon was grimly and stubbornly silent, as he listened to Narub who had deliberately set in motion a future that up until now, Simeon knew nothing about.

Quiet in its fashion, with an occasional cry from a faraway patient in distress, or the commonplace clatter of mishandled dishes, night had taken over the hospital. Simeon slipped into sleep sometime, but when he awakened again, well before dawn, he was not sure whether Narub had been there at all. His words lingered, more as ill-formed ideas than remembered phrases. Were there birds outside his window, singing at this time of night? What had Narub said, or implied? He was surely getting at something unusual and threatening.

Chapter 6—High in the Highlands

Two days later, Simeon sat once again in Dr. Narub's office, not sure whether a conversation had taken place, and forgetful of what they supposedly talked about. But it was no more incredible than finding himself invaded by cancer and yet all the while experiencing good health and anticipation of a future. He had been spared the death that seemed so certain a short time ago, while knowing that the disease could reverse once again, leaving Simeon on the brink.

He was given a second chance, incredible as it seemed. Could curing cancer somehow be a real miracle, a violation of natural law, like a sunrise at midnight? So far, he'd apparently thwarted death. But cancer, like some hibernating beast, could rouse and be hungry again, eager to devour another victim. Simeon settled for a reprieve, not denying that he was still gripped by a powerful adversary. A cat toying with a mouse tantalizes the poor animal with false freedom and release, only to catch it again, until through frustration, fatigue, and uncertainty, the mouse finally dies without actually being killed. Simeon could foresee just such a fate for himself.

Facing Simeon across the desk, Dr. Narub seemed to be his customary self, pleasant, articulate, and serious. Tentatively, Simeon knew that what was about to happen would be a continuation of their conversation, if that's what really happened. This time, he hoped, specific plans for his dubious future must surely be talked about. Lack of clarity was indeed too cruel for one in such need, yet with energy enough for almost anything. There is no more bitter fate than to be kept in limbo, dangling interminably between imminent death and hope for cure.

"I don't have an explanation for such a paradox," Narub conceded, as if taking up, without interruption, the conversation held in the hospital, "Nevertheless, when cancer has a foothold, it seldom gives up, although it allows you a little leeway, that is, until that time when…enough is enough. But that time, short or long, is to our advantage. We can use as much of your good health as possible." Narub was clinical in his manner, nonchalant, perhaps, but not at all indifferent. He seemed to care a great deal. Still, Simeon was dissatisfied.

"I can't deny that I'm loaded with cancer that's biding its time and I might get really sick anytime. What can you tell me about that?" Simeon said, "I feel like an insect preserved in amber and fixed in time, already dead but looking very well, indeed. I want to enjoy this delusion as long as I can. I don't want to push you to say how long I have, even if you could, before it starts all over. Let me ask you another question: Will I ever die of cancer?

I'm full speed ahead, but on a stranded ship, ready for a voyage but nowhere to go. When and where?"

Simeon took a long look at Narub's books, as if chiding them for not having a specific answer. For Narub, Simeon's journey to this moment had been providential. He needed Simeon, just as much as Simeon needed him, perhaps more. He needed someone with fully developed, indisputably widespread cancer, who was willing and healthy enough, desperate enough, yes, even rich enough, to face a challenge. This man, Simeon, seemed to fit such requirements. Advanced cancer and apparent good health, like upside down hypochondriasis, went well with a bleak optimism, just to keep him going, searching for cure that might not be there.

"We, I mean both of us, have a dilemma," Narub said, "There are parts of the world, you may already know, where cancer is unheard of, or so trivial that it is almost completely controllable. It is trivial or unheard of because people living there are not as enlightened about such things as we are."

Narub now began to be more circumspect. "To say cancer is unheard of means several things. There are various possibilities. It might exist but under another name. It really might not exist at all. Or it exists but amounts to nothing. Or it can be fatal at times, but methods exist to transform the disease into a curable complaint, never too late. These people are not immune to illness because they do get sick, recover or die. Other illnesses might immunize them to cancer, if they're not already immune. They may, however, have an antidote, a treatment that cures cancer at any stage, even the stage you're in, and more terminal than you." Narub seemed to be enjoying this didactic dance. Before he knew what proposal was about to be revealed, Simeon was getting scared of what Narub had in mind.

"What?" Simeon exclaimed, "An antidote for cancer? Sounds magical, like some bullshit testimonial from Mexico. Something that tames the beast, makes it into a pussycat, even destroys it? A cure that doesn't exist, except somewhere, not here? Why doesn't our world find out and do something about it, find out if it's on the level? It's hocus pocus. "Our world" sounded like the straight world. It reminded him of a time when Aunt Gina spoke about a world in which bisexuality would be the norm, and nothing was forbidden.

"Our world, the scientific world? I am not sure," Dr. Narub responded, "Our world has plenty of money; fat grants are out there. But our world doesn't have the resolve to follow such an exotic, improbable, unexplored lead."

Narub hesitated about tangentially damning the entire medical establishment, but added little to explain why somewhere else, far away, methods exist to stem cancer. He was carefully leading up to an even stranger proposal.

"Here and there, a few curious enough scientists are looking for jungle plants that have an effect on cancer, and they've discovered a few that relieve certain types of cancer, like ovary, pancreas, and lung, all still being studied. They hold back from the one I'm referring to. If they are aware of it or not, I can't say. If there were a promising cure for any disease common enough to matter commercially, drug companies would immediately open their fat wallets. That would certainly include cancer. There has to be the right time, place, and messenger. Otherwise, we're left with merely colorful anecdotes told by natives to gullible tourists. Reports are filed away, when the visitors happen to be scientists themselves. That's why such tales are wild enough to be under lock and key. They're too far fetched, too lurid and incredible for most people, including investigators."

"Well, not being a scientist, I have nothing against anecdotes, rumors, or wild stories that tell me what I want to hear. You see, I like to keep a balanced viewpoint," Simeon said sarcastically, not that a balanced viewpoint was typical of him. His optimism swelling, Simeon was becoming eager to hear a full account of what Narub still only hinted at. Just as he now knew that Barton and Narub selected him for the trip, Simon was equally certain that Narub knew exactly the place he was sending him to. Whether he was to be a pioneer trailblazer or an experimental dupe would never be settled. He was probably destined to be both.

"Keep me not in suspense, mighty one," Simeon joshed, not very convincingly, as if Narub would never be forthright. Narub straightened around in his chair, looking firmly at Simeon's face, as if trying to anticipate what was in this wastrel's mind. Would he be able to stand the rigors, suspense and pursuit of a bizarre remedy for cancer, one that also required endurance and faith?

"What if I told you that there are tribes living in remote parts of the world who don't realize that they have a means of controlling cancer?" Narub said, momentarily forgetting that he had asked substantially the same question a short time before. "They devoutly believe and practice sorcery. In fact, it permeates their existence. Magic is an everyday affair. For them, disease is an evil spell cast by an enemy." Simeon was already looking skeptical. Was this Narub's proposition and all that his secrecy amounted to? Magic and mumbo jumbo. Narub, sensing Simeon's imminent refusal, stopped, defensively, then began to explain himself.

"Remember how long it took for the bacterial theory of disease to be accepted. Before that, and still do, we practiced a goodly amount of magic. Only a fraction of what we do every day is scientific. Magic and sorcery, after all, are just a special unfamiliar attitude towards nature and the control of unforeseen events."

"If you truly know about such a place, don't fiddle around," Simeon said, forcefully, "I suppose you must equivocate and put a decent face on something, or you wouldn't be getting my hopes up. Tell me and I'll buy a ticket today! Sorcery doesn't scare me. I already feel that I'm under a spell. Put me under another. Kill or cure; but get it over with." It would not be extreme to call Simeon both dubious and ready to believe in the incredible.

"I understand your eagerness, and you're ready to go off somewhere, anywhere, without hearing more about the risks. I said magic and sorcery not to put you off, but to remind you that much of whatever goes on any place is far from scientific. And that certainly applies to far away, primitive medicine. It may be all fakery and superstition, but there is more to it than we're ready to accept. This is not a sure thing, only suppositions. But danger is a fact."

Narub had by now switched from being a committed advocate to a conservative, cautious physician.

"Naturally, I have a reason for telling you as much as I have. You've already guessed that. I'm considered something of an expert on so-called alternative treatments of cancer. It is not modesty, however, that keeps me from calling myself an authority. Actually, my information is quite rudimentary. I have very sketchy knowledge about the inner workings of primitive tribes and strange places, considering how different all of them are. Calling other tribes primitive and foreign places strange is a provincial viewpoint, one that even I suffer from. I am definitely not comfortable with aboriginal tribes or even the cults nearby. There are false remedies wherever there is suffering and ignorance. Every doctor worthy of trust is afraid of quackery." He paused; again Simeon glowered, incredulous and impatient with Narub's wavering, saying one thing, and then taking it back.

With full resolve, Narub then took a deep breath, transfixing Simeon with his gaze, and said, "All right, here it is, straight out. ***There is a cancer cure, and it is cannibalism!***" He let the pronouncement sink in. "There are tribes, far away, isolated even from other remote tribes, that regularly eat human flesh. And if they do get something that looks like cancer, and I know that they do, it is quickly eradicated by eating a soup-like preparation. Let's just call it a stew. Along with other things they use in cooking, the main ingredient is human flesh, mostly from enemies killed in war or executed prisoners. I told you about sorcery. Well, their belief is that eating the sacred stew breaks the spell, and the sick person recovers."

Simeon had been both enthusiastic and skeptical. Now he was astonished, shocked and thrilled, although he expected something no less extreme from the tentative tenor of Narub's comments up to this point. This, surely, was nothing so mild as a rare jungle plant or a bitter tea with potent properties. It was not teatime for aborigines. Simeon tried to visualize killing human beings and eating their flesh, whether in a soup or raw, with blood dripping down from corners of his mouth, as he chewed. Aunt Gina certainly never conceived of this taboo. If she had, she never mentioned it. Cannibalism was a crime, no doubt about that. Only perverts take part in such offensive business. He always avoided crime, of course, but in this tribe, evidently, cannibalism is not only practiced, but also hallowed, and cures cancer. What a therapeutic oasis that must be!

He had met insurmountable and repulsive taboos before, and often wondered what drinking blood would be like, instead of getting a blood transfusion. The thought of drinking menstrual blood, for example, was nauseating. He had once tried it just to shock the woman he was with at the time. But this idea, regular cannibalism, was more than shocking. Simeon lumped cannibals together with grave robbers, and for the same reason. Cannibalism would be beyond his tolerance and not liberating at all, only something grotesque. Even Simeon had his limits.

Nevertheless, despite his misgivings, Simeon was amazed to find himself now anticipating cannibalism as an acceptable, hallowed, sanctioned, and therapeutic form of alternative medicine. He was stirred and intrigued, with a new appetite for such an extreme taboo that would release him from a sorcerer's spell, and not merely from a serious disease. Then he'd be done, having accomplished the utmost, and thus would no longer be under an obligation to find the forbidden and challenge it. Simeon resolved to be candid with Narub who had probably already guessed that cannibalism was not such an appalling idea to his skeptical patient after all.

"Dr. Narub, I am not put off by cannibalism. I've never tried it, but always found something irresistible about violating any taboo. I am not a lawbreaker by the way, and the authorities are not looking for me. The taboo has never kept me from doing what I've wanted to do. Indeed, it has stimulated me. How do I become a cannibal?" For a brief moment Simeon was a little facetious, as if about to embark on a diverting excursion into a strange land that was just a little more exotic than tourists imagined. Simeon was almost giddy, and surely he sounded silly. Eating human flesh, especially of people recently killed, is pretty intimate and grim, not like buying a tasty tidbit labeled, For Human Consumption, wrapped in cellophane. It was a face-to-face confrontation with bloody death, of which he was still afraid. Simeon shuddered, expecting some kind of reproach and revenge from the ghosts who visit those who had eaten them.

"I'm glad you're so…open-minded," Narub answered, amused by his understatement. "But I don't want you to rush off, just for the thrill of it. There is no thrill, just an outside chance of benefit. Not many white men know these people, and the cannibals might take a fancy to killing you. This, I doubt, since sick white men are generally shunned. Don't for one moment deceive yourself. It is not a journey to a jungle cancer center run by little black people with bones in their noses, instead of stethoscopes around their necks. It can be risky, brutal, and disappointing, and don't confuse it with a safari just off the beaten path."

"How come you know so much about it, in spite of not being sure how and whether they cure cancer? After all, you're a cancer expert, and not a tourist." Simeon hoped for a straightforward answer from this pleasant but cautious doctor. After a visible effort, Narub became forthright.

"I told you about my interest in alternative methods for treating cancer. A long time ago, I checked out the story. Leaving the medical issues aside, I finally went to see for myself just this side of…never mind land. Never mind that it is very distant from here, hard to reach, and very risky. Hardly explored at all, just blank spaces on a drawing, surely not a map, but a body of guesses. Getting there is hard, and it will be for you, especially since you're a white man raised in our Western world. Not like me. You'll need a lot more than enthusiasm, first of all reliable guides who know the dialects, territory and the people. You need someone who is experienced, acceptable, knows the area as well as the tribe, and sponsors you. I had all that in my own visit, although I didn't stay there for long or sample the sacred stew. I didn't need it, and wasn't offered any. You will stay there, if permitted, and sooner or later, eat the stew, whatever it consists of. You can be sure it has human meat in it, besides lots of other things, probably unmentionable. The tribe can be unpredictable, hostile and brutal at times, without remorse, and does not hesitate to show it. At other times, they can be friendly, but on their terms. You'll still have to be very careful and don't break their taboos. I hope for your sake that they're friendly enough. Before you decide that this trip is for you, I want to say something else, emphatically. Under the best, most favorable circumstances, it will still be hard adjusting to the ways of a primitive tribe that mistrusts you, and if you're lucky will mostly ignore you. If you're very lucky, you'll get what you've gone for."

In spite of Narub's caution and caveats, Simeon almost trembled with anticipation. Had Narub consented, at that moment Simeon would dash out, lacking preparation, and launch himself in any direction that promised cannibalism. That would not only be foolish, it could prove fatal.

"I am telling you all this, certainly not to guarantee a cure," Narub said, "You might not get that far. Many things could interfere. Your expectations of cure might never come true. Consider this only a vision, at least for now. Cancer may be cured some day. Meanwhile it doesn't have to come from some exotic place that only a few explorers have heard about. Somewhere right now, in your country or mine, a young boy or girl, is going to grade school, never realizing that within a few decades, they will grow up to contribute their share to understanding cancer and all its processes. On the other hand, they may get cancer; probably someone close to them will. All I can tell you is that I did see cases that looked like cancer. Not instantaneously, of course, but within a short time, days or weeks, after eating and drinking that concoction, they were visibly improved and in comparative good health. I was more than impressed. I was amazed beyond credibility, even though as a scientist I knew it might only be an isolated case or two." Narub became more animated as he recalled his enthusiasm. He went as a believer wanting to see people in the throes of advanced disease, as he knew it, and found them. After eating the sacred stew, more than a handful of people showing signs of clinical cancer had recovered enough for Dr. Narub to see improvement, even restoration to good health.

"It was not snake oil. I was aware of first wanting to find and then finding what I did. None of these people, including the shamans, were out to make money. The idea of money, incidentally, is practically unknown. Of course, like any practitioner, shamans, call them medicine men, if you like, expect a reward for their services, even an enhanced reputation as a great healer, a great something or other. That ambition is not limited to their world or ours. Reputation may even help bring on the cure. No controls, of course, and the cures I was told about don't always happen so quickly, if at all. But when it does, there can be no doubt that something beyond our state of knowledge has occurred. The spell is lifted, open lesions heal, lumps do disappear, big bellies shrink, symptoms go away, and the erstwhile patient pretty soon is OK again. In the best cases, that is. But, I must say, the language barrier kept me from asking detailed and exact questions. Even if I could, the shamans are not apt to answer or report what Western doctors want to ask about. They are good observers for some things, not prepared for other questions."

Narub's eyewitness account testified to a valiant struggle with professional objectivity. Simeon was still incredulous, much as a skeptic at Lourdes might be flabbergasted if a sick pilgrim abruptly turned hale and walked away cured. Provisional recovery and gradual improvement are not the stuff of miracles, nor do they indicate positive absolution from a sorcerer's curse. Something spectacular and instantaneous is necessary to demonstrate the magician's touch and persuade his audience.

"You actually saw very sick people, looking like cancer, get well?" Simeon wanted to hear it again.

"Don't imply I merely took some resemblance to be cancer. After all, I am a doctor and a cancer clinician. Please remember that I am an oncologist. The treatment, call it that, doesn't work with everyone. I don't know why, but something worked for some patients, whatever it was. I was only there a short time, a matter of weeks, maybe a month, not longer, as recovery goes, not enough for even a crude investigation on my own. I saw what I saw, that's all. I made notes, and when I came back, looked into whether this had ever been reported before. I admit that in looking back, I could have fooled myself by expectation, just as you might be carried away, against your better judgment, because of strongly wanting it to work. Personally, I doubt that my wishful expectations work so dramatically. I couldn't write it up for a medical journal. That would be preposterous. Even a letter to the editor would be returned faster than it was sent. How do you study a sorcerer's spell?" With that, Narub reached up to a shelf, pulled down a thick loose-leaf notebook, and opened it up. The many pages looked as if they hadn't seen daylight for a long time.

"This is my journal," he said, "All my notes, unpolished and unpublished. No one has seen it, besides me. Take it and read it before you decide." Simeon knew that, besides his own reasons for going, he'd be there to fill in gaps in what Narub had not been able to see, or do. When he asked, Narub called it being a 'participant observer.' Simeon was, after all, a patient, sick or not, and not a physician.

That night, Simeon settled down to read Narub's journal. The notes were both typed and handwritten in the sketchy, almost illegible style doctors are famous for. Some paragraphs were scratched out. Many pages consisted of speculations, hazy and irrelevant. On the whole, however, not being a practiced writer, but merely someone making extended but educated observations, it was understandable as no more than an arresting personal document. Conspicuously missing were notes about how he found out about the tribe, where he happened to find an experienced guide to lead him, and who allowed him to stay and observe as long as he did. Although eager and fascinated, Simeon could only browse through the pages of an enormous manuscript.

The huge notebook began with a disclaimer designed to protect Narub from what he fervently wanted to declare, which was belief in the events he witnessed and heard about. Even though few people, if any, had or would read his journal, Narub was very cautious, lest it fall into unsympathetic hands. Nevertheless, his account could be condensed without doing an injustice, somewhat as follows:

If anyone happens across this report, my name is Arim Narub, a physician specializing in cancer. I set out in this trip to escape from the conservative parochialism of my colleagues, whom I respect in almost every other way. I happen to believe in other means of controlling cancer than what is currently practiced. In less sophisticated and more aboriginal parts of the world, I have read that certain tribes may use substances and practices that successfully deal with devastating diseases like cancer, still baffling conventional doctors. Narub was not afraid of sentences so long that they fall off the page, Simeon noticed.

Therefore, I chose to make a trip to the hinterlands of Papua New Guinea, a place I'd heard about as being filled with stories of remote tribes and strange practices. It was cheaper to visit Papua New Guinea, and just as promising for my purposes, than going to Africa, which I knew little about, or to Siberia, or the subcontinent jungles of Brazil. Although Papua New Guinea is not far from Australia, it is not next door, and preparations had to be made.

From my reading and talking to expatriates from time to time, New Guinea seemed to be a repository for primitive beliefs and practices. Narub did not say who these informants were, whether anthropologists, physicians, or government officials. Despite modern inroads, some tribes are so hidden away that life there is led according to long traditions, myths, legends, and sorcery. Evil spells, intertribal warfare, revenge, and other motives cause sickness, I was informed, although I later found that those professing intimate knowledge were almost as ignorant as I. Many had lived in the interior, along the rivers and in villages, but never went to the Highlands, except the foothills. Few explorers venture up into those jungles. These expatriate white men, even the citified natives, speak pidgin, but not many know native dialects, of which there are many. I speak a very clumsy pidgin. I went almost on my own, but stuck pretty close to the villages and hamlets, before getting to know a reliable guide and finding the best place to investigate.

I hope my words are coherent, which seems odd, since I intend to keep all that I've written very private. I do harbor a wish to publish, gain prominence, inspire others to repeat my trip, substantiate what I found, and discover even more, while still giving me credit. I'd like a promotion, but I don't think this is the way to get it. I want to decipher what is a deep mystery, and to share a mood that came over me as I traveled. I am frank that I saw what I wanted to see; and I was scarcely surprised, only astonished when my sanguine expectations took form. I cannot claim to be an anthropologist but my medical experience might make up for what I lacked otherwise. Simeon noticed the false modesty and fear of criticism, along with a very strong wish to be secretly famous and celebrated for his pioneer accomplishments. But Simeon pushed on through the journal, enduring even Narub's awkward literary efforts to depict the grandeur of the region.

High up in the Highlands of Papua New Guinea, there is uncharted territory, hundred of miles from better-known villages and towns. Here is the homeland of unstipulated tribes, speaking different languages and dialects, living apart and often at war with each other. The tribes may number no more than a few dozen members, while others, it is said, have numerous branches, with a hundred or so followers. They flourish and hunt, moving around like nomads, or settle down in collective hamlets and small villages to grow crops of yams. Stuff like that. They also hold strange (to me) beliefs, and practice rituals so old that only their legends suggest a beginning. They don't have calendars the way we do, but do measure time in their own way. There are no written records. Murder, thievery, kidnapping, all sorts of crimes, some not classified, take place, without a serious effort to stamp them out. Law enforcement as we know it is difficult when there are no laws or agencies to carry out arrest and punishment. Yet there are many tribal customs and regulations that are strictly obeyed. Visitors are generally not welcome, but every now and then, outsiders arrive, and are treated like curiosities or objects of fear and hatred, especially if they are white. My skin color might have spared me because I attracted no more than casual curiosity except as a stranger from elsewhere.

Sometimes, I was reminded, tourists come to places where they have no actual business except to stare and take pictures. Money buys a lot of things, including access, information, and assistance. Dread of the outsider prevents even more, regardless of money. The casual white visitor runs a risk because there are few visitors, anyhow. The boundary between Papua New Guinea and Irian Jaya, the other half of the island, is not well established, but a sharp political division, which I know little about, is taken very seriously. Indonesia is a hostile neighbor, and sometimes, mining companies venture too far. Raids and warfare can result. Violating the invisible, unmarked boundary is dangerous and invites capture and death on either side. Dense forests and jungle cover many miles over mountain ranges and deep valleys. Rivers and waterfalls without names are almost everywhere a person can see. Paths familiar only to the native hunters cut across the land, but even tribesmen are in danger at times, because of predatory animals and roving men from other tribes. Narub scribbled a long marginal note, as if to emphasize the wondrous but intimidating region. "I was awed beyond belief by this world. It was like a universe no one had ever seen before, although I knew different. There must be people who have never seen white men and therefore fear them. I, too, also fear the bias of white men, who really aren't so special, anyway. I fear their bigotry, but the natives fear them because they fear witchcraft and evil sorcery, which I have been spared. From my standpoint, there is good reason to fear because I am not quite a white man but not black." Narub could not put aside his bitterness about discrimination.

Narub interrupted his narration to speculate that if cannibalism were shown to have a beneficial effect on cancer, he can scarcely imagine its effect on the outside in the civilized world. Simeon paused in his reading to indulge in a little imagination of his own. As he thought about it, the more he was convinced that Barton and Narub had picked the right candidate.

Although officially banned, cannibalism is an ancient, sacred and honorable custom unlikely to be eradicated by a governmental decree. Inspection seldom occurs. The places and tribes that practice cannibalism are just too far and too devious to investigate.

For outsiders, cannibalism is a horrible deed, not only forbidden but criminal in every respect except, remotely, only under circumstances of starvation, and hardly then. It is surely a strong ban for us, but not for them. Narub wrote that he was never able to engage any tribesman in a discussion about cannibalism, especially its place in ceremonies and rituals. He knew, however, that while no one talked to him about eating human flesh, it was an acceptable, even honorable custom, especially after successful forays into enemy territory. Elders determine policy, and in many respects decide what is believed and practiced. They perpetuate tradition through oral history, glorified as well as factual.

Tradition has a license to revise itself and justify war. Elders stir up the cause, and young men act on it. Invading enemy territory has practical and historical reasons, too. Victors become heroes, live and dead, while live heroes become future elders. Cannibalism is therefore revered, and the first one privileged to eat a former enemy has a singular honor. It is surely not repulsive. Narub knew he repeated himself, with no editor to keep him straight, consistent, and clear. He was well aware, too, that the tribe had no obligation to tell him anything at all and that what they deign to say may be altogether fanciful.

Life is not easy, despite romantic notions of outsiders who picture some tropical paradise. Invasions and raids occur regularly, not always out of controversies that cannot be negotiated. The bounty is food, along with supplies and fertile young women to marry and replenish the population. There is little peace, as we know it, only an uneasy interval. Holy wars are hallowed, blessed by the spirits, and, as always, approved by the elders. Defeated men of the outside tribe are cannibalized, but if insufficient, women and children will do. The aged are not worth the bother, although some seniors are taboo, anyway. Death is avoided, of course, yet it is viewed as a necessity, but not exactly a fearsome thing. Seldom accidental, there is usually a firm reason for someone's demise, and, while regrettable, death is not followed by the kind of mourning Narub was familiar with. Only a person of high status was mourned openly and ceremoniously.

After a victory or successful foray, the heroes return carrying the fallen foe, or leading a line of prisoners. The dead bodies are soon carved up. The choice parts are the brain and heart, reserved for the leaders of a successful campaign. The remainder is then put into a large cauldron and added to what is already cooking. This is the sacred stew, actually too thick to be called a blessed broth but the religious or sacred element is never missing. Lesser members of the tribe will eat what remains of the former enemy but as a rule, there is also enough to replenish the stew. After a day or two, a feast of celebration is held for the tribe as a whole. Narub could not get his guide to explain further. Nor did he broach what happens if the tribe loses in warfare.

There are people who are allowed to drink the broth or eat the stew when they are very sick, but not everyone. Although Narub was principally interested in cannibalism as a cure for cancer, no one, of course, ever heard either word or an equivalent. A shaman is supposed to feed such people who are very sick and accursed, or at least someone in a high tribal position. In addition to ridding the victim of a spell, the stew heightens courage and character, which go together. Eating human flesh therefore makes for a better person, not merely a healthy person. Ceremonies surrounding the blessed cannibal stew also implore gods to intervene, offer protective immunity, and help in retaliating against future enemies who put curses on them.

The stew's aroma was apparently worth noting. It was very foul, in keeping with the belief that bitter medicine is the most effective in driving out something evil, and an evil odor, it was. Narub commented that if true, the sacred stew must be therefore strong enough to cure all maladies, as well as concentrated enough to drive a nail through a concrete wall. The gods must hold their holy noses before deciding to respond. However, as in other cultures, tastes vary, and if a medicine does its job, people will put up with it. Narub was not invited to taste the stuff, but joked that anyone swallowing the brew must be sick, indeed, or strongly yearn for a distinguished honor.

Narub's questions were seldom answered. A white man is suspect, a creature to be feared, a repository for potential curses, and probably is in league with other evildoers. Although Narub had his own complexion, why give him gratuitous information? In retrospect, he considered himself lucky to be there at all, because he might have been threatened with death, or dispatched in another way. Accordingly, Narub was very cautious about inferring more than he actually knew or was told. Throughout the journal he stringently tried to record only his biased opinion about skewed and limited observations, nothing more. Apparently this satisfied the scientist in him, while keeping his inclination to believe what he wanted. It was hardly an objective enterprise. Simeon became annoyed with Narub's equivocation. How Narub could know so much and conclude so little? It did nothing to support the risky journey that Simeon was supposed to undertake. Why didn't Narub just admit that everything he saw was questionable, and that therefore, there was no sure cure for cancer in cannibalism? For similar reasons, what kept Simeon pursuing the wild goose?

There were all kinds of sickness besides the cancer that drew Narub. Flukes and parasites, especially something resembling the chills and paroxysms of malaria, were common, judging by bloated bellies and big spleens. The drinking water was said to be "very good," and did have a cathartic effect. But practically everything else had a good and bad effect or was given supernatural significance. Spirituality and superstition were a common combination, and very few things were completely neutral. Practically everything had a meaning, often joined to another meaning, usually quite opposite. Naturally, as everywhere else, good and evil were mixed in together, and opposites regularly were attracted to each other.

Not adding to Narub's comfort were colonies of large purplish ants that worked overtime, talked to each other, climbed over him, and disregarded whatever meager protection was available. The ants had an advantage in that they had someone to talk to. Narub had no one except an incompetent, foul-smelling interpreter who was usually elsewhere when needed the most, and tribe members who communicated as little as possible in what pidgin they shared. Consequently, to his alarm, thrown back on his own reflections, Narub began to discover and attribute supernatural meaning everywhere. Something was getting to him. He was justifiably scared about becoming irrationally subjective and going native in a destructive way. His critical faculties were as soggy as the steamy weather. My judgment cannot be depended on, he reluctantly admitted, and faithfully recorded his dismay. One day, for example, his wristwatch disappeared. The soft regular ticking might have meant something magical to the thieves.

The tribe itself measured time only by seasons. Rutting and planting seem to be the same. If I sound silly, he noted to his unidentified reader, you are right. He witnessed the rutting season celebrated openly and without ceremony. Narub was embarrassed, but no one else paid much attention. "I'd rather be embarrassed than embraced," he dutifully wrote. No one apparently invited the austere outsider to participate.

Defeated and cannibalized losers are treated with much respect because former enemies become honorary adjunct members of the tribe. Respect for the cannibalized also helps the captured women feel more at home, so it is easier for them to marry again and become pregnant. While eating human meat during a celebration is supposed to help the acquisition of virtue, courage and character, not so, of course, for deaths due to poison, injury, victims of crime, or an overt curse. When a hero dies in battle the next male child born in the village is given his name, so that in effect, he lives on through cannibalism and a child. Death is not obliteration, but a bridge to someone else, making for a better person.

Nevertheless, for all his good will, Narub found it hard to credit these primitive people with compassion, spirituality, virtue, and immortality. Bias against black people, aboriginal or not, is hard to eradicate. Narub was ironically amused that to these people, he was almost white, but to his colleagues back home, he was almost black. His bronzed complexion made little difference, depending only on the standpoint of the observer.

Divinity is found in taboo animals, but Narub wasn't sure which animals were considered taboo. Lowly animals and vermin, shunned or disgusting, are not considered suitable receptacles for divinity. The divine spirit elevates, so birds that fly are taboo, while creeping animals are not.

The most sacred is a bird called the Ohwai, said to dwell only on the highest branches of the tallest trees, and is never seen or heard until the moment of death, and then only by a person of high distinction. It sings when the gods descend to claim the spirit of the deceased. Curiously, the Ohwai is also said to cannibalize its young. How it manages to perpetuate itself while eating the young was not made clear. Narub learned however that no one he spoke with had actually seen or heard the Ohwai, but it is bad form to inquire too closely about the matter. Inconsistency troubled no one, and there is much latitude for improvisation. Faith is stronger than logic and offers far greater rewards. Consequently, the Ohwai is revered, although it is probably mythical, at least seldom actually heard or seen, except by someone in high standing.

Narub was prepared for such flexibility. Back in India, gods with mixed, contradictory and arbitrary attributes never bothered true believers. Everything good is self-evident and needs no proof. The same goes for evil. True believers always give God or gods the benefit of the doubt, thanking divinity for good and excusing most gods from the blame of doing bad things, except, of course, for gods like Vishnu. Only an atheist would ask for proof, anyway. Narub's conclusions were that he found it hard to credit the tribe with consistent ideas about the gods. He puzzled over the connection between an evil force like cancer, and the custom of cannibalism, which is held sacred at times and reserved for the most worthy and distinguished members of the tribe.

Simeon found himself skipping, re-reading, and filling in gaps before concluding that it was far too long, repetitious, and rambling, rather than informative. Still enthused and eager, however, Simeon was far from inspired by the tendentious text, and certainly not persuaded that the journey would be successful.

Despite his central goal and purpose, Narub wrote very little about cancer, or cannibalism. He only hinted at how long he stayed. Important clinical information was curiously omitted, a strange elision considering the amount of information that had nothing to do with either cannibalism or cancer. Although this patient and that had signs of advanced cancer, he did not specifically describe those who lived or died, and the amount of the sacred stew each received. How many sick people had he actually observed, or did he depend on flimsy hearsay and native credulity? Perhaps cannibalism only conferred a nutritious supplement for sick people who had not eaten well. Perhaps there was remission, relapse and death after Narub left. In fact, there had to be.

If Narub expected to make a strong case for cure, he might only have found what he was looking for. Credibly, he recognized this and hesitated before going too far in any claim. No wonder Narub wanted a qualified emissary, someone with a stake in cancer cure, willing to travel, with an adventurous, perverse turn of mind who would willingly eat the flesh of another human being. The promise of an ultimate transgression still fascinated him, regardless of cancer.

After his return, Narub investigated historical references, which he briefly noted. Around the 1880's, a young priest-missionary lived for several years in an area not unlike the Highlands. Intent on bringing primitive souls to Christianity, he was not concerned with the tribes' health, advanced illness and death. That would have required more respect for primitive beliefs than missionaries are supposed to feel. Father Sylvester wanted to eradicate cannibalism, not to justify it. Devout and dedicated, he believed that the risk in being there meant greater glory for the convert as well as the priest. Cannibalism only signified how primitive these people were and how much in need of conversion. Natives called Fr. Sylvester "the white man who wears black and believes in other gods."

At one point, the priest wrote, "Unto the faithful, life will change but never be taken away." Did this faintly familiar paraphrase address devout Christians or the unconverted tribe? What did it have to do with the ceremonial cannibalism that endowed the dead with symbolic immortality? Eating human flesh could have, therefore, a sacramental significance. These issues were left dangling because Sylvester's journal ended abruptly. Much later, a fisherman found Sylvester's writings preserved on a shelf in a deserted hut. It had been wrapped in layers of thatch. How it got from up where Sylvester stationed himself, to a hut along an unidentified river was another tantalizing question. Presumably, Fr. Sylvester put it there. But what happened to the priest afterward? Narub shrewdly guessed that his predecessor found few people cured by any method, including cannibalism. Otherwise he would surely have claimed cures for faith and Christianity. How the University acquired Sylvester's document was not reported. According to academic sources, the account dating from the latter years of the 19th Century was always there, but few scholars had the interest to read it before Narub.

About forty years later, an anthropology student named Tilton studied several tribes in what was later called Papua New Guinea. He was scholarly, athletic, and enthusiastic, without a conceptual axe to grind. Speaking Pidgin adequately though haltingly, he was told about people with serious illness who ate human flesh and were cured, because they recovered. He was not a physician and it was doubtful if he personally observed the sick people. He did not describe symptoms that later students could have used to reconstruct illnesses that were cured or not cured. Had there been a medicinal stew, he did not mention it, and he probably would have. Tilton died unexpectedly shortly after returning home, never finishing the doctoral thesis that might have fleshed out his report. Narub's journal also included notes about personal contact with government officials and physicians familiar with the area's indigenous diseases. Nothing was said about the sacred stew or any other concoction and its effect on cancer. Public health records did not have information about the extent of cancer in the regions Tilton visited.

Medical authorities were sure that tribal shamans whom they called "medicine men" knew next to nothing about actual illness, except for self-limited maladies that cured themselves. In fact, they mistrusted shamans, declaring that they bilked the simple-minded peoples for their own gain. Quackery is everywhere, and hearsay is its agent.

Narub did not find much more about cannibalism from practitioners he met in larger towns, where interpreters were more reliable. Shamans spoke English fairly well and generally offered a set speech.

"No, no, Sir. Maybe in the old days. Not now. Nobody eaten. Sick people see government doctor, and get well or die. We are all civilized. Rascals do anything, even eat people, and kill them. Most people, no, no. We are now Christian peoples, go to top church, and believe in Easter and

Christmas. Big holidays. Santa Claus is fine big man, like Babe Ruth. Good times. I take off curse, too. Good medicines. Give penicillin."

Asking native practitioners specifically about cancer, Narub knew, would be like asking a Stone Age man about television. Far from prying government eyes, the old tribes still practiced older traditions like cannibalism. But this would not establish a link to cancer, at best only to severe sickness, which might be almost anything. When queried about sanctified soup, cannibalism, and cancer, tribal elders simply shrugged their collective shoulders and more citified practitioners smiled superciliously.

Narub got more information from occasional white men who told tales, sometimes very tall, about sacred foods and plants, some of which were in fermented form. Very sick tribesmen (and some women) had been revived and restored to extremely good health, they said. The stories repeated themselves over and over, different in details and deadliness of the reputed disease but sure in the cure. Such anecdotes were not even testimonials, but hearsay, with a little lying now and then about witnessing startling recoveries. "I was there when…" applies to any place where miracles are said to occur. No one would bother to report treatment that fails. Cannibalism was also mentioned as the vehicle of cure, but it seemed to be part of the fabric of a good story rather than a factual report.

Narub also learned about a curious but not unexpected by-product of a tribal food, possibly made into a soup, that causes patients (as he still thought of them) to go into a trance, even a delirium. They thrash about, mutter unintelligibly, and then when consciousness returns, claim to have spoken with the gods. These were far-fetched extensions of commonplace events to cancer cure, even though a kind of delirium was sometimes attached. Narub was objective enough to wonder if this were food poisoning or a toxic product in the soup. Narub, the consummate clinician, also noted that the delirium, which he had never witnessed personally, resembled the "crisis" of a serious febrile illness described by earlier generations of physicians. Very sick patients with high fever frequently developed delirium, often followed by a deep stupor or coma. Afterward, the fever broke and recovery took place soon afterward. Narub had personally spoken with others who recalled visions when very sick, before returning from death's door.

Simeon readily appreciated how difficult it must have been for Narub to maintain a semblance of objectivity. His fervent expectations for making the journey worthwhile often swayed his observations and conclusions, especially after listening to less than objective reporters. Nevertheless, Narub was there, and could not hallucinate the startling recoveries he actually saw and heard about, not all of which could be dismissed. Although

Simeon was just as fervent about a workable antidote for cancer, he hesitated about being duped, or being led on by extravagant hopes. After all, Simeon was an expert on using people's gullibility for his own purposes. He was already familiar with near-death experiences that some Western patients reverently talked about after coming through a grave illness.

All in all, Simeon raptly read Narub's narrative most of the night. Despite his doubts, reservations and Narub's caveats, he was not put off, but more certain than ever that he wanted to go there. There was nothing to lose but his life, which was likely to be lost, anyway, sooner or later when cancer got around to it. He was flattered, because Narub assumed he could make controlled observations while undergoing the tribulations of cancer. That he might die did not deter his resolve to take up the challenge. However, several nights later, before speaking with Narub again, while still mulling over the future, Simeon had an alarming but perhaps prophetic dream.

A turbulent river foamed and spouted dark poisonous waters. On the river's bank, snakes appeared from nowhere and slithered ominously, but ignored Simeon who tried to find a way to cross. As he stood motionless at water's edge, bloody feces streamed out of him onto the ground. Then, silently, a large pale pink creature with glistening eyes emerged from the water, looking like a fish that inadvertently had been caught in a net and, stubbornly resisting, just managed to escape. Simeon awakened, sweating and shaking, as if after all, he was doomed to die, and that Narub had only selfish motives for sending him on this mission. He was still stubbornly determined to accept the chance and go as far as necessary.

When he next met with Dr. Narub to report his decision, Narub struggled to conceal a satisfied smile. Then the cautious clinician took over, once again.

"I hope you understand that after all is done, the trip may end fruitlessly, and that there is distinct risk involved." There he was, paying a familiar tribute to informed consent. Like any very sick patient with few options, Simeon nodded, without exactly knowing much except that everything was provisional.

"I know that and accept the risk," Simeon said, "But I hope there's more to be found than the rumors you wrote about. I may end up dead, without hearing that bird sing." He picked out the most fanciful part of Narub's tale to confront the good doctor, knowing that if he did hear the Ohwai, he was as good as dead.

"Your irony and skepticism will be useful, Simeon. It might make you be more receptive to what facts there are. I was skeptical, too, but still there was much I wanted to be true, and couldn't confirm. I would not have let you read my journal if the stories were all a hoax. As a matter of fact, and this, I wrote about as hearsay towards the end, I did see sick people fall into a delirium. I was told they talked with spirits from the next world. I cannot vouch for that, since it was all in a language I didn't understand. It didn't seem like a hallucination, but I've seen believers at a revival meeting, talking with tongues, foaming at the mouth, practically, and then claim they've talked with Jesus." Simeon did not flinch or waver. He knew that this wasn't to be a scientific expedition, and that one cured patient was only that, and he hoped that fortunate person would be Simeon Benett. Narub congratulated him on his choice, and said it would be the experience of a lifetime, not mentioning that it could be a time for death, too.

"I'll put every contact I have at your disposal," Narub said, relieved, but in a formal tone. "It is absolutely essential that the trip is well-planned to the last detail. Unlike me, you must have the best, most experienced, and reliable guide to look after you, someone with lots of practical knowledge about the people, tribes, and the terrain, fluent in your language and theirs. Most available guides are at best, very simple, essentially uneducated, and mercenary to the utmost. Your guide should know how to deal with almost any contingency. Unfortunately, I know only one such man, whom I did not meet until my own expedition was long over. I would have learned more if Axel had been nearby. I hope he's still around and willing to take you on. It is a daunting challenge that I trust you are up to. I hope he'll trust you as much as you can trust him. I needn't go over his credentials. He's lived in the area for many years, knows the tribes, and speaks many of their languages, familiar with customs, so on. He has his private prejudices. If he doesn't cotton to you, whatever you call it, I guarantee you'll be back by the next boat. He is like that, very smart, opinionated, and absolutely sure of his rectitude, too. If all goes well between you two, he'll arrange for everything, food, shelter, transportation, introductions, protection from the rogues, black and white, that you'll meet along the way. His services don't come cheap. There are many ways to eat up funds, so be ready to pay up without haggling. But he's honorable, all the way. Bargaining would be fatal. It's his way or none. Don't for a minute let yourself be complacent, but follow the rules. If the tribe accepts you, it will be because of Axel. If he isn't available, I can't really advise you to go ahead. Cannibals aren't like us, don't forget, but it's up to you to find out how different they are." That would be the last meeting between Simeon and Narub for a long time.

Chapter 7—Axel

It is not a long trip from Sydney to Cairns to Port Moresby. But the plane was crowded, and the noise of the engines provided a wall that helped Simeon withdraw and enjoy deep solitude. The obliteration surrounding him soon filled up with a lengthy reverie, too random to be a review, of how he got from bloody urine to where he was presently going. He recalled Hermione that last night before the inspiring morning of self-congratulation and then to an abrupt onset of cancer and its consequences. From St. Thomas to Dr. Pochapin, then Dr. Carson, meanwhile losing his left testicle, then all the chemotherapy, his weeks of solitude and finally reaching Dr. Narub, the cancer doctor with a bent for exotic alternatives, and for mythical cures, such as cannibalism. All these recollections crowded in together. Each event fused with others until the prospect of the future joined in a mass of memory and expectation. He could scarcely recall the dreary and desolate days of chemotherapy, both his sickness and the monotonous intervals between injections and transfusions. Everything melded into disconsolate stupor, not unlike a special delirium of its own. Finally, there was an unsettled doubt about Dr. Narub, who offered a choice and chance to Simeon that he accepted. But it remained a questionable opportunity.

Without Narub, he would not now be going to Papua New Guinea and starting on an expedition in search of curing cancer and confronting a taboo worthy of being broken. He needed a cure, but his fate depended on an unknown guide, someone called Axel Bernstein.

First, however, he must meet this guide, sponsor, and spokesman to the Highlands tribe and whatever else waited in the future. True to his promise, Dr. Narub made the arrangements. It had taken several weeks of dealing with the bureaucracy, getting a visa, notifying New Guinea authorities, and finally negotiating with the busy and unpredictable Axel, whom he would depend on for weeks to come.

Much else went on unofficially during the preparations. Simeon never understood why the authorities were so involved, or why he had to get a visa. Usually, a passport was enough in that part of the world. Perhaps Axel insisted, knowing that his charge's destination would not be that of an ordinary visitor, there to see the sights and purchase souvenirs, but someone with a purpose that could not be talked about openly. Although cancer was mentioned in the correspondence, cannibalism was not. The omission, which was only prudent, did not keep Simeon from thinking about human flesh cooked in a stew or perhaps eaten bloody raw. In whatever form it was offered, he could not refuse. Indeed, he was eager yet hesitant. Maybe it was

125

no different than horse, donkey or monkey meat, all of which he had sampled, without a great deal of relish. With more trepidation, he had also eaten camel, snake, rodent, and various birds and beasts whose names he forgot. It was common fare in certain countries, and no taboo was attached except in the world Simeon left behind. He had not expected these exotic animals to confer any therapeutic value and at that time, he was not a cancer patient. Once he tried rhinoceros horn, said to be an aphrodisiac. It had no special effect on Simeon, whose libido needed no special boost, anyway.

All these samplings were far from cannibalism. Pretending that a dish of human meat would be only slightly different from, say, giraffe, did not make the prospect any more appetizing. Cooked human flesh would be easier to disguise, but even Simeon gagged slightly at what was, with luck, waiting for him. Indeed, there are dining clubs all over the civilized world that feature rare game and, allegedly, animal meat close to humans, like chimpanzees and gorillas. However, to be a downright cannibal is a distinction shared only with perverts and people from a remote primitive tribe. Naturally, as a world traveler and general sophisticate, Simeon used cultural relativism to ease his hesitation.

Simeon could not ignore the ostensible reason for the trip, cure of advanced cancer. He knew that he might never return, even to Australia. To die unknown somewhere in the New Guinea jungle or in a backwater settlement was not a welcome thought. There would be no one to mourn, however, or even attend his passing in any place, unless they were waiting to make sure that his estate was solvent. Nevertheless, Simeon decided with good reason that he would be grateful to anyone helping him, regardless of the outcome.

Simeon was hardly a callow innocent abroad. Travel had taken him to out-of-the-way places that tourists seldom hear about, visit or and are hardly noted by mapmakers. Nevertheless, Simeon still managed to find limited acceptance almost everywhere. Talent for fitting into new surroundings often earned access to private places that the ordinary outsider would know nothing about. He even picked up a rudimentary familiarity with local languages, sponging up enough in a short time to get along.

Before departing for New Guinea he tried to acquaint himself with its customs and culture through glossy guidebooks, magazines, and popular library books. These publications offered generalities about getting around better known towns and villages, hotels, foreign currency, and so on, most of which was informative but hardly what Simeon needed. For the professional, the library in Sydney had plenty of books, even scholarly monographs about sorcery and cannibalism. But just as Narub's crude journal yielded little cold scientific information, there was no mention of cannibalism's reputed therapeutic effect on cancer. In fact, most books simply glossed over cannibalism, calling it an old practice that these days is found less and less, even in the jungle. Although tribal diversity was accurately declared a fact of life in Papua New Guinea, most authors understandably wrote only about civilized tribes along well-traveled roads and places that tourists are likely to visit. Tribes in the interior were dismissed in a paragraph or two, mostly by platitudes.

Simeon hoped that he wouldn't be considered an enemy, although he had more than slight familiarity with endemic suspicion and mistrust of the intrusive white man. It was pervasive in urban centers where the white man lived and employed natives who themselves were thoroughly and lucratively accustomed to foreigners and their ways. Simeon concluded that diversity, bigotry, and suspicion were as widespread as the forest and rivers and found among all kinds of people who otherwise were friendly, hostile, suspicious, gullible, industrious, indolent, docile, aggressive, submissive, and assertive, with gradations and combinations. Easy generalities were not very illuminating, nor very useful guidelines. He therefore prepared himself to be suspicious of just about anyone, although he was not sure who the exceptions might be. This was easy for someone like Simeon, but only when he was genuinely healthy. What about a stranger like Simeon with an advanced case of cancer that could ignite at any moment without warning? A healthy outsider could be as wary as he pleased. But for someone so vulnerable, it was insufficient merely to be on the alert. He was well aware that adaptability might not be enough. Usually, Simeon made deception work to his advantage. In the land he was about to live in, he could not be sure. His own resources had to wait for the formidable Axel Bernstein, on whom he was supposed to rely completely. This was a disconcerting, even intimidating thought.

He might be escorted to unfamiliar and remote places, and then abandoned or exposed to such predicaments that life itself was at stake. Skinning a white man of his means was a common goal and livelihood for many. He needed protection and trustworthy guidance to ward off parasites of every kind. Merely knowing landmarks and speaking dialects, while indispensable, were hardly enough. Common sense told him that despite being very circumspect, he would probably not realize mistakes until he committed them and then be in serious trouble. Meanwhile, cancer kept him in limbo, unable to prepare for a relapse, should that come anytime.

Aunt Gina's indoctrination about meeting taboos and defying convention head-on seemed too simple-minded and risky. Most taboos in New Guinea had to be obscure and ingrained, with daily customs and expectations never directly announced. Confrontation and infraction could be an insult, with all sorts of unspecified consequences.

Tourists of all nations are usually quite comfortable in Port Moresby, a modern city where a traveler is easily understood and cultivated. Tourism is big and lucrative. Signs are in English and visitors are welcome, along with their funds. However, there were regular residents, including Australian expatriates who seldom tried to converse with outsiders. Furthermore, conspicuously unemployed young men hung around the major points of interest, watching newcomers, looking for fair game, and waiting for night to come. Hotel lobbies were not free of better dressed, but idling men and women who sought visitors for their own particular scam. Friendly or not, Port Moresby's gateway flavor added to whatever a visiting American suspected and was wary of.

Stores and hotels were busy, night and day, offering the usual inventory of artifacts and services. Luxurious accommodations at hotels sharply contrasted with the dilapidated outskirts, where, far on the periphery and almost hidden, were slums, stores, hovels, bars, and shacks for the underclass. A huge wooden parliament building stood empty, a monument to the aspirations of a native people, still to be fulfilled, striving for independence and respect, but long kept in semi-servitude. Periodically, parliament met to debate sundry issues, trivial and important. Besides practical problems of strengthening an embryonic democratic society, the jungle blood had not yet been subdued. Savage crimes were not infrequent, along with everyday offenses such as street mugging, robbery and assault.

Simeon did not pay much attention to the tourist attractions and noteworthy points of interest, because he wanted to move on as quickly as possible. His exclusive mission was meeting Axel Bernstein for the first time in Liaagam, a much smaller community about fifty miles away. It was there that final preparations for their journey were to be arranged. The exact location was unclear but Simeon hoped Liaagam was small enough to make any meeting place easy to find. Some people insisted on calling the town, Lima, but that was an inaccuracy brought on by differences in accented English.

On the day after his arrival a well-dressed black man in the hotel lobby promptly recognized Simeon. Axel had already hired a driver and a car to transport Simeon to Liaagam (or Lima). Because Simeon was so eager to start, he wasted no time and checked out promptly. He was alert and ready for any option, if he had any, despite total bewilderment about what awaited him.

The road out of Port Moresby was surprisingly smooth, with signs of recently being paved. The easy ride with a driver of limited sociability offered a chance for Simeon to entertain himself by casually inspecting the countryside and ruminating about nothing in particular. Out of nowhere, he suddenly remembered a young man visiting a small hospital where then-Simon was whimsically working for a time. While chatting with friends, the visitor, perhaps in his mid-twenties, suddenly complained of chest pain and died within a few minutes, much to the consternation of everyone else. Later, after a post-mortem examination, four recent partially obliterated coronary arteries explained his sudden demise, but did not account for his appearance of health just prior to collapse. Simeon needed no explanation to connect the young man's sudden demise to his own fears.

The smooth paved road, marked by just an occasional jiggle or two, made Simeon realize that a sudden accident with a less than careful driver could abruptly demonstrate how deceptive and futile the appearance of good health might be. It was a banal observation but everything, planned and unplanned, could be snuffed out in an instant. Fragility in a crust of well-being is silent and invisible until broken through. Simeon might never get a chance because cancer could always and without warning awaken and claim its victim. After all, he mused for at least the thousandth time, how different could human flesh taste? A shipboard confidant had once told him that human flesh was supposed to taste like kangaroo, or perhaps it was armadillo. Simeon would be an unappetizing item for a real cannibal's diet, despite outside appearance of health. They might feed him to pigs that are not so discriminating once he was found out. It was not a pleasant thought, either way. Whether sudden death from causes unknown, from cancer striking again, or being eaten by aborigines, he was not anticipating much besides an assortment of potential disasters.

As if attuned to Simeon's random thoughts of misfortune, the smooth road soon became rutted and far less comfortable. A few cows and a pig or two nonchalantly blocked the car, yielding the right of way only reluctantly. Simeon noticed a cemetery where a funeral service had recently been held, from all appearances. Flowers were there, along with a scattering of people and a freshly filled grave still surrounded by a few seats. Nevertheless, the dead person seemed already to have been forgotten by those still roaming around, conversing with each other, even laughing.

Impulsively, he asked the driver to stop, got out of the car, and walked over to a group of stragglers. They couldn't understand his halting Pidgin, and the driver did not share Simeon's wish to visit the new gravesite. Alone then, Simeon went to the new grave, just covered with fresh earth. The smell was pungent and sad, the ground having already taken the deceased for its own. Whatever tears were shed, by this time had already soaked into the grave. For a moment, Simeon felt a genuine pang, like a real mourner who knew the deceased. He recalled visiting empty country churches no longer echoing sermons and sounds of long vanished congregations. Like a sudden wind, Simeon felt a rush of kinship with anyone who lost someone or something essential to purposeful being. It was a curious series of events for a man schooled never to care. He couldn't be sure if he had just completed rehearsing his own funeral and interment.

Simeon's inclination to visit old churches was kept very private. He could not remember ever telling anyone. After all, who was there to tell? Typically, he would first look to see if anyone else was there in the church. In any case, he usually found the door unlocked, pews waiting for an assembly to arrive, and for a choir to sing. Alone, Simeon sat silently, not reading the prayer book, scarcely daring to breathe the lingering but dusty scent of flowers long withered and disregarded. It was an exercise in empty nostalgia for forebears unknown, now as he sat contemplating a future unfathomed. Still, in a way he could not comprehend, his silent presence communicated with the dead, who held the secrets.

Not for the first time, surely, Simeon had an expanding vision about cancer that then became Cancer, a way of life and existence, more than a sickness, but a grim magnitude. Its scope far exceeded the parochial disease being doctored elsewhere, and so casually nicknamed CA. Meanwhile, Simeon was on his way to an appointed destiny, like a penitent pilgrim. Not too inaccurately, he imagined a corpse discarded and left to rot alongside a foreign road. Standing now as he just did, staring at this freshly filled grave, death surrounded him with the scents of imminent mortality.

Gullibility and vulnerability are usually found together. The commonest gullibility practiced in a swindle is to convince the prospective victim that he is a lucky exception, even the favorite of the gods, a sure thing. It is a way of peddling the ruse. Lest he be fooled with false promises, Simeon resolved then and there never to be a gullible and therefore vulnerable victim, intoxicated with hope, or a confidence man looking to out-smart everyone else by sweet-talk. Simeon determined to imitate cancer by eating human flesh, just as Cancer is vanquished by cannibalism in return for the way cancer voraciously destroys its victims. It could be a life and death con game he was about to play, but that is the way he'd do it, not give in but use his vulnerability to get the best of a formidable enemy. Like the unknown corpse lying there in his grave, or abandoned by the roadside, his scent would survive. It was an empty resolution, making little sense, but, for no reason whatsoever, he trusted its absurdity.

Liaagam is a settlement far smaller than the other New Guinea town that shares its name, but not its spelling. While shabby and rundown, and certainly not more than an accumulation of shacks and shops, Liaagam also provides a small but adequate harbor for crafts not much larger than launches and motorized sailboats. Lying still further out, however, were vessels capable of carrying at least twenty passengers in spare comfort. For travelers who do not mind narrow bunks, rugged food and considerable inconvenience, Liaagam was a colorful haven, even a port for launching forays into the interior. Meanwhile, away from the docks, the settlement expanded into the village it was. A common central clearing served as a gathering place and focus for casual commerce and customary transactions. Small shops, lined up side by side, were at the edges of the central mall. Stores catered mainly to tourists, selling artifacts of native culture and other souvenirs. A few such hardy tourists now wandered around, looking at the populace as well as the goods that Liaagam's stores offered. An hour or two spent snapping pictures of natives were usually enough, except for those who patronized the hotel and sampled its victuals.

Several buildings were larger than the stores but none was more conspicuous than a three-story structure called the hotel, boldly located close to the town's center but still detached enough to preserve a shabby dignity. A garish striped canvas awning over a large verandah protected customers from the hot sun, while they sat, stared at others, and slowly drank the local potions. The elevated porch was separated from the street by a wooden railing.

Inside the hotel were a bar and restaurant on the first floor, and an assortment of accommodations on the two floors above. A few white men and older natives played cards and chatted in a small lobby. A little beyond, a mélange of customers sat at small tables, while others gathered at an adjacent bar in a much larger room. There was a well-worn pool table, a juke box, and for the more dignified, a billiard table. Despite their age, neither table was used frequently, since most patrons tried their luck on two ancient and noisy slot machines.

By standing on the verandah, a visitor could easily see a mountain range, its summit covered by clouds, off in the distance but still almost surrounding the village itself. At its foot were thickets and trees shielding the shacks and hovels where native workers lived in poverty. As everywhere, whenever natives and wealthy visitors come together, there is a sharp and bitter delineation between the huts and poverty and what passed for conspicuous prosperity. Nowhere was this clearer than in the hotel, rundown in some respects, but pretending to an elegance it could not truly achieve. There was no way to discover where the richer residents lived.

Simeon's uncomfortable automobile journey finally ended, just at the entrance to the hotel and café. Without a murmur of farewell, the driver simply dumped his passenger and the luggage, not rudely, but with impersonal finality. His mission was done, and he stopped just long enough before driving off quickly along a road that vanished among the trees. Simeon supposed that the driver had already been paid, so there was no need to feign a good-bye. He went up onto the verandah and sat a table where he could confidently expect Axel to show up. A multitude of buzzing insects disputed his choice, however, angry at being displaced from their gathering place. Simeon ordered a drink of the town's tawny but mild beer, and settled back, enjoying the sight of the passing population. From his seat, he could see almost the entire village and beyond up into the mountains. It was a familiar experience; he felt himself at the very center of activity without being a part of it. Scruffy dogs nosed around, looking for a piece of garbage. An occasional pig, fat and much better fed than the dogs, wandered among the swarms of people, but attracted almost no attention. The weather was steamy, and Simeon found that his broad brim hat protected him minimally. It was as if the sun was working hard to cook the surroundings before the afternoon settled down and cooled off. Only the natives seemed comfortable; they wore brief dungarees, without shoes or shirts, with an occasional bandanna. Visitors were dressed like Simeon, but with a camera or backpack.

Although Simeon anticipated a much longer wait in this oppressive atmosphere, he scarcely had time to finish his drink before a tall, tanned bearded stranger, looming above other people, approached and confidently addressed him by name. His imposing appearance and straightforward speech confirmed Simeon's quick assumption that this was Axel Bernstein, his all purpose guide, guru, and advisor, who would direct and sponsor Simeon on his trip to the Highlands. They shook hands solemnly, neither smiling but scrutinizing each other. Without being invited, of course, Axel sat down at the table, where without ordering, a drink was immediately served. The waiters knew Axel and his preferences. Simeon could not help staring at the man who was hired to play such an essential role in his survival.

Axel's Scandinavian heritage was unmistakable. He would have been noticed in any crowd, not only because of his height, gray hair, worn medium long, once quite blond, but by his manner and dress. Tanned, almost as bronze as Narub, his jacket and shorts, well worn and sturdy as he, instantly identified Axel as someone who spent much time in the tropics. A wide brimmed hat was at his side, covering his backpack. Eager intrusive tourists, who spotted Axel walking around, or just sitting on the porch, always wanted to take his picture, but Axel did not readily allow them the freedom of their camera. First, his permission was necessary. Otherwise, he would confiscate the film on the spot, and then politely return the camera, without comment. No one had the courage to dispute him. An aging veteran of the tropical jungle, islands, and rivers, looking like an actor authentically cast or a picture book adventurer, Axel played his part well. If he had dressed like a legendary Viking, there could have been no doubt that he was a close companion of Eric, or some other hero, straight out of an ancient saga. Axel could not disguise, exaggerate, or mute what he really was, a long time explorer/ guide/ anthropologist/ authority on New Guinea and the surrounding territory. He did not have to conform and play an expected part. His authenticity could not be disputed.

Were Axel inclined to speak of his past, he would match any romanticized picture that people who knew him expected or strangers could conjure up. He had credentials enough to qualify as a college professor, shrewd businessman, and rugged explorer, and probably much more that he preferred to keep undisclosed. Nevertheless, to rely only on his striking appearance would not have done justice to his resolute character, resourcefulness, and competence, honed after years both in New Guinea and in other parts of the world.

Born in a small city in Denmark, his surname, Bernstein, would ordinarily raise eyebrows, but that was, indeed, his family name. Axel came upon his Scandinavian mien legitimately. As an adolescent, schoolmates teased him about his Jewish name and prototypical appearance, laughingly questioning his legitimacy. Two Jews could not have managed to be parents to this strikingly gentile-looking youth who seemed to have sprung from this rugged Danish soil. During his boyhood, he enjoyed the outdoors, skiing, skating, sledding, and all winter sports. But he did not neglect the solitary pleasures of books and music, much to the pride of his parents, both of whom also played music and were teachers. In the tropics of mature years, however, books were few, hard to transport, and musical talent withered away, replaced by skills more appropriate to the jungle.

As a youth in Denmark, however, he was both an all-around athlete, and an outstanding scholar, even the brightest in his class. His father, Oscar Bernstein, a concertmaster of a symphony orchestra, traveled extensively, taught violin and viola, and was considerably more sophisticated and worldly than fellow-musicians and citizens of their city. Rachel, his mother, was a schoolteacher who survived a death camp. After World War II, she migrated to Denmark, a haven for dispossessed Jews even during the war, where she met and married Oscar.

Some fifteen years older than his wife, Oscar was attracted by her youthful appearance, despite the hardships she endured in the camp. Her family perished, but if any survived, Rachel often said, they must have settled in Israel. No one ever did contact the Bernsteins, nor did Rachel attempt to find her family. Already speaking several languages, she learned passable Danish without much difficulty. Consequently, she taught English and German in a local academy along with literature. There was no need to speak her native tongue, Polish.

Neither Oscar nor Rachel practiced Judaism, although they never denied their heritage. They were practically the only Jews in that part of the country, somewhat distant from larger communities where Jews were not uncommon. To the town, the Bernsteins were primarily Jewish, not Danish. There were negligible episodes of overt anti-semitism, but what they endured was merely social isolation, which they minded only slightly. Oscar was a native Dane, but his wife was always an interloper from a far away place, although she was well liked and respected by her colleagues. Rachel had few close friends, however, even at the school, but she was accepted and admired as a survivor of the Holocaust. Nevertheless, the Bernsteins appreciated such acceptance as they had, and Rachel never referred to the hardships in another country. The family was quite content with its own company, traveling during vacations and maintaining a loose connection with other countries. There were books on a variety of topics and in several languages, but Axel predominantly felt strongest affinity with the legendary heroes who traveled huge distances, discovered new lands and left a permanent heritage for future generations. Reading about their exploits and conquests, the young Axel grew up quite satisfied with his lot, proud of being Danish but exceedingly ambitious and restless to achieve what he could in the outside world. He did as his schoolmates did, and did it well, but knew that despite his Nordic appearance, he was not like them.

Rachel and Oscar agreed that when Axel was ready, he should attend a prestigious university in the United States, even if it meant not seeing him again for a long time. They were prepared for the sacrifice, since with his talents, neither parent could visualize Axel as a local established burgher. He was more than qualified for any first class university, prepared well and gifted in many ways, other than what he learned from his parents and instructors at school. Axel was eager to travel, and admired the English tradition for its reputed excellence in education and heroic history, which he knew well. Therefore instead of looking to the United States, he wanted to absorb the traditional culture at Oxford and Cambridge, where aptitude for language would surely be an advantage in studying philology. However, for reasons never divulged, neither institution accepted Axel. The sting of a double refusal was somewhat eased by admission with a generous scholarship to another Cambridge in the United States, Harvard University. This had been the very school that his parents admired from afar and approved for their son. Armed with great expectations and much reading,

Axel expansively anticipated life in the center of learning that Harvard signified. In his imagination, he conferred upon great Harvard professors some of the glamour that he ordinarily reserved for his Scandinavian heroes.

As an undergraduate, Axel established an outstanding record, but gradually grew restless at the prospect of an academic career, towards which everyone was pushing him. While still admiring his professors, many of whom supported his academic aspirations, Axel learned that they, too, could be very parochial. The sting of refusal by Oxford and Cambridge had not worn off. He preferred the idea of being an unaffiliated, informal wandering scholar, with roots nowhere, but able to learn from masters everywhere. Culture and education were not confined to the academic life, or to renowned colleges and famous professors. But even wandering scholars needed to live, fellowships and grants were meager, and Axel had few funds at his disposal, with no established way of earning a living. However, he did have unqualified confidence in being able to survive and get along well. So, against the urging of professors and parents, he put aside academic promise and decided to find out what the world had to offer.

The boundless beauty and primitive life of the South Pacific and Melanesia fascinated him. Worldly innocence in full bloom, despite his college years, had endowed this part of the world with an endearing, romanticized aura, unbesmirched by its bloody history, actual events, and evil people. For the still youthful and very energetic Axel, the aborigine was a Rousseau-like idealization, unsullied by civilization. Only later did he discover how totally wrong he was about these early assessments.

There were many ways for an educated and personable young white man to get along and make a substantial living. Axel's confident manner with an ability to speak several languages fluently and get by in others made him a natural for any large travel agency. In Melbourne, Australia, he was offered a job guiding parties of tourists around Australia and into the islands of Borneo and Papua New Guinea. It was not long, however, before his long-standing attraction to Papua New Guinea took hold and turned fascination into a commitment. Next to Denmark, Papua New Guinea became his home. Academic ambitions faded far behind, replaced by the prospect of adventure, which he subsequently found in abundance.

With the accumulation of years that passed ever quickly, he became well known and intimately familiar with the peoples and the region, especially as he ventured more and more into the interior, with its tribal intricacies, mixed loyalties, and ethnic challenges. Moreover, acquaintance with government officials and tribal chiefs gave him access and privileges that few ordinary guides could match. Practical always, Axel added to his fortune by exporting a number of artifacts unobtainable by collectors elsewhere. He hired a string of guides for tourists attracted by first hearing his name reverently mentioned by various agencies. By the time he met Simeon, Axel had become more than a highly reputable guide and businessman, but a storied sage. He was esteemed for languages and dialects, familiarity with local government, broad and deep acquaintance with tribes, and for such detailed knowledge that sometimes even professional anthropologists sought him out. Like the Viking idols of his youth, Axel became a legendary hero himself, without parallel.

Axel became so deeply immersed in Papua New Guinea that it seemed as if he had never lived anywhere else, especially after his parents died. Achievements, connections, and competence, braced with adventure, allowed a gratifying sense of success. The land itself became an inseparable part of his spirit and personality. Turgid mysteries hovering over the mountains and jungles intertwined inside Axel with unuttered fellowship. Axel belonged to the very earth and sky of his chosen land.

With due respect for a healthy profit, Axel added to his prosperity by cultivating collectors and businessmen who paid well for his unique expertise and access. Although definitely not a smuggler by any standard, he had connections that helped avoid export restrictions. It was widely rumored that Axel passed off various carvings, amulets, masks, and tribal regalia as older and more valuable than they were. He did not bother to deny these stories. If a buyer wanted what he had to sell, so be it. Since time is not the same for tribesmen as it is for Europeans, Axel's opinion of age automatically increased the value of merchandise. A century or two did not make that much difference to certain suppliers and customers. By carefully respecting custom and observing taboos, Axel was an honorable man in a practical profession who accommodated to an imperfect world without sacrificing his principles, a noteworthy if incredible accomplishment.

One of Axel's uncanny personal skills that could not help but polish his reputation was an ability to make intuitively accurate judgments and shrewd guesses about people he scarcely knew. Although he could be as wrong as anyone else, when he was right, people were impressed mightily. Like a magician who works according to subtle cues from the audience, Axel surmised with surprising accuracy what people would rather not willingly divulge.

In a highly superstitious society, his astonishing intuitions only amounted to quickly appraising another person's dress, speech and style, supplemented by a conjecture or two, and whatever other cues he picked up surreptitiously. Axel was smart enough let people think what they might. It was highly useful and he did not abuse private information, never betraying secrets he was supposed to harbor. Rightfully he was considered highly dependable and worthy of much respect, even reverence.

Axel needed nothing special to spot Simeon, a stranger sitting on the verandah, sipping a drink. Dr. Narub had already given him enough information to pick him out of a crowd of white tourists, on the ready, poking around. Simeon was not an ordinary tourist, nor did he look like an impressionable visitor. He was alone but with a private purpose made more conspicuous by sitting where he could see as much as possible, without an obstructed view. His drink, a local beer, was unfinished, and he tasted it slowly, signifying that he was there to wait, and not be in a hurry for the waiter or for the sun to go down. Axel did not introduce himself, assuming that people knew him anyway, and would not mistake him for someone else. Because he seldom engaged in trivial or idle conversation, while conversing with clients, or almost anyone, he managed to gather enough incidental information for a useful surmise. It was a thoroughly spontaneous habit, not intended to be artful or deceptive, but it was sometimes useful.

"You're a long way from home, Simeon," he said, unnecessarily, but by this casual remark implying that while most tourists are a long way from home, Simeon had traveled a very long distance for a singular and undisclosed purpose. "And you'll be here for quite a while." Information about the cancer from Narub suggested that Simeon might never make it home, wherever that was, but at best, his visit would not be short. Instantly Simeon concluded that Axel knew all. In just sitting there with his now and future mentor and guide, it was as if his goals were already declared, without putting anything further into words. He therefore fell back on strategic silence and said nothing.

"You will be here, in this place, this country for a long time," Axel said, again, explaining that Liaagam was not to be confused with its larger namesake, and that it was pronounced as if the name was "Lexington," not "Lima." Any further resemblance stopped there. He preferred to talk of Papua New Guinea itself. "This place gets into you, as you'll find as we travel away from the settlements along the river. It insinuates itself, without biting you. You may become a permanent visitor on an unlimited visa, which is far from being a fly away, here today, gone tomorrow. There are places where you'll feel a little risk, and the risks are real enough. This is not a jaunt or an outing. However, by the time we get very far up the river you'll start to smell the cinnamon and flowers. The foliage will reach over, almost touch you, and you'll hear and see a few crocodiles splashing into the water nearby. If you're careful, the crocodiles won't risk being killed. There will be tribes staring at us and you stare right back, if you can see them. But don't cry out or try to converse. You are and probably always will be a stranger, so act like one, and don't try to make friends. This is not Chicago. The steady flow of the river will seem quite familiar, even though you've never been here. Rivers are not the same as back home. Then it will turn from the familiar to the fascinating, I have never lost this sweet sense of novelty, even of everyday sights. After awhile, it will seize you, too. You'll feel possessed, whether you want to or not. It will happen, and you can't oppose it. How long you stay here is your affair. I've been here a long time and still feel myself melting into wherever I am. That's a long way off for you, but welcome, and I hope that our mission will be productive, and profitable."

This was a deliberately short introductory peek into Axel, the sentimentalist and the true professional, not attempting to mystify as much as to enlighten with a tiny paean about this land. He was a little more talkative than usual because he did not want to go into the high potential for disappointment, nor the rigors and utter loneliness that sometimes overwhelm an outsider. And he was clearly aware of the uncertain but extensive cancer in this stranger who seemed on the surface so well. He had called it "possessed," as if being here combined rapture with capture by native spirits putting in their claim.

"I am not sure what to expect, of course," Simeon said, "Dr. Narub is one of your admirers, and I'm sure he told you much about me." Axel chose to ignore this question and compliment, not accepting an invitation to talk about Simeon's search for a cure. Instead, he continued.

"After we get away from the customary stopovers, the wilderness opens up, and you'll meet very few people, perhaps roving bands not so friendly that we'll steer clear of. Maybe you'll run into a missionary or two, common as the bugs around you now, and just about as welcome. I tell you this because you must take care to observe the customs, which you don't yet know, and not ask too many questions of people you also do not yet know. It could be taken as crude intrusion, or an insult. Don't misread the apparent regularity and calm around here. Do not get close or even friendly with the native people, especially the women. You can be friendly enough by greeting them, but not friendly in the way you are familiar with. No seduction, whether you mean to or not. No eye contact." Axel was stern, firm, and considerate at the same time. This was not a casual conversation.

"When do we leave?" Simeon asked, rather hastily, interrupting Axel. "I suppose it'll take time to get ready. I'm anxious to get going." Of course, he should have known that Axel's admonitions were friendly warnings about being too eager or too ready. They would leave when Axel said so, not earlier and without good reason, not later. Simeon was acting as if he hadn't exactly heard Axel's precautions because he asked no questions about the people and the customs he might offend unwittingly.

"You won't have long to wait. Tomorrow is the time. Meanwhile, I've put you up at this fine hotel here," gesturing to the upper floor, earnestly, with a slight trace of irony. "I shall wake you early and expect you'll be ready." Simeon did not realize that their conversation was over. He wanted to go on chatting. Instead he had already begun his pilgrimage.

"You said something about being here a long time," speaking almost too casually, "How long has it been for you?" Axel's response was brusque, impatiently pushing his chair back. Simeon had wanted a story, and he wasn't going to get it.

"Never mind those details. Never mind how long I've been here and how I came to know Dr. Narub. Everything has its place and I've been here long enough. Everything past is in my memory vault, dead or sleeping. Memories are there but put aside, away for safekeeping. Some day you may be lucky enough to acquire a taste for this place, but that takes time and being open enough to let it get to you without trying to fit in, whatever that means, except that it doesn't work that way. I live here, belong where I am, and will die here. There are some people along the river, living in these tiny hamlets, who swear they already died and came back to life. I do not claim that. I am skeptical, but then I doubt a great many things and believe a good many more. This land cancels out the past for some, and it may do that for you, too. That can be a benefit, like the privilege of starting over with a second chance. Second chances are why a good many people, including expatriates, settle here. I haven't been impressed with what they do with their second chances. Nevertheless, forgetting is a skill that I urge you to practice and cultivate. Very selective forgetting, however. The past should be buried with the dead; otherwise you'll take a lot of shit to your grave. You learn it by yourself. It helps you get along without depending on what you already think is true. And if you really think you can get along without depending on what you already think is true, forget it. You're a hopeless case. You can use the past, or not. If not, forget it!" Simeon shuddered a little, because that's exactly what he was, a hopeless case following a vague promise of astonishing things.

A waiter brought more drinks, which Axel declined for them both. The intrusion bothered as well as interrupted Axel. He waved casually to an elderly passerby who saluted him by removing his hat. Simeon was reluctant to let him go. A group of tourists stopped just a few feet away from the railing separating Simeon and Axel from the main thoroughfare. The tourists looked as if they wanted to take a picture of a colorful character for their scrapbook back home. It was like snapping a photo of a native with a bone in his nose. Axel frowned, and then ignored them. Apparently, they got the message without being told and continued on without taking pictures. Axel had inconspicuously but firmly shaken his head.

"Simeon, one more thing. You are Narub's delegate as well as patient. But you have an agenda of your own, which may or may not work out for a lot of reasons." Simeon said nothing, waiting to find out if Axel knew about the cannibalism and his fondness for breaking taboos. How could Axel not know? After all, he was selected to guide Simeon, not for the scenery but for a special purpose, which Axel must have surmised, even if Narub held that back. Axel continued. "I do help strangers find what they're looking for, or think they're looking for. If it is possible." If he guessed about Simeon's fondness for breaking taboos, it was easy to guess; he would not have taken Narub's bait without it.

"And do they usually find it?" Simeon said.

"Some do, some don't. Like everything else. Most people, except plain tourists, have a personal reason for being here. Not everyone is on a pilgrimage. Some still don't know that they are on a pilgrimage. I call it a spiritual adventure, with a very uncertain outcome. My personal clients usually have a special reason, not just gawking at strange ways and exotic scenery. If I run across clients with a tourist mentality, I tell them to hire someone else, buy a few souvenirs, eat the food, take pictures, and leave. I am not rude, but it's more comfortable that way. And then there are people looking for things I can't help them with. They may want to hide out; they're fleeing from something. I don't particularly care unless it's a felony, or a legal problem they might want me to do something about. This is a good place for outcasts, but it isn't the only place to lose yourself and never be found."

Axel took people on their own terms up to a point. But they might not realize their actual terms until too late. If Axel didn't like the terms, that was the end of it. And he wanted not to waste his own time and skill for something neither feasible nor significant. Simeon recognized that this was an indirect compliment. Axel must think Simeon was someone worth bothering with.

"I am not exactly an outcast," Simeon said, "I am not being pursued. In fact, it's the other way round. I am a pursuer on a mission of sorts. No one cares where I am, or who I am, except Dr. Narub, and for his own reasons. I am in a hurry to get somewhere before I die. You must know that I already harbor my death inside me. It's advanced cancer, up until now not helped by anything medicine has to offer. I feel OK, but inside, it's another world." All this, Axel already knew, and said as much. Simeon did not add that he hoped cannibalism according to legend might cure his disease. Axel must surely know that legend, too. Even thinking it sounded outlandish. He was not at the point when he could nonchalantly call cannibalism an "alternative medical treatment." Axel seemed to understand without being given details.

"People with cancer have come here before, looking for a magical cure in the jungle, some secret remedy hidden in a berry or in an insect's wings, entrails, just for luck. It's just another upside down bias, that a primitive will know something never guessed by white men, with all their education. As a rule, practically always, I tell them to go home, somewhere else, save their money and hopes. Settle with fate or whatever it is without being here. I am not a magician, only a guide, and not a trickster. I refuse to let them become dupes of the rascals around here, who are all very willing to promote a cancer cure and get a buck or two. The native doctors are worse than the white bastards." Axel was firmly heating up, as if preparing to denounce whatever outrage he chose on this hot afternoon. "Look, Simeon, it wasn't just the advanced cancer that brought you here. I know that and Narub doesn't. And it isn't sex, either. I let tourists know that if they are after strange kooky, fancy sex, please go away. Bangkok is a better place, where there is a sex industry catering to white tourists of means. They provide everything and anything, including STD. There is no cancer cure there, either. Stay home, near doctors who know enough to help, if possible, although maybe no cure. I agreed to take you on because you are on a mission, not a tour, a pilgrimage, whether you know it or not. Please do not argue. I am not sure what the outcome will be. I can get you to the Highlands. But after that, my influence may not be enough. You may be refused on the spot, or be denied permission to stay long enough. It's a chance. There are a few tribes that observe and honor certain ways of life, including cannibalism that outsiders find grotesque and even criminal. They don't like white people, for good reasons. I don't know how they'll take to you. If a white man is a cannibal at home, and there are some who do come here to practice their perversion in peace, they are lawbreakers in their own country, and the tribes won't have anything to do with such an outcast. For that matter, neither will I." Simeon could only wonder if he'd come this far, only to be turned back. However, right now, cannibalism was only a weird unrealized fantasy, not a way of life, hardly as strong as his penchant for old women.

"I am honest with you. I have done things back home I'm not proud of," Simeon responded, "But I did not break any laws, or not many, not very serious. I'm against that. I am fascinated by the forbidden. I just have no appetite for crime. That's all. There are many things forbidden by our customs that aren't illegal, mostly unmentioned. But if eating human flesh has a hidden power to shake cancer loose and let me go, I'll be grateful and take whatever chance there is!" Had Axel already surmised this truncated confession? Indeed, Axel already knew that for Simeon cancer was more than an illness. It was a slumbering menacing ghost of a god, temporarily silent, but liable to stir up at any moment. Then it could become angry and devour leftovers.

Simeon said nothing further. Both men noticed a white man not far away gruffly yelling at a couple of natives to speed up their work. He cursed them loudly and unnecessarily. Simeon wondered which was worse, to be a slave with a master like that, or a cancer victim, also unable to control his own fate. Maybe the slave was better off, with the choices he had but didn't use. And he was just as annoyed by this new habit of always reflecting on his plight, always comparing himself to someone else. He wished he'd been born a beast of prey who simply and without forethought ate its own kind without qualms, just out of animal hunger. Do beasts of prey have a conscience?

Axel seemed ready at last to break off their talk. He turned to his fee, which was enormous, and wanted to be paid in full before going any further, just in case Simeon decided to leave and not come back. He was a practical man.

"I hired a room for you right here. It's not elegant, but it's as good as they have. Early tomorrow, we'll get as far as we can before stopping at a friendly settlement. That's how we do it until we get to where we're going." While speaking casually, Axel sounded as if he'd just enunciated a principle. With that, he got up and left Simeon to finish his drink, which was very warm by this time. Simeon spotted Axel a few minutes later, chatting and laughing amiably with an older couple a short distance away.

Chapter 8—Alphonz

A night spent in that seedy and bereft hotel was an instructive but hardly auspicious introduction to Simeon's new phase of life. The room was barren and hot, like an airless attic, empty except for a few basic used up furnishings. Odors of cooking as well as other unidentified smells seemed to have found their way upward through cracks in the floor. A single unwashed window with skimpy, transparent curtains tightly drawn permitted him to look out onto the junkyard at the hotel's rear. It was piled high and in no particular order with old tires, rusted machinery, crushed automobiles (despite the few roads), unstrung sofas, mattresses, broken chairs, tables, and abandoned oil drums. There were also a couple of discarded and rotting boat hulls, which had not been at sea for years. Simeon saw no graffiti, and surmised that the hotel either tried to keep its walls clean of visual scum or the potential culprits were illiterate and unable to write a few obscenities. Abundant stands of trees half-concealed the junkyard from passersby, although, from their rooms, guests had the dubious pleasure of seeing it whole.

Turning from his solitary view, Simeon scrutinized the room in which he was expected to sleep. It was not altogether dirty, just shopworn from generations of travelers. A wrinkled sheet retained something of the shape and scent of previous guests who slept on a narrow iron bed. Two thin blankets were folded over the foot of the bed. Prudently, he pulled back the sheet to examine the mattress in case that it might also be the permanent home of bedbugs and spiders. There were none, to his relief, although their absence might testify to the bugs' discrimination. The rest of the room, he decided, was tolerable enough for an overnight. He had known worse, but usually found them fitting his mood and therefore acceptable, much as the punishment comfortably fits the crime. There was an ancient armchair and a floor lamp with a shade in one corner. Surprisingly, the washbasin had both hot and cold running water. Three clean hand towels hung from a rack. A small bar of soap lathered with difficulty, a reminder to guests that soap wasn't cheap and cleanliness was low on the list of virtues.

As evening approached, he doubted if the creaky bed could be trusted to support him all night, should he accidentally fall asleep. The springs of the chair were as unreliable as they were noisy. He heard voices coming up from the bar, and considered spending the night talking with new acquaintances. But that option might raise personal questions about where he was going and for what reason. Axel might not approve of mingling with strangers. There were local customs to consider. Nothing was sure and everything was frightening. Although eager for the morning, Simeon had qualms. There was nothing to read, no radio, and certainly no television, nothing to distract him except wondering if Axel deliberately assigned this room as a contrivance to rethink his decision.

Simeon spent the night almost fully dressed, removing only his shoes. Fortunately, an overhead fan stirred grudgingly and fitfully, not merely quelling the stale humidity but sounding as if it were complaining about being overworked and underpaid. When he did finally fall asleep out of fatigue, a loud knock on the door woke him up slightly, but the banging stopped and Simeon went to sleep again. Then he had a dream, which seemed for a moment like a world to come. It was with him still, when he awakened. He was getting familiar with prophetic dreams.

Simeon was in a strange land and confined to a windowless maze of interconnecting corridors which went nowhere except to cross one another, without an exit. Despite the narrow confines, other people were there, but they seemed more comfortable and less crowded than he. They belonged, and he did not. That made a big difference. In spite of the crowd, he was painfully alone. He suddenly realized that the people communicated with each other only by telling lies. Anything that could be true or revealing was carefully avoided. Whatever they said therefore had to be contrary to what they meant. If, for instance, someone commented on the nice sunny day, they would all agree that it was night and raining. Insults were considered compliments, while a light innocuous observation stirred up immediate animosity. Complaints were regarded as jokes, but no one was smiling. Despite an atmosphere of laughter and fellowship it was grim and forbidding.

Everything was accepted as false, yet people seemed to get along by pretending and prevaricating. No one expected much else than duplicity and fictitious stories. Simeon, the stranger, with no exit and no reliable direction, discovered that he got along best by saying nothing. He was free to lie and mislead, knowing that no one would be deceived, but accurate information was nil.

Simeon knew that this curious world had more than a slight resemblance to the real world he left behind. Genial hypocrisy was far more welcome than candid truth, which could inevitably hurt and antagonize. Lip service about the virtue of speaking truthfully and being a reliable person whose word could be depended on were familiar but fictitious bromides, praiseworthy but used mainly to indoctrinate and mislead uninitiated schoolboys. No one really believed such nonsense. Morality rested on telling lies boldly and with conviction.

Since people expected the opposite could he fool people by telling the truth? Obviously, they lied as matter of custom, not expecting to be literally believed. Beyond bare facts of communication, most issues were trivial, minor, and limited to social platitudes and misdirection. Truth was scarcely an encumbrance since no one cared to hear facts, but only pretended to. Incorrect and misleading information might be very useful, and less intimidating than truth. Dictionaries gave wrong definitions, and fictitious chronicles were devised merely to entertain, not inform about history. Directives were prohibitions, and no one knew or cared otherwise. If you said that all people were liars, no one bothered to prove you wrong. And if you piously passed the opinion that basically people were good, there would be indifferent agreement. It made no difference to say everyone was evil. Everyone pretended to care, but with the unspoken premise that caring was meaningless and thus could be ignored.

Simeon did not forget his dream, which seemed to be an authentic guide to getting along in his new home, if that's what it really turned out to be. Strange as it was, even stranger was the close resemblance to the world he left behind. Consequently, Simeon would need little practice to fit right in. Aunt Gina taught him that there were no absolute standards and he had no reason to doubt that a good pretender with winning ways had it all over anyone who was sincere, honest, moral, and considerate. A deadly serious person with deep devotion to inflexible truths might as well be dead; indeed, so-called universal truths were doctrinaire but false, just in case it mattered. Where there were many standards, there were none to count on. Nothing was absolutely forbidden or forgiven. Exceptions were the rule, but, of course, not always. Any acceptable standard had to be trusted, which meant it should be mistrusted. And so on. Taboos were monuments to the dubious advantage of having inflexible principles. It was likely that taboos were established lies, honored by having believed them for generations. Taboos were commonly accepted policies, with no quarter given to truth or not.

The dream in fact was not as philosophical as Simeon's after-thoughts. He had to learn how to act in order to get what he wanted, how to cultivate and practice deception and misinformation, until he became skillful and convincing enough to make others accede to his wishes. He must be in charge of his game, no one else's. Even as a slogan, truth would be irrelevant. But wasn't that how he'd spent his life up until now? Maybe Axel couldn't be trusted, and would abandon him when convenient. Perhaps Axel's tall talk was just puffery, verbal foreplay just to set him up for a screwing. He was too hungry to cogitate further, so he carefully washed and went downstairs.

Axel was already waiting for him, while eating a hearty breakfast. His aide, named Sam, was at the docks, checking the equipment and supplies. Preparation for their journey was almost complete. There would be a long day ahead, but there's no hurry. No schedule to meet. No rush against a deadline. Things get done only when they are finished. Axel had seemingly forgotten yesterday's instruction about an early start.

Sam was a trusted helper and pilot who had gone into the interior with Axel many times. He was also a pretty good cook, and an interpreter whenever Axel's facility with native dialects faltered. Sam's real name was unpronounceable, so he was called "Sam," a practice that Simeon might have surmised from his dream. Just in case Simeon did not understand, Axel wrote out Sam's tribal name, Setatchkole, which still sounded different from the way Axel pronounced it. Workers were generally known by white man's names instead of their own. It was considered convenient, not derogatory. No one minded referring to native workers by the wrong name, however, neither the white boss nor the native worker. It was not offensive, only a custom that no one thought much about. A day's pay did matter. Simeon came to see that this was a commercial arrangement, nothing else. Tuno was Tommy, Poiva was Peter, Kutan became Kevin, and so on. Calling others by the wrong name was all of a piece with never being punctual and pretending that preparations were under way when they had scarcely begun.

The only sure thing was to be arbitrary and ambiguous, practices well known back where Simeon came from, and observed here too. Indifference to professed punctuality was also a privilege of important people. Disbelief, better known as skepticism, was the way to do business, but not let the other person know that you know. Make-believe was the political reality once it has been established. Simeon had once been Simon, and Simon, too, was a name given to him by someone unknown for reasons never clear. Simon Simon, where are you now, just in case you'd ever been? Simeon was beginning to feel at home. It was his familiar reality, neither more nor less than other kinds of dissimulation.

Then, to Simeon's surprise, instead of delaying their departure, Simeon, Axel, and Sam were quickly on their way within a few hours. The craft was a midsize shallow draft launch, with room enough for the three men and plenty of supplies. There was a cabin below with two sleeping bunks, a galley forward towards the bow, enough deck space back at the stern, and more comfort than Simeon expected. Sam, of course, was not meant to use a bunk, but to sleep on the open deck, near the galley, where he was to be always on the lookout, whether asleep or awake, for hazards and danger of all kinds. Although Simeon wondered about their destination, how far it was and how long the trip, he knew better than to ask. He could not expect a straight answer.

Sam scarcely looked at Simeon. He was just another customer to serve and ignore. But Sam and Axel chatted along amiably in a language both understood, neither seeming to mind that Simeon was excluded. Simeon tried out Pidgin on Sam, who was not impressed, and responded only with silence and an immobile expression. They passed what seemed to be small settlements, little hamlets where children waved from the shore. Large cranes feasted and looked curiously at the intruders, but never landed near the boat. Axel pointed out a crocodile or two nestling quietly in the mud near the shoreline. He warned Simeon about letting his arm dangle in the water. At night, there were loud noises from the heavy forest on both shores that turned the river into a menacing tunnel. Slighter, fainter, less threatening sounds were all around them, night and day. Nevertheless, the same surroundings acquired an exotic monotony as days passed that encouraged listlessness.

Axel spoke to Simeon about many pertinent things, especially local customs that seemed to change with every new tribe and bend in the river. He told stories about the people with the same off-hand geniality as how to identify local waterfowl. Although they had seen no women, Axel repeated an earlier caution about making eye contact. Obviously, he was worried about Simeon. Any woman who starts a conversation with a white man is presumed to be loose, Axel said, usually a prostitute soliciting trade. As a rule, the people shunned prostitutes, but habitually patronized them. The prostitutes were loathed especially for servicing white men, but business is business and often enough, their earnings were welcome additions to tribal economy. Axel need not have bothered to warn him, Simeon thought. The women he had seen in town and along the shore were, for Simeon, repulsive and ugly so that the thought of cohabitation felt like an unnecessary taboo that he chose not to consider. Their nakedness did nothing but revolt him, in case he noticed at all. Tribal tattoos had a negative effect, but this had been true back home with white women, too.

Simeon had always been strongly sensitive to rich aromas. The flowers along the river, redolent with heady perfume, actually had a stronger appeal to his senses than the women, but at first not at all sexual. His libido, damaged by chemotherapy, was evidently dormant, not entirely dead, because he felt a stirring with every new scent that the jungle offered. He did not discuss his specific plight with Axel, who explained how magic prevails among all tribes, guiding every type of conduct and decision, and that sorcery was everywhere. Simeon thought it wise to keep his appetites to himself, although Axel might have guessed.

Axel became more expansive with time hanging heavy. Several years before, a group of anthropologists were set upon, killed, and eaten. A common belief among certain tribes was that white men were capable of evil magic and could turn themselves on a whim into wild animals. This implied that any white man might be a sorcerer in disguise, out to commit an evil deed or cast a spell ending in death. Even a well-known, highly regarded river man like Axel was not exempt. He, too, was capable of sorcery, but only of a beneficial kind, unless, of course, he had a mind to do otherwise.

The launch was in no hurry, and neither was Simeon. Eagerness to get on with his project had already lost out to insidious tropical lassitude. To be and do whatever he was going to be and do would happen without special exertion on his part. Just like Simeon's mood, the river changed from the tree-lined tunnel to a watery course requiring careful navigation. The shallowness was a matter of concern about submerged rocks and tree branches until suddenly the river again became wider and deeper, almost too quickly. The shores gradually receded, and soon became barely visible. When Simeon hesitantly asked about risk of meeting headhunters, Axel sardonically said that headhunting was outlawed. Headhunting tribes and wandering thugs were surely in there, Axel commented, and they might be watching them now. But there wasn't any danger because the tribes were told that they couldn't hunt heads any longer.

Axel had anticipated narrower waters up ahead, and arranged to store his launch with a friendly tribe. They transferred to a smaller motorized canoe with a shallower draft that could go almost anywhere there was water, but there were no sleeping quarters. After spending another day storing provisions, including fruit, coffee, tea, and more fuel, they took off again. The following days were uneventful and apparently safe enough to sleep at night in a clearing on the riverbank, although Axel seemed conspicuously careful. Fog was heavy so Sam kept the speed to a bare crawl. On one occasion, a curious pig wandered into their makeshift camp at night while they were temporarily on shore. It was promptly butchered, making for a delectable, impromptu feast. Fresh fish followed the canoe, almost asking to be speared.

So it went until one morning, just around a wide sweeping bend in the river, the thick woods and foliage suddenly dwindled and were left behind, giving way to barren shores, largely gravel, rocks, boulders, and a few scattered tall trees, well below the timber line. Sheer bare mountains rose on either side to end in steep cliffs overhanging the river. Axel began to act as if their voyage was almost over. There was no doubt but that they were approaching the Highlands.

In a little while they came upon a broad stony beach where a group of men, perhaps a dozen were watching and waiting as the boat made its way to their rendezvous. They were clearly expecting visitors and Sam knew exactly where to land, although he could not have been there often, if at all. His instincts and experience with the river provided the guidance they needed, even about the intentions of strange tribesmen. Simeon was so surprised at the reception that he failed to ask how the men knew in advance, not just about their arrival, but the approximate time. Evidently their craft had been followed inconspicuously or some kind of pre-arrangement existed. Axel did not volunteer an explanation.

Several of the younger men waded out to pull in the boat and help the travelers disembark. According to custom all the men were dressed or underdressed in breech cloths or baggy clothing that covered their tattooed torsos only slightly if at all. Some men seemed to be decorated more ornately, even wearing large earrings, while others were all but naked, with only the slightest shield, probably a gourd, over their genitalia. No weapons were in sight. While the greeting party was helpful, they did not smile or talk more than necessary. The men spoke to Sam and Axel, ignoring Simeon, except to stare at him occasionally. The tribesmen were mostly stocky, heavily muscled, and shorter than their visitors, even Sam. Some were taller, wiry, and slender. But all were exceedingly black, indicating absence of miscegenation.

Axel seemed right at home. He quickly greeted the oldest man, recognized by strings of shells around his neck, and frizzled gray hair, as an elder of substance. The Chief was short, bent over slightly, thin, and deeply wrinkled. Like all the others, he was bare-footed and walked with no apparent difficulty, although the shore was rocky. He wore trousers that ended just below his knees, and an incongruous T-shirt, which bore the words, Philadelphia Eagles. Axel and the Chief embraced firmly, like old acquaintances, then touched foreheads before launching into a discussion presumably about Simeon, the Stranger. The Chief and Axel pointed to Simeon and chattered some more. While Axel maintained his calm, the Chief looked dubious, aloof, and negative about something that included Simeon. Finally Axel brought the Chief over to Simeon for an introduction. Even slowly shaking hands, up and down, he clearly showed misgivings by slowly shaking his head and turning away slightly. However, Axel seemed relieved by the handshake, and so informed Simeon.

"You have been given temporary permission to stay. The Chief granted that. But this first step does not mean that he fully understands what you're doing here. I've tried to explain the best I could, but preconceptions stand in the way. Why would a sick white man come all this way? And don't forget that for these people, sickness has another meaning. He is not sure but that you come bearing the power of bad deeds, even a curse carried over from another place. I vouched for you, of course, but until these people become better acquainted, you will have to stay in a hut at the edge of their settlement and be watched day and night. It's a start, learning to live here, eat their food, but otherwise you wait until you're invited to take part." Axel was pretty pleased. He'd been afraid that the Chief might turn them back.

"What do I do now?" Simeon asked, a little fearful about living quite alone at the edge of the village, if that's what the settlement was, and being scrutinized all the time. That meant he wasn't really alone but a prisoner.

"Nothing," Axel answered, "Just do as you're told and nothing more. See that taller man over there, the young man leaning against a tree? He will be your aide, helper, guard, guide, adviser, watchman, whatnot. Maybe he'll be your protector, too, though I hope that won't be necessary. He speaks only Pidgin and the local dialect, nothing else. You two should get along just fine!" Axel laughed at his spoofing. "His name in English is Alphonz, that's close enough. I've christened him for your sake. Don't make too much of that. Remember don't get too familiar with anyone. Don't speak to the Chief. Don't make any contact first. Don't even approach him. It would be taken as a threat, highly offensive. For now, you are taboo to everyone, except Alphonz. The Chief may address you but then again, he may not. Don't attempt to change or question anything."

Simeon saw that Sam was making preparations to leave, even though the canoe had just been unloaded. Axel explained evenly that yes, Sam would leave but in another canoe, while Axel planned to follow him the next day. The pair then would pick up the launch where it had been stored, and return together down the river. Simeon had already forgotten the name of the village they started from.

Simeon made no attempt to hide his apprehension. Separation from Axel, whom he expected would stay around for a while as a sponsor and translator, was too sudden. What if no one spoke to him? They were unlikely to, anyway. He was set down in a strange jungle, on top of a nameless mountain, it seemed, and suspected of being a purveyor of evil because he carried a sickness that the tribe considered likely to be an act of sorcery. It was hardly Welcome, Stranger. He was already exiled before settling in.

"Axel, don't leave me so soon! For all I know, right after you go, I may be their next meal!" Axel was unconcerned.

"That's nothing to worry about. I am sure they have better food to eat than some foreigner who may yet turn out to carry a curse. A sick white man is bad enough, especially one that doesn't seem very sick. You could be the devil, provided they believed in a devil. You are to be by yourself, just to be sure that you'll bring them no mischief, but the precaution may be indefinite. Alphonz will be there to watch over you and protect the rest of the people from you." Simeon could understand that he was a potential menace to a tribe of cannibals, whether or not he'd be eaten. Maybe they thought he'd suddenly turn into a goat, the traditional sacrifice, but this tribe might not know about goats. Why is Axel leaving so soon? He'd vouched for Simeon, and now puts distance between them, as quickly as possible. Maybe it's just that Simeon is one among many clients and he has other work to do. The entire retinue left the beach, carrying supplies and started the long climb up to the village.

It took several hours of carefully treading an intricate path between the rocks upward to the very high plateau where the settlement was located. Sam stayed behind and soon left, without a gesture of good-bye, even to Axel. Simeon was apparently human baggage to be dumped and paid for.

Climbing was difficult; the tribesmen helped Simeon whenever he seemed out of breath from the unaccustomed effort, as well as the increasing height and the dearth of oxygen. He managed to climb slowly by taking frequent breaks. Soon they came to a fragile-looking bridge put together with large logs, branches and fiber that Simeon trusted was strong enough. It permitted the party to walk one by one across a deep crevasse, not impressive by customary standards, but sufficient to separate the world below from what still lay above. After a short detour along another narrow path, the route turned inward through a kind of stone corridor covered by heavy branches. Finally, on reaching the summit at last, Simeon looked downward and saw the narrow ribbon of the river below. He was gratified about being able to survive the long climb, and felt reasonably well except for waves of fear, and by the prospect of being alone among wary aborigines.

About a quarter-mile away, set back securely from the edge of the cliff was a modest gathering of small cabins and huts clustered around a rough common area. Simeon had not known what to expect, but he foresaw and therefore expected a crude collection of lean-to shelters, impermanent, tiny, covered with thatch and mud, and on the ready to vacate. This was a more permanent settlement, indicating that the tribe was not nomadic.

This settlement was an established community, really a hamlet that could pass as a village, if size were disregarded. The huts were not all crude, and showed signs of being well constructed, with a number of people moving around, working or busy in other ways. Whatever the people were doing, it did not include staring at the new arrival, even though he was white, usually a sign for consternation. It was deliberate avoidance. While they conspicuously did not stare, it was not out of courtesy, but fear of Simeon's suspected baleful return of their look.

Glancing around, however, Simeon saw that there were no other white men, so their aversion was clearly protective. By not looking, it kept the stranger invisible. Meanwhile he noticed women tending a metal vat that was simmering and steaming in the center of the main clearing. The area was also large enough for people not engaged in cooking to gather for conversation and for children to play. Surreptitiously, he did notice the women's casual nudity. He was once again relieved to find no sexual response rising up. Nevertheless, he imagined Axel saying, "Look straight ahead, you horny bastard!" Axel had always been informal in addressing Simeon, since their first meeting. But for the present, there was no problem of violating an order.

Axel had somehow disappeared, probably to continue talking with the Chief and other elders. Meanwhile, Simeon's initial observations were interrupted by the approach of his newly designated companion and all-purpose advisor. Alphonz came over and gently took his arm. As they walked together towards the edge of the settlement, he pointed to a small shack, perhaps less than half-mile away. Simeon tried out a little River Pidgin and discovered that Alphonz was considerably more fluent than Simeon, indicating that Alphonz had probably traveled more than others of his tribe.

The hut itself was as simple and crude as any four walls leaning on one another could be, with holes on two sides serving as windows. The walls were made of clay and small logs with no furnishing except a stool and a mat. The door was made of woven thatch over flexible branches. A pot for cooking was just outside. His bedraggled room at the hotel in Liaagam would be opulently appointed compared with this mound of branches, mud and straw, containing a thin pad mattress to sleep on. It was here that the luxury-loving sybarite of not so long ago would be spending an indefinite length of time. Alphonz lived elsewhere under less primitive conditions, he suspected. Nevertheless, Simeon could not and did not complain. There was no central official to speak to, and he had to assume that as time went on, things would get better, because they could scarcely be worse.

With their sketchy language link, the two men conducted no deep conversation, but Alphonz did appreciate Simeon's shock at seeing his quarters. At least he was not an insensitive prison guard. His broad smile, unusual in itself, was reassuring in a way. As time went on, surprisingly, the two men developed an unusual means of communication, quickly conveying ideas and situations through simple imitative sounds and elaborate gestures that people speaking the same language might have difficulty understanding.

Within an incredibly short time, Simeon picked up a few simple words. English was useless, of course, and although they still mainly spoke in Pidgin, Simeon tried to understand as much as he could of the tribe's dialect. Alphonz was visibly surprised at Simeon's aptitude. A more suspicious person might have wondered if this white man was really a multilingual devil in disguise. Maybe Alphonz had no concept of a white devil, or demon, there only to bring misfortune.

Axel busied himself with talking to the Chief and elders without paying attention to Simeon. But he was by no means as casual as he pretended to be about Simeon's future welfare. Alphonz, meanwhile, had taken over and by intent set about establishing crude communication between Simeon and the few people Simeon came in contact with. Even at this early acquaintance, Alphonz would be what amounted to cook, guide, supervisor and factotum, although Latin was hardly their vehicle of parlance. It took many more weeks of sounds, signs and gestures, some very ingenious, before this was entirely understood.

Uncounted days went by, beyond the quick departure Axel had originally planned. Having fulfilled his contract, there was apparently nothing more for Axel to discuss, besides what had already been said. Yet, he tarried, wanting to make sure that his client was reasonably established.

Then, after another embrace of the Chief and a perfunctory handshake for Simeon, he walked down the path towards the river, there to follow Sam around the bend and out of sight. Later, after Axel left, Simeon and Alphonz went to the edge of the cliff. Seldom had Simeon felt so bereft and deserted as he did now, left alone among a tribe of cannibals. He spotted a tiny speck moving on a matchstick, and realized it was Axel in his canoe. Long ago he felt a little like this when Aunt Gina would depart into the world outside. Alphonz was now Simeon's only connection to the tribal world. Nevertheless, he was under surveillance all the time, night and day.

There was nothing to do by himself, and no opportunity to improve his knowledge of the local language, except through Alphonz. While at first, Simeon and Alphonz spoke Pidgin, accompanied by their private gestures, this changed later on as Simeon overheard scraps of talk among the inhabitants, then tried them out on Alphonz who corrected his mistakes. It was a cumulative experience. Alphonz permitted much more latitude about walking around and exploring what was nearby than Axel decided would be safe. With his natural aptitude, Simeon gradually found himself able to understand more and more. He and Alphonz visited other parts of the settlement, and even ventured along worn paths to encampments further away, where they observed and talked about the people living there. He learned that within a few miles in any direction there were affiliated branches of the tribe, but connected only by paths, seldom by social interchange, rarely by marriage. During hunts, Alphonz explained, the tribesmen could cover even longer distances through the heavy jungle in search of game.

Alphonz did not try to answer when asked what was being cooked in that large vat simmering constantly in the center of the settlement. While tended carefully, the contents of the cauldron were not the customary fare. Alphonz brought Simeon his daily fare from elsewhere. It invariably consisted of a vegetable stew, with small chunks of meat, probably local birds and small animals. Pigs and fowl, at least they looked like that, wandered around, domesticated and ready to be killed and eaten by the village at large. Once in awhile, Simeon ate an entire bird, which looked and tasted like tough shredded chicken or a flavored fish. The tame village dogs were apparently not eaten. Whether this was a traditional taboo, carrying punishment or simply an established preference was never established. One day, Simeon managed to ask if what he had just eaten was human flesh. Alphonz casually shook his head, implying that it might have been, but unlikely. Their mutual learning was generous and productive, largely because of a growing friendship between the two men.

Simeon went barefoot like everyone else. His original clothes were in tatters by this time, anyway. While he did not attempt to wear native dress, which combined nudity with decorative tattoos, he found out how to stitch makeshift trousers together from a rough native cloth. As a sign of glacial acceptance, several younger men gave Alphonz fresh game and clothes from defeated enemies to be turned over to Simeon.

One day, after long isolation, for the first time the Chief paid Simeon an unexpected visit. With delight and respect, Simeon stood up to greet him, only to be abruptly reminded to stay down, sit on his heels or kneel in the presence of the Chief. Only later, as a sign of tentative acceptance, Simeon would be permitted to stand when speaking with the Chief. Alphonz also told Simeon about the Philadelphia Eagles T-shirt, a gift from a traveler. Eagles are huge birds of prey known to be brave hunters with remarkable endurance and keen eyesight, and can soar even higher than the Highlands themselves. What about Philadelphia? They were told that Philadelphia was a large village far away, where Eagles are born and thrive.

On the Chief's initial visit, he addressed the stranger in their native dialect, having already learned about Simeon's skill in picking up the tongue. Up until then, it would not be possible to communicate except laboriously through Alphonz.

"You are foreigner from far away with sickness no one sees, hears, or smells. Bad sickness, Axel says. Inside guts. For us, that is bad trouble.

Touched by bad spirits, but not an enemy. You are no enemy. Your sickness is not like ours. You are not bad. Only strange white man we know. Axel wants to help you. Alphonz wants to help you. Axel is very good man to us. We want the same."

Alphonz was jubilant to hear that Simeon's status was now changed from that of suspect stranger to acceptance as a safe visitor. Now Simeon was allowed broad access to other parts of the compound, which informally and with Alphonz, he already had. He was able haltingly to speak with others; soon he could eat with the senior men in private groups. Alphonz did not always accompany him. By talking to other men, Simeon found that his awkward ability to speak the language improved enormously. Simeon, in effect, was trustworthy.

And so it was. During the times and seasons that followed, Simeon discovered that the indigenous speech was far more subtle and abstract than he had imagined. There were words and phrases he could scarcely comprehend, because the ideas depended on cultural experience and historical events. However, he learned enough to find that the language varied with the person addressed, and often by the status of the person who spoke to him. Simeon was told about matters such as festivals and celebrations, a little about religion, nothing about sex, and conspicuously less than nothing about cannibalism. He saw no one being slaughtered or cut up, so he wondered how often actual cannibalism took place.

Simeon's cancer appeared to be stationary, but his eagerness for human flesh was unabated, and still excited by the prospect of breaking an ultimate taboo. Because human flesh was not forbidden, that sense of violation did not exist in the village. His fellow meat-eaters asked nothing about his illness and said nothing about human flesh. Now, under provisional acceptance on terms he never understood, Simeon was allowed to witness the celebrations and understand the songs. The vocalizations might be called "songs," but they lacked the customary melody Simeon expected. He could see each person, trying their utmost to outdo one another by body painting and wearing ornately carved masks. They sang, danced, pranced, twirled and whirled to exhaustion. The traditional rhythms and shouts were loud enough to reverberate through the forest, and may even have frightened the boldest beast of prey, had any been around.

Ordinary hunting and foraging were simply parts of getting enough to eat, without ceremony or fancy preparation. The men went hunting while the women harvested and cooked, raised children and kept largely to themselves. But there were special occasions for group activities that apparently meant much to the tribe as a whole.

One day, bows, arrows, knives, and spears appeared. The tribe was about to invade another tribe miles away for booty of all kinds, including prisoners. Skirmishing with an enemy was a proud aim of any boy about to enter adulthood. The immediate pretext for this foray was a report that an intruder had been spotted nearby, probably preparing an act of sorcery. Whether true or not, such an incendiary excuse was necessary to declare war, which was often a traditional goal beyond that of food and prisoners.

Preparation was elaborate, day and night, with no apparent thought about the young men who would not return. The tribe made effigies of the enemy, burning, stomping, and stabbing make-believe corpses. The warriors anointed themselves with oils intended to make them impervious to wounds, a pious gesture indicating the righteousness of the invasion. Even if the oils didn't protect the warriors and men died, the act itself was still a ritual blessing that would insure a warm reception in the next world.

As a rule, after a long trip to enemy territory, wars between tribes did not last long, never more than a few days. A minor war could end in a few hours. There was no attempt to utterly destroy or humiliate an adversary. But for Simeon, now a close witness, the victorious foray turned into an elaborate triumph, and with it, finally, a chance to see people eating human flesh close up. A few warriors were dead, but no one seemed to pay much attention, because the returning heroes were glorified. The conquerors proudly marched back to the village, bringing along much food, nubile females, artifacts such as masks, spears, shields, and, yoked together, male prisoners, usually fifteen or twenty. Dead warriors on both sides were evidently left behind on the field of battle, to be disposed of quietly in unspecified ways.

There was scarcely any sign of bereavement: no weeping, no overt sorrow, scarcely any solemnity, and only triumphant joy. Alphonz clarified this. The glory in death is for the glory of the tribe. That is one of the reasons for war, a chance to prove valor and choose the leaders for the next generation, provided they are not destroyed before their moment arrives. According to their religious belief, the gods have already decreed who perishes, who survives and who becomes future elders. Hence, there is glory enough to go around. Names of the deceased are given to young boys with much ceremony, endowing the young future heroes with the courage and character of warriors by now elevated to another realm. Afterward, in traditional songs and impromptu impassioned speeches, they reminded one another about the wonders of life and death that the gods had granted. The celebration lasted into the night and the next day.

The climax came at night when captured female prisoners were brought to the central clearing, stripped of their skimpy clothing, and claimed by unattached heroes who had first choice, of course, before others. These young, unmarried women were the spoils of war and needed to replenish the tribe. When all the females were matched with a suitable male, there was public fornication, with encouraging shouts and cries from the dancing observers. The purpose of this display, Alphonz said, was to form marriages, not public humiliation or rape. Apparently, the girls were willing. It was an honor of sorts, and far better than being a slave or, like the men prisoners, executed with fanfare. Another generation would likely be harvested from this planting of seed.

When it was finally over and the ceremony ended, the captured brides were now ready to take their place in the tribe, and all seemed about to settle down. Simeon did not realize that a far more elaborate performance was yet to take place. It had a separate distinction, with supernatural significance, and therefore was entitled to a ceremony of its own.

The crowd gradually gathered in the public square where the tribal fornication had taken place. Indeed, visitors from friendly nearby tribes were invited and judging by their numbers, did not decline. The growing noise foretold what was going to happen. Then the ceremony began. First, the yoked prisoners were brought to the center, their bonds cut away, and the men lined up in straight formation, side by side. Their bodies glistened with lurid paint in red, green, and purple patterns. Figures and symbols were garishly different from the regular tribe, indicating special selection for the beheading about to take place.

The assemblage now became silent. The Chief came forward and despite his age began an impassioned oration. Simeon could not follow the Chief's speech, although it had a rhythmic, undulating flair not unlike a Western politician celebrating a patriotic holiday. As he spoke, the Chief walked along the line of prisoners, touching each man, loudly commanding him to kneel and put his head on a large concave stone block that four strong men had carried in. Each prisoner's head settled on the stone, and he was quickly beheaded, while his companions stared straight ahead, stoically waiting their turn. The same happened to the others, in succession, as the Chief slowly passed. The blood spurted in almost every direction, but was deftly caught in buckets made of heavy animal hide, until the beheadings were complete. The severed heads were placed on an elevated altar, while the bodies were laid side-by-side on parallel mats. The heads and the bodies were to receive special treatment.

The crowd once again began to stir after being silent during the executions. With murmurings of joy mingled with shouts and cries, they eagerly waited for what was about to happen, as if the beheadings were not climactic enough. Simeon's alarm added to his excitement. He began to tremble. Was he at last to witness cannibalism in this flamboyant, yet sanctioned violence? Would he be invited to eat the fresh bloody meat of another human? As it turned out, he was not ready for that distinction.

Prominent subchiefs and local shamans who were there in ample numbers flourished ceremonial knives as they approached the dead bodies lying in a row. Almost together and with skill derived from practice, each man made a lengthy central incision from the top of the chest down to the groin. An experienced medical examiner could do no better. The chest was opened, ribs pulled apart, the heart brought out from its sac between the lungs, and held up, dripping with fresh blood, as a remonstrance for all to see. The same went on until every body had been cut open and the heart extracted. The people cheered in sharing the celebration.

Nearby on the altar, after sawing through the skull, a more prestigious event was going on. The Chief and several elders removed each brain. Then, the two precious organs, heart and brain, were elevated for all to behold in awesome wonder. The tribe's doctrine held that the heart was the organ of courage, and the brain, the source of character and virtue. It was clearly a supreme moment, and just as victors had first choice of females, they also had the privilege of being the first to eat the heart and brain of their former adversaries, so recently killed. It was a privilege of almost sacred proportions. Symbolically, as the victors exercised their right, cannibalizing the dead foe made them spiritual kin, brothers in death, and honorary members of the tribe. Furthermore, eating the heart and brain enhanced each warrior's courage and character.

Simeon prepared for all this through reading and conversations with sundry experts back in the United States, although none had actually witnessed the ceremony itself. It was a privilege not to be shared unless with others specially invited for the occasion. Actual participation was still another honor delegated to the Chief and elders. Nothing he read or talked about could match this direct encounter with cannibalism, performed on the spot, but also magnified by Simeon's own surging appetites. In a little while, however, despite the atmosphere, the vast carnage began to sicken him, especially when he saw familiar people, like Alphonz, drinking blood copiously from a human skull. Distinguished members of the tribe avidly bit off, chewed and swallowed pieces of the hearts and brains, seeking protection against curses and future injury, as well as boosters for character and courage these organs contained. Clearly, cannibalism in this celebration of victory was more than simply sating an appetite; it was an act of communion with tribal history and with the gods.

After the more important people had their fill, the rest of the tribe was allowed to eat what was left. The entire ceremony might be horrendous to an uninitiated onlooker, but its primordial fervor overshadowed the shock of the blood orgy. Former enemies had been inducted into the tribe, the new women joined in marriage, and the victors were rewarded.

The uneaten flesh including almost the entire body except the entrails was carefully prepared for cooking along with other unspecified ingredients in the cauldron that never died down. Always tended by senior women, the sacred stew was alleged to fortify the tribal warriors' courage and rapid healing of any injury or illness yet to come. This was the first reference Simeon had heard of the healing property of the human flesh. Maybe the next reference would be curing a wasting disease? Would he ever get a chance to try it? He pictured himself at another feast of victory, savoring the flesh of a man recently decapitated. In his imagination, he watched that future Simeon eating heart, brain, and then the genitals. The latter had never been mentioned, nor given special therapeutic properties, but it was Simeon's personal contribution to a fantasy. The embellishment surprised Simeon, and it ended abruptly when he gagged recalling earlier escapades.

After witnessing the bloody panoply of cannibalism, Simeon continued to be enthralled and inundated with bloodthirsty images. His sleep was interrupted by vivid images of decapitation, evisceration, public fornication, and huge sacrificial altars awash with blood. Nevertheless, months were to pass before the celebration faded from memory, but he eagerly anticipated the next. Cannibalism was still forbidden to him, and he was no closer to cannibalism as a cure for cancer. As a privileged spectator, however, Simeon hoped that he'd be allowed to eat and drink soon. Nevertheless, he was understandably reluctant to relapse, knowing that he had to become conspicuously ill before being considered eligible for the sacred stew.

Chapter 9—Nyergy

One day, without a premonitory warning, as if making up for lost time and deceptive good health, cancer came back with renewed fury. It was not gradual and invidious, but suddenly, overnight, just like at its inception. Food of any kind became disgusting, he vomited the little he ate, and his body ached with renewed cancerous activity. His belly filled with fluid, puffed out; Simeon turned green with jaundice, itching and scratching madly, as he struggled to free himself from this sickly embrace. Waves of desperate nausea, retching, and vomiting periodically engulfed him. He coughed spasmodically, until exhausted. The only part of him not hurting was his remaining testicle. He was grievously and mortally ill.

Cancer at last had fully eroded poor Simeon. At a glance, even a casual witness would recognize that the signs of incipient death were upon him. Unable to do much more than lie recumbent most of the time, he broke out with ulcers on his heels and elbows. It was pitiable that having come so far and endured so much, Simeon was now on the threshold of death, without even a trial of the ultimate remedy.

Despite his parlous condition, Simeon was not left alone to die. Alphonz tended him with tenderness, devotion, and surely compassion. Even the Chief visited, standing at a distance, curious and aloof more than sympathetic. He might have been afraid of the miasma of deadly illness and the sorcery from afar that brought it on. There was no indication that the white man was any better off than a sick tribesman. Simeon did ask Alphonz about the sacred stew, but got no direct answer. The local shamans offered a variety of other potions and ceremonials that were without effect, except for a flurry of vomiting.

Then, during one fretful day, blurred by pain and numbed with sickness, Simeon jarred into wakefulness by the silent appearance of a stranger who quietly emerged from the nearby jungle. He was not sure if this visitation was an actual person or a tribal bogy brought on by hallucinatory debility and his wish for relief. The stranger spoke in a clear but rusty English that Simeon had not heard for a long time. However, Simeon understood most of the talk. Unlike other hallucinations, the visitor introduced himself. His name was Nyergy, a shaman, there to consult, which was also a term Simeon had not heard from the local shamans. Before he could explain himself further, Alphonz came running up, then stopped abruptly, impressed and surprised by seeing Nyergy. Although Nyergy was exceedingly disheveled, somewhat grimy, and unpretentious, Simeon was soon to learn that he was known and respected far beyond his own distant tribe. Alphonz immediately called out for the Chief who also greeted Nyergy respectfully.

Nyergy's general appearance and modest manner would have set him apart from the local shamans who tried to be neat and dressed with obvious care. Underneath his unkempt, shaggy look, Nyergy was clearly Caucasian, not all black, but still not altogether white. There were ethnic strains moving within him hard to identify, even by local experts. His skin was no darker than a slight tan, and his long brownish hair, while matted and unwashed, had the appearance of originally being straight. His English had long since grown stale, but with a little effort, Simeon could easily make sense of what Nyergy said. He was more proficient, of course, in tribal dialect, but he and Simeon together were still able to conduct a simple conversation. Nyergy was without doubt a product of miscegenation. It was also beyond doubt that he had high prestige and reputation as a healer, although he hardly dressed the part.

While not sure who summoned Nyergy in the first place, at the very first opportunity, Simeon asked Alphonz if Nyergy could get him a trial of the sacred stew. It's not possible, Alphonz wearily admitted, for unspecified reasons, implying that he had already requested it for Simeon. It was the sole decision of the Chief and Alphonz did not claim to know why the Chief had not consented to get the brew that supposedly helped so many others. Nyergy's presence and connection with the supernatural world did not sway the Chief's private resolve, although Nyergy said nothing when asked about the sacred stew. Consequently, Simeon had to accept Nyergy without the promise of human flesh. He was in no position to refuse anything that might help.

"Master," he learned to say, "I am honored that you come to see me. I am dying. That is for sure. There is nothing to help. I expect to die soon, and be the better off." Nyergy did not bother to show disagreement or assent.

"You are white man, almost like me," Nyergy said, "You are bad and good, like me. Much that I do in my time will be good or bad, maybe both. You are dying. That is sure like hell. All must sometime. You see only bad in death, no good in death. You are a stupid man for not knowing better." So they continued from that point, conversing from one day to the next, although Simeon debilitated and almost defeated, suffering sleeplessness and incessant pain, had a hard time remembering what was said. Nyergy sat on his haunches while Simeon reclined against the wall of his hut.

Nevertheless, and with surprise, Simeon found himself feeling somewhat better, engaged, and more alert than he ever expected to be before Nyergy materialized. Their conversation, while not memorable, made Simeon feel less alone. Nyergy's fragmented English also helped with its air of familiarity. They spoke about having a fatal illness, but without specifically mentioning cancer. Nyergy was a shaman, not a physician, and had no medical pretensions. Like shamans everywhere, however, he had potions to give and bizarre methods to try, but in Simeon's case, he decided to wait. Nyergy answered Simeon's questions in his own way, typically without giving much information. Simeon reminded himself that he could be lying, simply as a way of getting along.

"You ask what kind of man am I," speaking first in fractured English, then with combination of Pidgin and the Highlands dialect both were accustomed to. "I see you as man that makes sickness, even this your own. No, you don't make yourself a sickness, but you can make any sickness your own, and not like it." Nyergy sometimes made no sense, until Simeon put various disjointed peculiar statements together, like pieces of puzzle. "My father was mostly white," Nyergy once said, "My mother, I do not remember. I belong to this land, that's enough, with the spirits and gods who live in trees, and beyond all that. I am part of the ground we sit on, talking. The spirits know me well. We all belong to them whether we think so or not. But the greatest god of all is KA, master of masters, of life and death. I serve KA."

It might have been the first time Simeon heard of KA, reputedly the supreme spirit, father of all fathers, and a god for all men. According to Nyergy, everyone belongs to KA, anyway. He meant it literally, just as sons are to serve and obey their sires, always and forever. Simeon had not much thought about this curious affiliation. If he had, it was a true family connection, like direct descent from the gods. If faith were strong enough, then mortal man could take aristocratic pride in his spiritual forebears. It was a romantic notion, but much too Wagnerian for Simeon's taste. In his dire sickness, however, he was amenable to just about anything that offered an edge. Simeon shivered, despite the dank jungle heat. What Nyergy said more than puzzled him. It seemed to penetrate his body and stretch his mind, for no detectable reason.

"What of my sickness, Master?" Simeon said, "Have I created it, or did it come from what you call KA? Will I die without the sacred brother that might make me well?" He surely intended to say, "broth," but the mistake carried another connotation. "Sacred brother" could mean Nyergy himself, or by extension, be a holy link to KA. It was surely a plea for help addressed to the supernatural, or a devout petition stronger than his debilitated self could adequately muster about this world or the next.

"You have the sickness of men, not women. But sickness can be a gift from KA. I do not know. Mighty and wise KA, it is. Where are you at home?" Simeon wondered about this strange twist of words. What did

Nyergy mean? Where did I come from, what country, or where did I ever feel at home? He chose the simplest answer.

"I come from America, a long time ago. Do you know about doctors, not shamans? I saw many doctors at home, some help, but no cure. Masters of medicine." Nyergy had all the qualifications of a quack, and could pass as an untidy physician, except that he asked nothing and promised nothing, charged no fee, and wore no special regalia. He did have shaman remedies, however, and he attributed Simeon's sickness to a powerful god named KA. Was there more than a similar sound that linked KA with CA? Were KA and CA connected beyond mere abbreviations? Nyergy would be unfamiliar with the acronym, CA, and Simeon surely did not know the full range of KA's attributes. It was shortly after this exchange that Nyergy began his ministrations, showing off his bag of rituals and healing methods.

"I consult. I examine," he said, putting his hands on Simeon's head and moving them about, as if expecting a conclusive sign of illness to appear suddenly beneath his fingers. With no further preliminaries, he examined each nostril, and then put his finger inside of Simeon's mouth. He withdrew a small bloody clump and threw it away. This sleight of hand was a common conjurer's trick; a device that pretended to rid the sick body of an offending agent. Such behavior was surely beneath the dignity of someone with Nyergy's reputation. Fortunately, Nyergy made no boastful comment about his finding, but continued to run his hands down over Simeon's bloated belly, while chanting something almost inaudibly. It meant nothing to Simeon, who could only lie back, silent and compliant. Nyergy then reached down and took hold of Simeon's shriveled genitals, peering closely at the penis, as if expecting something sinister to come out, like the bloody clump he threw away. It was a strange and surely asexual procedure, as if equivalent to an orthodox medical examination. Nyergy slowly shook his head, like any other perplexed medical doctor. But he acted satisfied with his findings.

"Yes, my brother, KA has blessed you and you must soon die." His statement was matter of fact, confirming the obvious. Simeon found this commonplace conclusion utterly unacceptable, because it seemed to lack the compassion he had come to expect from Nyergy. "I know what it is to die. I sometimes die and come back from the dead. That is KA's gift. His power may mean bad things, but your desires may also be bad. Not everyone lives, but all must die. Only when good to die comes from KA. Maybe you are not ready for KA." Then Nyergy began to chant loudly, his voice rising to a pitch sounding like a plaintive wail. However, the village apparently heard nothing, nor did the alert and protective Alphonz quickly appear, as he usually did. They were undisturbed and alone, together in a secret rite.

Nyergy poured a liquid from his flask over Simeon's genitals. It stung and smelled like rancid oil of camphor. Nyergy slowly rubbed the lotion over Simeon's penis and swollen lower abdomen.

"Holy ritual or not, this man is now giving me a hand job, and singing at his work!" Simeon was quietly outraged. Saying nothing intelligible, Nyergy's chanting voice changed its tone, from an unnatural tremolo to a deep basso, which then dwindled to just above a hoarse whisper. Yet no one else seemed to hear. He was asking for spiritual guidance. Then he placed a small amulet on Simeon's chest.

"This will protect you...from the evils of the future...from the..." Nyergy spoke so softly that Simeon in his drowsy state thought he heard, "...from the Angel of Death." But of course that couldn't be, considering Nyergy's frank opinion that Simeon was inexorably slipping towards death. Besides, the Angel of Death could not be evil, but rather presiding benevolently over the passage from life to death. Nyergy had urged him to respect death as a good thing and not something to be protected against. He was reminded of the fresh grave he once stopped at and once again, imagined he smelled the odor of fresh earth, so close he was to his own interment. Nyergy's paradoxical belief about good and bad death spun gracelessly in Simeon's mind. After Nyergy's rituals, Simeon once again lapsed into sleep, but again woke up, alternating between drowsy wakefulness and fitful sleep, periodically dreaming or entering a reverie. He could not be sure which it was.

There was huge bird with an almost human head, larger than a raven, but clothed in a toga, like a Roman senator from ancient times. The toga hung loosely, revealing a thin naked body of indeterminate sex underneath. Maybe it was both male and female, but hardly human. Simeon had never known a hermaphrodite, but in the dream or reverie, the genitals seemed enigmatic. People of all races milled around the bird, which did not move or speak. It was a special day for remembering the dead. Simeon was present, unnoticed and dying, but no one noticed or mourned. Then, Simeon felt already dead, but unburied. Neither Nyergy nor Alphonz was around. The bird still uttered not a word, and did not move, like a piece of statuary.

Simeon then awakened completely, hearing a hubbub, then a tumultuous sound from the village, with people shouting and stirring. Alphonz now came running, excitedly announcing breathlessly that Axel had returned. There could have been no more noisy and respectful gathering if a god had decided to materialize. Something momentous was about to occur. More people clustered around the recumbent Simeon than had ever gathered there before. The throng parted, and into the midst, quick and resolute, looking only for Simeon, came the familiar and welcome figure of Axel, towering over everyone. The Chief was not far behind.

"I only heard a few days ago that you were sick again," Axel said, urgently, "Dying is the right word, now that I see you. I came as quickly as possible. You thought I'd forgotten you? You're sick and you're wrong. Both."

"I wanted you to be here," Simeon said, "But I didn't expect you. A shaman not of this tribe, named Nyergy, has been here and helped me turn from dying a bad death by myself to whatever is happening now. I dreamed that I actually died but no one noticed or cared because they were busy celebrating death in general." Axel did not acknowledge Nyergy's name or presence. Simeon admitted that he was becoming very alert and alive, the closer he came to death, as if it were an experience he didn't want to miss.

"I might not have come back," Axel said, "But when I heard you were dying and still didn't get what you came for, that was not fair. Not that being fair makes any difference. But you certainly earned a share of that sacred stew for sticking it out for so long. You've done your part, and more! Why you didn't get the damned soup, I intend to find out. This Nyergy, I know him. White guy, mostly white, that is, went native years ago and became a shaman, very odd fellow. I'm not sure how he did it. Maybe psychotic, too. I suppose he gave you the same old treatment, putting that smelly stuff on the belly and around your crotch. I know his methods. He sings so loud he wakes the dead or rouses those almost dead like you. Makes you feel better for a while. Plays with you and that might wake you up, too. But why no soup?"

Axel laughed sardonically, ignoring the crowd, and not hiding his fury about Simeon's not getting the stew. It was a tacit admission that even Axel had some confidence that this cannibalistic preparation might, after all his doubts, have some therapeutic use. Whether useful or not, to withhold the stuff offended Axel. It was downright discrimination. He turned to the Chief who had been standing by.

"They will not refuse me." A pronouncement could not be so firm and sure, without otherwise offending the gods.

Axel and the Chief began negotiating. Their conversation became agitated as it went on. At one point, Axel interrupted to address Simeon.

"You ought to get the sacred soup, since all of us treat KA with respect. If you do die, I want it to be in peace, a good death, not wracked with so much suffering." He spoke again to the Chief, who was joined by other elders; some were against giving Simeon the benefit of the stew. In a private aside Axel addressed Simeon in English, "I am pretty sure the Chief will relent and give you the sacred stew, blessed porridge, no matter. He claims that he thought you had a white man's curse. Don't try to figure it out. You've been here too long for that crap. It beats even me. He owes me. That's the main clout I have. He wanted to get rid of you even though you're a good white man. I can't count or name all the gods they have. Most have no names. But KA is the tops." Axel seemed to be calming down, his cause won. He shifted from angry argumentation with the reluctant Chief to the religious beliefs, here in the Highlands, like a lecturer with a single student.

"KA is the main god. He decides about life and death. I said, "He," but KA could be a hermaphrodite, like some of the Indian gods. Actually, there is an Indian god called KA, now that I think about it. He decides who shall live or die, whether in war, accidents, sorcery, and sickness. He is a god you want to have on your side. No one here commits suicide. That would be too audacious, takes the decision away from KA. You and I can understand the aboriginal mind only up to a point. Then I get baffled, but only because there is no idea of fair play, except for something like revenge. Maybe they thought you'd suicide, which they don't understand, and leave a legacy, which they surely don't need. KA has nothing to do with the white race. The Chief didn't know what to do, as you got sicker, so he called on Nyergy, a part white man but a big time shaman. I suppose the Chief was afraid you'd kill yourself, as white men do."

Simeon couldn't follow Axel's exegesis but he got the drift. He didn't feel like dealing with abstractions. He just wanted to get some human meat inside him and see if it made any difference. Simeon was now able to sit up, but also with surprising strength, got to his feet without assistance. Nyergy was not quite forgotten. Axel was not done when Simeon's strength gave out suddenly, and he quickly sat down again, bracing himself against a solid root.

"Nyergy is supposed to be very close with KA, who picks his own friends," Axel went on, relaxed now that he had persuaded the Chief to relent. "I'm not sure about KA's powers. I don't take to the born-again business, shamans coming back from the dead, and all that. I have heard that it happens, though, from people I think ought to know better. I mentioned it to you. The story usually comes from white men who have been a little too long in the jungle, and of course, it's part of what the tribe believes. One miracle is as good as the next, and I'll take them as I find them. Why Nyergy puts the stuff on your genitals is not for me to say. I've heard that sometimes he mixes semen with plants that burn and then rubs it all over you. Maybe you got off easy. I've heard of other kinky tricks. KA is supposed to be the one who decides who shall live and who shall die. Sometimes he gives a clue. A bird is supposed to sing from a place high up around the time of death. It might signal that a very sick person would recover or die, and might tip you off about what KA is planning. It all depends on what happens, whether the person lives or dies. Not logical, but who expects that? The bird sings anyway, except I don't know who hears it. I've heard it said that if a very sick person has a dream about KA, or the bird, or becomes delirious, pretty typical of extreme sickness, that's the equivalent of actually hearing the heralds sing, just like Christmas time, except no Santa. It means that someone is about to join the gods." Upon hearing Axel spout on in this way, Simeon decided not to tell about his own, very recent dream, which seemed to have the same imagery. What a dream, a prophecy all by itself! But he was now pretty sure that the humanoid bird with ambiguous genitals had a lot to do with KA and the spirits, including a sign that death was imminent. Did the obscure genitals have anything to do with Nyergy's hand job? Simeon wanted to be sure about the Chief, whether he was still adamantly against the stew. Axel was positive he'd already relented, the other elders notwithstanding. Axel ought to know.

"The Chief's no dictator, but he might as well be since he's a traditional ruler. He told me that you hadn't heard the Ohwai bird and therefore couldn't get the blessed broth," Axel said, "I guess you weren't dead enough for him, or still too white. The Ohwai only sings when someone is really about to die, which applies to you, or when KA decides that someone is about to recover. Pretty smart bird, having it both ways. A good story doesn't have to be true. No one is absolutely sure about ever seeing the damned bird or hearing it sing at all, ever. Well, people who usually die may first be in a delirium, or they could be delirious and then recover."

Simeon now reconsidered and carefully told Axel about his dream. Whether dream or reverie it looked like an omen of impending death, which no one needed to confirm, since Simeon was already so deathly sick. But there was no omen about recovery, only the bird, of all things, ready to orate, like a Roman senator or like Axel spouting off, still not singing. Axel did not respond to Simeon's dream, as if he knew without being told.

Axel went away, and then had a more serious and solemn talk with the old Chief, off at a distance from the crowd that dwindled during the negotiations. It was surely no holiday, but they might have been anticipating Simeon's demise. Simeon was not ready to accommodate them.

"When I die, as it looks now," Simeon asked Axel when he briefly came back, "Will they cannibalize me?" This was one of first questions he asked Axel after they met. "Until you came and put pressure on the Chief, I was sure I'd die soon, without the meat I came for. For that I could have stayed with Narub, Barton, or old Dr. Pochapin. No, I want more than a taste of that precious stuff. Maybe it'll turn out to be just another bowl of soup, coming from a cafeteria. But I have to know."

"No cannibalizing of you," Axel said, "They only eat someone whose good qualities they want to keep. He's not at all convinced about you. Not sure about your valor, I suppose, although he likes you pretty much for a white guy, enough to call in Nyergy. I told the Chief about your dream. That may have finally convinced him about the bird and you."

Axel's purpose was to convince the Chief that KA took a special interest in Simeon's case. Consequently, he might have embellished the dream a little. Simeon was not to be ignored and allowed to die, without the risk of offending KA. Axel was smiling, pleased at his persuasiveness. He had overcome objections.

"Finally, they will treat you like one of their own. Absolutely. The Chief was impressed with the dream. From now on, eat hearty! All the soup you can swallow, smelly as it is. At last, you can be a cannibal! Isn't that great?" Axel was gratified and sardonic, all at once. "You'll still be white. If you don't get the stuff, there might be hell to pay. I mean it. KA could wipe them out!"

Now, at last, Simeon was to be allowed his cannibalism, with no more delay or symbolism. It was incredible and yet satisfying, buoying hopes for a miraculous cure, no less than tangible acceptance into the tribe. At this moment, his head, heart, guts, and genitals quivered with anticipation, even in his present weakened state. In most societies anyone who ate human flesh would be considered a pervert, and be ostracized. Here, however, cannibalism was the most direct and appropriate method for combating an illness, especially in a distinguished person. Although frequently referred to as an illness, even cancer was primarily the consequence of a sorcerer's curse.

Simeon had not been able to hold down solid food during his most recent days. The sacred stew, now brought to him solicitously by Alphonz, had to be doled out carefully, and eaten in small amounts. The meat was tender enough, but the stench, combined with all the stuff that was added, was horrendous. Fortunately for Simeon, it was strong enough initially to blot out the taste of human flesh, and the others tastes as well. Simeon was even able momentarily to put aside awareness of what he was doing. Vomiting took over for a day, and then stopped. Within a few more days, the meat became much easier to accept and became quite palatable. Simeon then ate a full bowl of well-cooked and steaming stew, which went down without trouble. In succeeding days, the sacred stew became routine fare; losing the anticipatory thrill about breaking through another taboo. Neither disgusted nor enchanted, Simeon was now solely concerned with the state of his health, and looked daily for signs of improvement. This meaty infusion not only tasted pretty good by this time, despite its smell, but it surely should have other effects, too. It was the very last taboo that could legitimately be breached. After such a long preamble he felt a little letdown. He even laughed at his use of "legitimately."

Simeon's improvement was steady without setbacks in his state of health and appearance. Miracles should happen faster, he thought, grateful nonetheless. But he did feel better, little by little, day after day. The change was much more than in losing his symptoms, or drawing back from the grave. He thrived, gained weight, lost abdominal swelling, pain went away, and the ghastly green of his body became a healthy tan. Still surprised by the successful recovery, he was up and walking about, conversing, enjoying good health, eating the village fare, and always at least one bowl of the blessed broth daily. He switched from the sacred stew to eating solid food, steaks, and fried morsels he hesitated to identify. No gourmet, Simeon did prefer lightly roasted meat, with no blood oozing, only a healthy pink with a dark brown crusting on top. It gradually came to be no different than any hearty roast. He was afraid that this newly discovered taste, like that of young lamb and pig, might lead to cannibalizing children, a frightening thought that henceforth he kept privately suppressed in tight compartments.

Simeon knew he felt well, but was he cured? Did KA spare him for a reason? With the full devotion of an appreciative, grateful and obedient convert, he could scarcely wait until KA disclosed what next to do. He was ready for a holy directive. For the first time in his life, Simeon was a true believer, that is, besides what Aunt Gina taught him so well. Magic is not for everyone, and cannibalism can hardly become a popular and widespread human institution. Nevertheless, Simeon was convinced that KA had plans for him. Almost surely this must include the healing power of cannibalism and shamanism, in which Simeon now fervently believed.

Since his recovery, Simeon also acquired higher status in the community. The Chief and surely Alphonz enjoyed seeing how Simeon's once wasted frame filled out and the protuberant abdomen shrunk. That he was a white man of uncertain purpose did not seem to matter. Although Simeon, to his surprise at changing standards, began to notice and relish the sight of an occasional woman of the tribe, he also recalled Axel's firm admonition. There were no other temptations. Instead, as an honorary tribesman, he was invited to join with others in hunts. They taught him how to use a bow and arrow effectively, how to spear a wild animal, carve up game, what to forage for or let alone. He had already learned much, but now his aptitude showed itself again in treks through the woods in pursuit of food.

169

No longer in doubt about his cure and status, Simeon came to believe that he was a special kind of superior aborigine. One day, he found a strange young man prowling a campsite and rummaging through various articles that had been hidden. Not knowing what to do with the quaking prisoner, an older companion simply told him to run the culprit through with his spear. Simeon did so, despite misgivings, and found himself approved, not condemned, by his fellows. He was treated like a minor hero who had successfully protected the sanctity of the campsite. Although, afterward, nothing much was made of the episode, it was a key moment for Simeon, who found he could murder for the mildest of crimes, and be praised for it. Nevertheless, honorary aborigine or not, murder never became wholly acceptable to him.

Simeon sincerely became whatever his honorary and somewhat exalted tribal self called for. His gratitude towards Axel went beyond mere appreciation, and his devoted brotherhood with Alphonz was firmer than ever. Even the Chief, despite his early opposition about the soup, came to deserve a share of respect. Fulfilled as he might feel, and despite status of an honorary aborigine, Simeon remained an outsider, and he knew it. It was more than simply the indelible pigment of his skin. It was in his character firmly linked however tenuously to his past. Consequently, he refrained from some of the practices of the tribe that would identify a true member, which ranged from marrying to typical tattoos. He also remained celibate, an inconceivable achievement for the old Simeon. Among his secrets, carefully kept guarded, was that if he were ever to copulate with a woman, she could only be from his kind of civilized society, not a tribal woman, heretical as this thought might be. He was still a white man, with bias and taboos other than those of his adopted family. Although he had harmonious acceptance within the tribe, much of it depended on hiding these persistent prejudices and entrenched beliefs that he would like to disavow, but could not.

One evening towards dusk, for dinner, Alphonz brought Simeon a very large decorated fish head. The body had been cut away, and another much smaller was in its place, clearly not the body that the main dish was born with. It was not unusual to festoon meats and fish with local vegetables and fruit. But here, the fish head was by itself a special treat that Simeon was supposed to relish. This time, however, Simeon found himself staring with a sense of gloom into the clouded eyes of the fish. The fish though dead seemed to stare back with an unwavering gaze. It was not something to eat, after all, but an otherworldly messenger, presumably sent by KA. The unuttered message, which Simeon understood without equivocation, was that the fish had knowledge of good and evil that could not now be shared until Simeon deserved it. Their mutual gaze, meeting soberly, was so real that Simeon had to look away in subdued shame. The eyes reproached him for reasons yet unknown. Could this be how KA communicates, through the melancholy eyes of a dead fish? Had a sorcerer, bent on inflicting a curse, been responsible for the rest of the fish in order to send a portentous message? He asked Alphonz about the fish head. Simeon was mystified.

"It came from the river but a distance from here. The nearest tribe is kin, and I was given this fish special for you, the white man who lives like one of us. Fish heads are good to eat, but not this one, I think now. It was maybe the size that made it different. I should not have let them prepare it for you. I don't know about its missing body. Yes, the body was missing so I substituted the one that our cook prepared. Such a fish belongs in the river, and never eaten. Its dead eyes see into the clouds, which is why its eyes are cloudy. Fish see days yet to come." There was something else that Alphonz did not speak of, until Simeon pressed him. "The eyes weep, because soon you will leave and go back to white man's land." Alphonz was sad, and turned away. It was true, although Simeon had no thought of it until now and then with shame for abandoning his tribe.

Simeon acknowledged Alphonz's prophecy. It was an accurate prediction. He could not stay here until he died, not now. The purpose of his mission was clearly from KA, reflected in the fish head's cloudy eyes. Back beyond the bend in the river Simeon will tell white people in the civilized world about his miraculous cure. He also had an obligation to Dr. Narub. For now, at least, maybe for good, cancer had been foiled. His life was spared and now he was delegated for another cause. KA had spoken through the fish head with a message that although unspoken, seemed unambiguously preemptive. His journey back to white man's land was a covenant, allowing him to live, get well, and inform the rest of the world. Recovery was certainly a reason to return. Truly believing in his mission, Simeon's imminent journey could not be separated from his faith in KA. Alphonz, anticipating his absence, wept. Despite full adherence to this primitive god's order, but just to steady himself and retain a balanced judgment, Simeon tried to imagine what a skeptical Axel might say.

"So, now that you're better, at least for now, you decide to go back and tell the whole Western world, expecting that they'll stop, pay attention and make you a big man. Jungle man celebrity, Tarzan with a cure for cancer, a born again cannibal. The world must be breathless, just waiting for you. Especially the women who'll want a primitive man to make them squeal again. You think you're a benefactor, but you're wrong. You are just a very lucky guy, for a reason no one knows, who now wants to take credit and get famous. You're even convinced that a divine authority is backing you up. The stew, even the raw meat, maybe, isn't proven. People will still die and you can't help it. The only reason anyone back there will listen to you at all is because you have a freakish tale to tell. The tabloids will eat it up, pardon the pun. For a day or two, the story will shock some people, then be forgotten, because something even more bizarre will come along, like a two-headed cow speaking Esperanto, or a teen-age axe murderer, a choir boy singing an octave above high C. Only the very sick will care and can afford hope like this. And then where would they get the meat, not from the local butcher but from phonies out to cheat them, then they, too, will die."

Despite these reservations about what was ahead, Simeon's resolve did not waver. It was KA's imperative. Simeon must leave soon. Preparations for his return did go unusually well. Two young men volunteered to accompany him back to Port Moresby. At first, he refused. However, he finally listened to Alphonz and accepted the help. Simeon agreed, despite doubts, because he was a novice at seamanship, and almost entirely ignorant about the vicissitudes of a river journey.

The mountains, river and tribes along the way had not changed that much since he first came through the waterway long ago. He was not at all sure how long it had been, and didn't care. But his doubts magnified each day. He shivered ominously at night in anticipation of all that could happen, the closer he came to his destination, still a half world away.

Chapter 10—Prelude to an Aftermath

Nyergy had silently and inconspicuously faded back into the bush during the heated discussion between Axel and the Chief. Simeon had not heard from him since that decisive day. Alphonz could or would not explain where he had gone, except to say that it was Nyergy's way to appear and disappear without notice. Though still baffled by his methods, Simeon appreciated something about Nyergy's care but was satisfied not to search for his diffident shaman. He had more pressing obligations soon. The events before the cannibal cure receded.

Confident that he had a covenant with KA, Simeon was intent on bringing word of the cannibalism that cured him to the outside world. If the white man's world was dubious and disinterested, it was their loss. If they believed, then Simeon truly would be a benevolent messenger. Simeon did not imagine what an eager world might do about a sudden appetite and demand for human flesh.

He also had a one-sided agreement with himself that the cure was permanent, at least until the message was disseminated widely. But even if he relapsed, just turning a deadly disease into minor but manageable misfortune would be almost as good as a lasting cure. He felt authorized and empowered by KA's mandate. This is what inspired Simeon. How the knowledge of cannibalism would change the world's idea of good and evil was not his concern. He had been delegated by a power the world had yet to recognize.

The question of whether KA and CA had combined to bring about Simeon's cure, or if his recovery was only temporary before another relapse, this time perhaps the final, Simeon did not ponder. He had been pulled back from the edge, not merely to survive, but to resist death, regain full health, and carry back the glad tidings to his own world. Privately, he would have been content to enjoy his singular role of white man who thinks like a native, without leaving. But the episode of the fish head convinced him that he could no longer remain complacently grateful. He had to do more. Cannibalism strengthened his will, courage, character, and determination enough beyond the cure. Of that he was sure, and willing to face the risk that his message might arouse.

Nevertheless, the unsavory pairing of cancer with cannibalism meant personal risk on his return. There was a good chance of being heartedly condemned, if not destroyed in some unforeseen way. His religious and medical authorization by KA, with the apparent consent of CA, fortified Simeon for the risk. Vilification was acceptable, if necessary, along with martyrdom. There was no alternative. And so after taking leave, embracing Alphonz and, surprisingly, the old Chief, he began his way back, aided by his two pilots.

Although Simeon had misgivings about entrusting himself to these two volunteers, the trip went smoothly, with fewer adventures than when he, Sam, and Axel first embarked on his journey. He took this as a good omen. Tribes along the river welcomed the travelers, offering overnight shelter, food, and whatever supplies were needed. Even the crocodiles seemed quieter than usual, allowing the party to pass by, undisturbed and unthreatened. The peaceful trip was so uneventful that Simeon wondered, implausibly, if KA accompanied them, thus ensuring safety. He thanked his two tribesmen, when they reached a small settlement, and with other guides, went on to Port Moresby in a larger vessel. He stayed only long enough to buy clothes, reestablish his credit, get money, and buy passage on the next available plane. Simeon had not seen himself in a mirror for a long time, or worn western clothes. Even the sound of accented English seemed alien. It would take a while before the jungle man weathered the transformation back into a semblance of earlier but now obsolete behavior and then into a more modern version of himself.

His arrival in Sydney was far easier than before. He had no trouble finding the Cancer Center although there were many changes in the physical plant. Glistening new buildings decorated the site and honored donors. New medical towers dwarfed Narub's modest old concrete building, with its small offices and laboratory. Without realizing it Simeon believed with the many others that bigger is better and newer is truer. This must hold true for scientific research, reports of current progress, and inversely for Narub's unimpressive domain. That research and progress might be self-serving and unimportant but big never occurred to him. Therefore he had come to the right place for the latest and best in cancer, while holding Narub in somewhat dubious regard, even considering his influence.

Narub must have stagnated and been relegated to a backwater office since Simeon last saw him. This was ominous. He could not find Narub's name in the staff directory. It was then that he considered the repercussions of his message. Exposure as cannibal might overshadow anything else he had to say. Being ignored could be the least consequence of his expectations.

He could scarcely expect a welcome reception at the hospital and clinic. Perhaps lurid exposure was more likely than acclaim and appreciation of his cure. And Dr. Narub might not be the best sponsor. Although Simeon's recovery might be ignored, or greeted with scornful and dubious criticism, he was firmly determined not let his effort be spoiled by public antipathy.

Maybe only Dr. Narub would be pleased, and while not documented properly, Simeon's return and the report he'd give surely would add extra support to what Narub investigated long ago. Furthermore, to any fair-minded person, there could be nothing insignificant or commonplace about a patient with advanced cancer so close to death that made such an astounding recovery.

Simeon was grateful to Dr. Narub almost as much as to the people and the great god KA he left behind. But now he was not sure. Simeon almost turned back, leaving Narub, as he had so many others who counted on him. Where was Narub? Simeon had so confidently looked forward to their reunion that Narub's absence from the roster shocked him into doubting his entire mission.

Dr. Narub's old reception room that he evidently now shared with others seemed large but unprepossessing, judging by patients and families waiting impassively along the cold and barren walls. The doctors would be late, but this was standard protocol. Their time was too valuable to waste on punctuality. Nurses, technicians, and other employees, identified by different colored coats, bustled and strolled about. No one looked up. No one paid attention to Simeon. No one whispered "There is that white man cured of cancer by cannibalism," "He's a cannibal, and God knows what else, but free of cancer," "That jungle man claims to be cured, but do you know how?" "He eats human flesh, and now says it cured his cancer!" "Can anyone believe this pervert?" "What a freak! Why isn't he locked up somewhere? Imagine posing as a cancer patient!" These were Simeon's thoughts, as he felt his confidence sway. Then, confidence returning, he wondered if these anonymous patients were simply envious.

Simeon was prepared for disbelief, insult and revulsion. But he would resent ridicule or indifference. Therefore, regardless of scorn, those with CA still might pay attention and hear his message. He had come a very long way, endured travail too much to deserve antipathy and neglect. He was a man with a mission; at least that was how he judged himself, and deserved attention. There was no difficulty in finding the staff secretary who perfunctorily acted as if she expected him. There was no other greeting. To his relief, however, Dr. Narub was still there, despite his unexplained absence from the roster, and apparently ready to see him.

Dr. Narub emerged and firmly shook Simeon's hand, like an old friend. He quickly ushered Simeon into the seclusion and sanctuary of his office, unchanged but perhaps more cluttered than before. Both men seemed to realize that without the other, there would have been no jungle adventure. Narub's journal might have stayed unread, and Simeon could have returned to the United States or anywhere to do whatever else prior to certain demise.

Their meeting could have been a moment of mutual congratulation, yet it wasn't. It was surprisingly awkward when it should have celebrated a certain triumph. Despite a show of cordiality there was palpable distance between them. Nevertheless, Simeon, older and considerably changed, was there, while Narub looked changed, too, perhaps more than Simeon. His hair was much grayer, and he seemed to be gaunt and preoccupied. Years in themselves could have left their mark. In order to fill the uncomfortable gap, Narub conspicuously scrutinized his notes, which he probably already knew by heart. Simeon sat there silently, almost as uncomfortable as on his first visit. He waited for friendly conversation, probing questions and wise comments. When he did speak, Narub's words were phrased carefully; diction was perfect, and the quality and timber of his voice as resonant as before. He remained cool and contained, without saying very much. Unlike Nyergy, he was not apt to begin chanting something unintelligible. Yet both men, disparate in most respects, came from and even created their own worlds and had no reason to explain their ways. Simeon felt all alone, instead of in the presence of a benign benefactor and physician.

"I heard rumors about a man who cured his cancer by…but I wasn't sure it was you until you called the other day. I said nothing to my secretary, nothing to anyone else." It was a secret, just between them. Simeon could scarcely imagine why. He was more than a little disappointed that Narub seemingly kept his return somewhat clandestine.

"Yes, it was me all right. Here I am and with a tale to tell," Simeon said, with feigned enthusiasm. "Your journal hardly prepared me for what was going to happen and did happen! You couldn't imagine since you stayed in the area such a short time. I was without symptoms a long time, but the cancer did recur and I came as close to death as a person ever gets, without dying. Now that I'm back, I'm not sure what to do about letting anyone or everyone know. But my recovery should be known to others and give them hope, somehow."

Simeon might have been more comfortable with Nyergy or some other jungle sorcerer than with Narub. And Narub could not quite conceal his disinclination to ask about his time in the Highlands, even though both men had collaborated eagerly in sending Simeon off to an uncertain fate. Simeon knew that Narub had been scarcely more than a visitor to the tribe, that communication was rudimentary and second-hand through an incompetent interpreter, and that his stay was far too short to have more than a brush with sorcery, cancer, cannibalism, and everything else that Simeon spent a long time acquiring. Simeon hesitated about a bold word like "cure," preferring "recovery," lest he relapse right then and there. But he continued heedlessly, "I feel cured, and rejuvenated. I wanted you to know, first of all, and then ask you to decide whether cancer is still there. I've been fooled before, and done some fooling on my own." It was ridiculous, but he had trouble switching to English.

"Well, you're looking very healthy, indeed," Narub was cautious. "Jungle life seems to have agreed with you." What an absurd and belittling cliché! After all, Simeon had not spent a few weeks at some posh Florida spa for rest, relaxation, and a coat of tan, or been on a cruise stalking women. Narub's inane comment was as if Simeon just came back from the dead, and Narub had greeted him with, "Well, good to see you. How was the trip?" Nevertheless, not yielding to irritation, Simeon stayed silent, collecting himself, and turning on a false calm.

"I was very sick for a time, and now, you can see that I am well, strong enough to put up with...Well, whatever I did, I was still appreciative enough to come back." Simeon then lapsed into awkward silence again. What was going on with Narub? He should have been friendly and fascinated, urging Simeon to tell his tale. Instead, he was courteous, cool, and cautious.

Narub then narrowed the disconcerting distance by asking about the journey before and after cancer overtook him again. It was still far from personal. He asked nothing about the trip itself, nothing about Axel, and nothing but a few clinical details. He wanted to know what the symptoms, relapse and recovery were like, and conspicuously avoided asking about cannibalism and the sacred stew, which was, after all, the main reason for the daunting trip. Simeon was astonished by the deliberate omission. Without cannibalism there would have been no pilgrimage in the first place, in either direction. Lying in front of him was Simeon's medical record, cool, clinical and impersonal. By comparison with the actual events, Narub's clinical notes taken out of his sketchy journal were meager and irrelevant.

Simeon had an uneasy thought that Narub was both pleased and disappointed at the same time. Narub actually might have preferred that he not come back at all. Not that he was averse to patients who have remissions and feel better. That was what doctors look for, besides remuneration. And he could not help but celebrate vicariously the successful adventure that he inspired. But Narub looked at him like an unsavory character, who had come back to embarrass him in front of respectable colleagues.

"Dr. Narub," Simeon began again, deciding to find out what was happening, "Here I am after a very long time and a long joust with cancer away from regular doctors. I went through much, and all you apparently want to hear about are my current symptoms and the cancer. I haven't any symptoms, and I see that's a problem. I can't imagine you are indifferent to what happened, besides getting better. I expected more from you. After all, I wouldn't have heard about cannibalism and cancer without your journal and you. Dr. Barton must have known or he wouldn't have sent me all this distance." Narub put down his pen, looking abashed, but not disagreeing with Simeon's reprimand.

"Of course, of course, we'll certainly look you over and see what's going on. I'm pleased with your recovery and surely glad to see you again." At least he now showed willingness to listen, however belatedly, but his listening or willingness was still selective. Nevertheless, Simeon went over his former symptoms again, ending up in a careful narration about the parlous condition he called terminal. He did not mention the important people, the remote country where he spent so much of himself, and in its way, how he got so much more than remission, even redeeming himself. He knew enough not to speak of Alphonz, Nyergy, and the Chief by name. But he did cite Axel because Narub knew that Axel was indispensable. He scrupulously avoided any reference to the key tribal ceremonies that centered on ritual cannibalism and bloodthirsty orgies. This reticence was very strong. After all, Narub's journal gave Simeon more than subtle hints about ritual cannibalism. Simeon was actually an honorary tribesman, not merely a white spectator. Beheading, drinking blood, raw flesh, sacred stew, and sorcery had become part of Simeon's life. He was no mere visitor spending an exotic holiday among the aborigines. It was a story that just in listening even an experienced traveler might feel a rush of horror. Simeon had become a cannibal. This brute fact could not be blinked away or mitigated by euphemism. Simeon could not truly share what this was like. His dedication, which exceeded belief in KA, was certainly beyond the grasp of even sympathetic people like Narub. However, loyalty to the tribe prevented too much disclosure. Then and there, Simeon decided to be very impersonal, and selective about reporting daily life in the tribal settlement. How to talk about cannibalism without a mention of eating human flesh was absurd. There was also a temptation by selective omissions and additions to idealize the tribe, which was so absolutely incorrect, and disloyal in itself.

"Losers lose their life but become spiritual brothers, and get to be honorary members of the tribe. Different parts of the body when eaten promise more than recovery. They also believe in courage, character, immunity from future harm, so forth. Sometimes cannibalism is only for food, revenge for a fancied insult, or getting back a stolen article. Death is easy to come by. There is lots of murder in some parts of the Highlands. When provoked enough, any tribe can be as savage as the next. The veneer is thin, and thinner." Simeon felt as if he'd had his say, very tersely, about the aboriginal mind and the gory side of cannibalism. He was not about to say more, nor did Narub ask more.

"It seems to have agreed with you in every way. You could have stayed there and not come back. Expatriates get along very well, I hear," Narub was now quite amiable, loosening up considerably since the awkward beginning, but they were still at cross-purposes.

"I came back for a reason. I am more than an expatriate. I became really an honorary tribesman. Maybe you can appreciate what that takes. The only reason I came back, besides telling you, is that I have a duty. It is certainly not to tell a sensational story about savage headhunters. That would be a real bore and wouldn't do justice to a people who accepted me, that is, after they got to know the white man. I want to bring a message to every cancer patient who has been given up for as good as dead. I am not living in a fool's paradise. I know the risk. I am a cannibal now, but a healthy one. In the world's eyes, and in yours, too, unless I am mistaken, I am a pariah, something despicable. You knew that would have to happen, if the treatment worked. I am an unrepentant eater of human flesh. That's me. Believe me, when I was at my sickest, my greatest fear was that I wouldn't get a chance to be a cannibal!"

Once started, Simeon's reluctance peeled away and he insisted on telling his story straight, without censoring very much.

"There are far worse things than cannibalism. And for a cause like curing cancer, eating human flesh might be worth looking into, although I can't imagine people doing it, or how it could be done. I don't expect doctors to rise up as a philanthropic body and prescribe cannibalism in some diluted and indirect form for their cancer patients. Euphemism won't do. I expect to be denounced as a vampire or called a pervert of some kind. Maybe I deserve it. Something scandalous. That would be more accurate. If you don't already realize it, I'm not the same as when I left here."

Narub was restlessly shifting around in his chair. He started to get up several times, as if to relieve stiffness and cramps, quite unlike the calm, concerned, and reserved physician who came to the hospital room and talked late into the night about Simeon's future.

Narub was clearly puzzled by finding Simeon without a trace of the cancer, which had been so advanced when he last saw him. There was no sign of cancer whatsoever, remarkable enough when compared to what had been found earlier. Several nurses and technicians commented spontaneously on Simeon's glowing appearance of health. If there only had been a small scar or remnant of tumor showing former disease, Narub might have called this a remission and forgiven Simeon for feeling so healthy and looking so young. But as it was, claiming a cure was not only audacious but accurate. Nothing was there. Besides, this remarkable event, a physical miracle, came about by violating a taboo too extreme for civilized circles to emulate. Cannibalism could not and should not be ignored. But there was no acceptable alternative.

For all his sophistication and knowledge about alternative cancer treatment, Dr. Narub did not welcome professional challenge to his integrity, which was bound to arise when the full account of Simeon's recovery came out. He was no less ambitious than the next specialist or wary of risks in openly supporting anything about Simeon's saga, especially since he tacitly encouraged Simeon to undertake the trip. Proposing a clinical trial to test what happened was completely preposterous, even criminal. While Narub's original interest in the cannibal cure was prompted by curiosity, the living presence of a healed cancer patient was frightening, as if Narub had been caught in a scandalous escapade.

Narub was cautious for still another reason. Even after years at the hospital and in Australia, he was still subject to derogatory innuendo. If he wasn't white, then he was black. Academic promotion had been slow and difficult, and despite seniority he still had to share his hospital quarters with younger staff members. He did not welcome being the center of a controversy, especially about this reprehensible treatment. It might be disastrous. There was certainly no cause for celebration. While Simeon was understandingly jubilant, Narub was hesitant, inclined to do no more than describe the events in his private journal, and keep them there. The furor was waiting to erupt, if there was to be professional publication, and Narub was not up to the challenge.

Professional publication is essential for medical respectability. Without review by peers, medical claims are only as good as one-day newspaper items that attract public attention and then vanish without a trace. If a new medical treatment promising great benefit suddenly appears in the public press, patients promptly telephone their doctors, only to be told that it is still under investigation and not been approved. It is an immense bother and some patients start believing that the doctor on whom they depend is overly cautious or behind the times, which in some cases, amounts to the same thing. Often, the notorious break-through discovery is never heard from again. In this case, however, when cancer cure is yoked to such a companion, a sensational report followed by silence is only to be expected. Even more lurid stories regularly replace the cancer cures.

Narub had several options about Simeon's sensational recovery, whether cure, remission, or whatever it was. Absolute cancer cures are commonly heralded in magazines sold at checkout counters, not in prestigious medical journals. He could write a case report and submit it to an established journal, which might deem it worthy of publication only after it passed a rigorous editorial review. This was unlikely. Report of a single case is hardly worth publishing, and this would certainly arouse attention, predictably negative. Few journals would take the report seriously enough to consider publication. Because the world is full of weird people and curious testimonials, eccentric reports do occasionally slip by and appear in respectable journals, but not those in the top tier.

Narub had still another option, a Letter to the Editor. Without controls or medical monitoring the letter would be nothing more than a collegial anecdote that readers quickly pass over and forget. Narub was not that timid. He knew that what Simeon had to report deserved far more attention. Follow up study should be done, using human flesh, perhaps from cadavers, the key ingredient extracted from raw material, then given to volunteers with matching qualifications, and compared with a group of similarly afflicted patients, with and without a placebo. Reasonable objectivity would require so much further study that it was unlikely to happen.

Obscure journals with lower standards and limited circulation might publish an article with less reluctance. Narub hoped that no reporter would notice and sensationalize the story, which hardly needed exaggeration. Still other options would need the cooperation of an anthropologist with knowledge of Papua New Guinea tribal practices. Narub and the colleague then could write a joint report about tribal cannibalism said to be associated with alleged cancer cure. The anthropological perspective might forestall the tabloid treatment, since matter of fact reports of exotic practices in distant lands among strange tribes belong to the ledger of acceptable human diversity, not medicine. No moral outrage and scandal could be anticipated. The basic dilemma that Narub faced was how to report Simeon's cure without revealing very much and keep it all quiet.

A modulated, practically anonymous report of the bare, but incredible facts did not satisfy Simeon. He wanted to declare his mission openly, announcing the cure to the fullest, and drawing opinions from all over. Narub was firmly opposed, insisting on professional outlets that emphasize recognition, but no implied recommendation.

Simeon's way would surely have enormous repercussions and that was what he wanted. But for Narub, the outcome might end his career. Outraged conservative patrons and donors could be depended on for denunciation as well as for withholding funds. Cannibalism in a distant culture and deranged acts by an individual associated with a respected staff member would surely be counted as the same outrageous thing.

How to tell and not tell at the same time was the debatable issue. Even Narub had to smile at his hesitancy and hypocrisy. Impersonal academic language was imperative. Perhaps they could refer to a "customary tribal dietary component" which "seemed to be associated with an extended remission." But there was no way to fudge the facts. Medical information through professional channels takes months to appear, moreover, while newspaper stories come and go quickly. Journals only present, but tabloids inflate by shunning cautious qualification. While stories can be told in vastly different ways, it was especially hard to hold back on such topics as miracles, sorcery, young girls with holy visions, celebrities in scandals, and, of course, cannibalism. That was tabloid fare, not the stuff of conservative scientific publications.

Simeon did not want to vulgarize his experience. He understood that medical journals were very circumspect. He had not come this far to get laughed at, although he was prepared for severe criticism, such as might follow any offense. After all, he was or had been accustomed to transgressing taboos, or committing unforgivable offenses, although without much publicity. The new Simeon was afraid of gruesome jokes. "Eat your neighbor," "Cancer treatment? See your local funeral director." Simeon was beginning to worry for other reasons. In order to be a benefactor for cancer patients, he had to stay exposed to public notice. As time passed, what if he needed more human fare to stay well? He had no knowledge of maintenance meat. Where would he get it? Was he willing to become a furtive vampire, haunting funeral homes? Searching for human flesh in this society was much more reprehensible than back in the Highlands. It was a criminal offense. Again and again, he felt apprehensive, less heroic and dubious about KA's sanction away from the Highlands. He began blaming Narub for choosing him in the first place, forgetting his own fascination with the taboo.

"I chose you," Narub repeated, "Because your cancer had spread throughout your body and still left you healthy enough to travel. Besides, you're adventurous enough, and affluent enough, with no family to worry about, and no stranger to a wayward life. I guessed at that. That was it, and your willingness to give it a try. You had all the qualifications, but remember, it had to be your decision." Both men knew that the decision was Simeon's, but only after a concerted shove from Narub. They were beginning to fall out of their flimsy friendship, or at least, a working doctor-patient relationship was being stretched to a breaking point. Simeon wanted more, and Narub wanted less, practically nothing of publicity.

"That was only at the beginning, Narub," Simeon said, pointedly dropping the Doctor in his exasperation. "I've done things that the most world-weary adventurers, even Kraft-Ebbing or Kinsey would be shocked at, gone places the National Geographic couldn't find. My years in the Highlands went beyond what most people only fantasy about, if that. You just don't understand that. What I went through was certainly not just an adventure, but also a lot of lonely pain, suffering, and hardship under difficult living conditions. And now I am determined to get the results out there for a message, come what may."

"I'm not just a white man turned cannibal. And I'm not the Simeon you recruited. I'm not any old cancer patient who happens to be in the midst of an unexplained remission. I couldn't stay there, enjoying my good health, while back here are thousands of cancer patients suffering much more than I did. You see I've developed a conscience, which for me is just as miraculous as curing cancer! Maybe there are people sitting in your waiting room, right now, today, waiting for a chance at something that might help, too. Any choice. Even the choice of following me!"

Narub and Simeon were further apart than ever. Yet both shared a common and bizarre experience that they forgot in the dispute about publicity. However, their bickering was finally resolved quickly and unexpectedly, from a source in Papua New Guinea known to them both.

One night in a small but well-known village tavern along a river, far from the Highlands, Axel and an old friend, Nigel, were enjoying an infrequent reunion. An Englishman by birth, Nigel had long been employed by the Australian Government. His assignments over the years had taken him to New Guinea and Micronesian islands, besides the outback of Australia. Nigel retained his British citizenship despite living in Australia and New Guinea for many years, just as Axel held fast his United States passport and naturalized citizenship. In his official manner, Nigel was obliged to seem stiff, formal, and unapproachably bureaucratic. In Axel's presence he relaxed and no longer seemed the prototypical government bureaucrat. Nevertheless, Axel relentlessly teased Nigel about his certain Colonel Blimp manner. They were fast friends, however, and shared many private thoughts and opinions, knowing that confidentiality would be respected, without exception.

On this particular evening, after a lengthy interlude of joshing, conversation, and reminiscence, Axel chose a time near closing to unburden himself about Simeon's return to civilization. His concern was obvious, especially since Axel mentioned no names, dropped his voice, and ordinarily was disinclined to worry excessively, which was all right with Nigel. This however was an exception. Nigel's discretion could be counted on, and Axel needed to talk, although it took most of the evening before he was ready.

He told Nigel about his American client, still middle aged though looking much younger, rich, personally engaging, without showing signs of dissipation. Axel had many curious and idiosyncratic clients in the past, but this man was unique. Simeon had taxed even Axel's intuitive scrutiny and long experience by voluntarily living for years with a certain tribe and undergoing a series of events that culminated in cancer cure. Axel was careful not to identify either his client or his reasons for staying where he did for so long.

An Australian doctor that Axel knew and guided a few years earlier wanted Axel to introduce his erstwhile patient to a tribe in the Highlands that still practiced cannibalism. Axel agreed, and even took a liking to this odd man, although he customarily kept this side of himself under control. Cannibalism had been officially outlawed, but as both men knew, everyone in the know knew better. This man had advanced cancer throughout his body, yet seemed to be in excellent health, not sick at all, even robust enough to handle the rigors of jungle and river travel, and to stay with the tribe for an extensive period. Without being told, Nigel immediately understood. The stranger's quest was in search of cannibalism's storied effect on cancer.

The story was unusual in several respects. Proof or disproof of the legend was irrelevant. Nigel knew of no one who had successfully earned a place in that tribe, even without cancer. The stranger was not the first one to go off into the Highlands, but seldom did they get that far in search of the mythical cure. Their feeble physical status usually prevented them from ever leaving Port Moresby. Those who did soon turned back, intimidated by the jungle and the hazards of the trip. Others were able to travel, but fell into the hands of rascals who exploited them and took their money without recompense. Whether any visitors got near the Highlands was doubtful, and their fate even more uncertain. However, persistent stories about travelers seeking cancer cure were an open secret that hardly anyone spoke about. Government agents are usually prudent enough not to inquire or search the remote parts of New Guinea for every infraction of every law. No one knew if human flesh had any effect on serious sickness since according to the aborigines, illness was caused by sorcery, anyway.

From their years in New Guinea, Axel and Nigel understood that the difference between a tall tale and a factual report was sometimes so small that the embellished tale is more reliable than the basic facts, which often turn out to be just speculation and hearsay. Legend becomes hard information and the truth no more than an easy fiction. Consequently, provided that the cannibals spared white people, especially women and children, officials just looked the other way. It was a Live and Let Live philosophy, very practical, and easy to enforce. Sometimes they had to gloss over some gross forms of inhumanity, such as unwarranted cruelty, child abuse, ingenious torture, and sadistic pillaging. Occasionally, they would have to expose the culprits and demand suitable punishment. If, for example, they heard a rumor or report about a native woman said to have fornicated with a wild animal and subsequently giving birth to a child, their credulity might be stretched. But they did not dispute what was important for her tribe to believe, even when mother and child were killed in order to cleanse her family. After all, tradition everywhere is based on improbable events, like rising from the dead or crossing the Red Sea, which conveniently parted when needed. No true believer or religious zealot wants or welcomes doubt. People have been killed, ostracized, or severely punished for denying or denigrating the firm religious and political beliefs of sects and communities who happen to have the majority advantage.

Axel's story, therefore, did not seem that unusual, unless it was because of his client's tenacity. It was neither a tall tale nor hard facts, but rather an outsider's quest for an improbable cure through embracing an evil. For a white man, cannibalism is always considered evil, and strictly forbidden, regardless of the circumstances. For a native, however, eating another person is an acceptable way of settling disputes and marking major celebrations.

That was not what bothered Axel. The margin between good and evil is tentative, obscure, and variable enough to ignore most of the time, except and unless the evil is egregiously shocking and the good unanimously approved. Both Axel and Nigel agreed on that flexible code. Neither man was altogether surprised that Axel's stranger went to the brink of death, and then made an astonishing recovery after eating human flesh. Since the cannibal cure is known about but seldom documented, it has to be occasionally substantiated just to keep the belief alive. It was remarkable, of course, but most magical cures are. In fact, magic must be remarkable, unusual, out of the ordinary, and fast. Can a magical act be mundane? Is it possible for a miracle to take place slowly over a long span of time?

Nigel promptly understood when Axel finally came to the worrisome part of his story. This man, now a full-fledged cannibal, but bursting with gratitude and devotion for the tribal god, KA, now planned to leave the protected sanctuary of his Highlands home, return to the white man's world, talk openly about his experience, and become an evangelist for his cause. Axel was worried about the dangerous consequences. He did not expect news of the cannibal cure to have an instantaneous effect on cancer treatment. Several things could be imagined. At best, Axel's client would suffer ridicule, severe punishment at worst, or, perhaps worst of all, Axel contended, enough believers and converts to cannibalism would come to the island, hire guides of all types, and inundate the rivers, only to die in the attempt.

Neither man bothered making a medical distinction between cure and remission. But in the course of recovery, Axel's stranger changed conspicuously in ways that were almost as remarkable as getting over cancer, although not as dramatic. In contrast to his previous character, he acquired a conscience, stoutly believed in his mission, and with almost messianic fervor dedicated himself to telling the world about his good fortune. It was a dangerous decision, riskier and more doubtful than coming to the Highlands and living with cannibals. The white world out there would not welcome and tolerate such news, whether true or not. Surely the world of conventional behavior and established truth would be revolted. The pious messenger might be attacked, perhaps jailed, considered a perverted freak, and even lynched. Axel could already hear the uproar. No different than a vampire or an insane criminal, this intruder from New Guinea, wherever that is, could not be accepted, unless by a equally bizarre and desperate people who considered his oddity somehow sacred and deemed him appointed by God to heal mankind. Standard morality, in contrast to the converts, would insist on punishment, without concession. Most people would think that his secret motive was to get cancer patients and families to empty their pockets in a vain hope of recovery, and fleece the gullible.

"This man was about as close to death as you get, and from cancer," Axel said, "It was horrible to see. The doctor who sent him did all kinds of examinations and all were very bad. Still, this curious fellow felt well enough to travel. And he did, without complaints, except about the slow pace of accommodating to aboriginal society. After getting him settled and more or less accepted as a permanent visitor, I left and went about my business. But, as I recall, he got sick after a year or two, then very sick, and was pretty close to dying, all without that magical meat that he came so far to try. The Chief of the tribe knew him well enough, and liked him well enough to call for an itinerant shaman, called Nyergy, who has a reputation. You may have heard about this partially white guy shaman, gone native, who practices up there. He's really not white, but a mixture, speaks a fractured English pretty well, but also understands other languages and dialects, which as you know, are many. He's not a bad guy. The tribe, I mean the Chief, held back on the stew or whatever shape and form the human meat was in. And before he got the stew or soup, he suffered, and I mean plenty, without much relief. No doubt about it. I found out, came back, and raised hell. After all, I was responsible for the guy. I used my influence with the Chief, threw my weight around, a little, anyway. He got the soup and got well over time. Something else developed that I never expected, more dangerous than cancer. This conscience of his is a dangerous thing. It might kill him sooner than the cancer. Furthermore, it could be my fault, talking about conscience. Nigel, I got him that cannibal soup. The Chief of the tribe didn't want to waste it on a dying white man, you know. I insisted. I could make things uncomfortable for the tribe, and the Chief knew it." Both men laughed, because Axel was capable of almost any kind of coercion.

"Why didn't they let him die?" Nigel asked, "A bad disease is not a disease at all, but a damned misfortune and curse. They could blame it on the white man and probably make it his fault anyway."

"I am sure they didn't want him to live or die on the premises. A curse can be catching. The whole tribe might be contaminated, and I admit that I'd be a part of it if that happened! It took a time, I can't say how long, but it was not overnight. When totally healthy, he was grateful and went on to become almost a regular tribesman. Just like a naturalized citizen, he became one of them, although, of course, he wasn't. He'd join in hunts, all sorts of things. Learned how to use bow and arrow, spears, set traps. He liked the ceremonies, but forget that part. He didn't get married, or let himself be tattooed, nor did he have a girl friend. Before he came to New Guinea, he had plenty of women, and some men, too, I think. He behaved himself after I arranged for him to stay, but for a long time, he simply lived by himself, did what I had told him to do, kept out of trouble, and really learned their ways, even their language, which is hard enough. After the cure, it was different. It became a holy mission to be a special messenger appointed by KA. This fellow is asking for trouble, and I'm sure he'll find it."

Axel had told Nigel as much as he could about the stranger's recovery and newfound conscience. An excess of virtue can kill you, too, Axel said wryly. Without self-interest, unadulterated benevolence and altruism for the masses can be fatal. Axel and Nigel browsed on about the fellow, exchanging viewpoints, without arriving at any enforceable conclusion. Axel might have felt better just by confiding.

The evening was very late, and both men were winding down, tired and ready to go their ways until they met again. Nevertheless, Axel, still holding onto his pedagogy before it totally withered away, was unwilling to let his friend go without delivering a little lecture about the sacred stew. Nigel patiently let him continue, although he was already familiar with it. It was the professor in Axel that had never let go.

"According to this tribe, human flesh is good for a lot of things. It cures sickness, if you're prominent enough, controls wayward kids, reverses bad luck and misfortune, and so forth. Cannibalism, raw or cooked into a stew, is supposed to make a person feel better, get lucky in love, be a better person, and protected from very serious ailments. The tribe has a strict sense of what's supposed to be right or wrong, good and bad, by trying to be on the side of gods they believe in. What their gods approve of, they're prepared to do.

The sacred stew comes from the bodies of former enemies and prisoners. By eating them, the former enemy turns into an honorary brother. The ones who eat are supposed to become elite, compassionate, smart, courageous, and protected against further injury. More like the gods, these elected heroes are a kind of nobility. Whether it works or not, it's like a suit of armor that protected your medieval knights against slings, arrows and spears. Belief in protection is almost stronger than actual protection, just like strong faith. Reasons can always be found for something that doesn't work when you want it to work. Strong conscience is supposed to make a person stronger, more virtuous than anyone else, and our man became possessed, that's no exaggeration, with returning to the people he used to loathe in the white world. No, he really didn't loathe them. He was just indifferent, or, I guessed, he used them for anything he wanted."

The speech was over, and Nigel had already heard it all over and over, before dozing slightly. The bar was now nearly empty. A few employees were cleaning up. The proprietor counted the night's receipts. Despite the evening's noisy crowd and clattering dishes, it would have been surprising if Axel and Nigel had not been overheard. They might have picked a more secluded place, but they didn't. Besides, Axel was a local celebrity of sorts, and Nigel was a government representative. Eavesdropping was a common, very pleasant and sometimes, a profitable pastime. Hearing about a white man who came back from the dead after eating human flesh was a story too good not to be passed on. The fact that Axel's client wasn't dead at all, but only very sick provided the seed for prompt and sustaining elaboration, as it went from person to person.

A regular rumor route runs from the jungle and river byways to other settlements, out to coastal towns, with changes made along the way. Hearsay has no obligation to be true, and thrives on repetition and revision. Gossip grows and improves itself, the more lurid and extravagant the better. One version among many of the original story was that a white man had killed and eaten a native. Another variation was that a white man killed a native and threw his bones into a river, a heinous offense against humans and fishes. A large fish reported the crime to witnesses who then claimed to have seen the offender perpetrate that deed. Another fanciful tale was that a sick white man was about to die when given human flesh to eat. Immediately recovering, he became a full-fledged cannibal, but lived like an animal in the forest, preying on unwary natives for his daily food. The theme remained the same. A sick and dying white man recovers after eating human flesh, or a white man kills a native, which is a taboo offense, not the reverse.

Rumors change enormously during peregrinations. By the time the story reached Port Moresby and then leaped to Australia, a very sick but nameless white man got well after eating the genitals of unfortunate natives killed in battle or murdered. No one knew, of course, exactly where or when these events took place. But the elaborate story sensationalized every detail and where lacking, added new ones. First, the sickness was caused by a curse, then by a white man who defied the gods and committed a murder, then it was a bad sickness that killed the native, and in a later version, there was another homosexual twist. A famous visitor had killed and eaten several young boys after forcibly raping them. This was a highly objectionable but attractive rendering, like a vicious murder that has the public making bellicose noises of retaliation, as they salivate. No one is ever surprised by salacious rumors. The possibility of truth is delightful. By relishing gossip, people hate good stories to be disproved and contradicted. Appropriate facts are concocted just to solidify what people want. In this part of the world, nothing is too evil not to be credible, especially about a vagrant white man, or, better, a white man of high station. In larger settlements, as in most cities, native boys and men hang around hotels soliciting foreign visitors for homosexual purposes, so such a tale is plausible. There was something else that appealed to sensationalism. That extra ingredient was the cancer cure, not just cannibalism. It was good and evil, intertwined.

The good and evil combination of cancer cure became a major discovery, at least on news summaries coming from radio stations. Having a source in an exotic jungle far away made the tale outlandish, colorful, unverifiable, and therefore based on truth. Finally, the story reached and overtook Simeon and Narub, as they sat in Sydney, still debating the best way to publish a mild and respectable account. Further discussion was now moot. There was no obvious match between the rumor and the actual facts, but Simeon and Narub were forced to agree that some sort of publication was necessary before it all faded. They could not let it drop and disappear, Simeon was adamant. They could not long avoid being named, but, with an excess of innocence, Narub hoped that medical truth would conquer all and erase the tenacious stigma. In a last ditch effort, the basic story must be covered with a cloak of decent medical objectivity.

Nevertheless, the shock and titillation of forbidden sexuality and sadism combined with a sure cancer cure quickly made their way out of radio stations and into tabloids and talk shows. The final and persistent version was that a wealthy visitor with both extensive cancer and homosexual leanings had been given up by his white doctors, sent to New Guinea, where the medicine men in a remote area specifically urged the man to eat male genitals, after which he recovered.

That was enough to assure longevity for the story and make the reader's eyeballs bulge. Various pundits and self-anointed authorities weighed in with opinions. According to one columnist, with a vivid claim to metaphor, reminded the public that cancer eats away normal tissue. Therefore, when human flesh is eaten, the victim acts the part of the ravenous cancer and cannibalizes another human. Probably, he ventured, human flesh has a built in antidote to cancer, not unlike an immune response to protein in the cancer cells. The homosexual element was quickly lost because the promise of a quick cancer cure had to appeal to the population at large, not a tarnished group within that population.

Dr. Narub finally reported the real story to his superiors at the Cancer Center. He made it clear that Simeon did have advanced cancer, but that he sought cannibalism on his own and was by no means a confirmed homosexual. Narub's superiors spoke to their superiors and so on, up the scale until an executive decision was reached. The executive committee then ordered Dr. Narub to present a professional account of the case at one of the regular meetings of the local medical society, where it would be thoroughly discussed by selected authorities. For his own good, which meant theirs, the committee agreed that Simeon must be anonymous. Instead of being known as The Stranger, he was The Patient. The report had to be clean and the personal proclivities muted. There was no time to lose. Evil elements were gaining momentum. One fresh but persuasive rumor had already declared that the entire tale was a hoax perpetrated by an unscrupulous confidence man working with a greedy foreign physician, who was, moreover, not a white man. That, of course, pointed to Narub and the confidence man had to be an American.

The regular meeting of the medical society was moved up so that it was anything but regular. Newspapers announced that it was open to any interested person who wanted to hear about recent work in cancer therapy. However, despite efforts to contain the excitement, reporters and photographers were expected, along with distinguished members of the medical and religious communities. Since the customary lecture hall would be too small to accommodate the crowd, the presentation was held in the main auditorium of the university.

On the night of the meeting, officers of the Society enjoyed a little reflected glory by posing for pictures with Dr. Narub. The Chairman was himself a distinguished physician, Dr. Anselm Viets. He introduced Dr. Narub with a lengthy account of his credentials and achievements in cancer studies. Alluding to the cannibalism part of the anticipated report, he urged the motley audience not to take sides in the mounting controversy but let facts speak for themselves. He was decent and fair. The audience applauded.

Dr. Narub was at his urbane best, calm, professional, poised, and articulate. He first thanked the Center and the medical society for their scientific integrity and willingness to hear about a case that had, unfortunately, been erroneously reported and distorted by the public media. By distortion, he meant sensational innuendo and frank misstatements, purporting to be truths, but simply incorrect. He welcomed this opportunity to clarify and report at the very least a remarkable case. He did not mention Simeon except as "The Patient who…"

Warned in advance, everyone then seemed to be settling down to a dull evening. With proper medical objectivity, Dr. Narub talked about the natural course of a somewhat rare tumor, called a non-seminoma testicular cancer with extensions. He also emphasized that metastases often last for a number of years, and are by no means as ominous as with other tumors.

He outlined the treatment that The Patient received at different cancer centers, accentuating lack of response. The discrepancy between the extent of cancer and the absence of corresponding symptoms was unusual, considering its advance. However, The Patient's apparent good health made travel anywhere he wished quite possible. It was, nevertheless, a grim situation because treatment had not retarded the spread of cancer.

Dr. Narub glossed over his own travels to Papua New Guinea several years earlier, nor did he mention the journal he kept. He did not linger on the legends and myths that anthropologists report, especially about cannibalism and its effect on serious illness. Narub remained the consummate clinician as he described The Patient Who, reading about such practices, and adventurous with nothing to lose, decided to see for himself what was possible. Narub, in effect, removed himself from the decision. He reminded the audience that medicine is always searching for promising new methods of treatment from whatever source. Universities regularly sponsor expeditions to remote parts of the globe to gather and test whatever is said to have an effect on cancer and other diseases. He mentioned Periwinkle for one, useful in the therapy of ovarian cancer. He would have nothing to do however with mere nostrums or with methods that might hurt a patient. Like any cautious clinician he hoped that someday, good luck, informed exploration, experiment, and clinical trial would discover whatever plant or animal product had elements worth extracting. He implied that nothing was exempt.

He reiterated that his patient had learned on his own about tribal cannibalism, without hinting of his own early interest. Cancer diagnosis in the jungle without equipment and trained personnel is unreliable and dubious by necessity, although there is reason to expect that cancer does exist everywhere. Nevertheless, because the diagnosis was certain in The Patient's case, with ominous dissemination, despite treatment, Dr. Narub had no reason to discourage him. He then diverted the audience's attention by going into a hypothetical explanation of how human proteins, enzymes, and unspecified immune factors might have an effect on suppressing tumor growth. Dr. Narub was extremely cautious, distancing himself from the final act of devouring human flesh. He complimented The Patient for being a person who did not passively accept an unfavorable prognosis. Since his mind was made up, Dr. Narub put his patient in touch with a reliable guide in that part of the world.

As objectively as possible, considering that he was not present and clinical notes were not available, Dr. Narub described the later relapse and point where death was clearly inevitable. The Patient only then received a tribal preparation, regularly a part of the village food, consisting of human material along with local condiments. The exact nature of additional unidentified substances was not known. At first, the broth was not tolerated at all. The Patient could not keep it down. With the passage of time, however, he regained his appetite, ate carefully, and his swollen abdomen receded, indicating that ascites had gone. Narub emphasized that improvement had been gradual, not instantaneous, but quickly enough to be noticed. The remission and return to symptomless good health continued to this day. Recent examination has shown no indication of ever having cancer, a most remarkable remission, if that is how to describe it best. That was all. The presentation was brief, so was the polite applause. Scattered silence was noisier. Dr. Narub continued with a few informal and spontaneous remarks, as an addendum.

"Please accept this stirring account as a story, or anecdote worthy of your attention. We do not know what the outcome will be. Perhaps one day we will find that human tissue contains substances that slow down cancer cell division, if not destroy the cancer itself. That day may seem very remote, but vigorous cancer research is progressing on several fronts. I do not, of course, at all recommend this aboriginal treatment for every patient with terminal cancer. It violates much of our ethical and moral principles. Remissions do occur regularly, often surprising and baffling us by our ignorance of their mechanism. Every oncologist might have similar tales to tell, but our lack of explanation undoubtedly prevents further investigation for a variety of reasons. Before promising cancer cure, however, a longer follow up period with careful diagnosis and meticulous analysis is desirable, but frankly, I don't know how this can be implemented. We cannot accept one isolated, but fascinating outcome as anything more than an exotic incident. Ritual cannibalism, however repulsive as it seems to us, has been practiced according to a tribal tradition for countless generations. But let me suggest in the interest of future knowledge that we now try to separate biological implications from our moral principles and social distaste, in order to further mutual understanding of the processes that brought about this result."

This was a reasonable proposal and Dr. Narub sat down, confident that a balanced scientific discussion would follow. Many hands were raised, but Dr. Viets reminded the audience that this was not a public forum but a regular meeting of the medical society. The formal discussion, therefore, would be limited to a few selected participants. Another time, another place, and more open discussion of questions will be held, he promised. Some members of the audience got up and left.

The official discussants were all prominent. They concurred that medicine should always be alert for new ideas, especially for cancer, which is, by agreement, a scourge. Other platitudes followed, illuminating nothing in particular, and having little to do with the case. By ignoring Dr. Narub's carefully provisional presentation, they concurred that this was only a case of arrested cancer, not even a full-fledged remission. The negative findings at present, combined with the patient's excellent health, were not mentioned. The so-called cure or whatever did happen could all be understood as an unusual example of hypnotic suggestibility brought on by sickness, cannibalism, ritual ceremonies, skillful witch doctors, and familiar but ill-explained spontaneous tumor regression. The discussants were not exclusively medical. No women physicians were invited, probably, as explained later, an oversight. A prominent clergyman took up the issue of cannibalism directly. He was fervent in his moral condemnation.

"I cannot condone this report about a man who perpetrated an abominable and disgusting offense, even because of terminal cancer, which he might not have. Although I sympathize with a last-ditch, desperate effort to save his life, cannibalism is so extreme an offense against humanity that it negates the value of the life that might be spared. I do not care what aborigines do in a distant jungle. Their customs are theirs. I do care what people from our world choose to do. Traveling to a distant aboriginal land does not exempt a person reared in our culture from obeying fundamental moral and ethical principles. Does the cure of cancer in this man or in anyone, which I understand is not at all certain, justify an offense of this magnitude?" The good clergyman's point, aside from his unwavering scorn, was to question whether even a sure cure could justify such evil methods.

Sitting quietly unidentified in the rear of the auditorium, Simeon winced and shrunk down in his seat as he heard himself condemned. The clerical gist was that curing cancer through an extreme moral offense is unacceptable in civilized society. Any way a person looks at it, whether successful or not, is bad. And if it's bad, no possible good can come from it, not even curing cancer. Simeon shuddered to realize that this typified his entire life until grave illness and cannibalism brought forth contrition and compassion along with a cure. He did not mind the alliteration forming in his mind, knowing that KA would not be offended.

The final speaker among several who agreed with each other without adding much to the fray was a medical oncologist. At age 35, Dr. Niederland, already established as an outstanding cancer research scientist, had been offered lofty appointments all over the world. As he stood before the audience his poise and command of the subject could never be questioned. He was eloquent and informed. His youth implied open-mindedness about unorthodox practices and unconventional ways.

Dr. Niederland first praised his seniors and mentors who encouraged this open discussion and so judiciously refused to pass judgment until hearing all the facts. But how far should tolerance be stretched? He did not want open discussion abused in any way that condoned what people consider offensive, if not outrageous. There is a difference, he pointed out, between scientific discussion, pro and con, and soapbox oratory, which can be used for any cause, just to prattle on. He implied that the scientific format this evening was used only as a respectable screen for a heinous perversion that properly belongs to forensic psychopathology, not oncology. For us, cannibalism is a serious legal and moral infraction as well as an unsavory perversion. Cultural relativism is only a relative term, not a license to approve, if not advocate whatever it pleases. Claiming that cannibalism cures cancer without actual scientific proof is at best unwarranted, at worst, deceit. The Patient sullied the reputation of one of our outstanding physicians, Dr. Narub. If I were to fault Dr. Narub, it would only be for his generous gullibility, and for his willingness to accept what may only be a temporary remission as an excuse for reprehensible behavior. If violating a strongly held prohibition is a virtue, let us give up all our claims to morality and law.

Dr. Niederland's effective speech, enthusiastically applauded, paradoxically was more a diatribe than a scientific presentation. However, after this initial criticism, he turned to the case itself. Spontaneous recovery does occur, and very sick, even dying patients do not always die on schedule, according to a doctor's clinical and statistical expectations. Furthermore, it is not that unusual for a pathologist to find that a patient at autopsy was riddled with cancer but died of another disease. Similarly, an occasional cancer patient will not only be free of symptoms, but free of conspicuous confirmation of disease, using most tests currently available. The cancer is not discovered until after an unexpected relapse of an illness that did not make a patient sick, post mortem examination comes up with undisclosed cancer. Dr. Niederland continued, with an urbane smile, "I do not know for sure what happened or will happen to Dr. Narub's fortunate patient, but what may be good for him is not so good for science or for humanity. I would reluctantly recommend very careful study under close supervision before venturing on any form of an investigation, using human material. I can hardly do otherwise. There are other avenues of exploration right here, without mounting a dubious expedition that most of us would find offensive."

The meeting adjourned shortly afterward. Dr. Narub was left sitting alone, ignored by the other people on the stage. There was a conspicuous lack of enthusiasm, and no recommendation for further study. When the audience departed, he gathered his slides, which he had failed to show, and slipped out by a rear door. Simeon mingled with the exiting crowd, and returned to his hotel. He did not attempt to reach Dr. Narub.

But the reporters in attendance were hardly silent and did nothing to quell the incipient sensationalism that expanded almost immediately. In fact, the story now acquired new life out of its imminent disappearance. Freed of medical restraint, the story about curing cancer through cannibalism was to get even more attention from the press and media. The next few days would witness public fascination in the guise of moral outrage. Even some of the earlier and juicier versions were resurrected.

Man eats man - and cures cancer! So read one of the early headlines. Who is this unidentified cultivated savage who cannibalized fellow man but cured his own cancer? What brought him back, away from the jungle where he belongs? Is he here to find and eat someone else? How many converts does he aim to make? Pundits were called upon for post hoc opinions. Instead of settling problems, however, their guesswork only rekindled the fires of controversy. For some, the unknown stranger bringing good tidings of cancer cure was a benefactor, but for others, he was a beast not too different from those roaming the jungles he came from. It was curious but of all the people interviewed and polled, no one seemed to have interviewed cancer patients. Nor did reporters speak with families trying to deal with the impending death of a loved one. A high degree of insensitive crust would be required to ask a terminal cancer patient if he or she would be willing to eat human flesh, if they were offered a chance of cure.

Chapter 11—Not for Everyone

Simeon arrived in New York City from Sydney with two hopes. He wanted to remain anonymous, and yet spread the word about cancer cure as widely as he could. After the initial flurry, the novelty of his discovery died down. Less newsworthy than a mere two weeks ago, it needed revival and resuscitation, if any further notice were feasible. Although it had been freshly stirred up by the medical meeting in Sydney, a few people retained a casual interest in the dwindling story. Newer and much more lurid stories about scandal, sin, politics, and crime were coming along and naturally taken up by the tabloids.

Despite the fanciful publicity, Simeon had not yet been identified. Nevertheless, he was still counting on attracting attention of those struggling with cancer or witnessing someone close to them deteriorate from disease. For them, nothing was too far-fetched, bizarre or reprehensible, if relief and rescue were even distantly possible. While the cannibal cure was deplored by many, there were still those unhappy yet hopeful people who deemed his discovery promising, and if true, a monumental contribution.

A story like Simeon's was not meant for perfunctory amusement. Consequently, it soon polarized, either raising grateful hope or deserving nothing but scornful reprobation. People continued to ask questions. Was this a potential reprieve from a dreadful doom? Could it be another scam, intended to separate a desperate person from his money? Except for a fanatical few prepared to swallow magical solutions, reasonable people already knew that quacks never suffer from lack of clients. A predator on misfortunes usually finds a prominent platform to announce his lures, and has no trouble filling the house with credulous dupes.

Simeon's resolute anonymity did not fit the image of a charlatan capitalizing on publicity. Although true benefactors do not shun notoriety, some few stay modestly in the background. No one had a photograph of Simeon, or even was sure of his name, only that he came out of the jungle somewhere with an astounding message. He simply materialized, half a world away. Unrecognized by name or face, anonymity made it easy to register in a small but elegant New York hotel, nestled between tall buildings. The other guests also wanted privacy, and the inconspicuously expensive hotel was almost without identity itself. The staff was attentive but respectful of the guests' wish to be left alone, except when they wanted services.

Although the original tale may have lost its primary thrust, there were still many radio stations and print outlets always seeking to command an audience and advertisers. Even a somewhat shopworn story of curing cancer by cannibalism could be dressed up with freshly concocted colorful details and publicized further. High on the shelf, just about to be altogether forgotten, the cannibal cure had a few more dollops of attention-gathering controversy. Simeon counted on this residue to establish a foothold while maintaining his own privacy.

To his surprise, having crossed the oceans before Simeon's actual arrival, the story soon rekindled itself in the larger cities. Daily newspapers, ever on the lookout for readers, at first printed small comments, as if such a cure was already established, but understandably featuring the cannibalism, which was then described in colorful, often imaginative detail. Serious observers, such as columnists, lacking other pressing issues, also seized on cannibalism and the cure's authenticity, and daily delivered themselves of weighty controversial opinions. Here was a potential cancer cure from the jungle; why weren't medical authorities looking into it? Because so many need all the help they can get, they should be allowed to try it out, even if it means eating human flesh, provided that they can get it legitimately. No one ventured to guess where such fare could be obtained legitimately. There was no absence of influential opposition, insisting that the police stamp out experiments using human material, for whatever reason. Self-righteousness prevailed, both viewpoints adamantly insisting that morality and humanity were on their side. During the bleak nighttime hours, radio stations invited comments, which again were split between both extremes of the issue. Some listeners called in, begging to know where the jungle man lived, pathetically eager to try the cannibal treatment before it was too late. Presumably asleep, those firmly opposed seldom expressed their opinion at night. Gradually Simeon's story revived, not unlike the patients brought back from the nearly dead by eating sacred stew. No one seemed to mind that all the notoriety and dispute was based on only one person, one case, and one recovery.

News of a sure cure gained more momentum. The story's revival now depended more on a dazzling display of descriptive perverse sexuality, like a meteor shower released by cannibalism. The first fanciful reports from along the river were newly revised and adorned with Western fantasies. Celebrity now fell on the unknown jungle man who started it all, but whom no one seemed to know much about. Oddly enough, had people been able to identify Simeon by putting a face on him, the tale might not have survived very long. But now, this unknown nameless man gathered more mystery and credibility than a mere adventurer with a weird habit of eating his fellow man. It was like an alien from outer space with absolutely nothing to gain whose visitation brought good news about miracles that the human race had not yet achieved.

Simeon decided to keep the strategic ploy and remain silent and inaccessible. No one knew him, nor did they imagine he was living among them. He was a remote, abstract, and otherworldly character, still invisible, whether benefactor or schemer. However, there was an inherent savagery and prurience about the whole thing that inflated the hope of patients and tantalized many others, especially those without cancer.

His silence and anonymity soon had to be put aside however because success depended on being widely known. To get appropriate notice for the basic covenant, as opposed to the cheap publicity of tabloid quality, Simeon needed a superior sponsor, besides KA, and a respectable and dignified conduit. A public figure of unquestioned probity and unblemished reputation would get his message across to the nation and beyond ordinary geographical borders, and give the story instant respectability.

Such a famous and influential personage was Hiram Feigenmount, a distinguished savant and host of a public television program with an enormous audience of highly literate people. In his weekly program, Mr. Feigenmount interviewed prominent or noteworthy people who had an important message for an informed, affluent, and presumably educated audience. Nothing was contrived or contaminated by mere publicity and popularity. Celebrities from the sport and entertainment worlds were not invited. Questions were serious, timely, and of deep human interest. Viewers felt better about their own intelligence just by watching. "I must be damned smart and worthwhile if I'm a fan of Feigenmount's." Feigenmount had written several highly successful books, based on his program, and contributed to high-class magazines. He was exceedingly adept at clarifying complex issues and putting them in simpler perspective, without undue popularization.

Simeon was not surprised to find Mr. Feigenmount (actually he had several honorary doctorates but preferred plain "Mr.") unavailable at any time, even at the station where the program originated. His program was never called a "show," or an ordinary program, but always kept a special cachet, which lent distinction to an outstanding event. Simeon repeatedly called and his letters went unanswered, even after Simeon carefully identified himself. To be one of Feigenmount's guests required considerable eminence, usually a statesman, scientist, someone renowned for achievement, never a mere entertainer, unless it was an actor who had been knighted. A controversial, little-known transient figure like Simeon, possibly a mountebank, had no chance whatsoever.

After numerous calls, making sure that he gave his name, Simeon Benett, he was finally referred to an assistant who questioned him about the purpose of his message. Her manner was amiable but professional, and not inclined to welcome unendorsed individuals. He explained himself carefully, but she remained wary, telling him that he was perhaps the tenth person that month claiming to be the cannibal man cured of cancer.

"Madam, I understand your doubt about so many people calling and pretending to be me," Simeon said, laughing at her sally. "I am not from another planet, nor am I just seeking more publicity. I already have more than I really need, if all I wanted was notoriety. The jungle may seem very distant and exotic to you, but to the aborigines I know and respect, the world of New York City is just as incomprehensible. But I am also not the boy next door looking for a ticket to Hollywood. I have a serious contribution that the world and Mr. Feigenmount ought to know about. I have nothing personal to gain, except to accomplish my mission. I am looking for a respected outlet with a highly receptive audience. I am not proposing a cannibal peep show." By this time, having allowed him to speak, the assistant was impressed enough to inquire about calling him in a few days.

Simeon waited and waited. His polite compliance ended after a week. He then decided to talk with the editor of a highly regarded newspaper that had been quite even-handed in its brief reports about the jungle cure. He found it far easier to reach the editor, Henry Gould, than Hiram Feigenmount. Simeon was completely frank about his reasons for calling. Gould had worked his way up the organizational ladder, but kept the common touch and ready familiarity that typified his work as a reporter. He liked an unusual story with a bizarre twist, which qualified Simeon's saga. However, after speaking to Simeon, he was cautious, not wanting to be taken in by a two-bit scam artist, which had happened before, even to an experienced, big city reporter. Here was the jungle man himself, sounding like an educated and cultured gentleman, both of which were, of course, true. For a news story, there was no better angle than a cultivated gentleman with aboriginal tastes and wild experiences. A model predecessor with lasting appeal was Tarzan himself, raised by great apes, but also a member of British nobility. While still dubious, the cancer cure seemed to approve Simeon for a hearing. Moreover, Gould laughed when he heard about the cautious conversation with Feigenmount's assistant. He had a wild picture of the very proper and dignified Feigenmount interviewing a cannibal with a body covered by tattoos and a bone through his nose, nude except for a penile gourd. That would be some television program. None of these images, he knew, applied to the soft-spoken man on the other end of the telephone.

Simeon was still not sure that Gould took him seriously, until he began talking about his cancer, Barton, Narub, and the Cancer Center in Sydney, all of which jibed with facts easy to verify. A nonentity would not be familiar with so much scientific detail, regardless of a glib manner and an irresistible pitch. Gould realized that this man was on the level, if not wholly trustworthy. He had not delivered a set speech designed to part people from their money. Simeon emphasized that he wanted to set the record straight, without claiming full cancer cure, not like hawking a patent medicine. There was a needy public out there that might want to know the facts about what had been so widely and crudely sensationalized and distorted.

Simeon must have been persuasive because the next day, Feigenmount's assistant called back, identifying herself by name, apologizing for not reaching him earlier, and courteously addressing him as "Mr. Benett." They set up an appointment for the following week at Gould's newspaper, where Feigenmount worked occasionally and kept a private office. Simeon tried not to appear overly eager, which was difficult to conceal.

When the day arrived, Simeon went to the appointment punctually, dressed neatly and conservatively, nothing flamboyant, presenting himself as someone worth being heeded. Although he introduced himself quietly to a receptionist, he detected an immediate stir in the crowded office. Traffic seemed to freeze a little, but no one stared. In fact, sophisticated as the office people seemed to be, they kept their eyes deliberately averted. Evidently he had been expected. It might take a cannibal dressed in tribal regalia to evoke much more interest. Since Feigenmount seldom saw anyone at this office, this person had to be special. The receptionist punched a number on an instrument and Feigenmount immediately materialized at the end of a corridor, beckoning to Simeon, rather than coming forward to greet him. It was still pretty secret.

Feigenmount, rather Mr. Feigenmount, lived up to his reputation. He turned out to be correct, cordial, remote, and formidable, maintaining a distance between utter formality and casual ease, letting there be no doubt who was interviewing whom. He smiled quietly at nothing in particular, as if laughter would be out of place, while pleasant grace was acceptable. During the actual program, Feigenmount was very skillful at drawing people out and quickly getting to the gist of their message. Nevertheless, Simeon did not feel manipulated, although the distance between them was palpable.

Initially, Feigenmount motioned Simeon to a not too comfortable chair, slightly lower than his, a common ploy that Simeon recognized. Neither man expected or got a sense of collegial equality. This was a concrete mountaintop, not another office building. The noisy streets of midtown seemed far away. Simeon was significantly aware of Feigenmount's stature, but managed to hide his awe while gladly showing due respect for the famous man.

"Mr. Feigenmount," Simeon broke the preliminary silence. "You must understand how much I appreciate this meeting. I called because I need someone of your standing and reputation to help put my message before an educated public and into its proper perspective." Simeon was careful, while pleading his cause, not to be an eager petitioner. "My main message is just to report about slowing the course of terminal cancer, relieving deadly suffering, and for some people, reversing the course of terminal, end stage cancer, even bringing hope for a total reversal. It may sound grandiose but for people right on the edge of death, as I was, this has been no less than miraculous, although I use that word cautiously and regard my recovery with deep gratitude. I am cautious about long-range prediction. It is the other side of my cure or benefit that seems to have attracted, revolted or offended so many people who might be more objective. I understand why even those with cancer might be shocked and turn me into a menace. That is why I need a respectable means of urging more research or at least a careful hearing."

Feigenmount paid close attention, without cutting him off. Simeon became a little more confident, managing to speak calmly, clearly, and directly, pushing aside the thought that he was also the object of Feigenmount's appraisal. The least twitch of boosterism or having a secret axe to grind might be fatal. Feigenmount was a master at being politely noncommittal.

"Well, as long as you're here, and in your own words, please tell me frankly what brought you so far." Feigenmount deliberately ignored Simeon's opening statement, as if he hadn't heard or preferred to begin when he chose.

"My story is really about a far away tribe that has practiced ritual and religious cannibalism for generations beyond count, probably thousands. There is no way to measure. It is ingrained in their legends, history, and customs. It belongs to their tradition, and is far from what our society pictures as horrendous, perverse, criminal, and repulsive. I traveled so far because I was diagnosed with widespread cancer that even the finest specialists were not able to deal with. Not that they recommended going to this extreme. I was prepared, having no other recourse, to explore any avenue for getting help. Information about this tribe and their practices were told to me simply as a medical tale, without factual backing. I went there almost on my own. I needed a guide, of course, but from then on, for a long time, I was the only white man living with this tribe. How long? I am not sure. I spent several years with these people. I am adept at languages and even learned theirs. No, I promised to be frank. Without boasting, I learned their language well. I also came to appreciate their skills, customs, and virtues, such as bravery, and compassionately caring for the family. At no time did they try to convert me, although I came to respect their values, even if I didn't share them. They are not "savages," in the sense Western society casts them. However, and this has proved a serious sticking point, cannibalism is not an offense, not wrong for them, but a cultural act accepted and related to their religion. Sickness, however, is a curse, perpetrated by enemies or sorcerers, maybe both."

"If you were as sick as you claim, how did you withstand the trip, and put up with what must have been very primitive conditions?" Feigenmount inquired.

"I was fortunate. I understood that not every cancer patient with metastases feels that well. By no means. In most cases, it is an ugly situation of great sickness, incapacity, deterioration, and, of course, death. I felt fine. This happens occasionally, but how long it lasts is questionable. With me, it lasted several years, before I relapsed and from that point on, deteriorated and shortly I became very sick, and from all indications near death. I was ready to do anything, even trying their hallowed preparation reserved for the very sick. In fact, I wanted very much to try it, since that was my purpose in being there in the first place, in case I relapsed. I knew how it was made, and that among its ingredients was human flesh, as well as other, not so alarming stuff. I am sure you have heard about cannibal feasts. This became one of the methods to treat my sickness before I died, although there wasn't much celebration either way. Well, I didn't die. I got better, gradually. Otherwise, I wouldn't be here. My message might be called a mission, but I don't put myself on such a level, nor am I just another grateful patient. I have broken a taboo, but nevertheless, there might be something that our scientists have not yet discovered and that the informed public ought to know about." Feigenmount was still listening.

"I admire your candor and perseverance, even about a divisive topic," he said, "It's more than controversial. I am not unfamiliar with strange customs around the world. We have plenty right here in New York City that would shock our conservative citizens, without going to New Guinea to find them. We have indigenous neighborhood practitioners who also claim great results with weird and revolting medicines. From what I understand, even here, cannibalism or its equivalent can't be disregarded. It may go on here, undetected, of course. In your case, the public seems to be attached itself to cannibalism, without going into its religious and cultural foundations. For us, including the educated public, cannibalism is inevitably connected to other beliefs and practices, such as sorcery, orgies, beheading, blood sacrifices, Satanism, and so forth. I am sure many find links to the grossest promiscuity and, of course, homosexuality, as it did with your tale."

Simeon should not have been surprised at Feigenmount's calm acceptance of what others were shocked about. This was a sophisticated man who had been around the world in every sense, and not a pompous fool. He did not make up his mind without hearing different sides of a controversial issue.

"After all, I am a grateful patient, with much appreciation for good fortune. There may be an unknown immune factor in human flesh, at least in that place, among those people. I am not a scientist. I have heard about exotic viruses in the brains of people on other Pacific islands and that these unfortunates die slowly of a strange affliction similar to illnesses that are not unknown here. This other disorder is apparently caused by cannibalism, not through a curse inflicted by an enemy. I just don't know, but I think something deserves a hearing or maybe more professional investigation. If it is ignored, the reason can only be that people in power, holding purse strings, are as offended as any backwoods illiterate by what for us is a desecration. What about the very sick people with the most urgent demand for information? They are not scientists or clergy, but patients who may be terminal, and even suffering more than I did. I hope they have friends and family with a stake in their survival. They have everything to lose by our attitude." Simeon was trying to convert Feigenmount to his cause by avoiding words like "ought" and "should." "I happen to be a beneficiary. Nothing else. I don't want to go too far. You, Sir, are a model of respectful inquiry into a variety of controversial problems. This is one that I presume deserves your attention. I expect no more. Your eminence and reputation are far different than the way tabloids and commentators have treated the story. I have stayed away, been reclusive, just for that reason." Simeon was surprised to hear himself saying, "Your Eminence," which is a title for a high priest. But with Feigenmount's prestige, maybe the slip wasn't grandiose at all. What bothered Simeon was that he'd caught himself buttering up this guy with what sounded like overweening bullshit. Feigenmount must have sensed this because his unspoken attitude suddenly changed into impatience. It was like "Let's get on with this palaver!" Simeon had flattered him, and Feigenmount knew it, and didn't like it. Simeon was afraid he'd said too much.

"You make a strong case, Mr. Benett," Feigenmount finally said, "It is an intriguing story, not like anything I've heard before. Or been willing to hear. It is quite fascinating." Feigenmount was being disingenuous. Only the evening before, preparing for this meeting, he'd watched an old grainy black and white film made by anthropologists who'd studied cannibalism in South America. Feigenmount was in truth intrigued, but found it hard to connect those ugly painted tribesmen with the lofty ethical values and religious pieties Simeon avidly described.

"Perhaps it's a little too bizarre for my program," he said, "You can understand that many people seek me out with their own special causes to tout. They are evangelists, entertainers, some quite legitimate, and others have their own agenda. But yours is unique, and I don't doubt your sincerity. There are many very sincere people out there with a plan for beating the house in Las Vegas or out-smarting the Lottery. Not that you're in that league at all, but sincerity, dedication, and a sense of mission are just not enough, I regret to say. I refuse to be used, if I can help it. Some causes have limited appeal, or are so special that the millions who watch might not be interested. Phoniness is easy to spot, and I do not hesitate to believe you and your mission. Frankly, however, you seem to have a few messianic traces, traits of many other people seeking the publicity that the forum of our program provides. Considering your medical history, that you are or have been so full of cancer, you seem very healthy. Either the cannibal cure was every bit as effective as you claim, or your cancer doctors need to have another look. I want verification that things happened the way you say, and that your medical condition was every bit as serious as the doctors told you. Forgive me for being forthright but you are very persuasive, like a highly successful pitchman or a true-believing evangelist. I know that you are neither. If you were, we wouldn't be sitting here now. There is much more going on than meets my eye and the TV audience might be sharper than you imagine. They are not all boobs, and I depend on them. Some people might even recognize you from the past. I am sure that despite your wish to be anonymous, life did not just start when you returned from New Guinea."

He pointed to a leather attaché case Simeon brought with him, containing as much documentation as he could manage. Simeon handed over copies to Mr. Feigenmount who briefly glanced at them. Understandably, there was not much more than medical reports, all duly validated and signed. Feigenmount could spot the gaps and omissions. It was not, after all, a personal resume. Finally, after it appeared that Feigenmount would gently reject the bid, Simeon was surprised when his Eminence smiled. Simeon had not lost his touch; the appeal had not been wasted.

"I don't think of you as an out and out faker," Feigenmount said, indulgently and without apology. "Still, there is something opportunistic about you that worries me." Feigenmount smiled quietly, showing just the edge of his teeth, as if he were about to do something against his better judgment. "You have an excellent message and you present it well. Cannibalism is strong stuff, and you'll get plenty of criticism and insult, if you push too hard. My station will hear about it. I don't want to offend you, but something is missing from those files of reports you've given me, not related to the medical condition. I don't know what it is. It may be buried, and irrelevant, but perhaps not. Cannibalism is like an attractive poison, very risky for audiences, and I don't want to push it so far that its stranger bedfellows start showing up. The cancer cure has to be a very good cause and make everything else seem good, too. Your story is just too macabre and weird not to be true, or mostly true. I have reservations still about you, but that won't be part of the program. I'll still think about this privately."

They rose by mutual agreement. Feigenmount shook hands, and opened the door. Feigenmount had as much as promised, but then again, he cautioned about missing evidence that Simeon was not precisely the man with a mission he purported to be. Would his less than wholesome past be found out? Nevertheless, there was no brush-off, no perfunctory words about hearing soon, etc. Feigenmount was circumspect but interested. Simeon's facile speech, good looks, and ruggedly youthful manner were all in his favor. However, there were questions still unanswered. Was he out to make a score, a missionary seeking a larger flock, or an afflicted glib and grateful rogue saved from death, who now sensed an obligation to tell the world? The enigma itself might be intriguing for an audience that could make up its own mind about Simeon.

Simeon missed seeing Mr. Gould on his way out. Urgent business, it was explained. But he wrote him a gracious note for making the interview possible. Perhaps the note also did something else. Within a week Simeon was notified about his selection to appear on a segment of the program in the near future. Feigenmount paid nothing, nor did he ever pay anyone. The honor of appearing was sufficient recompense.

During the elapsed time since his interview, Feigenmount's investigators evidently did not reveal anything derogatory. Either the inquiries were too hasty or Simeon had been successful enough to disconnect from his past. No one had discovered unsavory items, such as his short career in pornographic films. Simeon would be asked about cannibalism, of course, but he could not make it too bloodthirsty, gruesome or too commonplace for the audience. Like a good politician, he had to sanitize a taboo topic, while being flexible enough to shift to something else, if he had to.

The evening of the program arrived. The very respectability of his cause made Simeon increasingly uneasy about coming out of his shelter of anonymity. Mr. Feigenmount could not have been more gracious, putting Simeon at ease while he asked probing questions. They conversed like two educated, sophisticated men of the world, neither shocked nor inured to brutal facts and exotic behavior. Simeon was ready for the cannibalism topic that could not be glossed over.

"I realize quite frankly that for the world we live in, what I had to do seems very offensive, even criminal, to some very good people. But these people must also be fair, and not condemn without a hearing or jump to judge me without understanding that I was desperate as well as beyond conventional treatment. While I was healthy in some respects, doctors cautioned that events might change and that I had to be prepared for anything. By that, they meant death from the cancer. How does one prepare for anything, particularly a grim outlook? I was afraid to die, too, just as I was afraid even to be among those primitive aborigines who finally turned out to be quite compassionate in their fashion. Perhaps I should have taken my medicine like a man right here, even though there was no medicine, and wait for death. I could not do that. Nothing was available for me, except stories of a tribe far away. If you're desperate enough, you consider everything. When I got so very sick and the tribe seemed unwilling to help at all, I felt my chances slipping away. I had come far, endured much, gone through years of waiting and serving my time. I was prepared to die like the stranger I was. The sacred stew, as it was called, might be too sacred for someone they suspected of being a sorcerer and evildoer, after all. Stranded and starving parties of men, women, and children in a wilderness are not unheard of, and at length they suspend their standards of decent society to make use of comrades who have already died. Emergency cannibalism does survive, and I was just as stranded and destitute. I did violate what from here seems reprehensible, but I was exhausted and clinging to a frail hope of living a while more. (Simeon, of course, did not refer to his excitement at the prospect of cannibalizing someone). After recovering, and it took a while, I knew how lucky I'd been. Even at the risk of being despised and condemned, I felt obliged, even a sense of duty about coming back and telling other unfortunate cancer patients and their devoted families. If I say so myself, with no pride whatsoever, it is also a humbling and humanitarian experience." Later in the program, he added, "I do not urge a similar choice for other cancer patients, however advanced, terminal, and beyond salvage they might be. For some, a quiet death might be preferable, surrounded by family and the consolation of another life beyond death. I had no such options. Had I somehow opted for suicide, instead of making a stand, I could not recommend that alternative for someone else. It was not my choice. It was an individual course of action, maybe unacceptable, but in my opinion, better than no choice at all. I turned into a cannibal in order to survive. But this is decidedly not for everyone, even the very ill and hopeless. Sick or well, you live and die by your own moral code. It cannot be suspended except under very severe circumstances. Sometimes your morality and sense of sin are stronger than the will to survive. At other times, no."

When the program was over, Feigenmount seemed pleased at Simeon's eloquence. He had been totally forthright, without equivocating, self-effacing yet responsible, steadfast, without trying to convert others to his way of life. Feigenmount's interview was also fair and responsible, without the marginal censorship and covert criticism Simeon expected. The program courted authenticity and respect by not being taped. It allowed spontaneous discussion, back and forth, fall-out and all, without correction. The staff congratulated Simeon as well as others who were also on the program that evening. He was not treated like a con man or a wayward freak. Two of the younger women asked if he were free the rest of the evening. He accepted the invitation of one and found a new and passionate friend. All at once, however, he became a public figure.

It did not take many hours, however, after the program aired, before dissenting and reproachful voices rushed to the attack. And it was not much later that anxious inquiries about his eventual cure were heard. Those who condemned outnumbered the appreciative needy callers. Some chided Feigenmount for having such a guest, while others praised his courage and insistence upon an unedited interchange, come what may.

Simeon was now out in the open, no longer the invisible stranger who came out of the jungle with a horrifying yet redemptive message. His picture with excerpts appeared in newspapers and television, looking like anyone else, only better than most and surely more articulate. But his critics were quick to point out that this was like the Devil himself, who could worm his way into credibility with urbane manners, wholesome good looks, and charm, all the better to deceive. For many, he had to be a charlatan, despite his noble and self-effacing sentiments, now freely voiced. However, a respectable number praised his courage and thanked him for his frank contribution.

Much money was to be made from a cancer cure, everyone knew, however unacceptable and near criminal. Letters to the Editor multiplied, as did editorials. Most condemned Simeon, calling him a perverted criminal, sneering at what seemed like hypocritical altruism, yet envying his good health. A few sanctimoniously wished him a good death, without predicting the time. Nevertheless, there were uncounted people sure that Simeon had divine sanction for what he did, and that his personal suffering and cure ordained salvation for the afflicted. A few observed that cannibalism had been a vehicle for good. After all, he hadn't done anything wrong. The bodies were already dead and he hadn't killed them in the first place.

Although patients and families wanted more information, Simeon thought that by now he had said and done enough. He would speak publicly no more and let knowledge of his conquest and mission spread by itself.

The entire story, even with enormous exposure, should have tapered off again within a few days. However, it did not happen that way, although he refused to make public appearances or give interviews, receding once again back into the shadows. He became part blessed and part censured. It made little difference. Mystery kept him alive as a mythic figure for both good and evil. People who never heard of Feigenmount had extreme and fixed opinions about this stranger.

Reporters and petitioners sought him out, but without exception, were turned away. Bundles of letters arrived at Simeon's hotel, which he once considered a private sanctuary. Pathetic notes, written by scarcely literate people, pleaded for help. Others berated him for raising hope while not giving specific enough directions for getting human meat for personal trial. A couple of letters invited him to satanic clubs, promising orgies that the old Simon might once have gladly leapt at. According to others, he was out to steal souls of innocents, sell them to the Devil, and keep dead bodies for himself and the medical research they did not trust. Although he answered none of the communications, he saved them all. Not unexpectedly, he had notes from couples wanting sex, and a few women proposed marriage. There was so much gossip that talk show hosts began to wonder whether his message for mankind had a link to the supernatural. Was his real purpose to cure cancer or to induce people to try cannibalism?

The most alarming consequences appeared soon enough. Eating human flesh for its own sake became a secret cult, associated with vampirism, sorcery, grave robbing, and the evil eye. Police were swamped with cryptic messages about desecrated cemeteries. Of course, talk about cannibalism, pro and con, filled the Internet. Praising the Devil became no more deplorable than advocating free speech. Books about Dracula and his counterparts sold out. Hearts, livers, and other organs were offered for transplant through underground networks. No one could guess where the supply came from. Simeon could do nothing. His mission had become so split and twisted that his original pious objective was lost.

More sinister events occurred. Soon after funerals, fresh graves were found opened, with parts of the corpses missing. Prostitutes were found dead by the roadside, carved up and cannibalized. Their patrons were interrogated so extensively that men simply stayed away from their usual haunts and became attentive husbands at home. Areas of the city known for crime were deserted at night. It was like an epidemic, but no one knew exactly what to call the public fascination with death and the mayhem surrounding Simeon's message. Lifers in prison, looking for parole points, volunteered to eat other human beings, although neither had any sign of cancer. A few cancer patients reported being solicited over the telephone by unknown persons offering to sell them human flesh for therapeutic purposes. No one knew if anyone accepted the offer, since complaints came only from people who refused. That an underground market existed could not be doubted. Funeral homes received anonymous messages offering to buy hearts and brains of newly deceased clients; the deal was cash and no questions asked and answered. Grieving families of newly dead relatives were advised to examine the body carefully before burial. Popular panic brought on magical superstitions long dormant, as if the population reverted to a medieval credulity.

Simeon was an unwilling celebrity, named Delegate of the Devil at this point, but unable to stop the crimes and return to the question of curing cancer. One United States senator, up for reelection, and in favor of capital punishment, made a speech, suggesting that executed criminals be used for cancer research, an idea that some convicts on death row approved. However, when asked if he meant cannibalism for consenting adults, he firmly withdrew, insisting that he was quoted out of context and meant something else, quite unspecified.

Police arrested a physician in a small town in Germany for feeding disguised human parts to late stage cancer patients. The patients died, but the story was a shocker wherever printed. Patients were advised to refuse new and unfamiliar medicines, especially when offered as a panacea. Rumors proliferated wildly. Not all blamed Simeon, because there were isolated reports of miraculous cures after cannibalized organs were fed to sick cancer patients. These were impossible to document or trace. A very right wing group claimed that Jewish doctors in New York City were prescribing human flesh at enormous fees, and that the raw material was processed in secret laboratories.

Here and there, newspaper editorials advocated that human cadavers be prepared under government supervision, given euphemistic names, and then given to controlled groups of advanced cancer patients. As always, charlatans prospered, selling sheep and pig brain extracts with disclaiming labels, "not for the treatment of known human diseases." The public promptly bought up these products, anyway, believing that the government had simply withheld information about their use in cancer. A rumor spread quickly that drug companies and government bureaucrats had already suppressed an unspecified cure for cancer in order to drive up the prices before approving it. The nature of the remedy was also left to rumor and speculation.

Meanwhile, back in Sydney, Dr. Narub was having his troubles. The Cancer Center frowned on derogatory publicity about unproved practices and remedies. His lecture to the medical society had done nothing to reassure his superiors that Narub was only a bystander to outrageous claims. The Cancer Center was expected to uphold high community standards, like churches and any other large corporation, especially because of conservative and generous contributors. Despite repeated denials, Narub was assumed to have encouraged his patient to explore cannibalism as a cure for cancer, and that Simeon was merely a gullible puppet. Envious colleagues did nothing to staunch the libel, even spreading the idea that Narub was likely to be guilty because he was a misfit, anyway, with an unusual interest in esoteric medicine. It was not long before his critics started to confuse ethnic background with ethical lapses.

Finally, without proof of any kind, Narub was asked to resign. While relieved that gossip and innuendo were now over, his research career was also over. No other center was likely to hire him. Dejected, Narub took to writing letters to various medical organizations, reiterating his role in this notorious adventure. Nobody listened or came to defend him. He was yesterday's culprit, hardly remembered, except by the few who feast on scraps of gossip long after the gusto is gone. He had no recourse except to set up a practice in a small community, already short on licensed doctors.

Back in New York, not even Hiram Feigenmount was spared. Why did such a prominent person agree to publicize this vile character in the first place? It gave that adventurer an undeserved platform for his perverted claims. One theory had it that Feigenmount was himself a cured cancer patient, but how was he cured? Irresponsible and lurid whispers elaborated their own exaggerations. Feigenmount was a closet homosexual as well as a cannibal. The public enjoyed the spectacle of a respected person having fatal flaws. According to the principle of enjoyable gossip, constant repetition of a rumor only reinforces the probability of its truth. An underground nostrum also made an appearance labeled Simeon's Secret Remedy and was recommended by a famous TV personality, but not named.

Anonymous donors continued to send money to Simeon, who without hesitation contributed the money to cancer clinics and hospitals, also anonymously. Despite such unforeseen notoriety, Simeon steadily lost much of his luster. To his loyal believers, he remained above it all, still almost a spiritual being instead of an ordinary man with flaws and faults, as well as admirable traits. Gradually, curling back into the anonymity of many yesterdays, the mission was over. The message was out there, not totally dead, not absolutely gone, but without its former glow.

Still feeling well, Simeon had no urgent appetite or need for human flesh. From time to time, however, old yearnings for an unidentified fresh taboo came back. Many nights he awakened with tenacious tingling in his loins, aroused by fantasies of old women working out their lust on his body. Nevertheless, contrary to his former self, he was content to restrict these images to the night, without seeking them to put into practice.

If he had ever dreamed that the scientific community would undertake a serious investigation, nothing happened. Very few people were now eager to see him. The mail tapered off and interview requests vanished. The minor madness had dwindled away. His popularity among Satanists was still strong but it made him wince with regret. Most discouraging of all, he realized that if the curative factor in human flesh were authentic, no one was about to find out. Even his cure was questionable. The covenant with KA was no longer obligatory and commanding.

Chapter 12—Lorenzo

Among millions watching Feigenmount's program, there was probably no one more intrigued by the guest from New Guinea than Bruno Lorenzo. He was not a fan of Feigenmount, disliking him as pretentious and infatuated with his own superiority. But on this evening, Mr. Lorenzo made an exception. He was eager to see and listen to Simeon Benett. For Bruno Lorenzo, Simeon was far from the celebrated jungle celebrity, recently emerging to talk about cannibals and cancer. Simeon was the boy Simon all grown up, although years had elapsed since they met at Gina's wake. Bruno remembered the few moments of conversation and was now sure that they would meet again.

Everyday that weather permitted, Bruno walked along the Boston waterfront, thinking long thoughts and enjoying solitude among the masses passing in both directions. Sometimes he sat on a park bench near the shore, now heavily commercial, watching ships in the harbor and tugs towing various vessels to the docks where cargo unloaded. On the day after the program, however, Bruno had special reason to think about Gina and the boy she raised. The funny name, Simon Simon, had been an absurdity without a reason, even then. There had to be a reason somewhere, known to someone, but it was a mystery no one ever explained. Name changes always mean something, usually to conceal or reject the past. Double names are uncommon. Surely there were enough names not to stint in this way, especially if there was something to hide. Simeon Benett was more like it. The last name honored Gina, but *Simeon* reminded Lorenzo of some obscure notable, possibly in religious history. In truth, Lorenzo had cause to wonder about Simeon's forebears.

Sitting today however as he watched people hustling by, Lorenzo mused again that everyone's moment is brief and quickly passes away, whether abruptly in haste or by tarrying until old age. Regardless of what they were and were not, their tiny importance inevitably withers, becoming the nothingness they were intended to be. In recent years the aging Lorenzo often faced his own mortality, the course his life had taken, and his reveries often ended with clichés that were strangely comforting. Ancient lines from the Persian poet reminded him of the uncertainty and fragility of existence, and that nothing could be changed. The power he once possessed belonged now to the past, although he still had considerable influence in several areas, business, political, cultural, and other places, some of which remain unmentionable. Mundane meditations, of course, but Lorenzo, with ample leisure, enjoyed what he still had. Simon or Simeon had once again come back into his life and brought aching memories and nostalgic pining for other choices he might have made.

Just then two workmen walked past, recognized him, bowed ever so slightly, and respectfully touched their caps. For whatever reasons, admiration or intimidation, he was remembered. What he liked best was respect, knowing that over time fear can turn into veneration. Money alone cannot command that kind of respect, nor did the fleeting prominence and reputation of Feigenmount amount to more than something utterly transient. In fact, much of Lorenzo's antipathy towards Feigenmount was envy of his fame, respect, and recognition by the public. Nevertheless, without money and its power, Lorenzo would be just another old man sunning himself on a park bench. A reputation for making decisions that still could be enforced meant lasting respect. He wanted and expected nothing less. Otherwise, aside from a few old business associates and fundraisers for cultural organizations, Lorenzo was pretty much alone.

Bruno Lorenzo was no longer engaged in day-to-day operation of the family business. He remained both a symbol of past power and a respected source of counsel. During a shady career with dubious eminence, he surely made many enemies, most of whom were gone. Of the competitors and rivals who once envied him, practically all were dead or harmless. His name and reputation, admittedly not savory, were still held in cautious awe by those who stood to profit from the family's illegal enterprises and from Lorenzo's philanthropy. From time to time, highly regarded patrons supporting the arts sought him out for advice and, of course, the generous financial contributions he often made. Frequently, politicians secretly consulted him looking for operational strategies and inside information.

For the small number that remembered a younger Bruno, he was still a sinister figure that society was better off without. Nevertheless, within the circle of organized crime, Mr. Lorenzo was a respected senior statesman of sorts, who had stepped aside, allowing younger men to take over in amicable succession. Moreover, when business or family animosity erupted, Bruno Lorenzo was the man to call on for mediation, before blood was shed unnecessarily. He rarely approved a hostile foray into a competitor's territory, even for rich booty, unless, of course, the promise of profit was overwhelming. Then a deal, profitable for everyone, was aptly arranged.

Considering his past, and lack of formal education, it was somewhat astonishing that through his own efforts over the years, he became a man of taste and cultivation. His colleagues found this amusing, and stayed away from the current nonprofit projects Lorenzo sponsored. The cultural community might have gladly recognized Bruno for the patron he was, were it not for who he had been. Still a person tainted by criminality, he enjoyed the secret role of counselor and contributor for artistic projects needing support and approval. It gave him vicarious satisfaction, and for a brief moment, a totally fallacious legitimacy as one of the artistic and cultural elite, which, of course, he never was and could not be. While so-called respectable people treated Bruno deferentially, his respect was based on lingering fear and a healthy appetite for what he could do for them. Those in need never refused contributions from questionable sources that they would rather not know about.

Had any of his beneficiaries considered it, Lorenzo might be compared to powerful renaissance patrons of art, inspiring and supporting the work of others, while dealing decisively with political enemies. Like them, he was once capable of ordering deeds of unlimited savagery. Nevertheless, with the reputed mellowness of advancing years, and equally gracious intervention, he brought crime and culture together in his own personal balance, while keeping each scarcely aware of the other. Lorenzo might contribute to good causes unrelated to the arts, even the established Church, just like the dukes of old.

No one knew for sure where his bountiful gifts stopped. He offered no apology for his life, but then no one dared to ask. His principles were flexible to the utmost. He was sure that evil might be an absolute good under different conditions, and that what passes for conventional virtue is likely to be a transparent mask for all kinds of mischief. All the same, he was not bothered by absolutes, firmly believing that those who proclaimed absolutes were probably absolute hypocrites. Feigenmount, for example, might be in this group, but Bruno never bothered to find out. Although he did not hawk his own beliefs, he often initiated projects that he expected others to support without hesitation. Whatever benefited him had to be good, but what seemed good to him typically concealed something suspect, sometimes criminal, and not likely to gain universal approval. Although he dealt with criminal organizations in his active career, he held them to high standards of efficiency and merit, illegal though his associates were. Those from other walks of life who were in his debt realized this and behaved accordingly.

Civic and law enforcement officials used Bruno as a benign resource when certain problems arose. But he was not yet a harmless relic. Consequently, it was their business to maintain an up-to-date account of his activities, on the record or off. While no longer a real danger, Bruno still could bear watching, like an old lion that keeps a few powerful bites in reserve. Never mentioned in the newspapers, he was, by designed default, a legend. He was publicly silent, but not deceased by any means. Small symphony orchestras around the country owed continued existence to his largesse. A long-time fan of opera, he offered generous endowments and scholarships, all without official recognition. While certainly not averse to gratitude, he realized that were his generosity openly acknowledged, recipients would be forced to refuse tainted funds, although he also derived substantial income from legitimate investments.

Urbane sophistication had not come easily. He learned and practiced to near-perfection the manners and methods of the educated, cultivated elite whom he met through the favors he granted. Looking back, he acknowledged that those who needed him were valuable mentors. Benevolence however was a virtue he acquired with difficulty. It was quid pro quo, enforced by a scarcely hidden sword. Mr. Lorenzo knew how to keep secrets, and kept them securely, ready to use. Mr. Lorenzo had long practiced the art of chicanery, at the same time despising those who did it for a living. As a result, people rash enough or unlucky enough to renege on an agreement or violate his trust were punished with a flourish that verged on art. As a dispenser of justice, he preferred a more intricate form of suspended punishment. While forgiveness was not in his nature, he never failed to retaliate, lest he invite future problems. But to his sorrow, revenge was seldom sweet, only a matter of principle.

Now, as he occupied a familiar bench, thinking about Simeon, he had a strange and sentimental notion that they were basically alike. For Bruno, absolutes were no different than loaded dice, appearing the same but basically crooked, and designed to deceive. In his opinion, based on this fancied similarity, Simeon must also combine philanthropy and altruism with a self-serving scheme to get his way and profit generously. Disinterested altruism was a fake. There was always a catch, a hidden scam, a lingering hook for deceiving the public and making a bundle. One made the other run. Cynicism could always make a case for itself and dark motives behind noteworthy contributions. This was not necessarily bad for either.

He liked being rich and could not understand people who did not feel the same about a profit in exchanging one service for another. That, after all, is what business is all about, whether in high placed boardrooms or in smaller quarters far from the hub of the city. His beneficiaries, then and now, were grateful, but would fool themselves mightily were they not to understand that they were obliged to reciprocate in some fashion. Favors might not be asked for, but indebtedness was still there, a lifetime obligation, never fully discharged. In effect, he owned them, as he might own a piece of art. He could also right a wrong, but only as he construed the offense and invented the retraction. A royal prerogative, self-endowed, provided him with warmth and a sense of abiding accomplishment. It was also a royal game in which he was always the winner.

Lorenzo was gratified and pleased with Simeon's polished performance on the program. Simeon was modest yet articulate, candid yet circumspect, and personable even while euphemistically describing what conventional people would surely consider gruesome, criminal, perverted, or just unspeakable. Lorenzo understood all that. So the little boy had become a cannibal and found an altruistic cause through his cure. He admitted as much to a national audience, especially that the cancer cure justified stepping beyond a strong taboo. It was no misdeed, but a misfortune turned into an advantage. It was not a violation or a crime, but a pitiful circumstance that now was ready to benefit other sufferers. Simeon was masterful, while indicating his hopes. This was praiseworthy because it turned vulnerability into a profit-making venture. What would others have decided when faced with such a life or death dilemma? Who opts for good or evil in the abstract without a specific problem? Those who act only from what is to their advantage must certainly tilt to help themselves.

As a practical businessman and hardheaded visionary, Lorenzo speculated about converting Simeon's mission into a profitable project. If Simeon would only join forces, it could be a momentous benefit and lucrative. A first step, then another and another; that was the way it always went, a law that justifies itself by the rewards. Harvesting human organs is not a revolutionary idea. Neither should harvesting human beings be unacceptable. The more he thought about it, the more appealing it became.

This is a world in which slavery and exploitation are sure moneymakers. Cannibalism curing cancer had a nice neat appeal, especially for those hopeless enough. Every successful project needs to capture and enlighten the public. The initial horror about cannibalism would soon be forgiven, forgotten, and transformed into a less gruesome necessity. The real thing was there to be purchased. After all, desperate people are willing to do anything just to survive, on almost any terms. Give them an acceptable reason to do what once might have been deplored, and they'll soon be steady customers, clamoring for what is for sale, just as with drugs and narcotics. It is not a matter of greed, but a fair exchange.

Bruno had no compunctions about drugs, prostitution, extortion, enlarging his fortune in all directions, and sponsoring still another artistic venture. Almost anything he had a hand in might turn out to be advantageous, even a cure that makes good and evil join hands with him and collaborate. Cancer patients will certainly buy what Lorenzo's family offers for sale. Lorenzo had always known that there is no inconsistency about doing things that are sometimes good, sometimes inordinately evil. It didn't make that much difference, once it works out. In his own life, apart from business and the arts, Lorenzo was capable of being compassionate, cruel, vindictive, tolerant, if only once in awhile, ruthless when called for, sentimental now and then, belatedly exterminating an enemy and then consoling the survivors. In a pinch, he found hatred and animosity easier to deal with than sentiment and love, which he managed to avoid. Strong attachments of any kind were dangerous pretexts for enslaving another person.

He recognized Simeon's courage in coming forward, while confident about hidden motives. There was, of course, a chance that Simeon actually believed in his holier purpose, and therefore might be a reckless fool with a conscience, always a dangerous combination. However, if Simeon had a scam going, that was fine; Bruno approved. But if he meant what he preached, Simeon was putting his head out to be chopped off. Simeon might already be looking for profit, and was not moved entirely by sheer benevolence. That was a comforting thought. No one with whom he shared a common code would be so foolhardy as to do much for humanity without a healthy profit, of whatever kind. Glamorous talk about the jungle and the worthy little black people inhabiting the cliffs might be window dressing to attract the crowds, but just bilge bent on bilking people out of something. With the right organization, and this came close to a universal rule for Lorenzo, there were always millions to be made in vice posing as virtue. It had to start with cannibalism. Success would be assured, and a new era might begin in mankind's quest to banish cancer. Bruno had to put his personal monetary sentiments aside and get to know Simeon personally.

Lorenzo conducted important business carefully, often late at night at home for special people. He did not relish narrow escapes, nor did he trust associates so far that they might be tempted to betray him, despite his senior status. There had been incidents when people presumed to be reliable failed to live up to expectations. The fewer people around when important matters are discussed, the more control can be exercised. He did not always enjoy retaliation.

Pasquale Carolino, known as Pat to his few true friends, was a trustworthy colleague, former bodyguard, and friend. Pat was dependable, ambitious, and ruthless, as well as efficient and genial. At present, he had been promoted over the years to a top position in the current family. Both Mr. Lorenzo and Pat understood, however, that a close friend is only someone less likely to knife you than anyone else. But Pat was unquestionably loyal to his former boss, whom he still called Mr. Lorenzo. He could not be bought and sold, like so many of their associates. Of that, Lorenzo was sure.

Late the next evening, Pasquale was there, drinking, reminiscing, gossiping and chatting as old friends do. He had the habit of laughing appreciatively at his own ribald jokes, but outside of Bruno's presence, Pat's ready humor and amiability could quickly give way to reveal the merciless thug behind the façade. His few superiors deliberately kept him down, the better to watch his behavior for tell tale treachery. Only money and power motivated Pat, like most of his associates, so that he knew Lorenzo had a purpose in asking him to visit, besides just getting together. Pat enjoyed moving people around, always devising new schemes for bending them to fit his aims. But he had to wait for Mr. Lorenzo to disclose what he had in mind. Finally, after talking in general about the family, its current projects and profits, his old chief came to the point. Pat was not surprised by what he heard. The family seldom talked directly when discussing an issue. If important enough, the subject was approached obliquely, so everyone could see what the senior person's disposition and direction were. The custom remained strong with Pat.

"Did you catch that asshole's program the other night?" Lorenzo asked. It was unnecessary to identify the program, because Pat already knew about Feigenmount. "You know who I mean, asshole is too good for him."

"Yes, I saw the program, and I get your drift," Pat responded. He had been a bodyguard at Gina's wake a long time ago, and had a clear idea about Feigenmount's guest. The asshole host was unimportant.

"What did you think about the guy who cured his cancer by eating human flesh?" Bruno asked, almost casually, sounding no more impressed by cannibalism than if Simeon had eaten a mouse and cured cancer.

"Imagine that! Curing cancer!" Pat said, "And by eating someone else! Wouldn't that be something for our girls to sink their teeth into?" A weak joke, but he laughed anyway, while knowing that Mr. Lorenzo had something else in mind. "Do you think he's on the level? It's a great scam, even if it's true. You don't usually show such interest unless it's a girl singer. You sound like you already know him."

"He was at Gina's wake, like us," Bruno reminded him. "I talked to him, and to Father Fogarty. You remember now?" Pat always remembered what he was supposed to, and forgot whenever it was prudent.

"Now I remember, he was a college boy or not much older. He looks a lot older now, but still looks young, but no more college boy." For Pat, any youngish man under thirty, not in his employ, was a college boy. "It's been a long time, even for us. I remember Father Fogarty, too, but that's another story." Pat was not very good at guessing ages or names, except that this, too, was tactical.

Bruno ignored the reference to Fogarty, although he quietly bristled. Right now, the subject was Simeon.

"He changed his name to Simeon Benett out of respect to Gina. I like that. But he can be a business partner for us, too." Pat immediately caught the drift, and wished he'd thought of it. Whenever Mr. Lorenzo or another superior talked about a new scheme to make money or consolidate their power, it was called a project.

"We could do the project," Pat quickly responded, "Use our contacts, no trouble setting it up. Simple. Much money. No risks. These countries have a hard time. No work, too many people and more kids on the way. No way to support them with jobs. Everything is for sale. The project could be a milk cow, too many children anyway." Pat laughed. He could foresee agents scavenging organs from children they'd bought on the open market. The project interested him, so he went on.

"Street kids are never missed. We'd need clean stuff, bought and paid for, no sickly stuff. Go to South America, somewhere. The Islands. No Africans. A little dangerous until we find who gets paid off. We could cut the government out by just spending money for some fucking cause down there. That way, politicians won't come to America, looking for handouts and complaining. We'll bring the money to them, off shore banks, you know. Down where the drugs are, fathers are still willing to sell their daughters. No question about that. Sons can be kept for work. We're over-supplied now with girls, who do a lot of street hustling. The politicians and generals like us and like our cash." Pat was expansive, as if he'd already planned out everything needed to launch another project. However, he hesitated before asking Bruno an important question.

"Why didn't this Simon, Simeon, whatever he calls himself, set up a project himself?" he asked, "Maybe he's a sap of some kind, or a wiseguy putting out a message that he wants to contact us. The market is there and the police are poor, too."

Lorenzo didn't answer because he wasn't sure himself. Pat continued elaborating the prospective project that they'd tell the family about for approval. Far beyond a mere brainstorm, it was almost a deal, pending a talk with Simeon. Sheer humanitarianism was probably just a cover. If not, then for sure, Simeon was a sap, someone who does good things for a cause, without a return. Nevertheless, preliminary planning without activation could go ahead. Pat would start the machinery, get approval by the family, even recruit the manpower but then wait until everything else was settled. Simeon was just the incentive, not a partner, no way, not right now.

Lorenzo already knew that he'd meet with Simeon for reasons having to do with Gina, unrelated to a project. He sighed with nostalgia. Pat noticed and said nothing. Lorenzo was in little doubt and surmised that Simeon would not join their project. He didn't tell Pat. For reasons hardly known to himself, he wanted it that way, keeping Simeon unsullied by family business; even being a sap was better than taking up with a criminal conspiracy.

"Go slow until I can talk to him," Bruno said," I'm glad you like the idea. Maybe, he's on the level about helping mankind or people with death from cancer staring at them. That could be trouble. Conscientious saps are always ready to spill their guts for a good cause. But I did think he was pretty smart about how he handled himself on touchy stuff. People want to be cured, lots of cancer out there, and they're all talking about the cannibal man. Make some inquiries, but easy. If he's not interested, we can go ahead without him. Perhaps we're better off that way."

For old time's sake, Pat quickly yielded, something he was not accustomed to doing these days. Mr. Lorenzo went on, talking reflectively to what amounted to an old friend.

"You know, Pat, I feel for cancer patients. I think about my parents and my wife, God rest their souls." Bruno seldom referred to God, his real family, and never to his dead wife, now gone for uncounted years. She was never very conspicuous, anyway. It had also long been rumored that Lorenzo had a brother who went into the priesthood, but nothing was said directly about this. Bruno never talked religion.

"I hope that Simeon is onto something. Even if he's not a sap, and the cure is just a hook for schnooks, there's a lot of money to be made. People like miracles, even if they should know better."

"Do you think he's one of us?" Pat asked.

"I don't think so, not yet, maybe never," Bruno said quietly, "Gina brought him up and she wouldn't let him be too different from us, or if he was too much like us, she'd do something about it. I don't really know how or why she brought him up. You knew her. From what I heard, of course, he was really a playboy growing up, lots of gelt and girls, maybe guys, too. I just don't know. He had a lot going for him, but maybe he's changed. Who knows what the jungle did to him? Sure, there was plenty of black pussy. Whether he liked that, I wouldn't know. Gina wouldn't let him get too square, too straight." If Bruno knew more, and he surely did know more than he admitted to Pat, he was overly reticent with his old friend.

It was about time for Pat to leave, and for Bruno to be alone with reminiscences. Few people knew about Lorenzo and Gina. They were lovers in a strange compact that recognized no love. In retrospect, Bruno hardly believed it happened the way it did. He was almost faithful to her, and for others in and around the business, it was hands off. She never questioned him about other women, nor did he ask about men, or women, for that matter. Had Gina acquired a stable of lovers through the years, Bruno would have been tolerant enough, without probing. She was very important in the business, especially for a woman, and Bruno, accustomed to ruling firmly, agreed to accept her as she wished.

Bruno was never absolutely sure whether he'd been the one to knock her up. When it happened, he was astonished. Gina never confirmed anything, never even admitting to be pregnant, although it was plain. After an extended leave of absence, she never referred to it, or said whether she gave birth at all. If Bruno had dared to ask, she'd tell him off, with something like, "Go back to your whore sopranos, and mind your own business!" She was very smart, a beautiful woman, and much more. No one was like Gina. And she could get so angry, that even Lorenzo shuddered when her sophisticated demeanor shattered. Just under that suave regal surface, she'd bite your head off and spit it in your face. She never seemed to be close to anyone else but him, at least Bruno hoped that was true. The others were just fill-ins for her private purposes.

Lorenzo clearly left her alone whenever she went back to Simon and her private home. We were lucky to have her working for us, he thought. She did her work thoroughly, promoted business we couldn't get otherwise. Started out as just a special whore, but only for a little while. She was different. All the names she was known by were phony, even *Gina* might have been made up. Should have had a French name, like Benet, something like that. Catholic, but not Italian. It was a new thing to have Gina in on family deals. Some wiseguys couldn't take it, and their wives raised hell. I supported her projects all the way. She never let her girls down, either. If a girl got pregnant, Gina arranged an abortion, though for some reason, she was against abortions on principle. If a girl wanted to keep a kid, that was all right, then out for good. She never let them whore again. Being a good mother makes a bad whore. Probably right. No pimps. Bruno smiled as he recalled a couple of recalcitrant pimps who were persuaded to get out and go into another line of work. He despised pimps, and Gina wouldn't tolerate them. No married girls, either.

Gina wanted agencies and clients to adopt more kids. The pill made the little bastards scarcer, and she got hold of foster kids and helped them as often as she could. She could really play the domineering duchess, but underneath, all determination and guts. Cross her when it counted and she'd roar back. But what a piece she was for me, Bruno Lorenzo. Made me feel like royalty, too. She had a good head, and very good head in bed. That is, for me, I hope. But kids got adopted, lucky for them. No one knew where they came from. Gina made up a pedigree. I offered to be the father when she got pregnant, but she wouldn't admit anything and surely not even appreciation for the offer. I meant it, too. She refused, and went away for a long time. Almost thought she'd left our life, because we couldn't trace her, anywhere. If another guy was the father, he'd better not say so. So, is this the kid? She did bring him up, but what a life he's had. Bruno was getting tired of rehashing the past. He still wondered why Gina kept Simon, instead of farming him out for adoption, like the others. The answer was beyond doubt. Simon was hers, and maybe his, as well.

More than a week later, while the response raged in Bruno's heart and the Program's publicity was high, a woman telephoned Simeon at his hotel, inviting him to meet with Mr. Lorenzo. Privacy and secrecy were no longer tight, and she apparently had no trouble locating him. The invitation was diplomatic, less a demand, but more than a polite summons. Simeon did not immediately recognize Lorenzo's name, although it had a vaguely familiar ring. At first, he thought Mr. Lorenzo was just another minor league celebrity wanting to cash in on some additional publicity, and almost refused. However, the invitation sounded like a command performance he would be unwise to refuse. He did not think of the urbane and somewhat glossy man he spoke with at Gina's wake.

In order to keep the message alive and the public's interest sharp, Simeon tried to maintain strict privacy ever since Feigenmount's program. But with his picture published and mail reaching the hotel, it proved impossible. He was afraid that the message might soon become hackneyed, and the cannibal man could be as worn-out as last week's news. If Simeon could somehow magically manage to rise above the mere celebrity and be a miracle benefactor, the story might gather its own momentum. The public would even forget sensationalism and turn the cannibal cure into an acceptable, even respectable topic. It was a vain and pious hope, of course, because the cure needed cannibalism to perpetuate the notoriety, and cannibalism needed the cure to keep the story popular.

Cannibalism would be easy to rationalize if there is something to gain like a complete recovery, and nothing to lose except biased morality. If human flesh can be eaten to save a life, surely it is better than being eaten away. This is what Simeon vaingloriously hoped about his mission. All that remained was widespread human sanction. Whoever he was, Mr. Lorenzo might be willing to lend some help. It was worth dropping the resolve about privacy and finding out what made this special invitation so hard to resist.

Bruno Lorenzo lived in an imposing condominium facing the Boston harbor. Once grim granite warehouses and factories, but then vacated by shifting economic tides, developers converted the deserted buildings into expensive and exclusive residences on the waterfront. Lining the docks and harbor, the buildings now clustered, impervious to intrusion. The wealthy occupants were seldom seen, except on summer evenings when they entertained aboard yachts and large cruisers tied alongside their homes. From a lofty aerie, topmost on one of the larger buildings, Lorenzo's view swept over the surrounding city, harbor, airport and even small towns miles away. He could ignore the rest of the waterfront, where visitors and tourists spent money in fashionable restaurants and boutiques on the principal pathways, still redolent in historical memories.

For his part Lorenzo never engaged his neighbors in a friendly chat. A courteous nod was enough. His reputation gave them a vicarious thrill, and no amount of cultural patronage erased the source of his riches. With only a little regret, he was destined to have few friends aside from former family associates, and people wanting something for their cause. Lorenzo had to be wary, just because his neighbors secretly disapproved in milder cases, and despised him in others. He was just an upscale hoodlum. Nevertheless, fellow-residents felt a little more secure just by sharing a building with him.

Simeon had traveled widely in civilized and developing countries, but never in this section of Boston before. Only by asking strangers for specific directions did he locate Mr. Lorenzo's building. There were few street signs to mark the place where he lived. An iron fence and forbidding gates to the premises set all the occupants apart, in order that only a select few were allowed to enter. A sturdy young man in a parking lot uniform asked Simeon's name, and made a call. Only then did he direct Simeon to a specific entrance. Another guard, dressed neatly but casually, met Simeon at the door and by private elevator took him to the top floor. Mr. Lorenzo was there to greet him.

As soon as the door opened Simeon immediately recognized Mr. Lorenzo. He was the man from Aunt Gina's wake who seemed to know her better than anyone else, with the possible exception of Father Fogarty. He had wanted to see him again. In his welcome, Mr. Lorenzo was casual but carefully formal. He shook hands and called him Simon, without hesitation, implying that their acquaintance went back before the Feigenmount program and the name change. Mr. Lorenzo was dressed as any prosperous executive at his leisure might be, in keeping with current style and the advice of expensive tailors. Nevertheless, momentarily ignoring Lorenzo's fine clothes, the furnishings and artwork of Lorenzo's spacious condominium, Simeon noticed an uncanny resemblance between Mr. Lorenzo and the old Chief back home. Skin color and tribal regalia could not have been more different, but they seemed at a glance to have similar facial features, such as a longish nose, black, somewhat curly, full head of hair, high cheekbones, steadfast eyes and a generous but restrained smile. Both men radiated authority and power. While their voices had altogether different tonality, their speech indicated that neither was accustomed to interruption, having their views questioned, or challenged without mortal risk. In the sense that everyone stems from a few primordial families eons ago, perhaps Lorenzo, the Chief, and Simeon as well, were all related, despite race, circumstances, culture, and state of being. It was a pleasant observation, establishing an amusing but antithetical link across the oceans and the span of circumstance.

Simeon followed Lorenzo down a corridor to a large study where at the bay window an observer could see and inspect the surroundings from a lofty distance. Still mulling and absorbing the resemblance of these two men, so distant in other respects, Simeon wondered which one was more aboriginal and made life and death decisions most easily. Without being told, Simeon assumed that Mr. Lorenzo was also a Chief in high standing, and could be compared with the Chief he knew. He had no doubt that both men could kill without hesitation, once they decided to unsheathe their power.

The study was apparently a working office and a small library, with several firmly packed bookshelves around the walls. A large desk and scattered leather chairs were intended for audiences petitioning Lorenzo for advice. The aura of a throne room made it the site of important conversations, and there were no other kind. It was the private sanctuary of a cultivated but unsavory gentleman, a throwback to the 19th century, or even earlier, to an age when private riches meant near-royal power, temporal and spiritual, and power was a reward for private wealth, however gained. Notorious families in Renaissance Europe wielded such power, but to compare one family with the one Lorenzo now represented would stretch imagination and falsely sanction the clean image Lorenzo fostered.

Lorenzo pointed casually to a designated chair, facing the window and the bright sun, so that he could no longer look directly at his host without squinting. Simeon considered moving the chair, before realizing that the position was deliberate. Glancing around, he could see a few paintings and noticed the bookshelves, but could not see titles. On the whole, the extensive apartment reserved its final grandeur for this room where only Mr. Lorenzo evidently read, worked, and studied. In truth, the wide windows betrayed another use. It was a watchtower. Both men quickly acknowledged that they met only once before, at Gina's wake, but then went on chatting casually about Boston and its antiquities. Finally, Mr. Lorenzo got around to Simeon himself.

"You are no longer that young man," Mr. Lorenzo said, "Even though you look and seem to be much younger than the age I know you are. Still, I recognized you at once when I saw Feigenmount's program. Your presentation created quite a sensation. Even this morning's Globe still mentions it. Its popularity is something rare for TV programs. I imagine you've been very busy, fielding calls and questions from all over."

Simeon decided to be quietly and modestly appreciative, and even surprised at the publicity. Of course, the response was exactly what he wanted in the first place.

"I was overwhelmed. Millions saw the program, I understand. I appreciated the chance, that is, I was glad to have a chance to get my message out there and let people know there's hope, even for very advanced cancer cases. I was afraid the sensational parts might queer everything, but after all, that's the message, and they have to take one with the other, that is, until science comes up with something less sensational, and perhaps finds the active ingredient. Cannibalism is a pretty shocking idea and it goes against what society accepts."

Mr. Lorenzo evidently decided not to get into the controversial side of the program, and said nothing about Feigenmount.

"I'm glad you had time to accept my invitation. There must be many demands for other appearances by this time." Bruno would have been very offended, had Simeon refused.

"For some reason, I didn't recall meeting you until now, but your invitation seemed special to me. I didn't consider not accepting immediately. Now I know why. You and my Aunt must have been very good friends, although growing up I never met any of her friends and surely never knew their names. I would have remembered you. I know now about your generosity, too, for the arts, music, so on. But I'm not sure how I learned about it. You are probably too modest to hear yourself described as Lorenzo the Magnificent but the comparison fits, from all I've heard." Simeon was not putting on the flattery as thickly as it sounded, but his words did have the ring of truth. He spoke correctly about knowing somehow of Bruno's generosity, perhaps from Gilday, but he couldn't be sure. Lorenzo smiled in appreciation, as if unworthy of such grandiose comparison, which he secretly liked anyway. Even so, Lorenzo was less amenable to praise than Feigenmount whose legendary ego always needed nourishment. Simeon wanted to get away from his cannibal cure but Lorenzo, seemingly non-committal, led him easily into the cure, putting aside for the moment, the main reason to meet, which was Aunt Gina.

"I suppose you need as much help in your mission as any aspiring artist or organization, but not financially, I am sure. Your cause is much more important than what appeals only to aesthetic or artistic tastes. Yours is an appeal for humanity, but it also has a side that can lead to prosperity, too, that all of us care about, unless doing good exclusively carries a person away, without payment of some kind. Your story has attracted so much publicity, and it has a lot of promise." Lorenzo said this in an off-hand way that he might have used in paying a much-needed compliment to a young musician or opera singer, without hinting at a business proposition. Simeon wanted to pursue Lorenzo's philanthropic bent, but questions about Aunt Gina dated much further back, more urgent even than his mission and all its promise. Simeon abruptly changed the subject.

"Mr. Lorenzo, I remember the wake very vividly. You said Aunt Gina worked for your family business. You had much good to say, but it wasn't very specific. You recall, maybe, that I never knew Aunt Gina's business or why she left me for so long from time to time. For years, I wondered, say, why she was away from home for weeks sometimes, never explaining where or when she'd come back. I supposed, later, after the wake, that it had something to do with the family business. When I was younger, I always felt abandoned, like an orphan left on somebody's doorstep. And for all I knew, which was practically nothing, I was an abandoned baby when she took me in. I could have been adopted, but I never knew. Aunt Gina didn't believe in being too candid."

Lorenzo smiled sympathetically but said nothing. He seemed to be staring at something just over Simeon's shoulder, but Simeon couldn't tell, facing the sun's glare from the windows.

"I hope you won't be offended, Sir, but after her death, I came into lots of money," Simeon said, wondering why in the world Mr. Lorenzo would be offended by talking about money. "I tried to find out where all that money came from, and whether it had anything to do with the family business. I found out finally what your family business is, but I'm not sure, although I was told what she had to do with it." It was a statement, not an accusation. Indeed, it was diplomatic, disingenuous, and informed.

"I suppose that means you couldn't believe all you heard," Lorenzo replied, smiling and sounding as if this were all a very old, somewhat tedious story that once again, he chose not to explain or apologize for. Underneath his formal but laconic manner, Lorenzo would welcome a chance to talk about Gina as much as Simeon wanted to know all about his parentage. But he did not intend to answer all Simeon's questions about Gina and the family. Instead, he told a little, and held back much more.

"That was Gina, trustworthy, loyal, devoted to you, and to the business. She could keep secrets until death's door, no matter who was knocking, even the devil himself, coming to answer. I wish I could tell you she never confided in anyone, but I wouldn't even know that for sure. It just seemed that way. But she'd never lie just to change a fact she'd rather not talk about. She would prefer saying nothing. Gina was without a question always the best, dependable and very diligent in whatever she did." Mr. Lorenzo began to sound like an employer giving a reference, without showing any personal affection. "The family appreciated all she did over the years. She did very well for herself, too, as you must know from your money. I know very little about her investments but they were also substantial."

"I appreciated my aunt, too, Mr. Lorenzo, in every way. I never imagined that she'd deliberately deceive me. She never did, except that she didn't tell me very much. I'm afraid, though, I didn't give her as much attention as she deserved, but she didn't mind, I hope. I wished she'd told me more about her health when it failed, and through my boyhood, about my natural parents, if she knew, especially how she came to take care of me, and raise me. She never talked family, whether your kind or mine."

Questions were out of him at last, like ghosts from a locked-up past. But Simeon's questions about family were far different from an unasked question whether Gina had ever been in a family way, or even a question about her own family. He assumed that Lorenzo kept secrets, too, that no one could pry out. Surely, Simeon could expect very limited information about Gina.

As if to confirm Simeon's assumptions, Lorenzo said nothing, but got up from his chair, turned around, and went to the wide window overlooking the harbor and nearby lands and towns. He beckoned to Simeon to join him, pointing out various ships, much like a favorite uncle might instruct a young boy.

"I know them all, Simon, after all these years. Most I remember; others I never cared much for. Out there, that cruiser, pretending to be a ship. That's the Desert Wind, registered here. Further out is the Soya Harbor from the Philippines. It carries a cargo, and inside the cargo is another cargo holding still other cargoes until we reach something forbidden. There's My Old Man, a funny name for a boat, but it does say something about one man's search for his father. I wonder if he ever found him. I guess not. If you look for a really dignified name, with lots of heritage, there's the Garibaldi. I don't know if you're up on Italian history or not, but he was a patriot who wasn't always sure which side to support, even his King's. And a little further out, slowly coming in, you can see the Halifax Queen. Nothing to do with the present Queen."

Simeon was nonplused about what the hell a distraction like this had to do with Gina and his family, this family of boats with evocative names. This surely had nothing to do with betrayal, loyalty, family businesses, and secrets. But it might illuminate something hard to speak of directly, provided that the ship names, complicated ownerships, passages, and cryptic cargoes could be deciphered. Perhaps these were Lorenzo's coded responses to Simeon's questions.

"I have watched ships from all over. They come and then leave. You know, I keep myself informed, not only these ships, but others, sometimes their secrets, too. Mostly, I just keep it all quiet, but watch, and they don't know it. It's sort of a hobby. I respected Gina's privacy, especially outside the family business, which was her business. It was her business, not our business. I never intruded, and came to respect your privacy, too. I knew a little, at least for a little while. I have sources, you know. I am always curious, but there's a problem sometimes about knowing and not knowing, and not knowing which is which, truth or convenient stories. I hope you understand that I sometimes tell, and sometimes not tell, and compromise by distraction. For example, I knew about your name, Simon Simon, and the reason for changing it, later on. But I didn't know why you had those names in the first place. No one ever told me. I also knew later that you never worked at a regular job, not a regular job for a living, but took made-up jobs with false identity. Why you did this is your business, too, but I couldn't have known. That is, until I realized that was your regular job, pretending to be someone else," Lorenzo continued.

"The chief reason I had for informing myself about *you*, especially after Gina's death, was for Gina's sake and her wish for, say, anonymity and secrecy. I didn't want you poking around into something that was not your business. Yes, I found out quickly about Gilday, a good man for the work he did. Whatever Gina did or didn't do, it didn't affect you. After your investigator, Gildea, found out more than I thought necessary, I needed to give him a message, as soon as I heard about it. He got the message. I am giving you no reason right now for anything that happened or didn't happen, except that our family is kept well informed and it respects secrets, too, whatever we find out. We betray no one. No, that's not true. We have had our share of renegades. I was amused by some of the capers and the company you kept. April Breeze, no less. That stint as a ship's doctor was very amusing, and the hubbub it caused when you left. I don't suppose you could make any more mistakes being a so-so fake ship's doctor than some of the medical dogs they'd had aboard in the past, or practicing somewhere now. But it was risky."

Simeon was surprised and resentful about being followed by someone he knew next to nothing about. What was Gina to Lorenzo? He was reluctant to pursue that right now. A fundamental question he wanted was about Simon Simon. Who was this child and how did Gina get hold of him? He was not plain nobody's boy, but somebody's, for sure. And then, why did Lorenzo take such an interest in Simon, since they'd had no contact?

"True enough," Simeon said, "Everything you've said, and more. I've been at loose ends, living an even looser life. That is, until I got cancer or, rather, cancer got me. Nothing meant much. I couldn't know how much Aunt Gina meant. What was I to her, I mean a formal relation? I suppose

228

that I didn't really want to know as much as I thought I wanted to know. It always hurt when she showed any feeling about anyone else. You're right about distractions, yes, but I was never a real fugitive, never a real anything."

Simeon couldn't believe that he was unburdening himself to a plutocratic thug, although a savvy, and perhaps kindly thug with a connection to Gina, but when and where, aside from general information about the family.

"No one cared where I was and what I did, except you, for your own reasons, your hobby, like knowing about ships coming into Boston Harbor. I don't suppose *you'll* tell me who I am, if Aunt Gina never did. No one chased me, except after I jumped ship, and then only because I deserted them. I've had no reason to be a fugitive, and yet I was." If Simeon expected any clarifying response from Lorenzo, he didn't get it. He talked about being a fugitive more than he understood. It was a fugitive's escape from permanency and from true identification.

Lorenzo again stared out the window at the tiny ships down below, like a child playing with toy boats in his private bathtub. Simeon felt the deep silence and knew it would never be penetrated. But he was enjoying this first real confession to someone who strangely seemed to matter and care, beyond Aunt Gina. Even with Sophia, he was recalcitrant to talk very deeply, keeping almost everything a secret, just as Gina wanted. Besides, intimacy aside, Sophia didn't want to hear anything personal. She kept herself aloof, except in bed, talking little about much.

"Yes, when I peed blood that morning, I stopped all the pretense and pretending. Nothing like blood to bring you back to earth. I had to find out what was wrong, and with that, what was right. One size didn't fit me at all, but I'd tried to fit into all kinds of jobs, none of which I truly believed in, just to see what it was like. It took a long time afterward, and not until the cancer cure did I seem to bring something into focus. All the chemo and stuff back here made me sick, and made me regret all that shit. I was an impostor and enjoyed the deception. Mr. Lorenzo, Sir, whoever you are, I am surely no saint. I do know better now what I am, at least for present purposes, thanks to cancer, the tribe, and cannibalism. Some of the poor cancer people want to think I'm more than I ever could be. I'm not a devil and God knows, not a saint! To make them well, that's all that matters. I am now called Simeon, but which one? Not Saint-Simon, not Saint Simeon. No saint at all. Simeon Benett is OK with me. It makes me feel permanently attached to Aunt Gina." Lorenzo slowly turned back to Simeon. The sun had gone down enough in the late afternoon for them to look directly at each other.

"I did ask Gina about you, once. She was raising you, and I asked. It didn't interfere with family business, so she told me to mind my own business. Since the wake, you've known that Gina was a closet Catholic, opposed to abortion. She was against abortion when I knew her, but went along with it, considering the risks of our business. She wanted to bring up a child but never did, until you came along. I never came right out and said whose child is this? Are you the mother, and if you are, am I the father? I wanted to know, bad enough, but I couldn't break through her silence and obstinacy; it was all taboo."

"She taught me about breaking taboos. I suppose you know about that?"

"Only certain taboos are taboo for us, Simeon. Otherwise we don't bother. For me, a taboo is just a policy that people are supposed to obey until it gets in the way of what you really want to do. For me, it has nothing to do with being a sinner. That is all crap to me. Anyhow, I stopped following you, or getting the word what you were up to, a long time ago." Simeon was now sure that Lorenzo had not known about the cancer until Feigenmount's program. What made him stop following him? When? Lorenzo shook his head, and then asked about Papua New Guinea, more about what and who took him there. It was another distraction, dissuading him from further questions.

"It took cancer to get me there, a disease and a dare. The Program must have mentioned that." He didn't expect Lorenzo to know about cancer and Cancer. Surely he couldn't know how far the reach of Cancer goes, or how hard it grasps you. Simeon couldn't have known about Lorenzo's parents, dying of cancer when he was young.

"Cancer brought you back here with a message for all humanity, at least that part of mankind with radios and TV's? No scrape with the law in New Guinea? No cuckolded husbands?" From all appearances Lorenzo wanted to get back to family business and their project, but Simeon had a few more things to say, enjoying a conversation with someone so responsive and yet so carefully modulated.

"The world, which means the part of Feigenmount's audience that remembers what I said, must think of me now as a would-be minor messiah bringing a special message, or, I hope not, some wild man from the jungle trying to promote cannibalism. I hope I'm neither, not that it's likely. They probably haven't any idea where I was, and what the people are like. Lots of things right here are much worse than curing someone of cancer through cannibalism. What about cannibalizing after someone is already dead? Some smart-asses call it necrophilia, something pathological, when it is no different than eating a sirloin steak and calling it bovinophilia. For some folks, I'm a freak, anyway, like someone from a sideshow, frightening kids.

I can't get away from one fact: I was as good as dead, or as bad as can be, when I ate the meat from other humans. Here I am, healthier than ever. I was rescued and I owe somebody a lot just for that."

Simeon was exhausted, but pleased. Late afternoon shadows were creeping across the rooftops of nearby buildings, preparing for another night of waterfront pleasure. Still, Lorenzo had scarcely alluded to the project he and Pat talked about at length and were prepared to launch. Without a signal, an elderly black man came into the room, bringing tea and little pastries, a treat for a little boy. They sat, munching, and serious talk stopped. Buoyed by still unspoken topics, they chatted about trivialities.

Simeon felt exceedingly comfortable, though he realized all too poignantly that Lorenzo's family was not the one he sought. It was like getting together with a favorite uncle after a long absence. Simeon could not help but notice that he was still being sized up. Did he detect a glint of affectionate amusement? Was Lorenzo just staring at him blankly, or was he about to drop more information, ever so casually? Lorenzo was like the old fish head, all over again, telling him to go forth, and know the difference between good and evil. But the fish head never did say those things. Finally, Lorenzo spoke, indicating that the afternoon had not entirely evaporated into good feelings and amiability all around.

"You seem to have spent much of your life, even after the cancer, looking for a past, Simeon," Lorenzo said softly, and not unkindly, like a well-seasoned psychoanalyst. "What a waste of what you might have done with yourself! Your jobs were fakes, you told me that. Gina raised you right, but on her terms, not yours. Gina could run away from her past, but she had a past that I didn't know very much about. She earned everything she got, and I backed her all the way. Breaking taboos? No one is more gullible than a fool who thinks he can't be fooled. And I am as foolish as the next person. I am what you know me to be. She brought you up to break taboos? Nonsense! Taboos are never banished, break one and another one pops up, even stronger, that you may not recognize. Did she ever allow you to do something with yourself, besides lots of fancy sex, which left you bewildered as ever? Yes, I had a strong idea about that, too! It was almost your undoing. Such freedom is hardly better than slavery. I exaggerate. It is far better than slavery. What made using your head and doing something useful so taboo? You wasted yourself until you got cancer and happened to recover. What you still want to know is no secret. The answers were not secret. Is the right word, *ambiguous*? At least until now. Who were your real parents? Right? Gina? Me? I suppose I should break a secret pact that Gina and I had, which was never to tell you. Believe me, I want to, because it will pull things together for you and cause you some pain, as well." Simeon held his breath, listening to Lorenzo who seemed to be toying with the idea of spilling the beans, but the beans were already spilt, one by one. Lorenzo was pretty sure he was Simeon's father, because Gina cut him out when she became pregnant, but she could not totally cut him out of what he felt.

Lorenzo had gone from the lightest mood in this late afternoon, late in his life when it no longer seemed to matter, to the resurrection of deep memories and still simmering suspicion, all without changing his conversational tone, just while sipping tea. It hadn't occurred to Simeon that he might be Lorenzo's bastard son until now. Incredible, he thought, and for that reason, like so much in his life, it is possible. By shedding the last uncertainty it was a tantalizing thought. No less disconcerting, however, were recollections of sleeping with Gina.

"Years ago," Simeon started to say, "Right after Gina died, I spoke with her lawyer, Burt. Of course, I learned about that money, never where it came from. But she was not what she seemed. Look at the contrast between a high executive, or chief whore in charge of other whores, and the faithful, retiring, generous churchwoman, still concerned about abused women and abandoned children, always ready with her checkbook and counseling. Who was this Fogarty, anyway? What made taboos so important to her? Is hypocrisy no more than breaking taboos when no one is looking?"

The venerable Lorenzo reprimanded the upstart.

"Gina gave you an upside down way of behaving, Simeon. You have a puritan's way of looking at the world, which may surprise you. You think that the only taboos worth breaking are sexual, as if sexual morals are the only thing to pay attention to. There's much more than the tyranny of sex. Well, it was only the way a wayward puritan might bring you up. If you really want to break taboos, the way our family does, you *ignore* them, and don't go looking for a prohibition. And you should, yes, 'should' is a moral word, always keep something hidden inside, something good, while you're breaking taboos, just to make you feel like a pious hypocrite. Indifference is a blessing." Simeon was shaking, as if he'd been abruptly unmasked. Lorenzo continued, just as casual and wise, not mocking, except in the indulgent tolerant style of old men who have out-lived almost everyone else. He knew that the fugitive had been apprehended.

"You came back to tell the world about your cure and for now, a lot of people are listening. But the world never really listens; it's too busy looking after self-interest to care about much else, even if it cures cancer. People do what they must or feel like doing, and only want to be shown how to do it easier, cheaper, more often, and for their own benefit. Where will cancer people get human flesh should they want to follow you? Did you think about that? You are like a preacher telling his flock to be good, without telling them how to do it. It makes the preacher feel righteous, and I suppose that's good.

"My family is just indifferent enough or cares enough in spite of the taboo, to supply all the human flesh any cancer patient needs, whether or not your treatment really works, and get a fair price. That should please the puritan in you." Lorenzo knew now for sure that he didn't need or want Simeon. His so-called mission would soon dry up. And the family will expand into this new project, rid of Simeon, gathering up more money, cure or not. Simeon is too much the moralist to betray anything.

Simeon surprised Lorenzo a little by promptly saying that the project was OK with him, he just didn't want to be part of it. While Lorenzo was waffling about a proposition, Simeon had anticipated and rejected being a part of that family's business. It confirmed the moralist in him, which Simeon accepted readily. Considering that people must die in order to provide the meat for cancer, he didn't bother with distinguishing between the already dead and those sold for human consumption. When someone becomes convinced that his cause is right and his behavior good enough, anything is feasible and excusable, depending on the package. Lorenzo's project was not much different than the policy of Simeon's tribal family. Killing for thievery and poaching was right, too, at least right enough. Legality always lags behind the taboo that supports it in the first place. Simeon wanted to avoid further allusion to the project, now that he was out of it, and to talk more about Aunt Gina, now much less likely to be his aunt.

"I can't imagine Aunt Gina working for the family and getting as far as she did without sleeping with you," he said flatly, "So where do you fit into my life?" Lorenzo did not have to answer directly. It was ridiculously obvious, and the lifelong secrecy was ludicrous.

"Who slept with whom, how long, and with what result is not your business, even now," Lorenzo said, sternly, "Gina was just about everything a woman could be: smart, beautiful, ambitious. She had it all. She could have had a real career, doing almost anything. Yet, at first, for a very short time, she was a young whore. She did what whores do and got paid for it. I never found out why she chose this way to earn a living, and do that to herself. Maybe revenge, to get back at someone, but that's too easy. She wouldn't take orders from anyone, even the committee, unless she saw a real advantage in it. She argued her case very well, and persuasively. The committee was often hard to convince. We had to be very careful with her around, though it's hard to believe. Perhaps that was in part because I was inclined to be on her side, although I was no dupe, you can be sure. I wouldn't have lasted very long or gotten as far as I did. If a pimp ever tried to get hold of her, she'd kill him right then and there. And I mean crush him, right away, like an insect. I had to wonder if she ever had killed anyone, and gotten into the whore business as an escape, like the fugitive you talked about. No answer, of course. I pride myself on getting information about anyone. Not on Gina. I kept her, how to say it, off limits to everyone except me. I suppose I fooled myself about that, too. The fact is that I didn't want to find out, that's the truth. I suppose there was a taboo about that. 'Respecting her privacy' is not an answer. But I didn't have to be very smart, just smart enough to know that something was gnawing at her, always. Maybe it was a taboo that had been broken against her will. Someone must have done something to her, really cruel, vicious or perverted. If she'd really killed anyone, I didn't want to know."

Lorenzo was now talking at an emotional crescendo, no more the world weary, benign uncle. Lorenzo spit indignation; hot words like cinders came from his mouth, searing his lips and memory.

"There was a wound inside her, a scar, that must have burned very deep. The whoring life for our girls is because they're broke and bitter. We train ourselves not to care, we demand it, and we don't care, except about big money. Few choose it as a job unless forced into it. The johns are just too repulsive. The girls don't last long, unless they feel that the johns are even worse than they are, which is easy to do. Most have been raped or abused by father, brother, even mother. They come into the life hating them, and hope that making lots of money will prove that they're worth something more than a piece of ass. With boy whores, it's usually money and they're too lazy to do anything else. They run away from home, and that's it, no home to speak of, and like earning bucks while they're still young. Drugs make it even easier for them."

Now Lorenzo was rambling, trying to pull himself back from recollections. By this time, Simeon learned enough and his few guesses could be wrong, but perhaps not. Maybe she'd had a child she'd given away, before going to work for the family. Maybe a rape by someone she expected more from: a father, priest, a trusted someone. Little Simon was to break every prohibition, especially sexual, for her freedom, even freedom that concealed their relationship. And she surely chose the most destructive way to do it, having incest with a kid until in healthy adolescence he wanted to screw her. Then she stopped. No gay stuff either, better have an affair with another old woman, past childbearing. That freedom stuff was basically all shit, cooked up philosophy, just to cover seduction of a child. And then, she secretly supported the Church, that most pious of institutions. Lady bountiful. Was she forgiven? Was Father Fogarty in on it? A priest? Women needing help got their help. Simeon's ruminations stopped when Bruno continued.

234

"When I found out you paid an investigator with a hot nose to look into things, we scared the shit out of him. He gave you a few scraps to keep you from doing any more investigating. It worked. He didn't know that Gina wanted to mother someone, whether she'd admit it or not. It had something to do with you, whoever you are. She despised a pregnant hooker. At the same time, she'd help them out. I told you all this before. She hated abortion and had a strong Catholic belief inside her. Up for adoption, OK. That was the better way. Gina was very tough when she had to be. The family never cancelled her decisions. Whores could be mothers, but mothers never a working whore. That was her taboo."

"Where do I fit in, a bastard that turned out to be me?" Simeon said, "I suppose I was someone's accident, even Gina's accident, a douche that failed. But why did Gina choose me to raise? Now I know. I was hers, and likely, yours? Never hinted that I was someone else's throwaway. No, she raised me to call her 'Aunt'. I meant something to her. I went along with her talk about love but lusted after old women."

"Gina deserves more than your sanctimonious skepticism and derision, Simon. She brought you up in the only way she knew. With all your name-calling, a true worldly man does not condescend in that way. You were jealous of her friends, men and women. Jealous of where she went. Did you ever feel like killing someone, for no good reason? Not from anger. Our family kills for business reasons, seldom out of anger, which is not the same as revenge. Killing with us is a business strategy that Gina understood." Of course, Lorenzo exculpated himself by presenting a rationale for Simeon's approval. But why did he go back to talk about killing? Like his namesake prototype, Lorenzo the Magnificent, this Lorenzo could readily order someone killed, but only for a principle and for convenience. He was ruthless and compassionate, all sorts of incomprehensible antithetical qualities thrived inside of this man. At this moment, more deeply than he ever thought possible, Simeon wanted Lorenzo's respect and affection. He wanted Lorenzo to understand and forgive him for wasting his life on profligacy, everything he had done and not done, until Cancer and KA showed him a way.

"I ran out of taboos a long time ago," Simeon said, "And never got a woman pregnant. That was evidently what Gina approved of. It was possible; there were a few young enough women who might have gotten knocked up. I had this hankering for old women. You seem to know that, for God's sake. Gina had her reasons. It's hard to explain but getting cancer of the penis was right on target. Cannibalism is something like taking communion, or keeping kosher, something like that. It upholds the law. I killed a man once, and not out of anger. It was something I had to do because according to the tribe's law, he deserved it. I did it to get respect, to be more like them than just another white guy. Maybe that's the principle you respect. Tell me, once and for all, are you my father by Gina or any other woman?" Instead of keeping silent, Lorenzo did not avoid the question at all.

"Yes, I suppose I could be your father, and not made-up uncle, like Aunt Gina. Through all these years, I have wondered, and then I realized I'd never know absolutely, for sure, but, my boy, it is very likely, knowing Gina as I did, and meeting you again. And I don't mean physical resemblance. I shall never resort to DNA. That would betray Gina's wish. She never said and I wasn't supposed to know about her pregnancy. It was all very secret. I was seeing her exclusively at the time, and there wasn't anyone else that I knew about. She would be very devious if she wanted to cheat, that is. If Gina was secretly your mother and I, your father, well, that's not important now, except to you, perhaps. What if you'd been the son of another woman, a nameless anyone, one of our whores? What if at that time, Gina just felt like having a male child to rear? She went away for a while, I must assume before you arrived. Anything could have happened. I don't know, and don't think I'd tell you, if I did. Gina wouldn't want me to, or she'd have told you herself. What difference would it make? What about all the other unwanted kids from indifferent parents? Would you like that, caught in poverty, where selling a kid makes it possible to feed the rest of the family? If a poor parent can't afford to raise another child, is it OK to sell that child, for a reason, even to be cooked into a stew, as you put it? Do you want to help others, or be left to starve, abandoned on the streets, or sell your young body to some creep, and finally when you're no good to anyone, allowed to die?"

Simeon was almost staggered by Lorenzo's sophistry, wisdom, honesty or whatever he talked about, beyond what he'd known. Children could be bought and sold for any purpose at a negotiable price. That was a fact beyond dispute and not a theory. Simeon could have been one of those dispensable foundlings, with parents known or unknown, but he preferred Lorenzo, his acknowledged sire, but unsanctioned by the law. Now he had a glimmering of understanding he could live with. Whether Lorenzo was his father made less difference than that Simeon wanted to mean something lasting to this man. He profoundly sensed a similar response in Lorenzo that went beyond parenthood.

"Simeon, we've talked longer than I expected. You're a pretty nice guy, no more, no less. Please have patience with our dear Gina, and how she earned the money you enjoy now. I mean tolerance for her secrecy. I have to live with that, too. You may prefer the jungle now, and belong there. But our family is as real and as much yours as those little black people way back there, up in the mountains, somewhere you're so proud of."

Simeon didn't know if Lorenzo were chiding, teasing, or really trying to disavow all they talked about. Regardless, however, he wished that in spite of themselves, Gina had been his mother openly, and Lorenzo his acknowledged father. Perhaps they were. No perhaps about it; they were likely parents. He could go no further. Lorenzo had come close but Simeon also understood Lorenzo's hesitation, beyond that of Gina's wish. If Gina *were* his mother, then Simeon would be forced to embrace an offensive taboo. If he, Simon, not so simple, *were* only adopted, she, aunt by common and unofficial consent, well, then, seduction of a child was a tolerable perversion for a woman inclined to have her way with either sex. Which would Simeon choose, had he a choice?

"Imagine, me, the son of a gangster and a whore, and no great person myself. If not you, then whoever she screwed when I was conceived. Some other hooker might have been my mother. Maybe my father was Fr. Fogarty, which would make me a true son of the Church. Fucking a priest would be taboo enough for Gina, just like teaching a boy how to fondle a woman."

"Enough of that! If we promise to cure cancer using human flesh, we'll not be more ethical if we just substitute pork, beef, or chicken. I can't praise or blame you for your upbringing. Whoever they were, you're stuck with the parents and upbringing you had. Just like me, just like Gina. Neither should you blame Gina. She did tell me how shocked she was when you actually fell for Sophia. It was all right to screw her, but not fall in love! She didn't plan it that way, just wanted to get you away from gays." Simeon should not have been surprised to hear Sophia mentioned.

"No, she wanted to keep me straight," Simeon said, "But Sophia was just right for me at that time, and for a time, I was right for her. You must know about Chester, too." Lorenzo held up his hand, stopping Simeon from confessing pointlessly.

"I met Sophia once, very casually," Lorenzo said, "My kind and hers do not mix very often or very well. Very cultured, rich, but she wasn't snooty, lots of good qualities. Good for you that Gina picked her out. Not just to keep you straight, but Sophia's oldest daughter and Gina were off and on lovers for a pretty long time. That's why I think she thought of Sophia. You didn't know that, I'm sure. Sophia knew it, and that's why she trusted Gina and her discretion. It was an exchange. She trusted Gina's judgment, without moral judgment about age difference. She was hot and curious." For Simeon, this was shocking new information. But for Lorenzo, it was mentioned casually, like a prosaic bit of gossip about mutual acquaintances. What doesn't this man know? If Gina was his Aunt, then Lorenzo is just a guardian angel. But the truth remained with him, like a shadow silently following him, having dispersed his uncertainty about parentage.

Now Simeon stood up, again, as did Lorenzo. Tea was over, and so at last, was their meeting. It seemed as if they were about to say good-bye much earlier, but Lorenzo continued to talk, no doubt to confirm what he had planned all along. By this time, Simeon, enlightened beyond what he'd imagined, was ready to greet the darkness outside.

"When shall we, or can we meet again?" he asked earnestly. Lorenzo's reply was equally sincere, but measured, now that the afternoon's meeting had settled Simeon's abiding questions with finality.

"Simeon," Lorenzo said, with a trace of hesitation, like a judge tempted to exceed his jurisdiction, "We shall never meet again." The decision was beyond negotiation, and yet, in a kindly way, tinged by regret, it was like a father bidding goodbye to an only son, about to seek his fortune elsewhere.

When Simeon reached the street, he felt a grave solitude. So these were his parents. That was more certainty than he'd ever felt before. Everything else seemed neutral, and every person indifferent to the jungle man's presence among them. Had Simeon sprouted wings and flown away, like a flying fox, no one would have noticed. Never to meet again meant that now he must grieve alone, as never before, for the father and mother hidden in the tangled, disreputable past.

Chapter 13—Two Gods for Simeon

Although Simeon and Bruno Lorenzo never met again, memory of that afternoon stayed with Simeon for the rest of his life. It was a decisive moment that Simeon recalled over and over again. Lorenzo did not firmly settle Simeon's speculations about his heritage, once and for all, but he came as close as prudence allowed. He had been candid, but gently and deliberately evasive, repeatedly stopping short of absolute and unequivocal information about Gina and Bruno. But Simeon now knew what he had always questioned. In all likelihood, they were his biological parents, with a slight chance of something else. The answers were not gratifying. There was incest regardless of whatever perversity remained after he and Gina desisted. What Simeon found most endearing was his feeling for Lorenzo, in all likelihood his father, and not just an Uncle to match Gina's alias of Aunt. Strange that for Simeon, accustomed to being remote and unattached, here was an older man, known only through his sinister reputation, who sparked a lasting sense of affection, respect, and affiliation. That Lorenzo was his father might have been settled by DNA, but never would be.

Simeon learned much more about Gina the woman, her antipathies, rebellion, non-conformity, generosity, and protection of pregnant hookers and abused women. Her own pregnancy still was cloaked in privacy. Nevertheless, she was clearly able to satisfy maternal disposition without revealing any further details. Of course, she might have said more on her deathbed, but Simon was not around. Whether Fr. Fogarty knew was something Simeon did not intend to investigate, and other questions about Fogarty were not to be asked. No one except Gina had claimed the infant. A nameless young prostitute, knocked up accidentally by a passing john, might have been his mother, but it was improbable. Gina found places for other unwanted infants, so her decision to keep Simon was as unambiguous as the persistent mystery was likely to get.

The lesbian affair between Gina and Sophia's daughter was something he hadn't suspected, but it didn't bother him. Homosexual affairs are far too commonplace to cause much concern or comment. Aunt Gina need not have been an exception to a familiar notion that the best whores are lesbians. That Simeon was seduced and trained to be attracted only to older women who could not get pregnant went beyond Aunt Gina's perverse disposition, as if she wanted him only to herself, without another child to deal with. Nevertheless, when Simon first told her about Chester, she was bothered enough to arrange an affair with Sophia very quickly. For this, she had to be well informed that Sophia would agree, and needed no persuasion.

Simon became Simeon, and fated never to have lasting love affairs with young women. His liaisons with April and for a short time, Hermione, were exceptions because neither woman wanted a permanent arrangement, and certainly not marriage. April was incapable of it, and Hermione had other plans. Simeon also understood why Aunt Gina had an insurmountable prohibition about intercourse between them. It would have been too incestuous. Theirs was true love, she insisted, over and over. Near-incest was evidently permissible, but actual incest, no. Evidently, only actual intercourse qualified as incest to Gina. Until Simon unexpectedly fell in love with Sophia, Gina was in no danger of losing him to another woman.

One evening, after attending a theater performance with an attractive older woman whom he had not yet bedded, Simeon returned to his hotel, and while preparing for bed, found it unusually difficult to urinate. After much effort, running water, and urging the stream to begin, he was aghast when at last, a torrent of blood splattered the wall no less explosively than when he first discovered cancer. He was afraid of bleeding to death, without control. Even as the bright red soon turned yellow, he closed his eyes to the terrifying realization that cancer, as if to make up for long dormancy, had announced itself with renewed vigor. Simultaneously, the cancer that he had presumed cured became Cancer, claiming a way of life and canceling his covenant. Recurrence thwarted the astonishing cure, now exposed as merely a remission, which could have spontaneously happened, with and without cannibalism. His mission disintegrated into something commonplace.

A few more days went by without further bleeding, but the preliminary explosion put Simeon on notice. Because he still felt well, Simeon almost persuaded himself that the episode was temporary and insignificant. He knew better, however, and while tempted, refused to be deceived. Then one morning, he awakened to find the bedclothes soaked with bloody urine. He had been fooled so completely, and had come on this long journey that he called a covenant, just to publicize a phony triumph over cancer. Cancer was back, and the immediate issue was how to deal with it. It was not a gentle reminder such as gradual weight loss, with a few nodules unexpectedly popping up here and there, but a crude demand for surrender. Then, after making its presence clear, the bleeding perversely stopped again, leaving Simeon the unwitting faker.

Everything he claimed was now spurious. Although he hesitated to consult a doctor, sooner, not later the secret would seep out. There was really no one at all to confide in except Lorenzo, but he decided against trying to see him. He was not sure why, since recurrent cancer would have been an excellent pretext, and he could warn Lorenzo, too, that the project harvesting human flesh for sale might dry up, like any nostrum that is eventually exposed. Nevertheless, unless he kept very quiet about it, the cannibalism rationale for cure was now insupportable. Opponents, long prepared, could be expected to rejoice, and say, *I told you so*. Supporters, and there were still many, certainly would waver, and ultimately turn on the false prophet. Only fellow cannibals, who were in hiding anyway, might sympathize and remain loyal. There was no more mission or message. The world wanted an easy and absolute cure, and he had, in effect, duped and disappointed the hopeful, once again. Most people, he surmised, had not as yet experimented with cannibalism, although tempted. The supplies were just not there.

Almost any physician knows about remissions, with and without treatment. Statements about curing cancer must always be voiced cautiously and edged with doubt because the course of illness is up and down, seldom linear and progressive. Predicting the future is easy, but hard to be sure about. Some so-called cures are merely extraordinarily long remissions that seem to vanquish cancer, but are really do not. Cancer is not easily defeated. Simeon, now the future agent of a notorious hoax, had to face cancer once again.

Simeon could simply abscond, like a real fugitive. He was unwilling to play the tragic hero, in whatever way he might make the announcement to the public. There were just too many experts out there, waiting to congratulate themselves on his embarrassment. They would be satisfied with nothing less than total capitulation and confession of chicanery. Tabloids might print a retraction, but primarily to expose a rogue who exploited human suffering.

The taboo against cannibalism is so strong that once breached would be difficult to give up. The appeal would outlast the presumed cure that failed. There were now more criminal cannibals out there than coroners could recall. Fresh graves needed still to be watched, just as prostitutes continued to be wary about customers who could mutilate, and then murder with impunity. Like many obsolete and ineffective patent medicines, demand for therapeutic flesh could well continue. Simeon had unleashed a recalcitrant appetite.

The urgent task for Simeon was to get treatment, not to fret about the demolition of his reputation. He wanted simply to vanish, just as anonymously as he had appeared, knowing that the secret would soon be out, like an ad in the daily paper. How it got out was a certainty, but he had no idea where the leak might occur. Nevertheless, Simeon had to meet with Dr. Narub and mend their differences. The relapse might help heal the split, although it was the implicit cure that helped shatter Narub's reputation, and that could never be reversed. The public might forgive a healthy retraction, and a rebuke from medical authorities might salvage Narub, but not likely, or much less than a public hanging brings forgiveness.

This time, however, he might not survive the arduous trip. If Narub could offer no help, then Simeon would surely go back to the Highlands, seeking more of the sacred stew. While retaining something of his faith in cannibalism, Simeon also imagined a new headline for a tabloid: Salvation Soup goes down the Drain.

Fortunately for Simeon, he remained well, without signs of progression, so he could not be sure of the extent of cancer inside. Like faithful converts to a dubious cause, Simeon preferred to overlook negative evidence and still believe that, basically, the relapse was slight and unlikely to return.

He hesitated about notifying Narub of his coming visit, and consequently made no appointment at the Cancer Center. Even after another long trip to Sydney, he decided to appear unannounced. Still unaware of Narub's disgrace and discharge, Simeon just walked up to the receptionist in Narub's office. "I'm Simeon Benett. I'd like to see Dr. Narub," he told her. She recoiled slightly, as if recognizing his name and its connection with Dr. Narub's transition from respect to banishment.

"Dr. Narub is no longer here, Mr. Benett," she said coolly, somewhat officiously. "Would you like to see someone else?" He asked about seeing the current Chief of Service, Dr. Hanover. Without questioning further, she directed him to one of the newer buildings, about a half-mile away, where Dr. Hanover's receptionist quickly informed him that the Doctor had a full schedule with no free appointments for weeks to come. That established Simeon's audacity and Dr. Hanover's importance. However, when Simeon mentioned something about being an old patient of Dr. Narub's, she took a second look, told an older assistant, who went inside, returned, and made an appointment for the next day.

Punctual as ever, Simeon still waited in the reception room for another hour. However, when the moment came, Simeon was taken to still another smaller office, there to sit a little while longer. As Director, Dr. Hanover was protected as diligently as Mr. Feigenmount. Simeon wondered why important people usually have their offices at the end of a long hall in a corner office. Dr. Hanover finally saw Simeon in a small cluttered office, apparently used for purposes other than interviewing patients. Photographs of colleagues and celebrities who, presumably, were friends and patients festooned the walls. The desk was piled high with documents and charts. Bookshelves were stacked with journals and unopened boxes that had no other place to be stored. No works of art were to be seen, not even a watercolor by an offspring. Among the pictures, Simeon recognized a Nobel Prize winner and a well-known jockey.

Dr. Hanover was brisk and middle-aged, with ample well-groomed salt and pepper hair to go with his senior status. Naturally he wore a white coat with a superfluous identifying badge. Instead of being terse, remote, and rushed, he seemed cordial enough, and exceedingly curious about finally meeting the source of so much trouble. There was no need for polite preliminaries. Hanover addressed Simeon directly, and without hedging.

"And what brings you back to us now, Simeon?" He was pleasant and relaxed enough to use first names casually. "You must have had many adventures since leaving the Center." The remark was not intended to be facetious. He smiled without amusement, as if recalling that meeting in which Narub tried to justify and explain his involvement in an otherwise startling case report.

"I didn't know that Dr. Narub was no longer here, Dr. Hanover. I arrived yesterday. The reason I'm back is that I've relapsed. I had bloody urine a little while back, otherwise feeling OK, but I know better than to continue believing in the miracle of cannibalism. I've relapsed, I think. I haven't consulted anyone, so here I am, presumably full of cancer, soon to be terminal again. I can't be sure what the future holds. I can't even be sure that bloody urine still means cancer." Simeon tried to be medically relevant and omit the controversy he stirred up by returning to the United States.

Dr. Hanover was not an unkind man. Away from his office, he was quite pleasant, decent, dedicated, and even witty. But this was a different issue, because the reputation of the Center had been at risk. He was judiciously restrained and stern about this patient's plight. Simeon was quietly asking for help, but he once lived among savages who were far more primitive and just as black as Australian aborigines. What's more, he became a cannibal himself, no less a savage, before undergoing a remission, which Narub audaciously implied was a cure. Simeon Benett publicized his condition, seemingly recommending the treatment, and now all had blown away like a castle in the air, when he relapsed.

In retrospect, Hanover conveniently revised Narub's cautious presentation and falsely imagined that he'd been much more unqualified in his advocacy. There would have been no reason for the lecture unless a good word for cannibalism hadn't been the alarming point of controversy. Despite the humanitarian pull towards helping Simeon, if possible at all, Hanover held him partially to blame for the deception and embarrassment to the Center. That couldn't be forgotten and condoned, as Narub's fate amply proved. After the entire hullabaloo, Simeon's fate demonstrated that Narub was wrong and reckless in such a misadventure. Simeon's relapse gave Hanover a certain grim satisfaction, knowing that he would no longer have to deal with questions about cannibalism. He would like to get rid of this unfortunate fellow, and get the affair over with, completely.

"I'd like to help you," Dr. Hanover said, "But considering the likelihood that cancer is back, we'd need an MRI, as well as several other examinations. Even then I couldn't be sure what we have to offer. The Center does have several experimental protocols you might be eligible for." Hanover implied that he might put Simeon into a non-treatment investigative program for patients who have run out of other options, but he didn't promise much. Not overjoyed by the bleak suggestion, Simeon nodded his head, then asked more about Dr. Narub. Dr. Hanover was not at all reluctant to speak of the departed without sounding unkind or righteous. He simply had to be careful, lest he be quoted out of context in a newspaper.

"It is really too bad. Such a fine physician is no longer on our staff. I can also say outstanding because he did achieve a lot, was very good to patients, and had an even more productive future ahead. However, the staff found that, as competent as he was, Dr. Narub was inclined to give more credence than necessary to unconventional and unproved methods of treatment. It was more than just liking to study alternative treatments. We are all interested in any established drug or method that might, some day, be found useful. I say established drug, but as yet unproven. You are a good example of why what seems an overly conservative attitude on our part turns out to be the best and only policy. It sometime happens that a doctor, with all good intentions, gets carried away by an arresting idea or tall story, then quickly puts it into practice, without proper scientific foundation."

"I suppose that's why he indirectly referred me to jungle doctors for treatment," Simeon responded, sounding resigned. "I must say that he was very careful in explaining options to me. Look, Sir, I have no appetite for arguing the case all over again. My relapse is refutation enough. But please remember that I had no other option at the time except chemotherapy which had already failed."

"I'm sure you were in the audience that night when he first reported your unique case," Dr. Hanover said, "I was not sure whether he simply made you aware of the cannibal treatment in the jungle, or if he actually advocated, even urged you to find out for yourself. Having a respected doctor even-handedly offer a set of options is almost impossible. He or she is bound to lean one way or another. In any event, it turned out to be a wild goose chase." Neither Simeon nor Narub had said anything to imply that the foray into the Highlands had been frivolous, whimsical, or a chase for the wild goose. But he hesitated about contradicting Dr. Hanover. There was no point in defending Narub or himself.

"I was there, of course, but Dr. Narub and I went in different directions. It was not his choice that I go to New Guinea. It was mine. I want to clarify that. It was not his decision that sent me back to America. All he did was make me aware of a story, not a factual medical report. He did not urge me to do anything, but I imagine that the medical staff is convinced that he did." Simeon avoided the inflammatory word, establishment.

It was certain, too, that Dr. Hanover did not want to argue the question. The matter was obviously settled, his original viewpoint justified, and he was not in the mood to learn more about the background of this incident. The telephone rang at that moment, and he firmly announced to the caller that he would be free very soon. Then he offered a few concluding remarks. Simeon understood that he was being rebuked for having cancer as much as for cannibalism. Few victims can defend themselves against that charge.

"At the Center, we are prepared to look into every legitimate and legal method that might help our patients. Treatment depends on using strict scientific criteria, based on rigorous testing in the laboratory, then on animals, and finally with patients who accept the risks, which are also investigated. While we will explore controversial treatment that has some scientific merit, we do not deal with the speculative or mythical. Dr. Narub was not that careful. He did not always regard the risks as seriously as we do, nor was he careful about rumors. He made us worry about patients under his care. Personally, I liked Narub. Not everyone did, and circumstances did not allow him to stay on. I am not sure what he is doing now, or where he is."

As Dr. Hanover got up, he added, "If you are interested in learning more about our protocols, let my secretary know." Simeon had come a long way, only to be dismissed. In truth, however, Dr. Hanover was just as well pleased that he did not have to contend with Simeon all over again.

Simeon had already decided what he was going to do, and it did not include the Cancer Center. As he left, he ran into a laboratory technician who recognized Simeon and remembered the stir about Narub. All she knew about Dr. Narub were unconfirmed rumors, which she gladly talked about. He had definitely left Australia. She heard that he took a government job somewhere in the United States. Maybe he'd gone back to England or given up medicine entirely. She shrugged. It was yesterday's tempest, hardly worth recalling.

Before embarking on another journey to New Guinea, Simeon did submit to several examinations, just to see how badly off he was. The tests only confirmed widespread cancer, not unlike what he predicted and feared. Yet he felt reasonably well, healthy enough to undergo a trip back to New Guinea, but still discouraged about recurrence and the failure of his mission.

Briefly, he considered participating in a protocol, but if he were the one to get a placebo it would do him no good, although it might help the investigator. He was sure it would be a waste of time and dissipate what energy and time he had left. Nevertheless, still vacillating about what to do, he did change his mind, and agreed to take part in a brief protocol. After about month, however, again without discernible benefit or damage, he quit without notice, true to the Simeon of old.

After dropping out he made his way back to Papua New Guinea, where he began preparations for another trip into the Highlands. He realized how little he actually knew about the tribe he left or how to get there. On the first trip, Axel had been responsible for every item of preparation, including maps, provisions, transportation, friendly and hostile tribes along the way, and the identity of that remote tribe where he would live. Simeon was only the passenger. Now that he was on his own, trying to get a crew together, stock up, find a pilot who knew the way, and where he was going, the tribe seemed no more real than what he might have imagined, even though he lived and learned much among them during a long stay. Simeon would not have been shocked, had the eventual experience been wholly vaporous, vanishing with the mist coming down from the mountains.

No one seemed to know of Axel or his whereabouts, and Simeon had few resources to arrange his own trip. Considering Axel's reputation, it seemed preposterous that he just disappeared, and that his name meant nothing. Finally, still looking for a clue to Axel's disappearance, he recalled a practitioner whom he briefly met previously in Port Moresby. The doctor's first name was Saul, an unlikely name here, and his last name eluded Simeon. However, he made a few inquiries and finally found Dr. Saul's office a few miles out of the central city, over a store in a modest strip mall. Yes, Dr. Saul knew Axel casually, largely by reputation, but hadn't seen or heard of him for at least a year. There were no rumors. He did give Simeon the name of a reliable guide service, but it was one he'd only heard about. Dr. Saul was no expert on river guides.

In putting a trip together for the Highlands. Simeon's inexperience made improvisation, luck, and good intentions indispensable to asking around. Liberal spreading of money also helped. No one even pretended to know about the specific tribe Simeon wanted, and Simeon got nowhere trying to describe his erstwhile family and where it lived. The ordinary guide was not accustomed to going very far, and certainly not into dangerous Highland country. Having no choice but to select almost at random, based on a little conversation and equivocal recommendations, Simeon at last hired a sturdy launch, equipped with two uninspired boatmen, including a withered skipper with a smattering of what passed for English, and ample provisions.

Predictably, on the third day after starting his expedition out of Liaagam, while docked overnight at a small hamlet, Simeon awoke to find himself alone and deserted. His crewmen disappeared into the forest, he was told. Only the aged skipper, the provisions, and the launch remained. No one had further information. It all reminded Simeon of his own habit of walking off a job. He didn't like it.

Simeon tried piloting the launch himself, not trusting the skipper who was more than old, and showed senility. He did well enough, luckily avoiding the submerged branches and keeping far away from shore, until he came to another settlement. At last, running into a streak of good fortune, he hired Hency, an experienced hand who had been up and down the rivers for decades, and spoke a little English, much Pidgin, and a dialect or two. The elderly skipper was indifferent about being let go, and merely sauntered away, possibly relieved. Although Hency had no idea about the tribe Simeon sought, his presence made communication much easier. He had been to the foothills of the Highlands and seemed trustworthy, which he turned out to be. Nevertheless, Simeon was cautious, afraid of again being deserted. He pushed Hency and the launch with scarcely any rest, night and day without respite. Hency had heard of Axel, yet they never met. Axel's disappearance was not unusual, according to Hency. He was a living legend, but like such heroic creations, seldom seen. Probably, Hency surmised, Axel was off in the jungle somewhere, shepherding tourists. Given the unpredictable temperament of tribes along the river, no one could be sure about Axel's safety, even for a seasoned guide. Meanwhile, Simeon gathered vigor during the journey and felt more refreshed just by spotting familiar sights, sounds, and smells. It was like a remission all over again.

Free of pain and cumbersome symptoms, he gradually lost the sense of immutable doom that dogged him. He began to thirst for the sacred stew, confident that he would get into another real remission, and just possibly, one that lasted long enough to be considered a cure. Nevertheless, he cautiously dismissed such fantasies as tantalizing but unlikely. This was his home, and these were his people. He would never be fool enough to undertake another trip to the United States or practically anywhere.

As the launch and its two passengers went further towards Highland country, the morning mists thickened daily and obscured vision. Indeed the hazardous fog became a personal adversary, wrapping itself around the launch, relenting from time to time, and then breezily going off elsewhere. The river provided constant reminders of life just back of the shoreline closer to the interior. On one occasion, tribesmen ran along the shore, shouting threats and insults, throwing spears that landed just short of the boat. Simeon and Hency were glad finally to outrun the spears and arrows.

Their only accident occurred one night while making very slow progress against a slight crosscurrent. They struck a protruding rock while trying to avoid several others and sprung a slight leak, which needed immediate repair. Fortunately, the people at that point were helpful, not at all hostile, and applied a pitch or glue that hardened quickly to the leaking hull. Everything after that was smooth and opportune. Simeon found himself looking for signs of the place he wanted and considered his home. But it was still several days before this happened. He could not remember enough of the first trip to compare the speed with this one.

One evening, after pitching overnight camp at a comfortable point along the shore, a few local people came out of the forest and quickly gathered around the visitors, including one young man who spoke a dialect with an accent not unlike the tribe Simeon was looking for. His destination was only another day away. True to the forecast, key landmarks appeared the following day, along with scattered tribesmen coming to the water's edge, waving in welcome. Simeon was remembered, and not merely greeted out of curiosity. It looked as if he was expected, too.

Hency had never been this far. Fearing that the strange tribe might still be hostile, he held back, and told Simeon he wanted to turn around before landing where the men had gathered. Simeon assured Hency that their reception had to be friendly. He counted on Alphonz and the old Chief because he recognized no one else.

At first, after wading ashore from the launch, Simeon was dubious about his rusty fluency with the tribal tongue. He immediately asked for Alphonz, again in terms that his hosts would be familiar with. At the mention of Alphonz, a common stir instantly rose up in the crowd, and soon Alphonz himself came down from the mountain through the tunnel of rocks and boulders, accompanied by a retinue of followers.

It was a changed Alphonz who flung out his arms and affectionately embraced Simeon. The old chief was dead and Alphonz, despite his youth, had become his successor. Not only was this a highly sought after and lofty position carrying much authority and prestige, but Alphonz was also required by tradition and personal admiration to adopt some of the mannerisms of the old chief, as if to perpetuate a long lineage. The Chief's ways and manners created an illusion that he was still alive inside Alphonz. Regretfully, while congratulating Alphonz, the old Alphonz would have been preferable, since Simeon remembered that the old Chief had withheld the sacred stew. The Philadelphia Eagles sweatshirt was gone, however, apparently lost to the depredations of time and constant wear. Accordingly, after greeting Simeon, Alphonz dropped his momentary joviality, soberly replacing high spirits with solemn authority. His voice became lower and speech fancier. He expected to be listened to by his subjects, and orders were to be promptly obeyed without hesitation. Nevertheless, his affectionate welcoming words were like the old Alphonz, friend and mentor, in spite of his new position.

Simeon remembered to bring Alphonz and the old chief honorific gifts, indicating mutual respect. He gave Alphonz a large and unnecessarily costly wristwatch, which he accepted with much gratitude. In return, Alphonz presented Simeon with carefully decorated woven garments and a necklace that identified him as a distinguished member of tribal and village society. It was indeed a rich compliment for a white man, but Simeon had already proven himself worthy. How long Alphonz held these gifts anticipating Simeon's return was not an issue. There had been only vague promises from Simeon, but he was expected to return some day.

In keeping with his new rank Alphonz was not as garrulous as before. He did tell Simeon about the old Chief's death and cremation. The precious sweatshirt had not just wasted away, but instead went up in the flames of the funeral ceremony. Tribes came and paid respects, bringing gifts, food, and other tributes. No warfare took place for a long time. How Alphonz came to be the new Chief over others much his senior was never explained; but choosing him was one of the Chief's final acts of authority.

Only the cycle of seasons and the occurrence of significant events, such as the old Chief's demise, connected time past and future events. Simeon's departure and return was a significant event. It meant either a long trip or death. Not being visible indicated that a person had either gone away after death, or departed for a lengthy absence with a doubtful return. Both alternatives amounted to the same thing. Simeon had definitely gone away and might have died, but his return was also held to be likely, just as Axel or the Chief might unexpectedly come back. Consequently, ceremonial tokens celebrating return could be prepared and held indefinitely.

Now that Simeon materialized after a long voyage or perhaps even from the realm of the anointed dead, he was also supposed to bring back an inspirational message. Simeon did not fail them, adding to his luster, respect and reverence. Although he omitted the real reason for leaving and returning, he copied the messages that others delivered, with a vivid description of where he'd been. It was an occasion of rejoicing throughout the village. After all, he was one of a kind, and threatened no one, except for the ingrained fear of white men. It did not take long for Simeon to immerse himself once again in village life. He was not only remembered with affectionate awe, but also now given better housing, almost a cabin, with two attendants.

The notion of servant or a servant class is unheard of among tribes in the Highlands. However, for Simeon's tribe and other tribes, the honor of tending the daily needs of a distinguished person is an assignment not lightly bestowed. Those selected to attend Simeon automatically were regarded as being on a higher social level, just by contact and appointment.

Simeon was nonplused, however, when distant villagers came over and touched him gently, as if he were now a sacred intermediary from another world. Regardless of these respectful gestures, Simeon was uneasy about how freely he mingled, and with whom. Too much respect and awe carried a risk of sudden reversal.

Meanwhile, Chief Alphonz remained his steadfast friend and companion. There was no rivalry between them. Simeon told Alphonz about his recurrence, and that he needed the sacred stew right away, although he seemed to be entirely well. As a result, the stew was promptly and amply provided. Simeon had first choice in fresh meat from recent victims. Cannibalism was not a serious question, and Simeon did not let them down. Despite his setback, Simeon kept staunch faith in the cure, as well as in KA, temporarily ignoring the difference between remission and cure. In the United States he was always afraid of needing fresh supplies, as well as not being sure about how to prepare the sacred soup. Here, he had no qualms about the right way to prepare the stew. There were other assorted local ingredients, also thought to be effective, which were harder to identify. Prisoners were apparently plentiful. An occasional unwary traveler was still another source, but the body had to be transported and this was a bothersome problem.

Simeon had no idea whether the sacred stew would be as beneficial as before, notwithstanding his faith. He guessed that the stew was effective but that maintenance was also necessary. That was why he relapsed. It was an encouraging thought. Before long however his hope and trust were justified. With negligible symptoms, it was hard to guess what, if anything, was happening inside, but he sensed steady internal changes for the better. No further bleeding occurred, and he thrived in all respects. For all he knew, the cancer might have stabilized, without exacting more or giving up its claim. He preferred to think of recovery. It was good to be home again, and that helped his morale, so badly damaged on his trip to the outside world.

During his nominal convalescence, Simeon had much time to think both about his cancer, which could insidiously extend its hold, and about the inevitable Cancer way of life. The distinction was the difference between a disease, and an existential calamity. He personalized cancer, imagining it as powerful, willful and unpredictable, more like a cannibal than a parasite. Wicked and implacable, when it has a mind to, Cancer seems contemptuous of efforts to restrain and retard its grasp. Like a hostile army, cancer might opt to invade at any time, occupy and then kill. Such a fantastic fable differed from the tribe's traditional notion of the sorcerer's curse. Consequently, unlike fatal sorcery, Simeon's version visualized Cancer's supernatural but autonomous existence, like a difficult god who is to be dreaded, appeased, controlled, or capitulated to.

No longer did Simeon plan to bring any message to the outside world. This surely included philanthropic missions and directives from KA. Now that he was beginning to understand the place of Cancer in a tribal universe, he adopted firm principles to guide his own behavior. Let the rest of mankind take care of itself and follow its own parochial truths and scientific fashions. What is true on the surface may not be a truth at all, but only current consensual opinion. Simeon wasn't concerned about truth, only utility, and the most useful rules were how to appease Cancer. He wasn't sure how to go about it because his own skeptical skill in dealing with Cancer, or CA, as he came to know it back in the States, had been manifestly inadequate. Faith told him that to cope with CA, there had to be an equally strong supernatural deity to grapple with and contend with CA. Like his fellow-tribesmen, he had faith in KA, a mighty, benevolent but unpredictable divine authority whom shamans of a certain status were qualified to converse with. KA made a covenant with Simeon before the first departure, which his recurrence rescinded, but now Simeon needed another link to KA in order to determine the future course of his life and the fate of coping with CA.

Simeon wanted to see Nyergy again. This strange ethnic melting pot of a man had silently slipped away after Axel arrived, either feeling ignored or that his mission was over. There had been no farewells, and Nyergy evidently returned to wandering from one village to the next, doing whatever superior shamans customarily do. His curious ministrations, exotic and not a little offensive, had not helped Simeon. Nyergy's authentic accomplishment was to support Simeon's morale when at its weakest. Chanting, ointments, and physical scrutiny had no perceptible effect. Nothing did, until Simeon was finally granted access to the sacred stew. Nevertheless, Simeon felt a tentative bond with this shaman, which had something to do with the traces of the white race that coursed through him. Principally, however, it was Nyergy's supernatural connection that made another meeting desirable.

Regardless of his ineffectual remedies, Nyergy was the one person who could intercede with KA, the supreme local god, and bring Simeon a lasting way to manage his plight and the other god called CA. Without Nyergy's presence, Simeon could have perished from sheer loneliness. He recalled, however, that although the old Chief denied Simeon the sacred stew, he sent for Nyergy in the first place, which amounted to a strong vote of confidence.

Simeon's wish to see Nyergy this time was not to support morale, voice gratitude, and renew old acquaintance. Simeon's morale was fine, his gratitude was modest enough, and they could hardly be called old acquaintances. The prospect of conversing in halting, scarcely intelligible English, cobbled together with dialects and vocabulary from all over, was not exactly entrancing. Nevertheless, there was a compelling urgency to find Nyergy and reap his still uncertain benefits. After all, through a sacred delirium, he was able to meet KA in the beyond, and once there, negotiate, and then return, unscathed. Nyergy would also voluntarily go into his trance, and claim to communicate with the dead in the next world. No one had the temerity to question it. The trance could last for hours, say, from sunrise until darkness, or continue for several days. When he came back to this world, Nyergy firmly reported extended conversations with such luminaries as KA or with the distinguished dead. To a skeptical outsider, this would seem like the simplest form of fakery, not unlike the mummery of table levitation or knocking on walls at spiritual séances. Here, however, in the jungle up in the Highlands, common sense, skepticism, and lack of evidence were meaningless.

Beyond question according to Alphonz, there were few shamans so amply qualified to go back and forth from one level of existence to another as Nyergy. There were, of course, shamans who profiteered, and the unwary had to be careful. Not so with Nyergy, who was not out to get rich. His was a most ascetic life, unaffiliated, and asking practically nothing but the most meager offering for his services. Simeon's strong yearning to meet Nyergy had to do with an entirely new ambition beyond curing cancer, but one that heavily depended on power, merit, respect and awe. His aim was startling and consistent with his prestigious status. Simeon wanted to become a shaman, and for that, he needed Nyergy.

After breaking the taboo against cannibalism, Simeon had steadily undergone a profound change in his character, even more than he realized. People do change in some respects over a lifetime, but not easily, and certainly not selectively. It cannot be done by an ordinary act of will, vow of repentance, or simple choice of what seems advantageous. Transition is usually so subtle and gradual that everything that changes seems natural, until recollection reminds us that some old attitudes and customary habits have largely disappeared, or at least become so attenuated as not to matter. Simeon was coming to that point where he hardly remembered his entrenched and scandalous behavior in the past or at least thought of it as no longer belonging to his major demands and desires. Shuttling and shunting from one job or person to the next, only to leave unannounced, as well as indifference to the bafflement and inconvenience he caused others could hardly be tested in the jungle. Nevertheless, former impulses and bizarre behavior contingent upon breaking taboos now seemed very dilute and scarcely worth acting on, should an opportunity arise. The jungle was far from Hollywood, and his more reprehensible actions, which couldn't be enumerated, dwindled and dried up. Simeon's old predilections had become atrophic from disuse. Here in the Highlands, taboos were common, but none with the preemptive drive to violate that had propelled Simeon in younger years.

According to the tradition of the tribe, human flesh strengthens both character and courage, just as surely as it helps recovery from a serious ailment, or from wounds. When curses are removed, or a sick person brought back from death, the events themselves testify to the divine intervention of KA. This auspicious event means that the favored person has been deemed worthy of KA because an ordinary person would not get such special attention. While physical recovery and future immunity to ills and injuries, of course, are of primary importance, superior character, high purpose, and strong courage are also divine attributes, bestowed generously by KA on the right people.

Simeon was already qualified to pursue this chosen vocation, but in order to become a higher order shaman he would have to perform many tests of courage and character as well as an extended apprenticeship with an established shaman and teacher. During his training the apprentice is supposed to learn secret things about plants and animals, ritualistic intercessions, and the essential ingredients of jungle medicine. Finally, if successful in all these trials and adept in learning what he must learn, the prospective shaman advances and undergoes whatever is required to induce a holy delirium, communicate with the dead and the divine, and become an intermediary between this world and the next. The training is rigorous and selective, and to attain such status, Simeon would be required to dedicate himself more completely than ever before.

Simeon was prepared to relinquish whatever remained of his previous life, renounce all outside ties, and live in the Highlands for the rest of his life. Memories must be locked up and fade away. In effect, the superior shaman, like a legendary hero of long ago, becomes the sterling representative of tribal morality and custodian of its history. The shaman's mind is holy, clear of evil, but responsive to the evil in others. Only noble sentiments, courageous deeds and eloquent desire to transcend earthly matters remain.

Despite deepening respect and affection for his tribe and its customs, Simeon had found it difficult to credit any of his aboriginal brothers or local shamans with such elevated goals. If these ideals were strictly adhered to, the shaman population would surely be very limited. After all, no amount of holy dedication changes basic human nature, with its flaws, violations, and deceits. Simeon's predilections had faded, but periodic reminders still were at the outskirts, ready to return, if Simeon questioned their viability.

Nyergy was nowhere to be found. All that Alphonz could say was, "He is gone away. No hear about. Nyergy is now the silent one." That was the first time Simeon heard a reference to the silent one. He was puzzled and questioned Alphonz what it meant. Dead, departed, or simply disinclined to speech? Alphonz could not explain it clearly, except that silence was something to be silent about. This did not seem very enlightening. For shamans of high quality, however, the terms *gone away*, and *the silent one*, have different meanings, one indicating that Nyergy might be dead, or living somewhere else, even on another plane. The other is that the shaman is close to the gods, an intimate of KA, and therefore, beyond human speech. However, still caring enough about those left behind, he acts as messenger and sometimes advocate to the world where gods reside.

Real shamans of quality are frequently away for protracted periods, supposedly on various journeys, whether actual absence or through a holy delirium, with its attendant inaccessibility. Their absence may be interpreted as a visitation with or by the gods. Either the gods come to this world, entering into the shaman, or the shaman travels to the world beyond. Simeon had a flicker of recalling Aunt Gina's periodic and unexplained disappearances. Shamans die, too. Others just wander away and disappear into silence. A shaman might choose to become a disembodied spirit after death, leaving an inanimate lifeless body behind. From time to time, the spirit might inhabit the body of a forest animal, and share its life. Certain animals are therefore taboo. As Simon discovered, it is hard to know which animals harbor a shaman. Even in death, shamans have options about how to spend eternity. Shamans who have just died supposedly hover between two worlds. After a career of great deeds amounting to miracles, certain shamans are later awarded extraordinary status.

Although Simeon could not honestly testify to the achievements of shamans like Nyergy, he aspired to higher status just the same, since it would demand the best qualities he had to offer. A good shaman brings relief to sick people through magical medicines and intercessions with the gods. Whether or not such intercessions forestall death, the suffering of terminal illness is usually reduced to an acceptable minimum. Terminal people are helped to turn dying to their advantage, thus putting themselves in good graces with the gods. How a dying person turns death to his advantage however was a lasting mystery to Simeon, ever since his early conversations with Dr. Narub. Yet, this was exactly what he had done. He was grateful for remission and return to the tribe he belonged to, something that once would have been incredible. Regardless of death which Simeon still felt was far away, his new-found character and courage might help turn death to advantage, say, by becoming a superior shaman and bringing better morale to those afflicted with terminal illness.

The truly gifted shaman is at his best in the period immediately before death and just afterward, when he tries to undo the evil sorcery behind the fatal illness, and prepare his client for the next world. Apparently, this was what Nyergy was doing when he carried out those strange maneuvers on Simeon. For the shaman himself, however, the ultimate ambition, being just dead, is to merit and receive the embrace of KA. If such an epiphany occurs, it will justify and repay all the rigorous training. But death cannot be hurried; that would usurp the gods, like KA. Death comes at its own time, whether prolonged into old age or honorably hastened.

Shamans of high achievement are always ready to ascend to another realm, but as they approach the moment of their death the gifted shaman is open to KA's presence. For Simeon, KA was already a reality more powerful and convincing than CA. The opportune moment of acceptance nearing death is the goal of a superior shaman, meanwhile earning his keep and recognition. Whether some shamans fail to get that recognition after death is a professional secret, since no one comes back and tells the bad news. The old Simon and a much younger Simeon had no ambitions whatsoever, beyond the whims of the day. Simeon in his maturity preferred to be remembered with awe and veneration as he approached being just dead and ready for the embrace of KA. He expressed this to Alphonz in various ways.

"Alphonz, my friend and Chief, you will know my wishes and I appeal for your help. I came back from gone away, a long journey to a strange land you do not know. I belong here, not with strangers. You and the old Chief made me well before I went away and now I will keep well again, with the sacred feeding. The gods want me back here to tend the sick, be a leader, banish pain, and undo the mischief of curses. I want to become a shaman."

Alphonz knew Simeon well and respected his wishes, even this ambition, which was highly unusual for a white man. He was in fact more than amazed, but said nothing to dissuade his friend. Simeon's return from the outside world was likened to resurrection from death to life, or from a higher realm back to the mundane. It was surely a capacity that true shamans are capable of. Alphonz remembered Simeon's dream when he was gravely ill, and the tale he told when awakened. Thus, it was easy to turn a vivid dream into a holy delirium. Everything therefore pointed to the preternatural wisdom, destiny, and obligation behind Simeon's aspiration, one that would surely be approved by the elders.

Alphonz had witnessed the suffering and ravages of cancer when Simeon and others were so desperately sick. He had no difficulty convincing the elders that Simeon be granted permission to undergo training. One of the early requirements was to show that Simeon had fortitude enough to challenge and defy the gods. This kind of heresy demanded courage and character. The blasphemy that was commendable in the Highlands was certainly opposite to the West where the profession of strong faith praising God testified to a calling and qualification. Here, it was praiseworthy to talk back to the gods and mock their teachings, but it was risky to do the same with elders. The gods apparently were more tolerant, less sensitive to insult, and even approved of brash criticism, far more than the elders who protected their own status. Gods strong enough to rule are able to tolerate blasphemy, and therefore admire anyone audacious enough to attempt it. Simeon did just these things, gladly. Mocking and cursing were tame acts of defiance. Carrying out what ordinarily would be punishable, such as taunting the gods, defying taboos, and breaking traditional rules was easy. In fact, it meant that gods had a sense of the ridiculous, besides forbearance. They did not need constant praise. To curse KA was part of a religious ceremony, and in effect, signified holy obedience and reverence. Underneath the solemn observances, it was great fun making up insults, but keeping them within bounds.

Teasing the gods and speaking rudely about KA were indications of respectful familiarity and admiration. Reviling the gods was a test of faith. Gradually, all manner of abusive transgressions can be turned upside down into pious readiness to meet KA, face to face. After a protracted period of training, the aspirant finally is prepared and ready to lead a holy life. Simeon came to ponder and admire the tolerance of this powerful god, KA, who could not be insulted and was therefore compassionate to an infinite degree. He recalled with a mixture of pride and disappointment how sincerely he once felt a covenant with KA. Having negated it all after his relapse, he now counted on KA's forbearance. Notwithstanding, KA had to be the ideal deity whose nature remained a profound paradox that could not be fathomed. Enlightenment was reserved for the privileged.

KA was depicted in contradictory ways, none of which was supposed to be an accurate portrayal. His countenance was too sacred for anything other than false images. Consequently, the acceptable way to refer to KA was to say something utterly false that could not be so. Despite being referred to in a masculine sense, because men were the dominant gender, KA was also ambiguously talked about by elders as a bird with a woman's face or a woman with a bird's beak. No one seemed to mention a link between KA and the Ohwai bird. Simeon's conviction about KA was firmly based on his vivid prophetic dream of long ago, and even further back, on the hermaphroditic apparition that materialized one afternoon.

Every would-be shaman, even those less ambitious than Simeon, needs a tutor, or master to teach what shamans have to know and justify. Nyergy would do, but Nyergy was not available. No one, not even Alphonz, knew his whereabouts. The elders recommended several outstanding shamans in the area. Clearly, Simeon, the future shaman, had become a project for the whole tribe.

How it came about was never fully made clear, but Alphonz and his elders brought an aged and honorable shaman from a distant tribe to be his mentor. Simeon never knew his name, and Alphonz for no discernible reason was forbidden to mention it. However, it was also likely that a very eminent master would have no name, and only be referred to as "Master." The Master spoke very little, and answered so few questions that Simeon got tired asking. His speech was soft and almost inaudible. Simeon wondered if the Master intended not to be overheard, even by the one who directly addressed him. Some might wonder if his silence was due to preoccupation with the other world, and that he couldn't be bothered. Moreover, such intelligible answers as the Master offered and could be heard were not relevant to what he was asked, nor did he comment on the divine mysteries with which he was supposed to be familiar. The Master talked randomly at times, without prompting, about a mixed-up assortment of topics. He would speak in fragmentary phrases or give miniature orations about plants, animals, the earth below and the sky above, the history of his tribe or any other matter. But he deliberately ignored most questions Simeon ventured to ask. Presumably this could have been a strategy that urged Simeon to find his own answers or to guess what wisdom the Master had in mind and was not about to share. Simeon wondered how this inscrutable fellow, well into his dotage, could teach anyone about anything, let alone leading him towards shamanhood and the holy secrets pertinent to the realm of KA.

Simeon elected simply to call his mentor, "Master", but privately thought of him as the Silent or Nameless One. Less politely, risking no reproof, he was vexed and to himself called the elderly sage by other unflattering terms, besides the Senile One. When Simeon at first asked the Master how to address him, he got no answer other than a series of amiable grunts. Simeon surmised that such responses might be typical of anyone so eminent, and decided that he wouldn't pursue the matter further.

Nevertheless, he knew that names had magical properties as well as being markers that identified class, region, and family status. Apparently, the Nameless One was above all that and quite silent about everything except what he chose to talk about. And even so, he was inaudible and off the mark. It was a curious form of instruction or indoctrination, and under less august circumstances, might have been a practical joke, except that it was utterly grave and deeply serious.

Although perplexed by his enigmatic tutor, Simeon was very eager to get on with his instruction in any way possible. He had no teaching in the ordinary sense except by osmosis and guesswork. If Socrates answered questions with other questions that allegedly led to wisdom, the Silent One answered questions and every other comment with no answers or a series of sounds that could have been words. Notwithstanding, the Nameless One was a holy person, and therefore exempt from almost any responsibility, such as practical instruction that might help Simeon. He could choose only what he chose to choose with no obligation to justify or explain what he was doing. Not the least question was how he achieved his exalted status. By default, he must be everything that he was supposed to be. Only Simeon privately questioned why this reluctant Master had been chosen and brought so far for his instruction, and then did little of it.

Simeon's central ambition was to become a superlative shaman, one who excelled at whatever shamans excel at. His aimless meandering and make-believe jobs were completely past. Totally devoted to his new vocation, he could not figure out how he was to be trained and tested. The quarry judges the hunters and warriors fight battles to enrich their booty. Tangible results were presumed beyond possibility. Inside, the apprentice Simeon had a deep yearning to attain what mystics always seek, serenity, enlightenment, and familiarity with the sacred world beyond this life. Hence, Simeon conveniently by-passed the uncommunicative Master, concluding that it was one of the paradoxes that KA was famous for. He would only know he'd arrived when he could talk with KA, which was a central practical ambition.

After awhile, however, Simeon became accustomed to the Master's curious ways. One day, to his own surprise, he began to make sense out of the Master's devious and disguised messages. Through unfamiliar sounds, gestures, words, and irrelevant remarks of the Nameless One, combined with flashes of something close to intuition, Simeon discovered how KA regularly reveals himself.

The elders all had their own ideas about KA, just as elders do authoritatively everywhere, about everything. Far more useful suppositions about KA came to Simeon through his own guesses and prophetic dreams.

By listening carefully, however, or inferring from what the Master only murmured, Simeon gradually compiled ideas that typified KA. Although definitely subjective, constant reiteration of this and that interpretation made his inferences seem more plausible and convincing. His notions about KA began to crystallize on their own.

KA makes the final decisions about who shall live or die at a particular moment, especially when older people become gravely ill. Curses through sorcery do not always work to extinguish a life, regardless of geography and interfamily rivalries. Hostile sorcery may just make people miserable, without causing a fatal illness. Because sick people respond differently as they near death, KA also decides who shall have distress and pain and who deserves a reprieve. How the decision is reached, what purpose suffering serves, are baffling questions asked by multitudes over generations, and they usually are left without answers, save for the comfortable rationales provided by earthly representatives.

Finally Simeon arrived at a watershed moment when practically everything the Master said or seemed to say fitted in with everything he knew or guessed by himself. It made the Master's voice intelligible and Simeon think that he was on the right track. He was not a miraculous healer who restored the very sick to ebullient health by word or touch. But through his manner and ministrations he seemed to help those who needed healing but could expect only death. With KA's implied permission, Simeon witnessed death many times, and managed to provide comfort to those whose destiny was to end at that moment. After that, it was up to KA to take over from CA.

The Nameless One instructed him in the lore of the forest, the rivers, waterfalls, heavens, and all things below, which plants to avoid, herbs to relieve pain and accelerate healing, how to recognize magic, make use of animals, and voice protective incantations. Frequently, younger assistants materialized and, more harshly than necessary, supervised a variety of skills Simeon might practice. In short, with the passage of time, Simeon began to learn from the Master's weird uttering the things needed by a shaman. The Nameless One, despite his idiosyncrasies, turned out to be a pretty good teacher, after all. Among his significant contributions were strategies for inducing a holy trance. The Master spoke about his own migrations with the same enthusiasm that a tourist just might show after returning from a trip abroad. The Master's talks usually illustrated the perpetual struggle between good and evil. His purpose was not to teach factual history, of course, but to glorify the tribal past and its relation to KA.

The Nameless One seemed to speak more clearly and coherently during the quiet delirium of his trances than when he was fully awake, as if for the moment, he became someone else in touch with another reality. The trance lasted for hours, sometimes only minutes, and on rare occasions, several days, an unlikely period for ordinary sleep or drug-induced stupor. During these absences, which seemed more like a heightened presence, the Master spoke as if he were closer to a higher spiritual being. Indeed, when he finally awoke, the Nameless One said that he'd actually spoken to KA, and even put in a good word for his student, Simeon. Convinced or not, Simeon nevertheless was grateful for the recommendation, thinking he must be getting somewhere at last.

"KA pleased," the Master reported, "He sees, he knows who makes spell, makes demons leave. Like the wind, he calms pain. Sick people will not remember. Like unborn child, KA takes those who die to be his own. He eats of their flesh, and makes the spirit flee to another." Since KA was not likely to be a cannibal, eating their flesh and releasing the spirit, Simeon thought, could refer to a more benign CA. The Master in his own awkward way began to wave his arms up and down, imitating a bird in flight. Perhaps he mimed the Ohwai.

In trying to induce the holy trance or divine delirium, Simeon recalled what he learned in India and from Zen monks in San Francisco about altered consciousness. It was more than self-hypnosis and successful meditation by an expert, which aimed to banish all troubling thoughts and emotions. So far as he could tell, no drugs or plants were involved. A favorable state of mind turned in and then opened outward with new and refreshing perceptions. At least, that was how the novice figured it must be. But that was just metaphorical stuff, without much to be used for guidance. Simeon tried to rid himself of extraneous impediments and distractions in order to become spiritual. This became an important goal, not unlike the spiritual hermits of old who lived for the near-moment of their death. Nevertheless, a by-product of increased spirituality would be exemption from death, or at least a conviction that death had either already occurred or paid a brief visit before restoration of life.

Deliberately striving to be spiritual was a daunting and ultimately futile task, like trying to think profound thoughts, be intuitive, or generate an unfamiliar emotion. From what the Master implied, the holy trance comes without specific encouragement, and without special rituals that facilitate it. It was a little like being prepared for serendipity, something that happens when it happens and at no other time. He did not explain how he managed to achieve trances at will.

Then, one day Simeon lapsed into what Alphonz and the Master described later as an authentic trance. Over the next day, Simeon seemed far away, and only gradually returned to consciousness. During the absence,

Simeon spoke incoherently, but without agitation and alarm. He seemed calm enough, but no one could understand what his words meant. Nevertheless, the Nameless One was impressed by Simeon's accomplishment. Whether he truly had conversation with KA was never mentioned, curiously enough, because everyone wanted to believe and did not seek details. Simeon would not hold back such an important break-through event. Yet he said nothing to the Master and Alphonz after returning to his usual clear conscious state. High quality shamans are able to explore many realms, assume guises, take up residence in an animal, and thrust themselves into the past or future. But there is always a qualification, a disclaimer that he must forget everything or not report it when he returns. The Master did not obey this decree when he spoke about his conversations with the gods. From these exceptions, Simeon learned that KA summons the very sick, but only designates special people for renewed life. He could not account for the Master's easy transition into a holy delirium, after which he reported conversations with KA and his own amnesia for what happened in transit to KA's world.

Despite his determination, whenever Simeon was called upon to glorify KA to the community through song, dances, sacrifices, and entreaties of all sorts, he could not perform as required. It was too much like public ceremonial religious claptrap all over the world, once again. The Master praised him for honesty, since debasement of religion and scoffing at ceremonials were part of his spiritual education, and therefore part of the training. He asked the Master about CA, cancer, and the sources of evil and suffering. The Master's only response was that at the moment of death, all would be made known. Simeon's questions *will* be answered, but not until then. Simeon wondered if a question about his parentage at or near death would confirm what Lorenzo said.

The trance was practicing being dead, a *thanatomimesis*. One night, lying naked in quiet supplication under the heavens, his consciousness open to influences raining down upon him, Simeon saw a meteorite abruptly streak across the sky, and then quickly disappear beyond the rim of the forest into the darkness. It was like an arching arrow carrying a special message that KA cared. Simeon felt a silent communion with whatever was beyond the forest and the night sky. At the same time, in contrast to the shivering cold of the night sky, the experience ignited something that seemed to glow inside without burning. If the Master knew about Simeon's experience, he gave no sign. In fact, afterwards, the Master showed how certain stones or gems, held to the forehead, while reciting a special incantation, could facilitate a trance, without waiting for a serendipitous occasion. This helped Simeon enter s trances by choosing to do so, using the aids given to him by the Master.

Simeon was far from a graduate, ready for a career. As training progressed, one of his duties was to perform a ceremonial decapitation. He was not only a designated executioner, but the first to open the skull, and drink the warm blood. However gruesome and repulsive, it was a highly privileged requirement to be first to eat of the brain and offer the heart to another, such as Alphonz. It enhanced courage and character as well as immunity from sorcery. No novice to cannibalism, this spectacle still offended Simeon. Nevertheless, as a white man who thought like a native and had undergone a rigorous training beforehand, he willingly accepted this duty.

A strange fate, he reflected. How far and unthinkable this was from his life just a few years ago. Eager as he was to become a shaman of high repute, he quavered. Simeon had witnessed many beheadings before, but now was expected to set an example for the tribe that was worthy of his coming status. However, he would not execute captive children, although his associates had no compunctions about it, as if it were what the gods required. Simeon the shaman tried to persuade the victors to adopt these children immediately, without infanticide. In most instances he succeeded. Otherwise, he participated as best he could in the blood orgies, and then left, going deep into the forest. Then, after making sure he was not followed, he vomited forcibly and spent the next few days secretly fasting. At times he would have preferred a quiet death from cancer, without such ceremonies designed to elevate his vocation. His incarnation as a practitioner whose courage, character, and compassion were strengthened and elevated by drinking blood did away with any semblance of guilt. This coincided with the early Simon who was not supposed to feel guilt, anyway.

One day, Simeon learned about still another public rite that a prospective shaman of the tribe was supposed to perform. It was almost as appalling as the public decapitation of prisoners. In an upcoming ceremony, he was expected to cohabit openly with an elderly priestess from another tribe. Although it was supposed to solidify and symbolize the continuity of generations and linkage of related tribes, his designated partner, a ruling matriarch of a distant tribe, disgusted Simeon. While of advanced age, appropriate both for the old Simon and new Simeon, the public fornication with this aged specimen was repulsive. Her painted countenance with ornate tattoos stretching across her chest, combined with ranting and prancing about, as she smeared obnoxious oils generously over her body would have made bestiality more acceptable. She embodied an ugliness he could not bring himself to overcome, not for moral reasons, but plainly because she stunk and looked as if she slept in mud and anointed herself with manure.

Alphonz was usually quite flexible about Simeon's duties, but this time he insisted upon tribal obligation, and would accept no excuses. It was a high duty and mattered to the linkage of one tribe with another over generations. His onerous duty was simply to remind Simeon that whatever he was delegated to do in the future might be equally repellent. His disgust and aversion were not reasons to withdraw, but to establish his dedication. The public act would be a powerful confirmation of tradition, offered only to a few, even though the job was surely repulsive and degrading. Alphonz tried to explain while knowing Simeon's response. For the sake of his goal, Simeon had to grovel in the dirt to find triumph. What his elderly partner privately thought of this ceremony with a white shaman was unknown, but presumably she was deeply aware of its significance. She was a dowager priestess, long in power, and after many years, quite accustomed to the ritual. In addition to having many partners and husbands, some of those still living were scarcely more than boys. Nevertheless, Simeon could not rise to the occasion and fully appreciate the honor.

After feasting abundantly, both tribes took up a chant, while forming a loose ring around Simeon and the Priestess. They called for the couple to come together. For her part, the priestess was an old hand. She danced rhythmically, swaying from side to side, pendulous breasts pulling her this way and that, in measured time with drum beats. Apparently enjoying her timeless appetite and ability to cohabit with a younger partner, she came closer and closer to Simeon who was quivering, but not from religious ecstasy. Meanwhile, Simeon went through a semblance of a ceremonial dance in order to distract himself from what was about to happen. He tried to focus on her tattoos and decorations, not on the odors emitted. He caught his breath as she came closer. The offensive scent of her body threatened to engulf him. Cleanliness was evidently not urgent. Anticipating a failure, Simeon could not rouse himself enough to engage fully in the ceremony. He vastly preferred holding his nose in disgust than fornicating with this ancient female. The crowd noticed and began to murmur in disbelief. The undismayed priestess was apparently not unfamiliar with this turn of events. Flinging herself at Simeon, she knocked him down, and with a noise sounding like a loud bray, flattened herself over him, all the while writhing, almost wrestling with her reluctant partner. There was no question about who was dominant, and this turned out to be the theme of the ceremony itself.

The crowd overwhelmingly approved of the outcome. The priestess continued to gyrate over the hapless Simeon, then raised herself and loudly proclaimed that he was a true shaman, and that the white man pleased her. Alphonz laughed as if in vindication. He teased the exhausted and mortified Simeon when the ceremony ended, telling him again that it was intended by tradition to be a spiritual ritual, not a physical ordeal. What Simeon regarded as humiliation and failure turned out to be, in fact, a triumph for all, a successful matching and mating. The weary Simeon could hardly believe it was other than absolute torture. It was a transgression, surely, but hardly a consolation to know that other shamans before him had gone through a similar test of faith. Learning that his sexual nonperformance was so eminently successful did not ease his distress. The best he could manage was a realization that the performance symbolized a sacramental union of opposites in the continuity of generations. In any event, it was a pretty smelly business.

Not long afterward, a young woman named Elina spoke with Simeon about becoming one of his attendants. It was neither a sexual offering nor a marriage proposal. Simeon was disposed to accept. Elina's duties would include supervising the household, which had grown in size in proportion to Simeon's prestige. Besides, he liked her and found her company more than pleasing, especially in contrast to the elderly priestess. There was no tradition involved. He was entitled to attendants, and Elina would be a chief administrator for a household that would undoubtedly increase when he became a full-fledged shaman of repute. Elina would also become a companion that he sorely lacked.

Alphonz was honored instead of feeling supplanted by Elina's favored position. In fact, he had encouraged Elina to apply because she was the eldest daughter of Alphonz's sister. The arrangement brought additional prestige to his already distinguished family. Simeon was also honored by the unqualified acceptance into a family of high status.

There was a legendary prophecy in this tribe that a white shaman would one day be sent by KA and bring good health and fortune to the tribe. No one now doubted that Simeon filled all the qualifications. The white stranger's special mythic significance enhanced his shamanhood and tribal authority. Hearing and receiving so much praise and adulation, Simeon found himself devoutly believing that he was on the verge of becoming one of KA's elect. Nevertheless, in the midst of his tribal glory, Simeon constantly feared that cancer might return. In time, Simeon acquired the reputation of a great healer, although like Nyergy, his actual therapeutic record was largely based on reputation, not cures. Simeon could do what he could in treating illnesses, and then travel to the other world and beseech KA to grant a remission. Some healers, including physicians in Western society, believe in personal exemption, and that only patients are sick.

Professional superiority endows them with a certain degree of immunity against falling ill themselves. It was different with Simeon who was very aware of his vulnerability, as well as having CA already within. His earlier experiences had only immunized him against arrogance, not cancer. He knew in his heart that despite his vigor, he lived only by courtesy of CA, who chose to remain inactive, and of KA who would select Simeon only when it was appropriate to do so. Because recovery is ultimately due to KA, every person really belongs to that mightiest and most benevolent God, KA who controls and dominates life and death. KA did not bother with ordinary illnesses or minor curses. Neither did Simeon, who preferred to delegate everyday illnesses to local shamans. This act of generosity helped maintain his reputation. Tribal healers appreciated referrals in which recovery was certain and therefore became Simeon's staunch supporters.

Simeon the Shaman not only avoided conflict with local shamans, he was also careful not to offend the tribe's politicians and elders. Any shaman of quality who expects to stay in power confines himself to spiritual matters. Nevertheless, while remission and cure did occur, recurrence did not always respond to human stew. Simeon accepted credit graciously when recovery did occur. Miracles followed him around. His reputation grew and the man behind the miracles became looked on as KA's anointed delegate.

Shamans were not expected to be monkish, and not a few shamans consorted with their devoted followers, grateful for the opportunity to share in both earthly and spiritual matters. Simeon's admiration and affection for Elina made her an exclusive favorite. It was a reward that others envied. Simeon was faithful in his way, too, allowing a few others infrequently to sleep with him for something well done.

Still, questions nagged him, especially at moments of congratulation. Was he only a hard-working charlatan who played on primitive gullibility? Or did he simply duplicate the practices of regular physicians over the generations and preside until patients got better on their own? To his credit, he did not make extraordinary claims for his skill, nor did he reject such stunning recoveries that occurred. Simeon wanted to believe that he was a favorite of KA who would naturally protect him against CA, and therefore, in effect, decree immortality. Consequently, he would never get old, fall ill, become decrepit and die, unless, of course, KA decreed. Despite fear of death, Simeon did gradually develop a comfortable conviction that confused his fame and power with automatic exemption from rules and illnesses. By transcending taboos, he could become a law unto himself. Transgression in the past and glory in the present might, he trusted, strengthen his body enough to be shielded against death.

Old age was not taboo. It was inevitable. The taboo came from defying old age. The Master taught Simeon tribal wisdom and much he'd learned on his own. But this did not include avoiding death. What he depended on, however, was preparation for meeting KA in the other world. He had achieved much, and much had been awarded. He now knew his parentage, and belonged to a devoted family, quite contrary to that of Gina and Lorenzo.

Chapter 14—Nunc Dimittis

One bright day, as Simeon wandered along the shore, having come down from his village, he spotted a small launch slowly rounding the river's bend. Even at a distance he saw two men, one at the bow, steering the craft, while the other stretched out at the stern. The boat maneuvered carefully, indicating that the pilot knew his way and had been here before. However, neither man noticed Simeon. After passing Simeon, who was now standing at the shore, the launch turned around. Even before it attempted a landing, Simeon recognized Axel as the man lying at the stern, but now sitting up.

It was an unfamiliar Axel, looking even from a distance to be gaunt and emaciated, seemingly very sick, and not the sturdy Axel he had last seen. As the launch came closer and closer into shallow water, Axel did not wave although he certainly must have recognized Simeon. The native pilot saw Simeon and threw him a rope to help landing, even though there was no pier but only a natural clearing between rocks. Axel did not get up until the boat was securely tied, and then with great difficulty rose to his feet and groped for support. He was indeed, a wasted version of the Axel he once had been, and who ordinarily towered over everyone else. The two men helped get Axel onto the shore.

At a glance, to Simeon's now practiced eye, Axel was losing the struggle with a devastating illness. Only after Axel was safely on land and standing more or less erect did he first seem to recognize his helper. They embraced gently, as Axel murmured a few words. Axel had made this trip mainly to see Simeon, now a reputable healer and first-class shaman. Unkempt clothes hung loosely on his haggard body, like a shroud on a skeleton. It took no special skill to see that Axel was already partially disengaged from life itself, and now clung to existence like the worn-out clothes on his body. He signaled that he wanted to sit down before continuing to speak. His voice had lost the bold firmness that gave the former Axel additional authority.

"I am sick, Simeon. That you can see. I am almost dead. You see me wasting away, but I wanted to talk with you, once again. Never thought it could happen. A little later if I can rest up a bit, I'll tell you more about it. I'm glad you're here, afraid you wouldn't be. I need help, just like you did." Even uttering these words left Axel breathless and hardly able to whisper. Simeon was afraid that Axel might expire right then and there, as if beyond struggle.

Simeon was vastly saddened by Axel's pitiful plight. To hear him asking for help, this remnant of the man he once was, seemed at first as if he simply wanted just to see Simeon once again before letting the last fragment of life depart. Disease can make a mockery of any man, but particularly those who find it hard to admit their incapacity and ask for help.

Simeon had always been grateful to Axel. But Axel's illness and debilitation was in such painful contrast to what he had once been—assertive, courageous, invulnerable, heroic, everything Simeon truly admired—that Axel's perilous state almost prompted Simeon to weep. Simeon imagined that he was Axel's last hope for healing and release, a seeming impossibility. He expected imminent death, not remission or recovery for Axel. Despite the fame and authority of healthier days Simeon was likely to be Axel's sole mourner. Perhaps back in Cambridge, there were survivors. Simeon knew nothing of that part of Axel's life. So far as Simeon knew, there were no next-of-kin to grieve.

There had been a long gap from the last time Axel saw Simeon until now. His recollections flooded back, with Axel still barely able to stand. Long before his aborted mission, Simeon had been on the edge of death. The old Chief for his own reasons had withheld the sacred stew that Simeon had journeyed to find. Then Axel arrived, insisting that Simeon be given the sacred stew. Afterwards, Simeon finally became a cannibal, and his recovery progressed, slowly at first but over time, completely. Now it was Axel who apparently returned to ask the same, although he might be beyond rescue. Simeon's obligation could not be shirked.

With effort, using two boys who wandered down from the cliff, Axel was helped to walk slowly, step by step, up the arduous pass between rocks and ridges, until reaching the top. It took a long, long time. He was put in Simeon's own cabin. Attendants rushed to make the visitor comfortable. Axel managed to speak once again with Simeon.

"I can't get much weaker than I am," Axel said, "But I'm here, so maybe there is a little time left." He was almost apologetic for being sick and feeble. Simeon wondered if Axel had ever eaten human flesh during his many years in the jungle. Curiously, the subject of Axel and personal cannibalism had never arisen. There was never an occasion. Simeon did not want Axel to become a first time cannibal against his personal wishes. It was still a taboo for a white man. Yet Axel by myth alone surely knew what benefited Simeon, and presumably many others. He had argued for it, without indicating his preferences.

Simeon wanted Axel to be healthy enough and more like himself when finally chosen by KA, if he had to die. The ailment was conspicuously cancer. Cruel and relentless as cancer might be, Simeon had to bargain with KA, who honored those deserving of being at his side. This was the way to make death appropriate and befitting.

"You realize, Axel, that the sacred stew is not for everyone; you told me that a long time ago. Nor is cannibalism," he said, hesitantly, not to build hope falsely, but to find out whether Axel would eat or had eaten human flesh. Somehow he doubted it. "What works for some people might not for others." Neither man was sure what worked, if it worked at all. However in the time since Simeon's return, before becoming a shaman, he had witnessed remarkable remissions from the sacred soup, besides his own.

Here was his prestigious former guide and protector, sick and beyond ordinary remedies, now willing to put faith in Simeon, at one time the very last person Axel would rely on. Simeon beseeched KA that the magic of human flesh would help his friend and rescuer, Axel.

Although Simeon worked hard and long to gain his present high stature, he also wanted Axel's good opinion. His arduous pilgrimage should have been testimony enough. Nevertheless, Simeon had not lost the white man's bias that automatically looks down on anyone who turns native, adopts tribal customs, and takes up tribal beliefs. Up until now, Simeon had successfully put his past behind, scarcely remembering the events that molded his life, but diffident about conversion to the tribe that once had been strange and alien. It was Simeon's disrespect for himself that mattered. After all, Axel knew, without being told, the general drift of what the former Simeon had been like.

When he and Axel talked in English, Simeon realized how rusty he had become, another sign of absorption into the native culture. Standing there a shaman in front of Axel made Simeon feel vulnerable and still a pretender, as if everything about his rigorous training had been a charade, not unlike taking on an assumed name for a job he was not qualified to fill. The past had not entirely disappeared. Axel must have sensed Simeon's hesitation, without exactly knowing why. His intuition did not let him down.

"I didn't come here just to admire your exalted status, Simeon," Axel managed to say, quietly. "What you decide to do with the rest of your life is up to you. Your reasons are good enough for you. I respect that. The sacred soup, always cooking in the cauldron, helped you get back on your feet again. Maybe me. I heard about your return and the condition you were in. Apparently, the effect of cannibal stew wears off after awhile, or it works only here where the mothers cook it right. That's what you came for, and I had to demand that was what you should get. I'm glad it worked, but I didn't agree when you decided to go back where we both came from. I need help, I'm sick enough to try anything, almost, whether I believe in it or not. The conventional stuff didn't work. I am even ready to embrace sorcery, since I have nothing and no one else to embrace. Nothing else worked for me. I am into the CA way of life and death, and I know what your remedy is. I'm willing. I have cancer of the bowel, the colon; you know, and it has spread all over me. It's an invading, occupying army; destruction and devastation the way I remember the Nazis. I'm an open city in ruins, expecting more looting and destruction."

Axel pulled the corners of his mouth into a rueful, unhappy smile, showing dry and decayed teeth, as uncared for as his tattered clothes, as incurable as his cancer. Simeon could scarcely believe that this gallant courageous man had turned into pathetic rubble. Axel decided to tell more about his illness.

"I went back and looked up Dr. Narub, the worse for wear after his experience with you. He did what he could, and made me promise not to say where he is now. He's doing all right, considering the beating he got in Sydney." Simeon wanted to ask more about Narub. Their rift had left unhealed contrition.

"We had a falling out, you know; but I won't push you about him," Simeon said, knowing that Axel would say very little about Narub. "I want to know more about the cancer." Axel sighed, reluctant to go beyond what he'd already said.

"Over a year ago, maybe more. I can't recall. It seems that long. I was on a vacation in Australia, down south, where I used to go. I met this woman traveling by herself. Not young but still very attractive, middle-aged, divorced, no obligations. I wanted her, not just for a piece but also for a friend, at least for a while. She had a charm about her I'd forgotten. And then I came down with something that seemed like a very civilized disease. I didn't know what except it seemed to hit the bowel, as I already told you. I never had anything like that before. I told her, but she left, didn't seem to care. Maybe she thought it was the usual clap, but it wasn't. I had no discharge. I saw a local doctor who treated me. You know my so-called intuition. I asked about Narub before I knew he was in that same town. I won't tell you where. Well, I thought I might have something else besides the clap, which I doubted, anyway. I was sicker than I needed to be. I let the doctor treat me, and then I looked up Narub and found that I was right about what I had. Why I hooked it up with that woman, I really liked her, I don't know. Maybe she was a witch who gives men cancer in addition to anything else. I didn't have the clap, though. I had a bad case of rapidly advancing cancer, and since then, well, just look at me. No operation. It had gone too far. I didn't want to wear myself out on chemotherapy, radiation, what not. Narub still practices regular medicine. Always did. He seemed to avoid talking about you, except that he didn't want you or anyone, I surmised, to know where he was. He never suggested that I go back to the Highlands. I did take some chemo just to make the doctor feel that I wasn't being neglected. But I could see that I wasn't one of his best cases. Coming to see you was my idea. The whole thing, how far I've come down in the world in just over a year, puzzles me. Must be growing fast."

Axel now wanted to know what happened after he sailed down the river and around the bend, leaving Simeon to undertake the cannibal cure. In talking, Axel seemed to become stronger, more alert, and less feeble. He even showed traces of his ability to size up situations quickly and make smart observations, even as he asked searching questions. Simeon wisely deferred talking about his adventure in New York and the failed mandate.

"What brought you to take up shamaning?" he asked, in a tone of voice he might have used if he'd asked about shoemaking. "You must believe all this about talking with the gods." He resisted using a judgmental term. "I wouldn't be here if I didn't think you were sincere. For all I know you and KA are by now buddies. It is not easy for you, a white man, to undergo what it takes. I know that you can play the crazy mystic as well as any other part you like. But I think you've really joined up this time. I respect these people and you, too. They want a miraculous cure, and so do I. But I still want to know if you're for real."

For the first time, Axel laughed with just a hint of his old sardonic timber. Simon recalled how Axel used to needle him, and was glad to discover that his sense of humor hadn't wasted away. Axel had heard about Simeon's cure that turned out not to be a cure and evidently also knew about Simeon's recovery after coming back for a successful booster course of the stew. He also knew about Simeon's training for shamanhood. The training hadn't been easy for a white man, especially a long time libertine and dilettante.

"I am all right, Axel. I'm for real; even if I can't understand everything I've learned. One thing I've learned and must tell you. I'm serving at the discretion of the top god, KA. You know about the tribal gods, especially KA, just like the Egyptian spirit called Ka, except that's far away and a long time ago. How can you 'almost' believe something? Well, these people can do that, and the gods, especially KA, like to be doubted! I don't have to be a true believer, but I've had reason to believe. Being an 'almost' believer isn't good enough. I've had the chance to be in KA's presence, too. I've learned that KA actually wants you not to be too holy, that blasphemy is OK. In fact, sacrilege is encouraged. It shows you have a mind of your own. Telling KA to kiss your ass, that's a sign of something, not much, but a sign. It won't get you admitted to the holy sanctum. I've conducted myself in ways that KA would approve of." Simeon spoke about KA as if he were a generous broad-minded CEO of a big company, without a Board of Directors to outvote him. However, he was prudent enough by this time not to tax Axel's credulity with details about the holy trance and KA. Being 'in KA's presence' was enough. He could be skeptical, and still consider doing KA's will. But a non-believer like Axel who is ready for cannibalism needs all the credulity he can muster. Doubting KA's existence and using disbelief to needle KA is not a private joke, but a way to qualify belief and, not incidentally, whet his appetite for the cannibal stew.

"You've changed," Axel said, "And for the better. That's clear to me. You're not that weird horny outcast who threw money around, as if no one else had any." Axel was right, of course, but he couldn't realize how far the training had transfigured Simeon. The world of KA was very real to him, despite that skeptical joshing. He was also respectfully silent about KA and guarded the calling that prompted him to dedicate his remaining life in this manner. Prolonged meditative silence was no less a virtue than candor. Undoing sorcery was a strong part of his vocation but his spiritual adventures far transcended jungle medicine or sorcery. Not even Axel could understand what he had experienced.

There was no need to prove anything. Both worlds and worlds beyond those were real enough to exist at the same time. However, KA's world could wait for what Simeon accomplished in this one, and then at KA's discretion. It sounded too mystical to believe, and he had to spare himself from Axel's scathing doubt, if that was possible.

Right now, there was the matter of Axel's illness, his sufficient faith to travel so far, and his lingering near death. The sacred stew was all that remained for Axel to try. It might earn him a remission. Miracles and cures were not for Simeon, but he had no doubt that only cannibalism through the holy stew stood between Axel and his death. Axel's critical condition made the situation even more urgent. Alphonz gave his prompt and kindly assent, in contrast to the adamant reluctance of the former Chief. The stew was promptly made available, without the embarrassing rituals of Nyergy's curious interventions.

Tribal chieftains differ in how to prepare cannibal stew; one batch might be different from another, and therefore not as effective. Perpetual tending changed the ingredients, but human remains were always there, simmering along with additional contributions. Besides, like everything else with a religious tinge, ceremony is everything, even if the mummery were deliberately left out.

Simeon wanted to skip the chanting and the rest of the rigmarole. He put his faith entirely in the prospective potency of human flesh. There had never been a specific proportion of this or that in the broth, stew, or soup. Hearts and brains were the principal organs used most directly for enhancing courage and character, but as a rule heart and brain were eaten raw, just after the donor was killed. Given the gluttony of the celebrations, there seldom was enough heart and brain left over for the soup. The remaining effectiveness depended on the rest of the body. According to Elina, no one made the stew as well as her mother, a universal culinary compliment. Consequently, Simeon decided that the Elina stew, added to the always ready traditional preparation, would have to do, since there was no other way to determine which preparation was best for Axel. Before Axel started, Simeon first went on a brief retreat during which he got KA's permission to feed Axel the cannibal stew. Simeon then presented Axel with the alternatives, cannibalism or simply comfortable care. Axel did not flinch but had expected to be offered the sacred stew. But he would have resented not being given a choice.

For all his residual skepticism, Axel gladly cooperated, day after day, drinking the broth, and eating the meat without complaint. He did not go into a trance, like a shaman, but finished his daily allotment, protesting only that he was still hurting and extremely nauseated. Later, as he became more accustomed to the scents and tastes that never were appetizing, Axel bravely consumed as much cannibal stew as possible. He had lived off the forest before, and found the stew and its nameless contents not altogether objectionable. It was not much different, he said, from eating grubs and insects, and much better than some animals he chose not to mention.

At last, signs of improvement began, gathered momentum and infusing Axel with some of his old energy. It was not miraculous, not a sudden magical transformation but a steady renewal, typical of how an ordinary patient with a self-limited disease at last finds himself recovered. Simeon was satisfied, and so was Axel. It worked on Axel as it once had for Simeon. And there was no doubt that Axel had been rescued. CA had been persuaded to let him go, at least for the moment. KA's intervention was not to be mentioned to anyone not already one of the elect.

Periodically, Simeon the Shaman renewed himself. Aside from a regular allotment of sacred stew, he had secret rituals to observe and ceremonies to perform far away from the tribe. Sometimes he walked hours still further into the interior, or went down along the shore, until he found a hidden cave, tucked inconspicuously between two boulders known only to him. There, he stayed for several days, generally living on whatever fish and animals he could catch, along with vegetables and roots he foraged. While on such a retreat he spotted Axel's return.

Simeon practiced asceticism in spirit as well as body, enduring the rigors of scarce food and bad weather as good for enrichment and nourishment. In addition to this spiritual and therapeutic regimen, he regularly went into trances that fostered transport to another realm. KA was satisfied that Axel had the full cannibal experience, raw flesh besides the stew, omitting only tribal celebrations. No religious beliefs were necessary. Simeon got an indelible impression that KA liked to cure a skeptic more than a pious believer. That included Axel's cure.

Axel's steady but slow recovery became faster and faster. Not only did he eat more of the sacred stew, but supplemented his regimen with generous amounts of regular food, however exotic. He looked and acted more like the old Axel, asserting himself often, clearly, and with authority. Spirited and robust once more, the old skeptical Axel began to question whether he ever had cancer in the first place, conveniently disregarding the examination and treatment he had been through. Simeon wasn't to be drawn into further discussions about KA and CA even though Axel seemed determined to test him by insistent challenges.

"How do you know that I didn't have some sickness that sooner or later would get better on its own?" he demanded of Simeon. By these questions Axel was struggling to regain his former confidence and minimize his vulnerability. It was all a sign of health, denial and optimism. Axel taunted Simeon the Shaman about everything else, as well. Although he spent years in the jungle, preferring it to his earlier attachments, Axel chose now to separate himself from the indigenous people and their culture. In healthier moments, he respected most of the tribes he associated with. Nevertheless, he now showed signs of a budding wish to return to early roots, at least in the USA, if not in Denmark. However, it had to do with a stunning remission, not disdain for the tribes. While similar to Simeon's wish to return and carry a mission, for Axel it was an ambition to turn time backwards and become young enough to deserve a second chance, canceling out the choices he made in the first place and using renewal to rectify what had gone on before.

Simeon acknowledged that whatever cannibalism does or does not do, sorcery is usually involved. He refused to go further than this ambiguous statement, because that was all he knew. He answered Axel's questions cautiously and compassionately, saying that the evil had been banished. While far from a believer, Axel had philosophical respect for other ideas, including magic and sorcery. But arguing and disputing, even against himself, made Axel feel vindicated and renewed. Alphonz proved to be wiser than either Simeon or Axel in dealing with the aftermath of Axel's recovery.

"I do not know what your medicine men believe" he said, "But over and over, our sick people are cured from a curse put on them by enemies. It is easy to put a curse on someone, if you don't care about having the same done to you. Some people are killed for trying to curse someone, or trying to do magic. Who did this to Axel?" Simeon told Alphonz about the woman from whom Axel might have caught a venereal disease, which was never established, but then the discovery of cancer of the colon, already widespread. Was this not a curse, a hateful destruction of Axel's character and body? Maybe she was a witch who first entranced him and then cast a spell. That version was strange enough to have some validity, too.

"It is always up to the spirits," Alphonz said, pulling a piece of bark from a nearby tree. Under the bark was a large crawling agitated insect, suddenly exposed to light and annoyed at the intrusion. The yellow and black striped body squirmed ominously. Its large head was dotted with many eyes; the dorsum had a large phosphorescent spot. The antennae flayed around, as its claws sought a secure foothold in another secret place to hide. Opportunistically, Alphonz seized the animal, picking it up without apparent hesitation and gave it to Axel.

"Here, the spirits live inside this frightened animal," he said "It looks evil, but if you eat it, the insect will take away a bad curse without killing anyone." Axel was not a stranger to eating bugs, grubs, and a variety of jungle life, as much for experimentation as for food. He did not hesitate. With a smile that neither mocked Alphonz nor demonstrated bravado, he bit off the insect's head, then popped the rest of the still wriggling body into his mouth. He had in this fashion passed a test of faith, without a qualm. When he finished chewing and swallowing Axel bowed gravely without a sign of triumph, first to Alphonz, then to Simeon. The ceremony was far more eloquent than Axel's arguments. After his years in the jungle, Axel strongly believed in benign spirits as much as in witches.

"There," he said, "I am protected from evil. But maybe this huge bug has something in it that protects me, ugly as it is." He left his comment unfinished, but then the old Axel couldn't resist making another speech, like the professor he might once have been.

"If man can create gods then it's no trick to believe in the gods he creates and no trick at all to create angels, like the Angel of Death, and believe that, too. I think that the Angel of Death got bored and went away. That's why I got better. Maybe KA was responsible for that. I might have been getting well anyway, so his services were no longer required. Make no mistake. I believe your god was on my side, this time. A dog will follow its master, not because he shares the master's beliefs, but because he cares nothing for them. I follow you, Alphonz and Simeon, though neither of you is my master, and I don't trust your gods, either. Spare me a harangue, trying to convince me, although I repay you with a harangue of my own. Some gods, I like; others annoy me. Too pretentious, or their believers are too righteous. I am well enough now to leave. Maybe a curse was on me but

I'm OK now, ready to do whatever I decide." This was said in irony, everyone knew.

He knew of his vulnerability, and while seeming to deny he had been sick, asserted that a curse might have also afflicted him, not that a god had graciously intervened. Axel was a man of the forest, jungle, and river, a proud though not arrogant maverick following his own lead, without declaring allegiance to any god whatsoever. He retained much of the anthropologist's feigned and fractured objectivity, respecting other ways while not sure of his own.

All that Simeon wanted had been realized. Axel did not die. KA spared him and repulsed CA, whether anyone acknowledged this or not. Knowing that others would come along, just as sick, and die, Simeon could not be blamed or take credit for any unforeseen outcome. Whether Simeon was a super shaman or a counterfeit claiming to make deals with KA made no difference. Belief in KA was irrelevant. Cancer made a difference, however, because it was clearly a curse and calamity. Whether CA was also a deity with capriciously mean motives, or just an unknown and impersonal biological process remained an ambiguous question whose answer left the outside world just as mystified, and just as dependent on its own metaphors.

In fact, Axel recaptured so much of his former strength and self-confidence that Simeon was moved to wonder what other magical process had been unleashed. His recovery exceeded physical expectations. Next to his physical rehabilitation, another astonishing transformation took place. More than an expectation, an actual rejuvenation took place. The cure had gone beyond building courage and character, which Axel already had in abundance. The cannibalism seemed to turn back the clock by decades, as if whatever accounted for the recovery outdid and overshot its aims and accomplished much more. The old Axel had been self-confident yet compassionate, more than most men. His intelligence and intuition had been part of his ample gifts and personal endowment. But what happened now was a bizarre age reversal to somewhere in his talented youth. He became an Axel unknown to Simeon.

The rejuvenated Axel was on the lookout to learn. Simeon marveled at what might have been the brilliance and promise of his youth. Like many other bright college students, Axel also began to dispute, and often test his elders. Alphonz, along with a few elders, were offended by what was so unlike the mature Axel, who needed to prove nothing and would never try to score intellectual points with respected teachers and friends. After all, these were primitive people, learned only in the ways of the forest, not given to abstract polemics. For the new Axel, this did not seem to make a difference.

Simeon was disturbed by Axel's ambitions and extravagant plans. Regularly, Axel spoke about leaving the village, going back to some unspecified place in the United States, perhaps Cambridge, Massachusetts, where he had made fateful career decisions that now might be undone. He could begin all over again with a second chance to do what he once had failed to do, and to correct earlier mistakes, as if intervening years did not matter. Without elaboration, Axel talked of people that he wanted to see once again, even alluding to a woman, nameless, but so tenderly mentioned that it might have been a young wife.

Whatever happened in the course of recovery had changed the mature Axel into the Axel of years ago. Like Faust, few people would resist rejuvenation if offered, even by the devil. Interventions that promised to stem the advances of old age would be welcomed by almost everyone who wanted to turn back the clock and start fresh. But Axel's remission, if that was what it was, went beyond the youthful appearances of modern plastic surgery. He actually looked and acted much younger, having lost the weather beaten creases and clefts of his aging body and regained the musculature and flexibility of an athletic youth. Simeon could only stand by, incredulous at the miracle of rejuvenation. The transformation could be sorcery but it was sorcery different from what had afflicted him with cancer.

Simeon was fearful of Axel's future if he persisted in trying to regain the life he had long ago chosen not to follow. The likelihood of making new mistakes during second chances was almost certain. As with anyone else regretting past choices, there is no evidence that another path might have been better, had it been taken. Second chances are fantasies, imagined in advance to have a better outcome but seldom reached in reality. It was not like the covenant with KA that led Simeon to believe he had a mission to fulfill.

Axel firmly believed that rejuvenation entitled him to forsake his present life and get another chance and another choice. He had been successful with his first choices, becoming almost legendary in the land he chose. But he had many choices as a younger man that he chose to reject; some of the details were still in his memory vault. While the fountain of youth is and always will be a vain dream of aging men and women, frustrated by the passage of inexorable time, no one can fully restore a life built on fragments of old regrets and rueful experience. Painful episodes, embarrassing events, and unavoidable indiscretions of youth could outweigh the other benefits of being young again, new opportunities or not.

Perhaps KA had deliberately played a practical joke on the defiant Axel, or tempted him with another, even stronger taboo, yet to be broken. Simeon just wanted him to leave quickly. However, eager or not, Axel stayed on, enjoying his audience, like a self-absorbed adolescent rebellious yet reluctant to leave home. Perhaps too his fabled intuition warned of potential disaster.

"Mighty Simeon, healer and redeemer, Captain Courageous, proprietor of my soul, my rescuer, I owe you much. But what have you done to me? I am more than I ever was, all over again, again, and again. Once I thought I could be whatever I wanted, but soon learned better. Now I am that young man I once wanted to be and never was. You want the after-life, old man? I don't need it now. I will go back where I started, but where was that? I want to say yes, when once I said no, and say no, when I made a mistake and said yes. I'll do better this time. Make no mistake about it, because I'll have no regrets with my new paradise, and a garden of opportunity."

Axel kept up these exuberant tirades, tactlessly teasing Simeon about his licentious past. He seemed to have guessed much more than Simeon ever confessed. Simeon had put his own past in the memory bank Axel told him about. But Axel, riding his well established guesses like an unruly horse, acted as if he'd opened up a candid, uncensored diary and now was reading it aloud to an audience. He needled Simeon about his preference for old women, laughing and kidding about the dry crotches that Simon (he even used that name) enjoyed moistening, once upon a time. How he knew or even surmised Simeon's secrets was hardly possible for a gifted adolescent, and extremely unlikely for the mature Axel. It was an enhancement of his talents buoyed by rejuvenation.

To Simeon, this mocking betrayal was an abusive perversion of Axel's intuitive skills, once so arresting and perceptive. It was not like the generous Axel who once rescued Simeon and proved a competent mentor in other ways. In another misguided jest about Simeon and KA, Axel started to call him Captain AKA, also known as Assistant KA, the pilot with many names, an agent of KA who cures cancer for KA's sake.

It was not at all amusing to be called an impostor, libertine, bastard, and rich kid when that part of his life had faded away. How Axel knew all this was as mysterious as why he turned Simeon's past against him. Ordinarily, it would only be one youth jealous of another, but now, Axel's ridicule eroded Simeon's hard won liberation and degraded his shamanhood. If an impostor admits his fakery, does that make him an honest man? Axel's taunts found their mark. Simeon shrunk back, dreading painful memories, now worried that he too might revert to the older version of himself, lose his dedication, and, indifferent to all he'd gained, seize an opportune moment to abandon his tribe.

"Tell me, mighty Captain," Axel went on in a typical harangue, "Does KA ever sleep at night? Is he in favor of large families? Does he wipe his ass when he takes a shit? Aren't we all related to KA and that cockroach Alphonz gave me off the tree? It tasted good, but not as good as..." Simeon tried to be serene, but this was as impossible as being steadfast in his vocation. He wanted to ignore the sarcastic abuse and pretend that Axel was challenging just to find out what was true and valid, not to torment him.

"You're testing to see if KA approves of a taboo about second youth," he said, "KA sanctions or tolerates many things. Some, I have no idea about. He doesn't encourage evil in anyone, not even you who ridicule what very decent people take seriously. He has no tolerance for evil magic or for magicians who think they can abolish evil. It would be enough if KA just taught us the difference between good and evil. There is nothing so good that someone, somewhere, will not consider evil, and no depraved act that someone does not regularly embrace and finds good. I am still vulnerable. You were once my rescuer, and I'm still grateful. But now you're acting as if you've been spared not only from death, but from getting old. CA can make you very sick, but this is going too far. You don't think about death any more, just like when you were listening to your father play the violin." Not considering himself very intuitive, Simeon wondered how he'd come up with that piece of Axel's early life, which he'd never been told about. How can one person share another person's memories?

"Axel, I've learned that death is not always something to regret. Sometimes, it can be postponed until another time, whenever that is, but seldom by choice. That way, we get rid of time and getting feebler, impaired, and old enough that we only look for deliverance. There are other worlds, but not necessarily second chances, like the ones you want and imagine will give you a new triumph, or a chance to see how it might have come out. I've spoken with KA. Yes, I admit that. I couldn't become a real shaman without coming face to face with KA. I've heard his answers to questions I might have asked. What is the purpose of life, if there is one? That question is one any god worth his salt should at least make a stab at. What if there is no purpose except to live as long and as well as possible, and then die? There's no good reason to think that anyone's life has a purpose, anyway, beyond what is apparent, healthy survival, which is only a means, not an enlightened end. KA never told me the purpose of life, but did say that until I found out, I could pass the time thinking about good and evil, while the search for the real purpose goes on. I'd like to just be dead long enough to get a little look into what's around the corner, that is, just over the edge of death into wisdom, whatever you call regrets for past mistakes that you're not likely to make again. A sneak peek into what's hidden for everyone else."

Simeon did not like talking this way, this holy stuff, word twisting, fake piety, false assumptions, phony conclusions, banal lectures, and riddle wrestling. It made him feel just as adolescent as Axel. But his vernacular was consistent with what KA sanctioned.

After that declaration, Simeon no longer responded to nettlesome teasing. He had been going on like a preacher; as if he knew something for sure that really wasn't so. Once upon a time, he believed that telling lies was the only true way to get along. Now he knew that even careful lies have a certain validity, and that always telling the truth is impossible, likely to be no more than a pious posture. Those who claim to tell truth, whatever the outcome, are pious hypocrites seeking extenuating exemptions for mischief on the sly.

"What, me and KA pals? You mean he wants me not to get old, but not any younger? For what purpose?" Axel was enjoying himself, unabashed, "I hope he has better taste in the friends he makes. I'll die soon enough, but not now, not now. I don't have to for a long time, if ever. That's how I feel. Let me stay young again, with the world open at my doorstep, ready to go out and be something more than ever I could be. I even had a wet dream last night, you rascal. Soon I'll have pimples again from pulling it off!

"How about you, Simon or Simeon or whatever you, the shaman, call yourself? I'm not satisfied with these little black girls around here; their frizzy hair always bothered me. I've nowhere else to put my friend here." He grabbed at his crotch, like Chester, not like the dignified Axel of old. "Sorry that's all there is for you. I want to leave and find myself a nice lady tourist without the clap." Simeon resented this line of talk. He had struggled with asceticism, except for periodic fornication with Elina, but didn't like finding old memories in everyday occurrences.

Axel spoke about going back and having a second chance to rectify and accomplish what he'd done or not done, but there was a conspicuous amnesia and lack of details about his original past. His was simply an overarching plan without form or body, like an empty ambition spun out of youthful fantasies and a newly constituted body.

"I'll leave," he finally said to Simeon, who was becoming just as impatient as the elders and Alphonz about the new Axel. "I act as if I've all the time in the world to do whatever I have to do. And I don't know what I'm supposed to do! And that can't be true. That river and these people, I used to know them well, and speak their language. I don't now. I can't be young and old at the same time. I can be young, but have to let go what I've learned growing up, and the rest of the baggage I've carried for so long. You can't have it both ways. They are all unfamiliar to me. Even you are someone I've just met. Maybe I'll go back to Cambridge, get a museum job, become a campus character. Have I said this before? Then there's home again, back to my parents who must miss me as much as I do them." That his parents were dead for many years did not occur to him, so full of the youthful illusion that everyone, including his parents, was alive and the same age as when he last saw them.

As he neared departure, Axel ceased mocking Simeon the Shaman. Simeon became the guide and mentor to this youthful incarnation. This version of Axel was docile and inexperienced, needing reassurance and firm directives, in contrast to the mature Axel around whom adoring legend formed. Other than Simeon, Axel truly had no one. Simeon hesitated, never having been in such a singularly dominant position with someone he revered and even feared. It was not at all like Simon Says. And now Axel, whether old or young, sober and subdued, enthusiastic and uninformed, was about to leave again. Simeon tried to picture Axel anywhere else but in the Highlands. Could a young Axel really do it all over again, only better? What would a young Axel do with a second chance? Not only had he been restored to health, but looked as if he were his own grandson. Axel, the sage of the river, was not, after all, a youngish graduate student about to do and be something other than what he was in Simeon's eyes. It was a free ride, with bonus attached, but a ride where? Second youth was what untold generations pine for, but when compared with rejuvenation like this, coming back from the dead would be anticlimactic. Only an Axel could aspire to the miracle of this final taboo, established as beyond attainment so firmly that no one could call it evil.

Simeon found the prospect of Axel's rejuvenation and return deeply disturbing. The Axel of just yesterday would disappear and forget his later life in a camouflage of youth without the encumbrances of memory. Liberated to make new mistakes and hurt endless people, yet to be met, Simeon shuddered at this horrendous taboo that no one adequately comprehends. Conceivably, science fiction might install unused genetic seeds into someone in order to bring off this change, but Axel was the first to have second youth actually superimposed upon cancer recovery. What was this second chance? If Axel simply wanted to atone for past mistakes or penalize himself for offenses yet unrequited, that was understandable. However, it could be done without an outlandish retrogression. Simeon himself had such a list too long to enumerate. Undoubtedly, Axel will go back to Cambridge and find that everyone he'd known was gone, dead, the dust blown away, even the young bride he'd abandoned, if she happened to be real. Who would remember, or if even vaguely recalled, care for a revenant anachronism claiming to be someone he was not? The whole project might be a fiasco. Axel would be wiser to pass himself off as his own grandson, if indeed there were such a person. Simeon was truly alarmed, dreading Axel's mistakes, yet to be made. He might falter in the same old way, even with new rules and fresh taboos.

Simeon remembered how his own mission had been abruptly negated by relapse. Axel might also relapse in the midst of his return. Simeon's message about curing cancer through cannibalism now seemed ridiculously naive and grandiose. Only his brief meeting with Bruno Lorenzo indelibly mattered. Had the urbane Lorenzo actually been as compassionate, informative, and wise as he seemed that day? Did he really all but say that he had been Simeon's father? Simeon momentarily forgot that Lorenzo admitted that fact, to the best of Lorenzo's knowledge.

Simeon was close enough to his own demise to reflect upon the ultimate mystery of another world, closer to KA. Even Simeon the Shaman must face the edges of his imagination. What if a person could linger a little while after dying? It meant a small extension of life, death plus a little more. He had called it a peek. Wisdom and justice are not things that matter to the just dead. Such ideas are abstract and moth eaten enough. Few among the living truly care about such things. In the jungle, man and beast regularly exchange places, according to myth. Maybe this happens too in rejuvenation all over again. Simeon, still fearful of anonymous disintegration, recalled the strange odors redolent in that cemetery; a scent lingering on after the body was buried. This strange arresting aroma might have heralded the just dead, who for a fleeting moment were able to straddle the abyss between the living and dead, and can do nothing about either.

The day arrived however when Axel finally departed, with only Simeon in deep gratitude and Alphonz with lingering respect at the shore to bid him good-bye. Simeon and Alphonz helped Axel by arranging for suitable transportation, with helpers hurriedly hired because his favorite river pilot was nowhere to be seen. It was a sad and ominous ending for one who had confidently roamed jungle paths and rivers for so long. Another boatman claiming to know the river well enough to navigate safely was also recruited to replace the lost pilot. No one knew if the new pilot was capable. Qualifications could not be checked, an uncertainty that reminded Simeon of his adventure as ship's doctor. He hoped his recollection was not prophetic. Axel embraced both Simeon and Alphonz before starting out.

Then Axel was gone, standing in the bow, a hearty contrast to the feeble specter that once landed sick enough to need both assistance and a miracle. Axel and Simeon had mutually agreed to keep one another informed about their whereabouts, knowing that nothing of the sort would happen. Alphonz said nothing, except to return Axel's good-bye wave.

The following morning Simeon awoke with heavy foreboding that Axel would never live to use his rejuvenation. In reverting to a younger self, Axel had also lost his vast knowledge and experience of the river, jungle, tribes, risks to watch out for, and his fluency in local dialects, even Pidgin. There was only a void, and no look at the immediate future. Although Axel had completely recovered from cancer, there was also no assurance of a lengthy survival. Axel might have given up too much to be young again. The young Axel in all his ignorance could again be a victim, with so much erased from the noble Axel he was, the first time around.

Several weeks later, as jungle time is measured, rumors came floating back that his new pilot disappeared one night, abandoning Axel to marauders from the interior. Another bit of information reported that Axel reached Port Moresby, but never left New Guinea. That was highly disturbing because his intention was to embark as quickly as possible. There had in fact been no sighting of Axel since his departure. He had evidently not reached Port Moresby or anywhere else on the map. According to the flow of rumors, Axel was said to have taken a wrong turn in the river, which he had once known well, and lost his way among unfamiliar tributaries. He might have stumbled into hostile territory populated by criminals hiding from authorities. Robbery and murder occurred regularly, and the culprits were rarely found. Although Axel carried a weapon, his newly restored inexperience in the jungle did not arm him with the skill to use it. Rumors are never asked to substantiate themselves, so Simeon and Alphonz could only hope that every rumor was wrong and they'd soon hear from Axel, the indomitable, not the innocent voyager who left them not long ago.

Nothing further could be verified, but harrowing stories continued to flow. He simply disappeared. Had he been captured and killed? A sense of invulnerability was part of the burden that Axel carried with him, and that, Simeon feared, carried him straight to doom. Those who practice cannibalism frequently believe in their immunity to illness and injury, thus strengthening an illusion of invulnerability and undying youth. Axel's return to youth, however, was literal, not an illusion. Such fearlessness has its own risks and penalties, the most absolute of which is death. It is the revenge of old age upon the young and the youthful.

At last all rumors ceased, and Axel was forgotten. Inquiry yielded few facts, and meager speculation. Simeon returned to his shamanhood and great renown, becoming famous in his vocation, as Axel once had been in his. At times, he wondered if he could keep this man alive indefinitely, simply by imagining that Axel's spirit was still thriving somewhere, intangibly, perhaps on another dimension, but not yet dead.

Years were uncountable and unchanging, as Simeon flourished and grew older, then unmistakably old. There were only unending seasons and cycles of enlightenment, which gradually dimmed as if wearing out with Simeon. How much enlightenment can any human hope for and tolerate? Simeon never became accustomed to visitors who made a special pilgrimage to draw upon his supernatural reputation. Alphonz died unexpectedly. He was honored and Simeon again presided, grieving deeply for a loyal and true brother. The new Chief had not yet been born when Simeon first arrived. Simeon was alone again, sustained by the warmth and esteem of his tribe, there, up in the highlands and along the river.

Another year or two passed and others in the tribal family also died, including Elina. Devoted and loving for these many years, she had spent her youth and maturity attending Simeon. In magisterial solitude, Simeon belonged to many worlds, but to no one person. No one replaced Elina or Alphonz. But while Simeon needed fewer and fewer people, he did seek frequent spiritual renewal in his visits to KA. These journeys came about through holy trances and by secluding himself in his favorite cave along the river. Simeon was ageless in the eyes of the tribe. However, solitude allowed him greater responsiveness to the birds that sang and the fish that swam silently in the river. He was amply satisfied with his adopted aboriginal family. There would be no return to the world he once knew. He owed his life to KA and all the consequences that came. Simeon had faith, but no obligation to prove or praise anything.

Periodically, his thoughts wandered back to Dr. Narub. Whatever happened to this misunderstood stranger, almost a pariah wherever he went? It was Narub who started Simeon on the path leading to this moment. There were no compelling temptations, and therefore no transgressions, unless, perhaps, an injunction by nature itself that no one can restore youth. Consequently, like many mystics before him, Simeon found that he spent his days, aside from shamanic duties, contemplating his demise. His mission was accepting death's inexorability. His goal was to encourage a death appropriate for others to choose, had they a choice. When such a happy consequence did come about, Simeon marveled at the readiness with which very sick people slipped into and away from their earthly existence.

He had several mild relapses of cancer. Each time CA reminded him that death was not a special province, nor was Simeon the Shaman exempt. With each relapse Simeon found that the sacred stew was less and less effective. KA was asking him to stay but a little longer. CA and KA were negotiating the best and most propitious time for Simeon. Perhaps as a first class shaman he had done enough and it was time to move on. The best time could not be foretold. Simeon was alone with his meditation, just as he traveled alone to meet with KA. The balance between recovery and compliant acceptance of death gradually favored a quiet exitus, without fear and suffering, only repose. Where was KA? This was an unfamiliar question because Simeon firmly believed he knew. He once thought that Nyergy was returning, but it was only a rustling in the forest.

One small dawn, no different from countless mornings past, Simeon awakened in that limbo between night and morning in a quasi-trance that allowed quiet entry into KA's domain. Around him was the familiar jungle, with its sounds and smells rising to herald the coming day. This time, however, he heard faint but unequivocal sounds of a bird he did not recognize. It was not a dragonfly, not a noisy insect, nor a strange visitor looking for him. He saw nothing to locate the song.

The habitual noises of forest animals just beginning to wake up yielded to this song of a bird high up in a tree. The animals became unnaturally quiet. This was the right time for the Ohwai. Simeon was not sick, nor did he willingly acknowledge that his time on this earth was drawing to a close. In fact, he was alert and appropriately responsive to every sound and scent. It was an odd, yet compelling interlude that joined the dawn of another day and the serenity of his anticipating spirit. Who made the decision, he did not know. It had to be KA. The Ohwai had been dispatched.

The trees rustled like the tongues of an imaginary conversation. Simeon yearned to talk again with Axel, Gina, Lorenzo, and Sophia. He stirred himself to awaken more fully and look for Alphonz, who had already died. It was becoming lighter, even in the darkened jungle. The Ohwai had been there, high up in the tallest tree but he heard nothing now. Strident sounds drowned out the faint song he waited for and managed to catch, fleetingly.

From deep in the vaults of memory, he heard scattered sounds softening into strange words in another language. The words became clear and vaguely familiar, almost a phrase. Again, they faded away. He could only guess where. When the phrase recurred, then he understood fully. He heard *Nunc Dimittis*, over and over, as well as the faint Ohwai song. Simeon stood up, wanting to walk, soar, or swim, to join with everything inhabiting the earth, air, sky, and water. Nunc Dimittis, it was permitted to die, allowing Simeon to take another step on his journey. Simeon had arrived at that point when taboos no longer mattered, but he knew there were more to come.

Cannibalism is not the last taboo. We age inevitably, but the next taboo keeps us from total rejuvenation. It is a taboo because rejuvenation, like reincarnation, is a forbidden journey into second chances, with regrets, opportunities, mistakes, and incessant bad judgment ready to be revised, then repeated. The dream of being someone else, only more effective, or another version of ourselves, perfected by foresight and unerring judgment is the last taboo, but it is as inviolable as death itself.

About the Author

Avery Weisman is Professor of Psychiatry emeritus at Harvard Medical School, retired Senior Psychiatrist at the Massachusetts General Hospital, former Principal Investigator of Project Omega, a research study of how cancer patients cope with illness and its ramifications. He founded the psychiatric consultation service at the MGH, which now is known by his name. His many honors and appointments are cited in Who's Who in America. He is the author of several books and numerous articles on existentialism, psychoanalysis, death and dying (thanatology), vulnerability, and coping with cancer, but this is his first novel.

Prior to becoming a physician, Dr. Weisman studied philosophy and science at the University of Michigan, graduating with honors, three degrees, and a lifelong inclination towards a philosophical viewpoint. After several years in residencies in Pittsburgh, Detroit, and Boston, he settled into a clinical and academic role at Harvard Medical School and Massachusetts General Hospital. He is unique in having three specialty certifications: neurology, psychiatry, and psychoanalysis. Currently, he and his wife, Lois, are both retired and living in Scottsdale, Arizona.

His novel is based on accumulated experience with a wide variety of people, known professionally and personally. "They are people I have known," he says, "people I have heard about, people who would want nothing to do with me, and people conjured up through assemblages. If there is anything autobiographical, it is inadvertent and accidental."